Emotions:
Essays on Emotion Theory

EMOTIONS:
Essays on
Emotion Theory

Edited by

STEPHANIE H. M. VAN GOOZEN
NANNE E. VAN DE POLL
JOSEPH A. SERGEANT
University of Amsterdam

LAWRENCE ERLBAUM ASSOCIATES, PUBLISHERS
1994   Hillsdale, New Jersey   Hove, UK

Lawrence Erlbaum Associates, Inc., Publishers
365 Broadway
Hillsdale, New Jersey 07642

Library of Congress Cataloging-in-Publication Data

Emotions : essays on emotion theory / edited by Stephanie van Goozen,
   Nanne Van de Poll, Joe Sergeant.
      p.   cm.
   Based on lectures presented at a colloquium sponsored by the Royal
Netherlands Academy of Arts and Sciences in honor of Nico Frijda.
   Includes bibliographical references and index.
   ISBN 0-8058-1207-5 (hard : alk. paper). — ISBN 0-8058-1208-3
(pbk. : alk. paper)
   1. Emotions—Congresses. I. Goozen, Stephanie van. II. Poll,
Nanne Van de. III. Sergeant, Joseph A.
   BF531.E516   1993
   152.4—dc20   93-6708
                                                            CIP

Books published by Lawrence Erlbaum Associates are printed on acid-free paper, and their bindings are chosen for strength and durability.

Printed in the United States of America
10 9 8 7 6 5 4 3 2 1

Contents

PART III: SOCIAL INTERACTION AND EMOTIONS

Preface

This volume is a collection of essays on emotions, their significance, and how they function. For most of us, emotions are simply what we feel. They give our lives affective value. Scientists, however, approach emotions differently, some considering the "feeling" aspect to be of little relevance to their research questions. Some investigators consider emotions from a phenomenological perspective, others believe that the physiological bases of the emotions are of prime importance, still others observe and study animals in order to generate hypotheses about human emotions. This volume contains essays that represent each of these approaches. It is, therefore, in one sense a heterogeneous collection. Nevertheless, the variety of approaches and interests come together, since these scholars are all operating from a more or less cognitive psychological orientation and use the same conceptual reference scheme. These essays are written by experts in their own area and they reflect the richness of research in emotions. Whether these approaches and opinions on the emotions can be harmonized in a single theory of emotions is a question that the future will have to answer. Thus, although it is obviously desirable at this moment in time that there be "cross-fertilization," we are not yet ready for a complete synthesis of concepts and approaches.

We offer a brief summary of the main issues raised in each of the essays. Before we begin, we first point out that the essays have been grouped together under three general sections: the energetic and structural aspects of emotions, the expression and consequences of emotions, and social interaction and emotions.

In the section on the energetic and structural aspects of emotions, the issues discussed are the anatomical and neurological bases of the emotions. Cognitive psychophysiology provides a bridge between these levels of research.

Some researchers confine themselves to a limited number of hedonic states (positive and negative feeling states) and use a structuralist approach. Zajonc describes how subjective emotional states can be produced by emotional efference governed by changes in hypothalamic temperature. Emotional expressions have been explained sometimes as an adaptively valuable development because they enable an animal to broadcast information about its internal states to others in its vicinity. In Zajonc's view, outward behavioral actions, and especially facial efference associated with an emotional episode, may have a different function, namely the modulation of hypothalamic temperature. Zajonc presents evidence for his thesis from human research on, among other things, facial efference, phonetic utterances, and music appreciation, as well as data from animal research.

In his research, Gray, using animal models, argues that emotions may be conceived of as central states elicited by reinforcing events; different emotions may therefore be regarded as corresponding to a specific subset of reinforcing events. Each emotion, thus defined, is mediated by a separate subsystem in the brain. The key areas are the limbic system and the basal ganglia. From this general approach to the neuropsychology of emotion, Gray proposes that the mammalian brain contains three fundamental emotion systems: a fight/flight system, a behavioral inhibition system, and a behavioral approach system. This model is used for a taxonomy of several psychiatric conditions including anxiety, panic, addictive behavior, depression, schizophrenia, and obsessive-compulsive disorder. Gray suggests that his model can also serve as a framework for understanding the relationships between normal variation in personality, mood, and reinforcement.

The essay by Lang functions as a bridge between the *structural* approaches and the cognitive approach to emotions. He postulates a motivational continuity from reflex reactions to complex, cognitively elaborated emotional expressions. Responses are motivated by either the positive-appetitive or the negative-aversive brain systems. Lang uses the "startle probe reflex" as a method of evoking automatic emotional reflexes. Reflexes evoked during emotional processing are augmented if their affective valence (positive or negative) matches that of the active motivational system and inhibited in the event of a mismatch. Lang shows that probe responses are reliably potentiated during perception and imagery of unpleasant events and reduced during pleasant events. The essay concludes with a presentation of the neurobehavioral foundations of this conceptualization and an elucidation of the implications of probe analysis for theories of emotion organization as well as the assessment of mood and memory.

One of the liveliest debates in the field of emotions is the relation between affect and cognition. Some hold that affect determines cognition, others that cognition determines affect. In the section on emotional expression and consequences, Bradley argues for a dimensional view of emotion. She presents evidence from her own work and that of others that emotional stimuli can be profitably viewed as varying along two primary dimensions: affective valence and arousal. The issues addressed in her chapter exploit this organization of emotion to determine the influence of the two dimensions and their interaction on emotional processing using psychophysiological response and performance in memory tasks where affective slides or sounds varying in pleasantness and intensity are used as prompts to emotional experience. The influence of these dimensions is then assessed using several different measures of memory. Bradley's conclusion, that arousal (intensity) plays a key role in memory performance, leads to a discussion of neurophysiological and cognitive processes possibly responsible for these mnemonic effects.

One of the most important sources of information on emotions is the recall of significant life events. Reports of emotional experience are replete with information about the time course of individuals' responses to emotion-eliciting situations. Gilboa and Revelle use such data to study the temporal structure of emotional responses and their interaction with personality. Specifically, they describe a study designed to examine the relation between personality and different characteristics of affective reactions to positive and negative life events. In this study, subjects read descriptions of naturally occurring life events which varied widely in their emotional significance on both positive and negative dimensions. They then rated various aspects of their expected emotional responses on both types of affect. With regard to the temporal structure of affect, considerable differences were found between responses to positive and negative events, thus supporting the independence of differently valenced reactions. As for the interrelationship of affective response and personality dimension, neuroticism was related not only to the amplitude but also to the duration of negative emotions. Impulsivity, in contrast, was related only to the amplitude of positive emotions.

Two important channels for communication of emotions are the human face and voice. Following a discussion of some of the differences between facial and vocal expression, Scherer's chapter introduces the notion of *affect bursts*, brief, discrete expressive reactions that consist of synchronized changes in the facial and vocal channel of communication in response to affectively charged events. Although the vocal part of such affect bursts (interjections) has received some attention from students of language, the phenomenon as an integrated vocal/facial expression is curiously underresearched. Scherer's discussion focuses on the origin and function of affect bursts, on whether they are produced spontaneously or intentionally, and on their appearance in raw or conventionalized (emblematic) forms.

Because people can communicate their emotions to those around them, it is evident that social environment may play an important role in determining which emotions may arise and be expressed in a given culture. Section III addresses the topic of social interaction and the generation of emotions. One aspect of social comunication is ritual behavior, which van Hooff and Aureli examine from an evolutionary point of view. In their view, the reason for the manifestation of emotions and their ritualization is to manipulate the larger group. This requires reaching a balance between social harmony on the one hand and the disruptive force of social competition on the other. Conflicts of interests, especially when they lead to agonistic interactions, should not be allowed to disturb relations that have other values. Recently, reconciliation behaviors have been studied in primates. Van Hooff and Aureli present studies that suggest that by offering or withholding reconciliation an animal can manipulate the levels of social uncertainty and stress of its partners, depending on the value the relationship concerned has for the animal in question.

In human research on social emotional interaction, Taylor, Aspinwall, and Giuliano present a theoretical analysis and data concerning the emotional consequences of receiving information about other people. As research on social comparison processes indicates, comparisons of one's self with others can produce emotional consequences. The authors suggest that automatic reactions to social comparison information produce contrast effects, including positive emotional reactions to those perceived to be worse off and negative emotional reactions to those who are perceived to be better off. More thoughtful responses to social comparisons produce assimilative emotional reactions, negative responses to downward comparisons and positive responses to upward comparisons. Their chapter also details situational and individual difference moderating factors that are likely to influence emotional responses to social comparison information, such as threat, self-esteem, empathy, and perceived similarity.

In the last three chapters, the binding and disruptive forces of social interaction and their effect on emotions are discussed. Human social behavior is governed, in part, by the cultural values to which people subscribe. In Mandler's discrepancy/evaluation theory, arousal and cognition are the bases of emotional experience; values are addressed as the cognitive contribution to the constructed emotional experience. Values arise from the discrepancies and contradictions we experience, as well as from the sense of comfort we derive from the expected and the familiar. After a brief presentation of some applications of this theory, this analysis is extended to the psychological aspect of freedom. A distinction between natural and constructed liberties is presented, and the emotional aspects of natural liberties are discussed in terms of the experiences of feeling free and unconstrained and their converse, experiences of constraint and inhibition. Power relationships impose constraints and negative emotional experiences on the powerless and a lack of inhibitions and positive emotions on the powerful.

In his chapter, Frijda explains why the desire for vengeance poses a challenge for emotion theory. It is a universal and often extraordinarily strong instigator of action, yet there is no satisfactory account of both its universality and strength. Whereas current emotion theory views emotional impulses as in some way adaptive and rational, vengeance would seem to bring the individual no obvious gain: Vengeance usually cannot undo the harm that has elicited the desire. Frijda proposes first that the desire for vengeance involves a universal, and perhaps innate, disposition to answer harm received with harm to the antagonist, and for that reason (and in that sense) has a claim to being a "basic emotion." Second, Frijda suggests that desire for vengeance illustrates a class of emotions the utility of which goes beyond coping with the eliciting event as such. Finally, he contends that the desire for vengeance is rational and adaptive in tending to restore power inequality, self-esteem, and sense of identity, and thereby provides some relief from the pain caused by harm or humiliation.

Solomon also addresses the notion of vengeance in his chapter. The question, "What is justice?" has been answered by philosophers since Socrates in terms of the supremacy of reason and rationality. Solomon's thesis is that there can be no adequate understanding of our sense of justice without an appreciation and understanding of the emotions. This includes not only benign "moral sentiments" such as sympathy, care and compassion, and other "fellow-feelings," but also the nastier emotions of envy, jealousy, resentment and, especially, vengeance. In his essay he analyzes compassion (what used to be called "sympathy") and vengeance, which he defends as an essential aspect of retributive justice. In his opinion, one cannot develop a theory of justice without a substantial grounding and engagement in the empirical knowledge of how people actually feel and behave. Solomon thus claims that philosophy needs psychology and that an adequate founding of justice cannot but be grounded on both.

This collection of essays reflects current approaches and issues in the study of emotions. Behavioral scientists have in the past emphasized the need for objectivity in their research, sometimes to the extent that objectivity has become an end rather than a means in scientific enquiry. By virtue of the fact that emotions contain a large element of subjective private experience, it appeared to many behavioral scientists that they were not a proper domain of interest. This perspective has changed. Emotion is now seen simultaneously as a subjective experience and a domain of objective inquiry. This has only become possible by viewing emotion in a way that makes it open to testable hypotheses.

This volume is in honor of Nico Frijda. One of Nico Frijda's major contributions has been the development of a model of emotions that presents a set of constructs that can be experimentally investigated. Most models of emotion are restricted in the amount of subjective experience that they describe and can handle, because they confine themselves to the study of appraisal patterns. The unique contribution of Frijda has been to draw attention to another distinguishing feature of emotion, namely the experience of action readiness. He argues that emotions not only differ in how the emotional situation is construed but also in the accompanying action tendencies or other modes of action readiness.

The recent resurgence of interest in emotions has brought about a reconsideration of the influence of the emotions on other psychological processes. This can be seen in the relation between cold and hot cognitions. In this volume it becomes evident that an adequate account of memory requires acknowledgment of the influence of emotion on recall and retention. Similarly, the formation of human attitudes and social relations can only be properly understood when the role of the emotions is taken into account. Finally, the intensity of emotions and the differentiation between emotions is seen to be related to (neuro)physiological and biochemical processes. Although clinicians have long been concerned with emotions, the recent development of emotion theory has offered new approaches to studying clinical phenomena such as anxiety, depression, and even the taxonomy of mental disorder.

This volume represents a brief and up to date overview of the field of emotions. It indicates what has and has yet to be done.

ACKNOWLEDGMENTS

This volume is based on lectures presented at an invitational colloquium of the Royal Netherlands Academy of Arts and Sciences in honor of Nico Frijda. This colloquium was made possible by support from the Royal Netherlands Academy of Arts and Sciences and the Institute for Emotion and Motivation at the University of Amsterdam. We offer our sincere thanks to Andrew Ortony for his encouragement and support throughout the process of editing this book.

Stephanie H. M. Van Goozen
Nanne E. Van de Poll
Joseph A. Sergeant

Emotions:
Essays on Emotion Theory

ENERGETIC AND STRUCTURAL ASPECTS OF EMOTION

1 Emotional Expression and Temperature Modulation

Robert B. Zajonc
University of Michigan

The contributions of Nico Frijda to the study of emotions are so broad and they cover so many aspects that there is little to add. After having looked at the writings of Frijda on the subject, one is convinced that all the important things have already been said *by him.* It is therefore both a great honor to be associated with this event that honors his work and at the same time a challenge. For on this occasion one needs to say things that at least approach in depth of insight those things that he has discovered, conceptualized, clarified, and integrated. One is proud and humbled at the same time.

I wish to begin this chapter with one of those insightful Frijda thoughts. In his volume, *The Emotions,* Frijda had something very important to say about behaviors that are usually called "expressive." They are those that are

> evoked by events that an observer, or the subject, understands as aversive or desirable or exciting. They serve no obvious purpose in the same sense that instrumental and consummatory behaviors do. They are called "expressive" because they make the observer attribute emotional states to the person or animal concerned. They do so even when no eliciting event can be perceived by the observer. They make a mother look for the undone safety pin in the baby's diaper, or cause a child to be frightened of the dog someone else is frightened of. (1986, p. 9)

There is a great deal of insight indeed in this short quotation—insight and wisdom. For this brief thought alone incorporates almost all of the most important aspects of the theory of emotions. It does so by what it does not assert. For it does not assert that expressions are the manifestations of internal subjective states, and very carefully does not assert or imply that they are the effects of autonomic processes. It does not assert that they are voluntary or involuntary

3

communicative acts. But it does very clearly begin the story by focusing on the fact that their quality of being "expressive" lies in the ability of the observer, and even the "expressor," of attributing to them a connection to internal emotional states. There is an enormous difference between saying that the so-called expressive behaviors manifest internal states and saying that they can be used by observers to make inferences about these states. There are only indirect grounds to justify any of these assertions that some scholars take for granted.

The second very important insight in the short paragraph makes expressive behavior part of an important social process. An expression may "*make* (italics added) a mother look for the undone safety pin," Frijda said. Later (p. 11) he said that "'expressive' movements *produce actual effects in the interaction with environment*" (italics added). "Expressive behavior is behavior that establishes, weakens or breaks, some form of contact with some aspect of the environment" (p. 13). These statements assert, without making any prior decisions about the origin of expressions, that they have true and significant social effects. Frijda's view makes emotions inevitably social phenomena that are to be treated with the concepts of social psychology.

This short, deceptively simple and innocent introduction to Frijda's volume in *The Emotions* presented us with insights that changed the study of emotions. We will never be able to think of these phenomena as isolated neural programs underlying distinct emotional categories. We have looked for these programs for 100 years and Frijda is telling us that we have little chance of finding them. We must now look at the emotions as rich aspects of social lives—aspects that implicate almost all psychological phenomena. For we can find a significant participation of emotional elements in psychological processes ranging from classical conditioning to social conformity, from memory to collective representations.

In this chapter I concentrate on the expressive aspects of emotions, taking as my point of departure Frijda's very careful definition of *expressions* as behaviors that might allow an observer or the participant to infer the presence of emotional states.

PREEMPTIVE CONCEPTS IN THE STUDY
OF THE EMOTIONS

It is very important to be careful about the term *expression of emotion*, as Frijda was, because *expression* is one of those preemptive terms that provide us with a ready-made theory or explanation before all the facts are in, and often before any facts are in. These preemptive terms taken from everyday language will make us look at a phenomenon with a great deal of prejudice. There are quite a few such preemptive terms in psychology. Take the term *retrieval*. It implies that there must be a "store," that there must be a "search" through that store, that the store holds intact distinct items, that there is a way of "locating" the item being searched, that this item remains unchanged and stable in the course of the search, and that it is somehow brought into consciousness as a communicable and intelligible response. There is hardly any evidence for these strong assumptions.

Expression is such a preemptive term, as well, and it has been with us for centuries. We have taken its meaning for granted, and Darwin used it taking it for granted that there is something internal that is being manifested by expression. The meaning attributed to *expression* by Gratiolet (1865) and Piderit (1867) made less claim about it representing internal states, for it was more closely tied to the sensory system. Thus, for example, the protrusion of the lower lip in disgust was considered by Gratiolet as a simple generalization of the instinctive instrumental reaction emerging when an unsavory substance enters the mouth—a reaction designed to expel the substance. To Gratiolet, the lower lip protrusion upon hearing an absurd idea was not a manifestation that an intellectual examination has terminated in a feeling of contempt for what was presented, but an instinctive gesture of disgust seeking to expel the idea from one's consciousness as one expels a rotten oyster. From Darwin on there was a theory embodied in the word "expression." It meant (a) that there is a distinct internal state for each emotion, (b) that this distinct state seeks externalization of a distinct form, (c) that there is a one-to-one correspondence between the internal state and its outward manifestation, (d) that there is to be found a "triggering" neural process that can connect the internal state to its externalized output, and (e) that the internal process has sufficient energy directed toward its own externalization, but that under some circumstances it can be "suppressed" by a process requiring even greater energy.

That is quite a bit of meaning and theory to be contained in one word. I call *expression* a preemptive term because it preempts a theory yet to be developed. In the case of the emotions, there is yet to be solid evidence about any of the above five points about the emotions when we speak of their "expression." It is indeed quite difficult to resist the temptation to use the term *expression* in its rich meaning. So much more immediately comes to mind. But very little of it is confirmed or known. Clearly, Frijda was well aware of this temptation and he took great care in his explication of the emotional processes and their expressive correlates in his work.

An important fact that complicates our understanding of the emotions and that was recognized explicitly by Frijda (1986), is that the correlation between the so-called expressive movements and internal subjective states or their autonomic correlates is very unstable and quite low (Stemmler, 1989; Wenger & Cullen, 1958; Zajonc & McIntosh, 1992). There are internal states that do not manifest themselves externally either in motor behavior or in autonomic activity. Equally, there are emotion-like external movements that have no underlying internal correlates. You say CHEESE and you look like you are happy. But it is only an utterance. Or is it? We shall see that there is in fact more than just the utterance.

For these reasons, I chose in my own work (Zajonc, 1985) to replace *expression* with the clumsier but more neutral term *emotional efference*. If we for a moment avoid using the term *emotional expression* and substitute for it *emotional efference,* we can ask some new and interesting questions. For example, we asked questions about the consequences of emotional efference, examining instances where there was what "looked like" an emotional efference but being fairly sure that no detectable underlying emotional process accompanied this efference. If such instances exist, and common sense as well as the empirical data suggest that they do, then perhaps emotional efference functions not only to externalize internal emotional states and communicate them to others, but it has other functions as well. Its evolutionary provenance may not be found fully it its communicative value (Andrew, 1963) but in another function. In all fairness, it must be acknowledged that Darwin himself did not insist that expressive movements were selected primarily for their expressive purpose. No muscle, he said, "has been developed or even modified exclusively for the sake of expression" (1965, p. 354).

In the rest of this chapter I also use the term *emotional efference* instead of *emotional expression.*

IS THERE A PRIMARY FUNCTION
FOR EMOTIONAL EFFERENCE?

If emotional efference has functions other than expressive or communicative, what are they?

Waynbaum's Vascular Theory of the Emotions

The answer to this question is supplied by an obscure French physician, Israel Waynbaum (1906, 1907a). Waynbaum had no laboratory, no academic appointment, no connection with psychologists. He was an amateur scientist in the true sense of the word. All this was when science was more a hobby than a legitimate pursuit institutionalized by such supportive organizations as the National Science Foundation in the United States or CNRS in France. But he was extremely well read and had fabulous insight. Waynbaum rejected the idea that emotional efference had primarily or even mainly a communicative purpose. He attributed to it an entirely different function. He offered instead the revolutionary hypothesis that facial gestures, in general, and emotional gestures in particular, have first of all regulatory and restorative functions for the vascular system of the head.

The main clue for Waynbaum's hypothesis was the curious organization of the vascular system supplying blood to the head. He observed that the brain—the most crucial organ of the organism, which has undisputed priority in receiving scarce support in all domains—is not supplied by blood directly and independendently. Rather, the main carotid artery is divided at the neck into two branches: the internal, which supplies the brain, and the external, which supplies the face and skull (Fig. 1.1).

It was this configuration that spurred Waynbaum to look for a connection between facial gestures and their effects on blood supply to the brain. Because blood supply to the brain must remain at a fairly constant level—it can neither be much reduced nor increased—why wasn't the brain supplied independently and directly? Why was it sharing its supply with the face and skull? Waynbaum thought that the branching in the main carotid artery must be there to act as a regulator. But how? And what had all this to do with emotional efference?

First, Waynbaum observed that all emotional experiences produce disequilibria in the vascular processes. For example, in the case of fear, blood is redistributed to supply skeletal muscles to meet the demands of an incipient response, say a sudden flight. It is therefore less available for other functions. If there was a branching of the supply close to the brain, adjustments could readily be accomplished; if the brain suddenly needed blood, it would receive it at the cost of the supply to face and skull, which are less critically dependent on blood supply. Thus, Waynbaum conjectured that this vascular architecture exists to allow the facial branch of the main carotid artery to act as a safety valve.

How could this work? The muscles of the face can press facial arteries against facial bones and thus shunt blood away from the brain when there is an oversupply. They can equally relax and allow greater inflow when there is not enough. Waynbaum thought of the facial muscles as tourniquets that could constrict the diameter of the facial arteries and hence reduce uptake of blood in these regions, or allow freer flow when open.

And what has all this to do with the emotions? Waynbaum was quick to relate blood flow to hedonics. He offered the interesting conjecture that brain hyperaemia, within certain limits, is pleasurable, whereas anemia is experienced as a negative subjective state. A sudden lack of inflow feels bad, more as a discomfort that seeks restoration of a previous state. Therefore, resumption of ample flow feels good by contrast.

Freeing himself from the semantic network in which the term *expression* was embedded, Waynbaum was able to look at emotions not as ending with the motor externalization of the internal state, but was able to think of the possibility that facial efference was itself capable of producing subsequent events, that is, subjectively felt hedonic consequences. So, like James (1884), Waynbaum contradicted the common notions about the order of the emotional sequence, but unlike James, he proposed a specific process that would explicate such a sequence.

Waynbaum's ideas were so implausible at that time that when he presented them at the *Académie* he was summarily dismissed by Dumas (1906) and Piéron (1906). Neither found the idea to have any merit. Piéron took Waynbaum to task for offering a "finalist" explanation of facial expressions, asserting that it is quite dangerous to explain physiological processes by their alleged usefulness. He

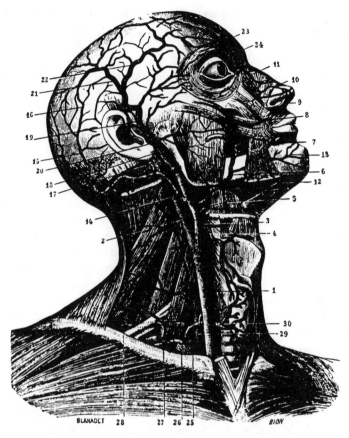

1. Artère carotide primitive droite. — 2. Artère carotide interne. — 3. Carotide externe. — 4. Thyroïdienne supérieure. — 5. Linguale. — 6. Faciale. — 7. Labiale inférieure. — 8. Labiale supérieure. — 9. Artère de la sous-cloison. — 10. Artère de l'aile du nez. — 11. Rameau par lequel la branche nasale de l'ophtalmique s'anastomose avec la partie terminale de la faciale. — 12. Artère sous-mentale. — 13. Partie terminale de la dentaire inférieure. — 14. Occipitale. — 15. Branches terminales ou cutanées de cette artère. — 16. Anastomose de l'occipitale avec la temporale superficielle. — 17. Auriculaire postérieure. — 18. Origine de la maxillaire interne. — 19. Temporale superficielle. — 20. Transversale de la face. — 21. Branche postérieure de la temporale superficielle. — 22. Branche antérieure de la même artère. — 23. Artère sous-orbitaire. — 24. Artère frontale interne. — 25. Sous-clavière. — 26. Mammaire interne. — 27. Sous-scapulaire. — 28. Scapulaire postérieure. — 29. Vertébrale. — 30. Thyroïdienne inférieure. [D'après SAPPEY, *Anat. topogr.*, Masson et C^le, édit.]

FIG. 1.1.   The vascular system of the head. Note the branching of the main carotid artery (1) into internal that supplies the brain (2), and external that supplies face and skull. (From Waynbaum, 1907a).

addressed the *Académie* in uncertain terms: "Je crains, d'une manière générale, outre des difficultés physiologique et anatomiques très sérieuses qui s'opposent à l'adoption de cette thèse, que M. Waynbaum n'ait abusé du principe d'utilité" (p. 475). Given the stature of these scholars against Waynbaum's modest credentials, Waynbaum's career was essentially finished at the point of that meeting. And he published only one other paper in 1907, which must have already been in press at the time of the meeting (Waynbaum, 1907b). Dumas, who later (1933) wrote the definitive psychology text, devoting three chapters to emotion, did not mention Waynbaum at all. And Waynbaum's work remained uncited between 1907 and 1985.

Blood Flow versus Brain Temperature

Piéron and Dumas did not touch on most of Waynbaum's misconceptions and false assumptions. They could only avail themselves of the physiology then known. Not surprisingly, therefore, they missed several of Waynbaum's assumptions that are now questionable and others that are now outright wrong. For instance, arterial flow is unlikely to be much affected by muscular action of the face because it can be controlled directly by vasodilation and vasoconstriction. However, if modified, much of Waynbaum's thinking can be useful. For instance, facial muscles might not have a significant effect on arteries, but they can affect venous flow. More importantly, facial action might alter the temperature of blood entering the brain by interfering or facilitating the cooling process of the brain. Such a process may in turn have subjective effects through its impact on the neurochemical activity in the brain.

Here then is a testable hypothesis that we can derive from the type of thinking liberated from the constraints of the term *expression:* Facial action can produce changes in brain blood temperature that, in turn, have significant hedonic consequences. Hedonic consequences are obtained for a variety of reasons. For instance, subjective changes can be obtained because changes in hypothalamic temperature can facilitate or inhibit the release and synthesis of a variety of emotion-linked neurotransmitters. Thus, for example, if a certain action of facial muscles results in raising hypothalamic temperature, and if consequently norepinephrine is released, the individual might experience excitation. Similarly, if the individual engages in facial efference that affects hypothalamic temperature and thus releases serotonin, the effect will be correspondingly depressant.

In brief, anything that the person can do to change hypothalamic temperature may have subjective effects. And within some limits, one can change hypothalamic temperature at will. These voluntary temperature changes may be achieved mainly through facial gestures or changes in the person's pattern of breathing. Lamaze is an analgesic procedure relying on deep breathing, and so is Yoga and Meditation. Qigong (pronounce Chi gong), an old deep-breathing technique has seen a revival in China such that 40 million people are now said to be practicing it. Qigong has been attributed remarkable successes in a variety of domains ranging from weight loss to the destruction of cancer cells. Vocal output, because it involves vigorous muscular facial action and because it also must alter breathing patterns, can affect brain temperature. And because exercise affects breathing rate, it will affect hypothalamic temperature as well. Of course, because of the increase in cardiovascular and metabolic activity, exercise raises core temperature, and has been shown to have significant mood effects (Roth, 1989).

How can Yoga, Meditation, or Qigong have these effects? The explanations of the effectiveness of these procedures border on the mystical. *Qi* is said to be a form of bioelectricity generated within the organism in interaction with the environment that can be manipulated mainly when it is guided by a Qigong master. Meditation and Yoga are equally mystical in offering explanations for their effectiveness, as is Lamaze. What is common to all these techniques, however, is that they all are capable of altering brain temperature because they rely on variations in facial efference and breathing patterns (e.g., Fried, 1987, 1990). Biofeedback is a procedure that often relies on variations in finger temperature. It is entirely possible that patients using biofeedback successfully engage in facial action that has analgesic effects.

We need to discuss now *how* breathing patterns and facial efference can change brain temperature, and *how*, in turn, brain temperature can affect our mood by acting on brain neurochemistry.

Cooling of the brain is a crucial physiological function. Because of its immense metabolic activity, the brain is a heat producer many times more active than any other tissue. In the adult, 20% of body heat is produced by the brain, which represents only 2%–3% of the body's mass. In the infant, whose brain mass ratio is greater and metabolic rate higher, as much as 80% of body heat comes from the brain.

The brain is an organ that cannot tolerate temperature variations as readily as other organs. In the upper limits, the human brain can tolerate temperatures up to about 40.5°C, whereas the trunk often reaches much higher temperatures. For example, trunk temperature during marathon running goes as high as 42°C (Cabanac, 1986). The hypothalamus is a crucial structure in this story because the hypothalamus is profoundly involved in *both* temperature regulation and the emotions. The lateral hypothalamus is the seat of bodily thermoregulation and the anterior hypothalamus is the seat of brain thermoregulation. Moreover, the two temperatures are fairly independent (Caputa & Cabanac, 1988; Fuller & Baker, 1983).

Interestingly, many responses that are involved in thermoregulation— shivering, sweating, pilo-erection, and many others—are also involved in emotions. Shivering, sweating, and pilo-erection are all parts of the fear response. The hypothalamus is also heavily implicated in the control of aggression, eating,

and sex, to mention just a few behaviors that have substantial emotional components. All this cannot be accidental.

The Cavernous Sinus and the Cooling
of Arterial Blood Supply to the Brain

Cooling of the brain relies heavily on heat exchange whereby venous blood
cooled by evaporation exchanges heat with arterial blood that enters the brain
(Hayward & Baker, 1969; Taylor & Lyman, 1972). In addition, brain temperature is controlled by the temperature of venous blood that reaches the cavernous
sinus, a venous configuration enveloping the internal carotid just before the
carotid enters the hypothalamus. The cavernous sinus, which is the only structure
in the body where an artery passes in the interior of a vein, participates actively
in the regulation of hypothalamic temperature (Caputa, Kądziela, & Narębski,
1976; Dean, 1988).

The cavernous sinus (Fig. 1.2) is able to perform this function because its
veins drain blood from nasal mucosa and are therefore air cooled in the course of
normal breathing (Scott, 1954). In some animals, the angulates of the desert, the
gazelle for example, arterial blood does not enter the brain in one vessel, such as

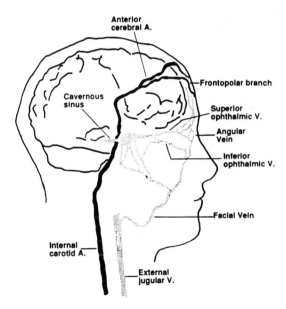

FIG. 1.2.   The cavernous sinus and the veins connecting it to nasal
airways.

the internal carotid artery, but it enters it in an immense number of very tiny vesicles—like in a radiator, presumably to effect the cooling more efficiently (Adams, 1957; Baker, 1972; Baker & Hayward, 1967; Cabanac, 1986; Du-Boulay, Kendall, Crockard, Sage, & Belloni, 1975; Edelman, Epstein, Cherniak, & Fishman, 1972).

In an elegant experiment, Kluger and D'Alecy (1975) studied the cooling of the hypothalamus by the cavernous sinus. Using a reversible tracheal canula, they observed rabbits that were either allowed to breathe normally through their noses, or had to breathe directly through a tube implanted in the trachea, thus bypassing the upper nasal passage and, therefore, also the cavernous sinus. They found that hypothalamic temperature increased when the cavernous sinus was bypassed. When the rabbits were breathing normally, the hypothalamic temperature was .3°C lower than rectal temperature (see Fig. 1.3). They showed therefore that allowing air into the nasal airways cools the blood that supplies the hypothalamus. Others have found similar effects (Sugano & Nagasaka, 1980).

One clue to this process is to be found in the discomfort we experience during the common cold or nasal congestion. Under these conditions, the cooling action of the cavernous sinus is severely restricted and, as a result, we feel distinct discomfort. Individuals with a deviated septum often suffer recurrent headaches. At the extreme end of the continuum, many patients who for various reasons must breathe through tubes inserted directly into the trachea, and thus bypassing the cavernous sinus, experience severe emotional shock. In some cases of chronic nose bleeding, a procedure is performed that consists among others of packing the nose with gauze tampon. The pack is so tight that no ambient air reaches nasal mucosa and the patient is essentially incapable of taking any air through the

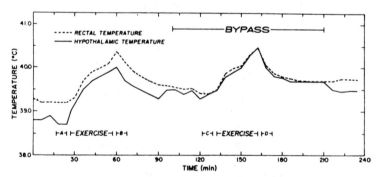

FIG. 1.3.   Rectal and hypothalamic temperatures taken under normal breathing and breathing through tracheal bypass in one rabbit. Period A is preexercise (treadmill) normal, Period B is postexercise normal, Period C is preexercise bypass, and Period D is postexercise bypass. Note the 0.5°C difference between rectal and hypothalamic temperatures in Period A, contrasted with an increase of hypothalamic temperature during bypass exercise, due to the absence of cavernous sinus cooling. (From Kluger & D'Alecy, 1975).

nose (Fanous, 1980). In some cases, especially if the nose packing is retained for a few days, there is a violent emotional reaction, quite often that of severe panic (Bendixen, Egbert, Hedley-Whyte, Laver, & Pontoppidan, 1965). This procedure, of course, eliminates the possibility of any cooling through the cavernous sinus. Upon removal of the pack, the patient experiences exceptional relief. In one case, a patient known as an affectionate and warm person, developed an intense hatred toward the surgeon when her nose was packed, and 2 days later she felt an equally intense love for him when the surgeon removed the pack (Carol Porter, personal communication, 1990). Monkeys whose nasal airways were packed developed severe distress symptoms, and to some rats this procedure is fatal only after a few hours (Peter S. Vig, personal communication, 1990).

Brain Temperature and Breathing

Ninety percent of people breathe exclusively through the nose. Yet one gets exactly the same air through the mouth. The so-called nasal-pulmonary syndrome, which has as its one feature the panic felt by the patient, has commonly been attributed to hypoxia. This hypothesis is now rejected because research indicates that there are no differences whatever in oxygen desaturation between patients with and without nose packing (Taasan, Wynne, Cassisi, & Block, 1981). Why, then, is there a distinct preference for nasal air intake? Because breathing through the nose allows cooling of the brain, something that cannot be accomplished by oral breathing. A simple experiment will demonstrate the importance of nasal breathing, for it is much more uncomfortable to breathe exclusively through the mouth (by holding one's nose) than to breathe exclusively through the nose (by holding one's mouth).

Even when nasal breathing is made very difficult and effortful—say by artificially restricting nasal air supply—people still prefer to take air through the nose (Drake, Keall, Vig, & Krause, 1988; Spalding & Vig, 1988). Together with a colleague from the University of Michigan Dental School, Peter Vig, we tried to see whether air taken through the mouth will increase if we gradually obstruct nasal air. The experiment was conducted by means of the Simultaneous Nasal and Oral Respiration Tester, an apparatus designed by Keall and Vig (1987) that measures exactly and separately air taken through the mouth and air taken through the nose (see Fig. 1.4).

Breathing patterns were observed in a number of participants when nasal air supply was obstructed in various degrees by means of a valve. It can be seen from the data in Fig. 1.5, which shows the results of a typical participant, that when nasal airflow is obstructed by a valve, the participant continues breathing through the nose even though nasal breathing becomes extremely effortful. This is true even for occlusions approaching zero availability of nasal air. Because the proportion of nasal breathing is largely unaffected, we conclude that nose breath-

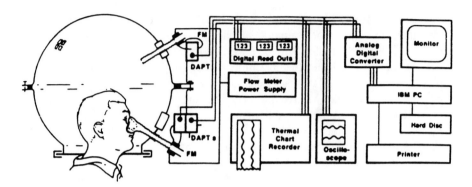

FIG. 1.4. Schematic view of the Simultaneous Nasal and Oral Re-spirometer. FM—flowmeter. DAPT—differential air pressure trans-ducer. (From Keall & Vig, 1987).

ing serves another function besides taking in air: very likely that of cooling the cavernous sinus.

The next step in this rather complex process involves the relationship between brain temperature and neurochemical activity. Curiously, there is relatively little work relating brain neurochemistry to temperature. Most neurochemical experi-ments with mammals are run under 37°C, with temperature held constant. There-fore, the assumption that changes in hypothalamic temperature can influence brain neurochemicals that are associated with subjective emotional states still needs more empirical documentation. But it is consistent with the fact that *all* biochemical processes are affected by temperature. For example, many bodily processes increase three-fold or more when core temperature is raised 10°C (Precht, Christophersen, Hensel, & Larcher, 1973). Some thymus-dependent antigens, for example, are released 5,000 times faster when the temperature is raised only 10°C (Jampel, Duff, Gershon, Atkins, & Durum, 1983; Miller & Clem, 1984).

FIG. 1.5. Composite of oral and nasal flow rate. Left side shows a patient with low nasal resistance. Right side shows a patient with a high nasal resis-tance. Note that oral intake be-came active with high nasal re-sistance, but nasal intake did not stop. In contrast, in the ab-sence of nasal resistance, there is no oral intake at all.

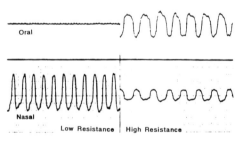

An important fact to consider in the process that relates facial efference to emotion is that facial veins can change the direction of venous flow. They are the only ones capable of changing direction of flow. They drain either into the cavernous sinus or into the external jugular vein, and even more significantly, they change their direction depending on temperature (Caputa, Perrin, & Cabanac, 1978). In fact, very small differences in temperature are sufficient. It has been shown in vitro, by Winquist and Bevan (1980), that changing the temperature just 1°C reverses the direction of the flow in facial veins of the rabbit.

SOME EXPERIMENTAL EVIDENCE

Facial Efference and Phonemic Utterance

A number of studies from our laboratory generally support various aspects of the process that we believe connects facial efference to temperature and to the emotions. Note, in this respect, that no assumption is made that subjective feeling states are occasioned exclusively by facial efference. In all our work, facial efference is considered to be a sufficient condition for the evocation of mood and emotional changes. No claim is made that it is also necessary.

In some of our studies (Zajonc, Murphy, & Inglehart, 1989), we attempted to discover if facial action *alone*—without an accompanying emotional excitation—is capable of changing subjective states. Is facial efference sufficient for inducing hedonic consequences? In order to do this we used facial actions that very much resemble emotional expressions but are not in themselves emotional. Our procedure was based on the photographer's trick of eliciting what appears to be a smile by asking the participant to say CHEESE.

Instead of inducing emotional expressions in participants by letting them recall emotional experience or forming emotional expressions using the Ekman-Friesen technique, we relied on *phonetic utterance*. In each of these experiments, facial action was induced by means of phonetic output, temperature was measured, and subjective feeling data were collected. Temperature was measured by thermography, and we focused on just two points on the forehead, midway between eyebrows and the hairline, and right above the pupils. It is here that the best external indication of temperature of the arterial blood that supplies the brain can be obtained. Under these points is located the frontopolar branch of the anterior artery, which is a direct branch of the internal artery.

A number of experiments showed that those phonetic actions that resemble positive emotional expressions generate lower temperatures and positive affect, whereas those that resemble negative emotional expressions generate higher temperatures and negative affect. For example, participants were asked to pronounce vowels that they heard in a specially prepared recording.

Note from Fig. 1.6 that the change in temperature varies across the vowel

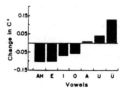

FIG. 1.6. Changes in forehead temperature during the utterance of various vowel phonemes. (From Zajonc, Murphy, & Inglehart, 1989).

phonemes. Those sounds that require a configuration of the facial musculature that is associated with positive emotions, *ah* and *ee,* produce a drop in temperature and those that are associated with displeasure or pain, for example, *ü,* produce a temperature increase. The affective ratings for these vowel sounds (shown in Fig. 1.7) correspond closely to temperature changes.

Ambient Air Temperature, Brain Temperature, and Affect

In another experiment, designed to determine whether cooling and warming the nasal airways and thus the cavernous sinus is related to feeling states, participants were invited to take part in what appeared to be an experiment in the psychophysics of olfaction. They were handed little tubes, which they put to their nostrils. They were told that subtle smells would be infused through the tubes, which they were to smell and judge for pleasantness. There were in fact some smells. But there was also plain air, either slightly heated or slightly cooled.

Their forehead temperatures and subjective ratings of mood were recorded. Again, there were quite clear increases in forehead temperature when warm air (in very small amounts) was inhaled through the nose and decreases when cool air was passed through the nostrils. And these changes were correlated with their feelings as previously: cooling with pleasantness and warming with aversion.

Direct Cooling and Warming of the Hypothalamus and Hedonics

Direct tests of the relationship between cavernous sinus temperature and hedonic state are not possible in humans. However, some animal models are suitable for such experiments. There is some earlier work that shows hypothalamic cooling to be a rewarding event (Corbit, 1969; Dib & Cabanac, 1984; Satinoff, 1964),

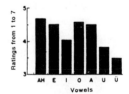

FIG. 1.7. Subjective ratings (1 = "Bad," 5 = "Good") for uttered vowel phonemes.

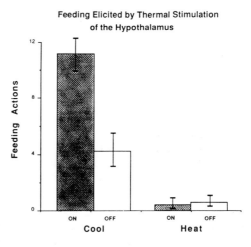

FIG. 1.8. Feeding elicited by thermal stimulation of the hypothalamus (From Berridge & Zajonc, 1991).

but there is much more literature on the effects of electrical stimulation of the so-called pleasure-center (e.g., Olds & Milner, 1954). Recent work in this vein by Berridge and Valenstein (1991) indicates that electrical stimulation of the lateral hypothalamus augments the animal's response to the natural elicitors of pleasure, such as food. When the rat's brain was so stimulated, Berridge and Valenstein observed four times as many feeding actions in response to food as in the control condition. Berridge and Zajonc (1991) used the identical procedure except that we substituted cooling and heating of the hypothalamus for electrical stimulation. Virtually the same results were obtained when the hypothalamus was cooled: three times as many feeding actions were observed with cooling than with the brain at normal temperature, and 40 times as many as with the brain heated (Fig. 1.8).

Recall that the hypothalamus is a structure that participates heavily in the control of the emotions, in aggression, in sexual behavior, and in eating—in fact in several behavioral domains that have a heavy emotional element.

SOME IMPLICATIONS

Why Do we Like Music?

That music elicits substantial emotional excitation requires no evidence. But how is music capable of having an emotional effect on the listener? In a recent experiment, McIntosh, Zajonc, Vig, and Emerick (submitted) measured participants' forehead temperatures, breathing patterns, and self-reported affect while music known to have positive or negative mood effects was played to them. Temperature changes, nasal volume, and affective ratings were found to be associated with the different pieces of music (Albinoni's adagio and Madonna's Vogue). Not all participants, however, showed the same pattern of music-

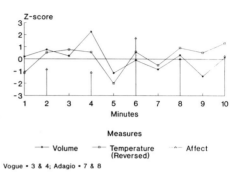

FIG. 1.9. Nasal air volume, forehead temperature, and affective rating in response to two musical presentations. (From McIntosh, Zajonc, Vig, & Emerick, 1993).

temperature change correlation. Those that like the given piece of music better, regardless of what piece it was, showed a decrease in temperature. Conversely when a disliked piece was played we noted a rise in temperature. More importantly, forehead temperature was found to vary inversely with volume of nasal air (Fig. 1.9).

Recall in this respect that more effective cooling of the cavernous sinus (a condition associated with positive affect) can be obtained by inhaling greater volume of ambient air. Table 1.1 shows the nasal breathing data of one participant who announced a decided preference for Madonna's Vogue. It is suggested by these findings that in listening to music the person's breathing rate and vigor are affected, perhaps by following the meter of the piece.

In another experiment, Wolff (1991) sought to explicate the basis of music therapy. Her hypothesis was that if music can reduce stress, then it must do so via changed breathing patterns and resulting temperature changes. Thus, she induced stress by having participants fail what appeared to be an intelligence test. Five groups were examined, including a control group, which did not listen to any music. The remaining four groups listened to the same piece of music played either in a major or minor key or fast or slow. The music was played immediately after the participant was escorted out of the intelligence test situation, ostensibly having nothing more to do with intelligence but being part of another independent experiment, this time concerned with music. As can be seen in Fig. 1.10, there is indeed a substantial rise in forehead temperature when we compare the pre- and post-stress measures. However, in this situation music was not effective in preventing temperature rise of the participants. At best, it did not make it

TABLE 1.1
Changes in Nasal Breathing Patterns to Music

	Albinoni	Natural	Madonna
Rate per min	14.5	15.5	18.5
Volume (ml/min)	5697.9	6259.8	7733.6
Rate in first min	13.0	15.0	19.0
Sec not breathing	20.5	3.7	3.2

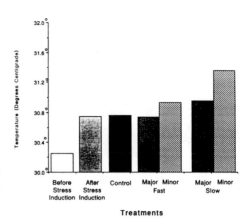

FIG. 1.10. The effect of music on forehead temperature following stressful experience. (From Wolff, 1991).

worse. The pattern of results shows that the major key is more positive than the minor key, and fast music more effective than slow music.

Biofeedback

Why does biofeedback work? It is interesting in the light of the relationship between temperature and hedonic enhancement that several biofeedback procedures depend on the control of temperature (Mathew, Largen, Dobbins, Meyer, Sakai, & Claghorn, 1980; Taub, 1977). However, I believe that there are no biofeedback studies where the facial efference or breathing patterns of the patient are closely monitored, for it is virtually certain that one would find those patterns of facial efference and respiration that cool the hypothalamus. Under thermal biofeedback instructions, the person must engage in some muscular action to bring about the neurophysiological change, and that action may well consist of changes in breathing pattern or in changed venous blood flow to the cavernous sinus. It is these changes that may induce analgesia or, as Mathew et al. suggested, affect regional cerebral blood flow. Future biofeedback research might profitably take measures of facial efference and breathing.

Placebo

The same processes that make biofeedback effective, may well make placebo effective, although it has been suggested that the process triggered by placebo involves imagery (Lundh, 1987). Kojo (1989) reported finding placebo being 1/3 effective and nocebo (a harmless pill presented to the participant as inducing pain) 2/3 effective when imagery suggestion was used together with administration of the harmless pill. But how can imagery by itself trigger the appropriate neuro–physiological and neuro–chemical processes? The possibility then exists that some form of action on the part of the patient, say facial efference or respiratory change, elicited by or accompanying imagery, might alter temperature so as to effect the desired change. In the case of the immunogenic effects (Ader, 1981), the patient would induce increase in temperature. In other cases, facial efference may work to decrease temperature, and possibly thereby augment the release of enkephalins.

Nonexpressive Facial Efference

It is in the same vein that we can now explain why people make various facial grimaces—why they cringe when they are in pain, or furrow their eyebrows when they are making a physical effort, why the weight lifter or the karate expert screams when lifting weights or breaking bricks. All these facial actions alter air access to the nasal airways and by altering facial venous flow, alter the temperature of the cavernous sinus. Again the hypothesis suggests itself that the change in hypothalamic brain temperature so achieved acts to release or synthesize neurotransmitters that allow greater effort or reduce the sensation of pain.

And in line with this hypothesis, we can also ask why people bite their fingernails, chew gum, or keep toothpicks between their lips? All these actions restrict air access to the mouth and direct all air intake through the nasal airways thus affording the individual some pleasurable experience. For the same reason, thumb sucking is so difficult to extinguish even long after all reinforcement has ceased. Also in the case of thumb sucking, the infant *must* breathe through the nose. Recall that the infant's brain produces 80% of body heat and it is crucial that there be ample cooling. The augmented nasal air intake, whose temperature is lower than that in the facial veins, cools the cavernous sinus and thereby the hypothalamus. In turn, the behavior because it is pleasurable is hard to extinguish. It would be interesting to take temperature measures of infants during thumb sucking and compare it to normal resting temperature.

Tics

It is a curious fact—not thus far seriously noted—that tics occur principally in the face (Leckman, Riddle, Hardin, & Ort, 1989). There are few knee tics or shoulder blade tics. Why not? Tics are facial motor responses, frequently involving the zygomatic, corrugator, and orbicularis oculi muscles (Azrin, Nunn, & Frantz, 1988; Golfeto, Loureiro, & Ribeiro, 1988)—the same muscles that are heavily involved in emotional efference. It is not impossible that they might help regulate brain temperature. The person with a tic must suffer some form of a chronic neurochemical imbalance, and the tic has been invented to correct this imbalance. Perhaps for that reason tics are fairly resistant to therapy, for eliminating them would merely bring about the malfunction that recruited them in the first place. Temperature measures during a series of tics and in their absence would reveal whether the hypothesis has some merit—an experiment that is quite easy to perform. It is possible, for example, that the temperature changes produced by means of tics may implicate, say, dopamine activity, serotonin levels (Goodman, McDougle, Christopher, Price, & Riddle, 1990), or monoamine oxidase, an enzyme that regulates serotonin levels. All these are temperature sensitive and all are involved in deep depression, suicide, crime, and hyperactivity. To my knowledge, no studies exist relating temperature variation to tic activity, even in the case of the LaTourrette syndrome of which tics figure as a significant component. However, there has been some interest in the relationship between breathing patterns and tics. For instance, Kuang, Lang, Yang, and Zhang (1991) reported that children who tend to hold their breaths tend also to develop tics and twitches.

Crime, Aggression, and Temperature

There are a number of studies linking crime and aggression to ambient temperature (e.g., Baron & Ransberger, 1978). There are many metaphors that connect raised body temperature to aggressive and decreased temperature to serene mood: "Boiling mad," "Hot under the collar" for rage and anger, and "Cool customer," or "Cool headed" for calm and emotionally controlled. Not all research replicated the aggregate correlation between ambient temperature and the likelihood of riots and mass violence (e.g., Carlsmith & Anderson, 1979; Tyson & Turnbull, 1990). However, there seems to be some likelihood that on the whole the original hypothesis has substantial support (Anderson, 1989). The last word on the matter is an analysis of 826 major league baseball games for the number of times the batter was hit by a pitched ball—an event considered as an aggressive act (Reifman, Larrick, & Fein, 1991). Figure 1.11 shows the relationship between such events ("hit by pitch" or HBP per game) and ambient tempera-

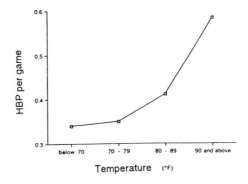

FIG. 1.11. Mean number of players hit by a pitch (HBPs) in games played below 70°F (n = 176), between 70° and 79°F (n = 315), between 80° and 89°F (n = 224), and at 90°F and above (n = 111). (From Reifman, Larrick, & Fein, 1991).

ture during the game. There is a strong rise in HBP with rising temperature. And this is so, according to Reifman and his colleagues, even when all possible confounding variables are held constant.

INDEPENDENCE OF AFFECT FROM COGNITION

There has been something of a controversy over the relationship between affect and cognition. In an earlier article (Zajonc, 1980), I claimed that not all affective reactions require the active participation of the cognitive processes, such as the appraisal of the eliciting event. The assertion was disputed on *a priori* theoretical grounds (Bischoff, 1989; Lazarus, 1982). The new findings reported here and considerable literature that has been accumulating since the original assertion was made are now presenting a convincing picture.

There are two processes that, although occurring jointly in the vast majority of cases, are quite distinct and independent. From our data we see that mood changes can be induced simply by changes in hypothalamic temperature, regardless of how such change is produced. No cognitive correlates are required. Recent neuroanatomical work is entirely congruent with the two-system view. The older view of the emotions regarding the process as beginning with the thalamus relaying information to the sensory areas of the neocortex as the first screen in the emotional episode is no longer viable. Recent work by LeDoux (1987) proffers the idea that before the organism can react emotionally, the meaning of the eliciting stimulus must be extracted from the information processed earlier by the sensory areas of the neocortex. This unlikely theoretical sequence does not appear to be viable. The previously assumed requirement that meaning of the eliciting stimuli is extracted from the information thus processed by the sensory areas of the neocortex before the organism's reaction, or even the signal to the amygdala, turns out not to be necessary. LeDoux found direct pathways between the thalamus and the amygdala that bypass the neocortex altogether. Interesting in this respect is the fact that the thalamo-amygdala pathway is only one-synapse long whereas the thalamus-hippocampus pathway has several synapses. Given an eliciting stimulus that evokes a thalamic response, the reaction in the amygdala is 40 ms shorter than the reaction in the hippocampus. With such a neuroanatomic structure, the participation of the hippocampus, and therefore of cognitive appraisal, memory process, and so on, is not required.

Confirming this view of the matter is an important study by Zola-Morgan, Squire, Alvarez-Royo, and Clower (1991) in which amygdala or hippocampi or both of monkeys were removed. The animals were then tested for responsiveness to emotional stimuli and for memory. For emotional reactivity the animals were observed while responding to fearful and aversive stimuli, as well as to appetitive stimuli. Cognitive functions, on the other hand, were examined while the animals were matching objects to sample objects. The data are reproduced in Fig. 1.12.

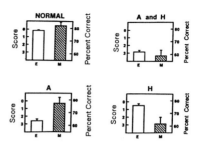

FIG. 1.12. Emotional reactivity (left ordinate legend, E) and cognitive performance (right ordinate legend, M) for monkeys with hippocampal and amygdaloid lesions. (From Zola-Morgan, Squire, Alvarez-Royo, and Clower, 1991).

It is clear that with both the hippocampus and amygdala removed, there is neither emotional nor cognitive responsiveness. With the amygdala removed there is no emotional reactivity but the cognitive capacity remains intact. Conversely, when the hippocampus is removed, emotional reactions remain intact but memory functions suffer a decline. It is quite clear from these data that affect and cognition can be regarded as two separate systems that can function independently of each other.

Self-Healing

The vascular theory of emotional efference and empirical findings reviewed in this paper have a compelling research agenda. What is being suggested here is that the face is a neurochemical plant—a plant that can produce on demand neurotransmitters, biogenic amines, antigens, neurohormones, and neuro-enzymes. Perhaps that is how the writer and editor Norman Cousins recovered from a collagen disease. His claim that a positive attitude and laughter played a major role in his recovery was a case in point, and he was taken seriously by at least one immunologist (Ader, 1990). Could laughter induce immunogenic reaction? Changes in noradrenaline and cortisol levels were found to have been achieved through the Chinese fitness exercise Tai Chi (Jin, 1989). Associated with these effects were also pronounced changes in mood and heart rate. And Yang, Cai, and Wu (1989) reported an experiment with acupuncture, finding consistent emotional effects even in the absence of any changes in the sensory response to pain.

   Much of what was said in this chapter must be taken with some caution. Even though there is a great deal of consistency, still a lot is to be learned. The ideas presented here offer a fairly specific agenda of research, for some of which methodology is fairly simple. For more definitive answers, research is more difficult. The payoff, however, can be very significant. If we can determine how various neurotransmitters act on emotional reactions, if we learn how these neurochemicals respond to temperature changes, and if we learn how such temperature changes might be brought about by breathing patterns and the muscular action of the face, we will be able to turn the face into an efficient personal neurochemical plant. And in the process of discovering these questions, not only emotions but a variety of illnesses may be responsive to voluntary temperature control.

REFERENCES

Adams, W. E. (1957). The extracranial carotid rete and carotid fork in Nicticebus coucang. *Annals of Zoology, 2*, 21–38.

Ader, R. (1981). *Psychoneuroimmunology.* New York: Academic Press.

Ader, R. (1990). Norman Cousins (1915–1990). *Brain, Behavior, and Immunity, 4*, 267–268.

Anderson, C. A. (1989). Temperature and aggression: Ubiquitous effects of heat on occurrence of human violence. *Psychological Bulletin, 106*, 74–96.

Andrew, R. J. (1963). The origin and evolution of the calls and facial expressions of the primates. *Behavior, 20*, 1–20.

Azrin, N. H., Nunn, R. G., & Frantz, S. E. (1988). Habit reversal vs. negative practice treatment of nervous tics. *Behavior Therapy, 11*, 169–178.

Baker, M. A. (1972). Influence of the carotid rete on brain temperature in cats exposed to hot environments. *Journal of Physiology, 220*, 711–728.

Baker, M. A., & Hayward, J. N. (1967). Carotid rete and brain temperature in cat. *Nature, 216*, 139–141.

Baron, R. A., & Ransberger, V. M. (1978). Ambient temperature and the occurrence of collective violence: The "Long, hot summer" revisited. *Journal of Personality and Social Psychology, 36*, 351–360.

Bendixen, H. H., Egbert, L. D., Hedley-Whyte, J., Laver, M. B., & Pontoppidan, H. (1965). *Respiratory care.* St. Louis: C. V. Mosby.

Berridge, K. C., & Valenstein, E. S. (1991). What psychological process mediates feeding evoked by electrical stimulation of the lateral hypothalamus? *Behavioral Neuroscience, 98*, 652–660.

Berridge, K. C., & Zajonc, R. B. (1991). Hypothalamic cooling elicits eating: Differential effects on motivation and pleasure. *Psychological Science, 2*, 184–189.

Bischoff, N. (1989). Emotionale Verwirrungen oder: Von den Schwierigkeiten im Umgang mit der Biologie [Fuss over the emotions: Difficulties in relation to biology]. *Psychologische Rundschau, 40*, 188–205.

Cabanac, M. (1986). Keeping a cool head. *News in Physiological Sciences, 1*, 41–44.

Caputa, M., & Cabanac, M. (1988). Precedence of head homeothermia over trunk homeothermia in dehydrated men. *European Journal of Applied Physiology, 57*, 611–615.

Caputa, M., Kądziela, W., & Narębski, J. (1976). Significance of cranial circulation for brain homeothermia in rabbits (2). The role of the cranial venous lakes in the defense against hyperthermia. *Acta Neurobiologica Experimentalis, 36*, 625–638.

Caputa, M., Perrin, G., & Cabanac, M. (1978). Écoulement sanguin réversible dans la veine ophtalmique: Mécanisme de refroidissement sélectif du cerveau humain. [Reversible blood flow in the ophtalmic vein: Selective cooling mechanism in the human brain]. *Comptes Rendues de l'Academie des Sciences, Paris, 287*, 1011–1014, Série D.

Carlsmith, J. M., Anderson, C. A. (1979). Ambient temperature and the occurrence of collective violence: A new analysis. *Journal of Personality and Social Psychology, 37*, 337–344.

Corbit, J. D. (1969). Behavioral regulation of hypothalamic temperature. *Science, 166*, 256–258.

Darwin, C. R. (1965). *The expression of the emotions in man and animals.* Chicago: University of Chicago Press.

Dean, M. C. (1988). Another look at the nose and the functional significance of the face and nasal mucous membrane for cooling the brain in fossil hominids. *Journal of Human Evolution, 17*, 715–718.

Dib, B., & Cabanac, M. (1984). Skin or hypothalamic cooling: A behavioral choice by rats. *Brain Research, 302,* 1–7.

Drake, A. F., Keall, H., Vig, P. S., & Krause, C. J. (1988). Clinical nasal obstruction and objective respiratory mode determination. *Annals of Otology, Rhinology and Laryngology, 97,* 397–402.

DuBoulay, G., Kendall, B. E., Crockard, A., Sage, M., & Belloni, G. (1975). The autoregulatory capability of Galen's Rete Cerebri and its connections. *Neuroradiology, 9,* 171–182.

Dumas, G. (1906). Communication a la Société de Psychologie. *Journal de Psychologie Normale et Pathologique, 3,* 475–476.

Dumas, G. (1933). *Nouveau traité de psychologie* [New treatise of psychology]. Paris: Alcan.

Edelman, N. H., Epstein, P., Cherniak, N. S., & Fishman, A. P. (1972). Control of cerebral blood flow in the goat: The role of the carotid rete. *American Journal of Physiology, 223,* 615–619.

Fanous, N. (1980). The absorbable nasal pack. *Journal of Otolaryngology, 9,* 462–467.

Fried, R. (1987). Relaxation with biofeedback-assisted guided imagery: The importance of breathing rate as an index of hypoarousal. *Biofeedback and Self-Regulation, 12,* 273–279.

Fried, R. (1990). *The breath connection.* New York: Plenum.

Frijda, N. H. (1986). *The emotions.* Cambridge: Cambridge University Press.

Fuller, C. A., & Baker, M. A. (1983). Selective regulation of brain and body temperatures in the squirrel monkey. *American Journal of Physiology, 245,* R293–R297.

Golfeto, J. H., Loureiro, S. R., & Ribeiro, M. V. (1988). O sindrome de Gilles de la Tourette: Estude de um Caso. *Neurobiologia, 51,* 189–202.

Goodman, W. K., McDougle, C. J., Christopher, J. Price, L., & Riddle, M. A. (1990). Beyond the serotonin hypothesis: A role for dopamine in some forms of obsessive compulsive disorder? *Journal of Clinical Psychiatry, 51,* 36–43.

Gratiolet, P. (1865). *De la physionomie et des mouvements d'expression.* Paris: Hetzel.

Hayward, J. N., & Baker, M. A. (1969). Comparative study of the role of the cerebral arterial blood in the regulation of brain temperature in five mammals. *Brain Research, 16,* 417–440.

James, W. (1884). What is an emotion? *Mind, 9,* 188–205.

Jampell, H. D., Duff, G., Gershon, R. K., Atkins, E., & Durum, S. K. (1983). Fever and immunoregulation: III. Hyperthermia augments primary in vitro humoral immune response. *Journal of Experimental Medicine, 157,* 1229–1238.

Jin, P. (1989). Changes in heart rate, noradrenaline, cortisol and mood during Tai Chi. *Journal of Psychosomatic Research, 33,* 197–206.

Keall, C. L., & Vig, P. S. (1987). An improved technique for the simultaneous measurement of nasal and oral respiration. *American Journal of Orthodontics, 91,* 207–212.

Kluger, M. J., & D'Alecy, L. G. (1975). Brain temperature during reversible upper respiratory bypass. *Journal of Applied Physiology, 38,* 268–271.

Kojo, I. (1989). Placebo and imagery. *Medical Hypotheses, 27,* 261–264.

Kuang, P., Lang, S., Yang, Z., & Zhang, F. (1991). A study of infants' breathholding spells and their mechanism. *International Journal of Mental Health, 20,* 56–63.

Lazarus, R. S. (1982). Thoughts on the relations between emotion and cognition. *American Psychologist, 37,* 1019–1024.

Leckman, J. F., Riddle, M. A., Hardin, M. T., Ort, S. I. (1989). The Yale Global Tic Severity Scale: Initial testing of a clinician-rated scale of tic severity. *Journal of the American Academy of Child and Adolescent Psychiatry, 28,* 566–573.

LeDoux, J. E. (1987). Emotion. In F. Plum (Ed.), *Handbook of physiology: The nervous system* (Vol. 5, pp. 419–459). Washington, DC: American Physiological Society.

Lundh, L. G. (1987). Placebo, belief, and health. A cognitive-emotional model. *Scandinavian Journal of Psychology, 28,* 128–143.

Mathew, R. J., Largen, J. W., Dobbins, K., Meyer, J. S., Sakai, F., & Claghorn, J. L. (1980). Biofeedback control of skin temperature and cerebral blood flow in migraine. *Headache, 20,* 19–28.

McIntosh, D. N., Zajonc, R. B., Vig, P. S., & Emerick, S. W. Temperature, affect, and nasal breathing: Tests of the vascular theory of emotional efference. Manuscript submitted for publication.

Miller, N. W., & Clem, L. W. (1984). Temperature-mediated processes in teleost immunity: Differential effects of temperature on catfish in vitro antibody responses to thymus-dependent and thymus-independent antigens. *Journal of Immunology, 133,* 2356–2359.

Olds, J., & Milner, P. (1954). Positive reinforcement produced by electrical stimulation of septal area and other regions of the rat brain. *Journal of Comparative and Physiological Psychology, 47,* 411–427.

Piderit, T. (1867). *Mimik und Physiognomik.* Detmold, Germany: Meyer.

Piéron, H. (1906). Communication a la Société de Psychologie. *Journal de la Psychologie Normale et Pathologique, 3,* 475.

Precht, H., Christophersen, J., Hensel, H., & Larcher, W. (1973). *Temperature and life.* New York: Springer Verlag.

Reifman, A. S., Larrick, R. P., & Fein, S. (1991). Temper and temperature on the diamond: The heat-aggression relationship in major league baseball. *Personality and Social Psychology Bulletin, 17,* 580–585.

Roth, D. L. (1989). Acute emotional and psychophysiological effects of aerobic exercise. *Psychophysiology, 26,* 593–602.

Satinoff, E. (1964). Behavioral thermoregulation in response to local cooling of the rat brain. *American Journal of Physiology, 206,* 1389–1394.

Scott, J. H. (1954). Heat regulating function of the nasal mucous membrane. *Journal of Laryngology and Otology, 68,* 308–317.

Spalding, P. M., & Vig, P. S. (1988). Respiration characteristics in subjects diagnosed as having nasal obstruction. *Journal of Oral and Maxillofacial Surgery, 48,* 189–194.

Stemmler, G. (1989). The autonomic differentiation of emotions revisited: Convergent and discriminant validation. *Psychophysiology, 26,* 617–632.

Sugano, Y., & Nagasaka, T. (1980). Effects of tracheal bypass breathing on heat balance in rabbits. *Japanese Journal of Physiology, 30,* 701–708.

Taasan, V., Wynne, J. W., Cassisi, N., & Block, A. J. (1981). The effect of nasal packing on sleep-disordered breathing and nocturnal oxygen desaturation. *Laryngoscope, 91,* 1163–1172.

Taub, E. (1977). Self-regulation of human tissue temperature. In G. E. Schwartz & J. Beatty (Eds.), *Biofeedback: Theory and research.* New York: Academic Press.

Taylor, C. R., & Lyman, C. P. (1972). Heat storage in running antelopes: Independence of brain and body temperatures. *American Journal of Physiology, 222,* 114–117.

Tyson, G. A., & Turnbull, O. (1990). Ambient temperature and the occurrence of collective violence: A South African replication. *South African Journal of Psychology, 20,* 159–162.

Waynbaum, I. (1906). Communication a la Société de Psychologie. *Journal de la Psychologie Normale et Pathologique, 3,* 467–475.

Waynbaum, I. (1907a). *La physionomie humaine: Son mécanisme et son rôle social.* Paris: Alcan.

Waynbaum, I. (1907b). Les charactères affectifs de la perception. *Journal de la Psychologie Normale et Pathologique. 4,* 289–311.

Wenger, M. A., & Cullen, T. D. (1958). ANS response patterns to fourteen stimuli. *American Psychologist, 13,* 423.

Winquist, R. J., & Bevan, J. A. (1980). Temperature sensitivity of tone in the rabbit facial vein: Myogenic mechanism for cranial thermoregulation? *Science, 207,* 1002–1002.

Wolff, T. (1991). *Effect of music on stress reduction.* Unpublished manuscript, University of Michigan, Ann Arbor, Michigan.

Yang, Z. L., Cai, T. W., & Wu, J. L. (1989). Acupuncture and emotion: The influence of acupuncture anesthesia on the sensory and emotional components of pain. *Journal of General Psychology, 116,* 247–258.

Zajonc, R. B. (1980). Feeling and thinking: Preferences need no inferences. *American Psychologist, 35,* 151–175.

Zajonc, R. B. (1985). Emotion and facial efference: A theory reclaimed. *Science, 228,* 15–21.

Zajonc, R. B., & McIntosh, D. N. (1992). Emotions research: Some promising questions and questionable promises. *Psychological Science, 3,* 70–74.

Zajonc, R. B., Murphy, S. T., & Inglehart, M. (1989). Feeling and facial efference: Implications of the vascular theory of emotion. *Psychological Review, 96,* 395–416.

Zola-Morgan, S., Squire, L. R., Alvarez-Royo, P., & Clower, R. P. (1991). Independence of memory functions and emotional behavior: Separate contributions of the hippocampal formation and the amygdala. *Hippocampus, 1,* 207–220.

2 Framework for a Taxonomy of Psychiatric Disorder

Jeffrey A. Gray
Institute of Psychiatry, London

Psychiatry is the branch of medicine that addresses disorders of behavior and the psychological processes that underlie behavior. Much of what it deals with consists in disturbances of emotion and emotional behavior; though, to be sure, cognitive, motoric and perceptual symptoms also loom large. Now, the cornerstone of my own approach to psychology is that all psychological processes, as well as the behavior that they underlie, are a product of activity in the brain (an assumption that is rarely questioned openly, though often implicitly abandoned in contemporary psychological science). It follows, therefore, that an understanding of the neural processes that mediate the psychological processes underlying emotion and emotional behavior—that is, an understanding of the "neuropsychology of emotion"—is fundamental to psychiatry. If so, such an understanding should yield a rational approach to the very difficult task of constructing a viable taxonomy of the psychiatric disorders. This task is at present largely left to committee decisions on operational definitions of words to describe symptoms, symptom-clusters, and syndromes, with the principal aim of permitting consistent communication between different clinicians and research workers. The purpose of the present chapter is to offer a preliminary sketch-map of what an alternative, rational taxonomy, based on current understanding of the neuropsychology of the emotions, might look like.

Before we embark on this endeavor, three introductory comments are called for.

First, the neuropsychological approach to the emotions is neutral with respect to questions of aetiology. Whether excessive anxiety, depression, and so forth, arise from genetic or environmental causes, whether they are triggered by a harsh word from a friend or metabolic disturbance in the brain, and whether there are or are not structural abnormalities in the brain to which they can be related, these and other emotional states *must* at the time of their occurrence reflect processes going on in the brain; to abandon this assumption, implicitly or explicitly, is to embrace a Cartesian dualism that is alien to most contemporary science. Thus I see no necessary opposition between this approach to the emotions and approaches from more purely psychological or, indeed, social-science perspectives.

Second, the construction of maps of brain systems subserving different emotions has perhaps seemed hitherto a purely academic game, and one not warranting much attention from those who do not play it. But the advent of human *in vivo* neuroimaging, using positron emission tomography, magnetic resonance imaging, and the like, radically alters this situation: Any proposed neuropsychology of the emotions is now in a position to influence the direction of clinical studies and, at the same time, the shortcomings of such a neuropsychology will rapidly become evident as data from clinical studies become available.

Third, the neuropsychology of the emotions cannot be separated from the neuropsychology of other psychological processes. This point can be illustrated in many ways taken from the psychology of the emotions: At the level of perception, the detection and interpretation of stimuli are known to be deeply influenced by emotional state; at the cognitive level, it is widely accepted that appraisal of a stimulus (e.g., as threat or promise) plays a vital role in the initiation of the appropriate emotional state; and, at the motoric level, it is equally accepted that the emotional state is intimately bound up with action tendencies (Frijda, 1986). The same point can be illustrated from studies of the brain: there is, for example, no structure implicated in the control of emotional behavior that has not been implicated also in a variety of perceptual, cognitive, and motor functions. Thus, the sketch-map that follows is not only one of the neuropsychology of the emotions, it is simultaneously a map of the neural structures that subserve a number of these other functions.

There is, of course, a danger inherent in this close interweaving of the emotions with other psychological functions: How can we construct *their* neuropsychology without committing ourselves to constructing the neuropsychology of everything? Is there anywhere we can draw a line? A line can, I think, be drawn with relative precision in brain terms: There is increasing evidence that most disorders of emotion (and psychiatric disorders generally) are related to neural activity in the limbic system (including frontal and temporal regions of neocortex that are closely related to the limbic system) and the basal ganglia. To be sure, these make up a substantial part of the brain; but we can nonetheless largely leave out of account lower brain systems mediating mainly vegetative functions, the cerebellum mediating mainly motor function, and areas of neocortex mediating mainly sensory, motor, and language function (though these each of course necessarily influence and are influenced by the limbic and basal ganglia circuitry that appears to be primarily involved in the emotions). In psychological terms this line corresponds, albeit fuzzily, to a distinction between two kinds of cognitive function, one phylogenetically old, the other more specifically human. The evolution of cognition has not waited until human beings were around wishing to converse about the weather or play chess; on the contrary, it has been a vital ingredient in Darwinian survival ever since animals first needed to learn and remember how to obtain nourishment or avoid danger. Cognitive function of the latter kind—that is, linked to the appraisal of reinforcers—is an essential aspect of emotion, and appears to be mediated largely by the limbic system and basal ganglia (Gray, 1990). This type of cognition, then, is inside our line; more intellectual accomplishments, such as speaking a language, doing algebra, riding a bicycle or playing the piano, lie, broadly speaking, outside it.

THE ANALYSIS OF EMOTION

The role of appraisal of the significance of a sensory input in the instigation of emotion is widely accepted (e.g., Frijda, 1986; Lazarus & Folkman, 1984; Lyons, 1980). Couched somewhat differently, this approach has a long and valued history also in animal learning theory (e.g., Miller, 1951; Mowrer, 1947). In the terms used in theories of this kind, emotions can be regarded as states of the "central" or "conceptual" nervous system (CNS), that is, simultaneously psychological and neural states, elicited by stimuli or events that have the capacity to serve as reinforcers for instrumental behavior. Thus the starting point for an analysis of the emotions is the notion of an instrumental reinforcer. This has its standard Skinnerian definition: A *reinforcer* is any stimulus (or more complex event) that, if made contingent upon a response, alters the future probability of emission of that response. Figure 2.1 presents a more or less exhaustive outline of the possible variants on this definition, created by the intersection of: (a) whether the putative reinforcer is presented, terminated, or omitted (when otherwise it would have occurred) contingent upon a response (the rows in the figure);

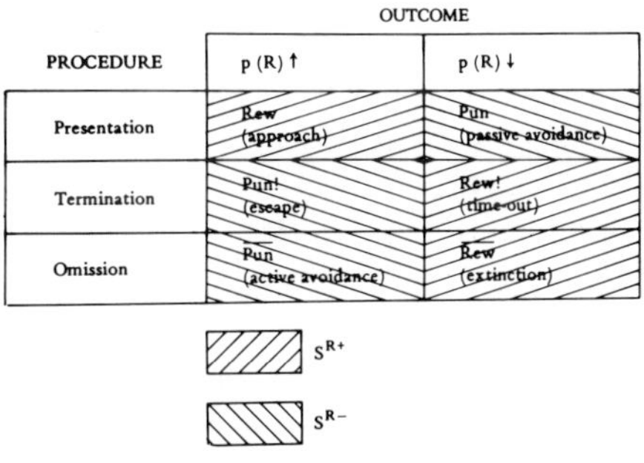

FIG. 2.1. Possible reinforcing events as defined operationally. Events may be presented, terminated, or omitted (rows) contingent upon a response, and response probability—p(R)—may in consequence increase or decrease (columns). S^R+, S^R-: positive and negative reinforcers, shown by crosshatching.

and (b) whether the observed change in the probability of emission of the response is an increase or decrease (the columns); if no change is observed, the stimulus is not a reinforcer at all. As a matter of empirical fact, it turns out that stimuli (if they are reinforcers at all) come in two kinds: those that, when presented contingent upon a response (top row), increase response probability and also, when terminated or omitted (bottom rows), decrease response probability; and those that, when presented, decrease response probability and also, when terminated or omitted, increase response probability. This gives rise to the distinction (cross-hatching in Fig. 2.1) between (in various terminologies) positive (the former class of stimuli) and negative reinforcers (the latter), rewards and punishments, or appetitive and aversive stimuli. Because the termination and omission procedures (bottom two rows of Fig. 2.1) usually give the same results, the figure may be collapsed into a 2 × 2 table: Rewards, when presented, increase response probability and, when terminated/omitted, decrease it; punishments, when presented, decrease response probability and, when terminated/omitted, increase it. To this 2 × 2 table one further complication has to be added: Reinforcers may be primary (unconditioned) or secondary (conditioned). The former are stimuli or events that, without special learning, have innately reinforcing properties for the species concerned, for example food, water, a sex partner, pain. The latter are stimuli that are initially neutral (do not alter response probability), for example a tone or light of moderate intensity, but take on reinforcing properties as a consequence of entering into an association (most probably by Pavlovian conditioning; Gray, 1975) with an unconditioned reinforcer.

We are now armed with most of the tools of conceptual analysis that we need. They are to be used to address the following questions: How many separate emotions are there, and how is each to be defined? Or, in terms of the argument being developed here: If, in general, emotions consist of states of the CNS elicited by reinforcing events, can we parcel out the total set of reinforcing events (as defined by Fig. 2.1, together with the unconditioned/conditioned distinction) into subsets, such that each subset of reinforcing events corresponds to a different emotion, elicited by members of only that subset?

At first sight, to someone steeped in human psychology, this question may seem simplistic to the point of absurdity. After all, if one looks into any good dictionary, one will find hundreds of words describing (apparently) different emotions. Consider: regret, nostalgia, indignation, schadenfreude, and so on. Yet, on the analysis advanced here, there is only a maximum of eight (the multiple of our 2 × 2 × 2 orthogonal distinctions) separate emotions possible. This problem, however, is more apparent than real. The analysis developed here is not aimed at human linguistic behavior. How we name emotions is as separate from the way the CNS produces emotions as is how we name colors from the mechanisms that underlie color vision; and, in both cases, the words we use reflect as much the particular circumstances that give rise to the experience (e.g., "nostalgia," "shocking pink") as the experience itself. Just as, in the case of color vision, a mechanism based initially on just three color pigments is able to give rise to the great variety of experienced colors and thus to provide the basis for the even greater variety of color words, so (it is contended here) just a few emotion systems in the CNS are able to give rise to the variety of experienced emotional states and then to provide the basis for the vocabulary that is used to describe those states (Gray, 1985). How, then, are we to arrive at subsets of reinforcing events, each corresponding to a separate emotion and therefore to a separate system in the brain responsible for that emotion? The distinctions we have made above are largely of a purely operational kind. It is a matter of experimental convenience that we decide, for example, to measure changes in response probability separately as increases and decreases (the columns of Fig. 2.1) or to classify stimuli as positive or negative reinforcers (the cross-hatching). But we do not know in advance whether the brain makes the same distinctions that we do: It may or may not use different mechanisms to acquire new behavior and to suppress the old; or to respond to positive and negative reinforcers; or to do both these things. Moreover, quite different theoretical positions have been taken on just this sort of issue. Thus, some theorists suppose that the brain has a "reward system" for dealing with positive reinforcers no matter how they affect behavior, together with a "punishment system" that similarly deals with negative reinforcers (e.g., Olds & Olds, 1965); whereas others suppose that there is one system for the acquisition of new behavior and another for behavioral inhibition (e.g., Gray, 1975). These theories are quite different. However, they overlap if only the top row of Fig. 2.1 is considered in isolation; in consequence, they have often been confused with one another.

To take a position on these complex issues in the short space of this chapter inevitably appears arbitrary. In fact, however, the specific model I now present is based on an extensive data base, culled from a wide variety of experimental approaches in the study of animal learning and behavior, psychopharmacology, neuropsychology, and neuroscience (e.g. Gray, 1982a, 1987). A number of alternative models can be ruled out by data from one or other of these disciplines; the model that remains is, by contrast, at least consistent with (though far from proved by) the bulk of the data from all of them (this multiplicity of sources of critical data is, indeed, one of the great advantages of the whole neuropsychological enterprise).

The model posits in the mammalian CNS three fundamental emotion systems, each of which (a) responds to a separate subset of reinforcing events with specific types of behavior, and (b) is mediated by a separate set of interacting brain structures that processes specific types of information. The three systems are termed the behavioral inhibition system, the fight/flight system, and the behavioral approach system. A description of each of these systems requires specification at (at least) three levels: behavioral (input-output analysis), neural (brain structure and function), and cognitive (the information processing functions discharged by the relevant neural processes). To these it would naturally be desirable to add a fourth, subjective level; but empirical research still lacks a viable approach to this level (verbal report is a behavioral output, not a window on subjective experience). Analysis of both the behavioral inhibition system (Graeff, 1987; Gray, 1982a, 1982b) and the behavioral approach system (Gray, Feldon, Rawlins, Hemsley, & Smith, 1991a; Gray, Hemsley, Feldon, Gray, & Rawlins, 1991b; Swerdlow & Koob, 1987) has proceeded at all three levels; the fight/flight system has been extensively analyzed at the behavioral and neural (Adams, 1979; Graeff, 1987; LeDoux, 1987; Panksepp, 1982, 1990) but not the cognitive level. A major problem in this field is terminological. Neither the system names I use, nor the names of the emotional states to which the systems are linked, are necessarily the same as those used by the authors cited above; for examples of the confusion to which these different usages can give rise, see Gray (1990, 1991). For the sake of simplicity, I shall in this chapter use only my own terminology. In addition to these terminological difficulties, however, there are also major differences of opinion about a number of substantive issues in the field (see, e.g., Gray, 1990, for a number of points of view). Important though they are, it will not be possible to enter into these controversies in this chapter; nor will there be any attempt to present the data on which my own model rests (for portions of these data, see Gray, 1975, 1977, 1982a, 1987; Gray, Feldon et al., 1991, Gray, Hemsley et al., 1991; Gray & McNaughton, 1983). Here I offer only a brief summary of each of the three systems, followed by a consideration of how a number of normal and abnormal emotional states and predispositions may fit into the conceptual space that they jointly define.

THE BEHAVIORAL INHIBITION SYSTEM

This is the best worked out part of the model. The input-output relations that define the behavioral inhibition system (BIS) at the behavioral level are presented in Fig. 2.2. The critical eliciting stimuli are conditioned stimuli associated with punishment, conditioned stimuli associated with the omission or termination of reward ("frustrative nonreward"; Amsel, 1962), and novel stimuli. The appearance of novelty on this list may cause some surprise, because it is not at first obvious that this counts as a reinforcer at all, given the definitions set out in Fig. 2.1. In fact, however, novel stimuli possess rather complex reinforcing properties that change as a function of the degree of novelty and also interact with stimulus intensity as well as a number of other factors (Berlyne, 1960). At high values of novelty and intensity, the stimulus principally elicits the type of behavior shown to the right of Fig. 2.2; as (with stimulus prolongation or repetition) these values diminish, the elicited behavior shifts to approach (see the section on the Behavioral Approach System, later); with still further stimulus prolongation or repetition, complete habituation sets in and the stimulus ceases to

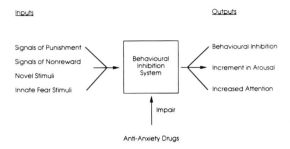

FIG. 2.2. The Behavioral Inhibition System (BIS) as defined by its inputs and outputs.

elicit any response. The transition from behavioral inhibition to approach is not sudden; thus, over much of the range of values, novel stimuli elicit an approach–avoidance conflict (Gray, 1982a, 1987, chapter 9; Zuckerman, 1982).

The behavior elicited by these stimuli (right-hand side of Fig. 2.2) consists in behavioral inhibition (interruption of any ongoing behavior); an increment in the level of arousal, such that the next behavior to occur (which may consist in a continuation of the action that was interrupted) is carried out with extra vigor and/or speed; and an increment in attention, such that more information is taken in, especially concerning novel features of the environment. There are a number of compelling empirical reasons for regarding the BIS as constituting a unified system, rather than a fiction based on a number of separate relationships between each of the inputs listed to the left of Fig. 2.2 and each of the outputs listed to the right. Among these reasons are, first, the fact that each input elicits all of the outputs; and, second and more important, the fact that a range of interventions in brain function affect simultaneously all of the outputs to any of the inputs. Furthermore, such interventions may leave intact other input–output relationships, including some involving either an input or an output (but not both) to or from the BIS. For example, a drug or lesion that impairs the ability to inhibit behavior in response to a stimulus warning of punishment (the input–output relationship specified at the top of both the left and right-hand sides of Fig. 2.2) may simultaneously leave intact the animal's ability to inhibit behavior in order to obtain a reward (for details of this kind of experimental result, see Gray, 1982a). Thus the BIS indeed behaves like a system, and one that is separate from other systems.

Among the interventions that specifically abolish the input–output relationships that define the BIS is the administration of drugs, such as the benzodiazepines, barbiturates, and alcohol, which reduce anxiety in human beings; indeed, the study of such drugs was a major impetus to the formation of the concept of the BIS (Gray, 1982a, 1982b). On this basis, one may tentatively identify the subjective state that accompanies activity in the BIS as anxiety. This identification gains plausibility from the fact that it leads to a face-valid description of human anxiety: that is, a state in which one responds to threat (stimuli associated with punishment or nonreward) or uncertainty (novelty) with the reaction, "stop, look, and listen, and get ready for action" (right-hand side of Fig. 2.2) (Gray, 1982a, 1982b).

Neurologically, the set of structures that appear to discharge the functions of the BIS are as illustrated in Fig. 2.3. The (tentative) identification of the BIS with activity in this set of structures depends on a variety of sources of information (Gray, 1982a). Now, from the point of view of a psychologist attempting to understand emotion, it is on its own of no great importance to be told that one set of brain structures rather than another mediates the functions of the BIS. Indeed, there have been a number of valuable attempts to test, at the human level,

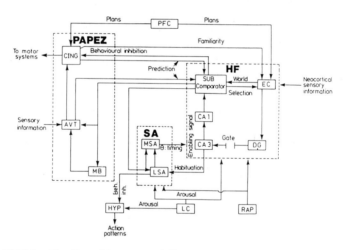

FIG.2.3. The Septohippocampal System: Major structures composing the neural basis of the Behavioral Inhibition System. The three major building blocks are shown in heavy print: HF, the hippocampal formation, made up of the entorhinal cortex, EC, the dentate gyrus, DG, CA 3, CA 1, and the subicular area, SUB; SA, the septal area, containing the medial and lateral septal areas, MSA and LSA; and the Papez circuit, which receives projections from and returns them to the subicular area via the mammillary bodies, MB, anteroventral thalamus, AVT, and cingulate cortex, CING. Other structures shown are the hypothalamus, HYP, the locus coeruleus, LC, the raphe nuclei, RAP, and the prefrontal cortex, PFC. Arrows show direction of projection; the projection from SUB to MSA lacks anatomical confirmation. Words in lower case show postulated functions; beh. inhib., behavioral inhibition.

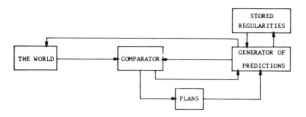

FIG. 2.4. Information processing required for the comparator function of the septohippocampal system.

predictions derived from the general concept of the BIS, together with related ideas, without reference at all to its supposed neurological underpinning (e.g., Boddy et al., 1986). There is, however, a value to the psychologist in such "neurologizing." First, in the actual construction of a concept such as that of the BIS, the utilization of data from the neurosciences as well as from psychology is likely to lead to a more robust basis for further, purely psychological theorizing. Second, understanding of the neural basis of a system such as the BIS can lead to specific psychological questions or hypotheses that would otherwise be unlikely to arise; we shall see some examples of this later. Third, the neurological level leads inevitably back to mainstream issues in psychology. For the main function of the brain is to process information, and the task of describing how that information is processed, in other than neurological terms, belongs to cognitive psychology. Thus, faced with the kind of neurological flow diagram shown in Fig. 2.3, one should ask not only how the structures illustrated therein produce the behavioral outputs of the BIS (Fig. 2.2), but also what cognitive (i.e., information-processing) operations they perform in order to do so.

The information-processing functions attributed to the interlinked set of structures depicted in Fig. 2.3 are themselves illustrated in Fig. 2.4; detailed justification for the ideas that enter both figures can be found in Gray (1982a). At the cognitive level, the key concept is that of the comparator, that is, a system that, moment by moment, predicts the next likely event and compares this prediction to the actual event. This system (1) takes in information describing the current state of the perceptual world; (2) adds to this further information concerning the subject's current motor program; (3) makes use of information stored in memory and describing past regularities that relate stimulus events to other stimulus events; (4) similarly makes use of stored information describing past regularities that relate responses to subsequent stimulus events; (5) from these sources of information predicts the next expected state of the perceptual world; (6) compares the predicted to the actual next state of the perceptual world; (7) decides either that there is a match or that there is a mismatch between the predicted and the actual states of the world; (8) if there is a match, proceeds to run through steps (1) to (7) again; but (9) if there is a mismatch, brings the current motor program to a halt, that is, operates the outputs of the BIS (Fig. 2.2), so as to take in further information and resolve the difficulty that has interrupted this program.

In the application of this model to anxiety, the focus of the analysis was on step (9) and the further consequences of this step (Gray, 1982a). More recently, Gray, Feldon et al. (1991) have been concerned with the details of the monitoring process itself and the way in which this interacts with the running of motor programs; we turn to this aspect of the problem later, in the section on the Behavioral Approach System.

Figure 2.4 depicts, as it were, the software of the comparator proposed by Gray (1982a); the corresponding hardware is illustrated in Fig. 2.3. At this neural level, the core structure is the septohippocampal system (SHS, composed of the septal area, entorhinal cortex, dentate gyrus, hippocampus, and subicular area). Here we note only the following points. First, the heart of the comparator function is attributed to the subicular area. This is postulated (1) to receive elaborated descriptions of the perceptual world from the entorhinal cortex, itself the recipient of input from all cortical sensory association areas; (2) to receive predictions from, and initiate generation of the next prediction in, the Papez circuit (i.e., the circuit from the subiculum to the mammillary bodies, the antero-ventral thalamus, the cingulate cortex and back to the subiculum); and (3) to interface with motor programming systems (not themselves included in Fig. 2.3) so as either to bring them to a halt or to permit them to continue. Second, the prefrontal cortex is allotted the role of providing the comparator system with information concerning the current motor program (via its projections to the entorhinal and cingulate cortices, the latter forming part of the Papez circuit). Third, the monoaminergic pathways that ascend from the mesencephalon to innervate the SHS (consisting of noradrenergic fibres originating in the locus coeruleus, and serotonergic fibers originating in the median raphe) are charged with alerting the whole system under conditions of threat and diverting its activities to deal with the threat; in the absence of threat, the information-processing activities of the system can be put to other, nonemotional purposes (Gray, 1984). Lastly, the system depicted in Fig. 2.3 needs to be quantized in time, to allow appropriate comparison between specific states of the world and corresponding predictions, followed by initiation of the next prediction and next intake of information describing the world. This function is attributed to the hippocampal theta rhythm, giving rise to an "instant" within the model of about one-tenth of a second.

Much of the above analysis is inevitably speculative. Even so, the existence of a reasonably detailed sketch map of an emotion system covering several levels of analysis—behavioral (Fig. 2.2), neural (Fig. 2.3) and cognitive (Fig. 2.4)—together with a plausible identification of a subjective state associated with the activity of this system (i.e., anxiety), has, I believe, heuristic value in indicating what a developed theory of a particular emotion might look like. In particular, we can now flesh out a little the notion of an "emotion system." Behaviorally, this consists, as we have seen, of a set of outputs jointly elicited by any one of several types of input. The plausibility of attributing such input–output relationships to an underlying system is increased by evidence that, say, certain drugs (e.g., Gray, 1977) or lesions of the brain (e.g., Gray & McNaughton, 1983) selectively alter these but not other input–output relationships; especially if one can show by independent arguments from neuroscientific data that the drugs and lesions concerned affect function in only a particular subset of neural structures (e.g., Gray, 1982a). The concept of a system gathers further strength from a consideration of the particular cognitive (information-processing) functions that it is likely to discharge; especially if such ideas can then be tested at the human level.

As an example of this process of theoretical and experimental evolution, consider the "increase attention" output of the BIS (Fig. 2.2). In the human literature on anxiety, it has generally been considered that anxiety impairs the capacity to attend to and process environmental stimuli (e.g., Spence & Spence, 1966). In the light of the effects of antianxiety drugs in animals (Gray, 1977), I proposed instead that anxiety *increases* attention to environmental stimuli, provided that these are related to the anxiogenic event or are of a generally anxiogenic nature (Gray, 1982a). Research with human participants has since confirmed this derivation from the BIS model (e.g. Mathews, 1988). Further important evidence at the human level comes from the recent application of imaging techniques to the living brain: Using positron emission tomography, Reiman, Raichle, Butler, Hersovitch, and Robins (1984) showed that patients diagnosed as having panic disorder differed from normal controls in only one brain region, namely, the region containing the entorhinal cortex (the major input to the SHS) and the subicular area (the major output station from the SHS). Thus the program of research that commenced with the study in animals of drugs that reduce anxiety in human patients has come almost full circle back to the clinic.

THE FIGHT/FLIGHT SYSTEM

The input–output relationships that define the fight/flight system (FFS) are set out in Fig. 2.5. Whereas the BIS responds to conditioned aversive stimuli, the FFS responds to unconditioned aversive stimuli; and whereas the BIS responds with "Stop, look, and listen, and get ready for action," the FFS responds with unconditioned defensive aggression or escape behavior (Adams, 1979). Moreover, to these different patterns of behavior there correspond different pharmacologies. Thus, as noted above, the antianxiety drugs reduce the responses of

FIG. 2.5. The Fight/Flight System (F/FLS) as defined by its inputs and outputs.

the BIS to its adequate inputs, but these drugs do not reduce responses to unconditioned aversive (painful) stimuli; conversely, analgesics such as morphine reduce responses to painful stimuli but do not affect reactions to conditioned aversive stimuli (for review, see Gray, 1982a). Correspondingly, the BIS and FFS have different neurologies (which is not to say that they have little interaction; see later). There are three important levels in the neuraxis at which stimulation and lesion experiments have pinpointed structures that appear to have the functions of the FFS: the amygdala, which has an inhibitory influence on the medial hypothalamus, which in turn has an inhibitory influence on final output pathways in the central gray of the midbrain. The latter region receives afferents carrying information about painful stimuli, and both the central gray and the amygdala have high densities of opiate receptors. Thus the analgesic effects of both exogenous and endogenous opiates are likely to be mediated through these regions. More detailed analyses of the neural structures concerned, and their behavioral functions, can be found in Adams (1979), Graeff (1987), LeDoux (1987) and Panksepp (1982, 1990). Of particular importance in the present context are Graeff's observations of the similarities between the autonomic responses to electrical stimulation of the central gray in animals, on the one hand, and the symptoms of human panic attacks, on the other; and of the inhibitory control over the neurons responsible for these autonomic responses variously exercised by systems utilizing as their neurotransmitters serotonin, gamma-aminobutyric acid and endorphins.

THE BEHAVIORAL APPROACH SYSTEM

The input–output relations that define the behavioral approach system, or behavioral activation system (Fowles, 1980)—in either case, BAS—are set out in Fig. 2.6. In essence, this depicts a simple positive feedback system, activated by stimuli associated with reward or with the termination/omission of punishment ("relieving non-punishment"; Mowrer, 1960), and operating so as to increase spatiotemporal proximity to such stimuli. By adding the postulate that conditioned appetitive stimuli of this kind activate the BAS to a degree proportional to their spatiotemporal proximity to the unconditioned appetitive stimulus ("goal") with which they are associated, we have in Fig. 2.6 a system that is in general capable of guiding the organism to the goals it needs to attain (food, water, etc.) for survival (Deutsch, 1964; Gray, 1975, chapter 5). At the neurological level the last decade has seen rapid progress (see Gray, Feldon et al., 1991, upon which

FIG. 2.6. The Behavioral Approach System (BAS) as defined by its inputs and outputs.

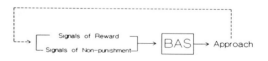

this section is closely based; Groves, 1983; Penney & Young, 1981; and Swerdlow & Koob, 1987) in the construction of plausible neuropsychological models of the BAS (though, in the relevant literature, this phrase has not itself been used, terms such as "motor programming system" being preferred). The key components are the basal ganglia (the dorsal and ventral striatum, and dorsal and ventral pallidum); the dopaminergic fibers that ascend from the mesencephalon (substantia nigra and nucleus A 10 in the ventral tegmental area) to innervate the basal ganglia; thalamic nuclei closely linked to the basal ganglia; and, similarly, neocortical areas (motor, sensorimotor, and prefrontal cortex) closely linked to the basal ganglia. These structures and their interconnections are set out schematically in Fig. 2.7 (based on Gray, Feldon et al., 1991; Groves, 1983; Penney & Young, 1981; and chiefly Swerdlow & Koob, 1987).

It is useful to see this overall system as being made up of two closely interrelated subsystems, centered on the dorsal striatum (caudate-putamen, CP in Fig.

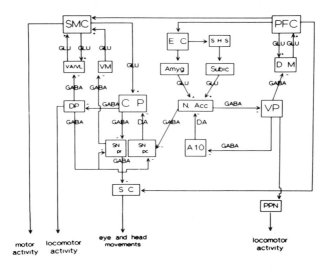

FIG. 2.7.   Major structures composing the neural basis of the Behavioral Approach System and its interrelations with the Behavioral Inhibition System. Structures: SMC = sensorimotor cortex; PFC = prefrontal cortex; EC = entorhinal cortex; SHS = septohippocampal system; Subic = subicular area; Amyg = amygdala; VA/VL = n. ventralis anterior and ventralis lateralis thalami; VM = n. ventralis medialis thalami; DM = n. dorsalis medialis thalami; DP = dorsal pallidum; VP = ventral pallidum; CP = caudate-putamen; N. Acc = n. accumbens; SNpr = substantia nigra, pars reticulata; SNpc = substantia nigra, pars compacta; A 10 = n. A 10 in ventral tegmental area; SC = superior colliculus; PPN = penduculopontine nucleus. Transmitters: GLU = glutamate; DA = dopamine; GABA = y-aminobutyric acid.

2.7) and ventral striatum (nucleus accumbens, N. Acc in Fig. 2.7), respectively. The caudate subsystem relates together non-limbic cortex (motor, sensorimotor, and association cortices), the dorsal striatum, the dorsal globus pallidus, nuclei ventralis anterior and ventralis lateralis of the thalamus, and the ascending dopaminergic pathway from the substantia nigra to the caudate-putamen. This system appears to be concerned with the detailed sensorimotor content of motor programs. The accumbens subsystem interrelates limbic cortex (prefrontal and cingulate regions), the ventral striatum, the ventral globus pallidus, the dorsomedial nucleus of the thalamus, and the ascending dopaminergic projection to the nucleus accumbens from nucleus A 10. This system appears to be concerned with the more emotional aspects of motor programming, namely, goal direction and incentive motivation. Importantly, the nucleus accumbens also receives projections from the amygdala and from the subiculum (output station for the SHS). According to the model proposed by Gray, Feldon et al. (1991), the former projection (as supported by much information from, for example, single-unit recording; Rolls & Williams, 1987) conveys information about associations between successive subgoals and the final biological reinforcer to which the whole motor program is directed; whereas the latter conveys information from the comparator system depicted in Fig. 2.3 and 2.4, earlier, indicating whether successive subgoals at each step in the motor program have in fact been attained or not. A key coordinating role is also played by the prefrontal cortex, which is connected to all the other major components of the system depicted in Fig. 2.7.

A detailed model of how this system acts to discharge the behavioral functions of the BAS (Fig. 2.6) is set out by Gray, Feldon et al. The chief assumptions on which the model rests are as follows:

1. The caudate system, by way of its connections with sensory and motor cortices, encodes the specific content of each step in a motor program (e.g. for a rat, press the lever on the right; or, for a human being, say the word "cheese"); for reasons set out by Gray, Feldon et al. (1991), a motor step has a duration of about one-tenth of a second.

2. The accumbens system operates in tandem with the caudate system so as to permit switching from one step to the next in a motor program.

3. Both the establishment of the sequence of steps that makes up a given motor program, and the subsequent orderly running of the program, are guided by the projection to nucleus accumbens from the amygdala; this projection conveys information concerning cue-reinforcement associations.

4. The septohippocampal system (Fig. 2.3) is responsible for checking whether the actual outcome of a particular motor step matches the expected outcome (Gray, 1982a, 1982b); this information is transmitted to nucleus accumbens by way of the projection from the subiculum.

5. The activities of (A) the caudate, (B) the accumbens, and (C) the septohip-pocampal systems are coordinated and kept in step with one another by the prefrontal cortex, acting by way of its interconnections, respectively, with (a) the cortical components of the caudate system, (b) nucleus accumbens, dorsomedial thalamus, and amygdala, and (c) the entorhinal and cingulate cortices.

For further details of this model of the BAS, the reader is referred to Gray, Feldon et al. (1991) and Gray, Hemsley et al. (1991). Recent research with human participants has related this system to the reactivity of the autonomic nervous system (Fowles, 1980) and to behavior, especially in children (Lahey, McBurnett, Loeber & Hart, in press; Quay, 1988), but there has been little work relating it to human emotion as such. Given the functions with which it is attributed, we might expect it to underlie such states as pleasurable anticipation ("hope"; Mowrer, 1960), elation, or happiness.

AN APPROACH TO TAXONOMY

This section explores how these three emotion systems (the BIS, FFS, and BAS) can be used to provide a framework for the taxonomy of human emotions, emotional behavior, and emotional disorders. Note that, if this approach is suc-cessful at all, it will not result simply in the type of factor-analytic dimensional taxonomy familiar from models both of mood and emotion (Tellegen, 1985) and of personality (Eysenck & Eysenck, 1985); though, as we shall see, these models bear an important relation to the approach pursued here. The reason for the greater complexity of the present approach is that emotions and their disorders can be seen as reflecting variously: over- or underactivity in one of the three systems; dysfunction in one system; combinations of over/underactivity and/or dysfunction in more than one system; or dysfunctional interactions between more than one system. These various possibilities cannot readily be translated into expectations concerned with the relative similarities between different emotions and emotional disorders that are captured by multidimensional statistical tax-onomies. Thus, in what follows, the emphasis will be on relating particular conditions to the three emotion systems in the manner outlined above; though this endeavor will certainly have implications for the relative closeness of differ-ent conditions in "emotion space."

Anxiety

As will be clear from the discussion above of the BIS, the easiest condition with which to commence our taxonomy is that of anxiety. Both in concept and in its data base (Gray, 1982a, 1982b), the BIS is so closely interwoven with this emotion that it follows almost axiomatically that anxiety consists in a high level of activity in the BIS. However, it is not the case that this statement is immune to empirical test. Indeed, it is already clear both that some experimental findings at the human level are in agreement with the theoretical structure that relates the BIS to anxiety, and that others require important qualifications to be made to any statement of identity between the two concepts.

One key empirical test is that of sensitivity to antianxiety drugs, because it was initially on the behavioral effects of these compounds in animals that the input–output relationships depicted in Fig. 2.2 were based. Because it was known before the concept of the BIS was developed that such drugs do indeed reduce human anxiety (e.g., Rickels, 1978), it is surprising to find that further research on their effects has given rise to one of the ways in which any equation between high BIS activity and anxiety needs to be qualified. Klein (1981) has reviewed much evidence that a key group of antianxiety drugs, the benzodiazepines, which are effective in most forms of anxiety, are not usually so in the treatment of panic attacks. The latter do, however, respond to treatment with serotonin-uptake blockers. These pharmacological data have persuaded most authorities that panic has a different neural basis to that underlying other forms of anxiety. Clearly, therefore, one cannot attribute both panic and anxiety to the BIS; panic must belong elsewhere (we shall see where in a moment).

On the other hand, in agreement with the view that the neural structures mediating the BIS (Fig. 2.3) are related to human anxiety, it has been found in a PET scanning study already mentioned (Reiman, 1990; Reiman et al., 1984) that a group of patients suffering from an anxiety disorder differed from normal controls in only one brain region, namely, the posterior parahippocampal region, containing the entorhinal cortex (the major input to the septohippocampal system) and the subicular area (its major output station), where they showed heightened blood flow lateralized to the right hemisphere. But this gratifying observation poses a further problem for the BIS model, because the patients concerned had a diagnosis of panic disorder. This puzzle appears, however, to be amenable to solution. The differences between the patients and the normal controls were established at a time when they were not actually experiencing a panic attack. Now, it is known that, between actual attacks, patients with panic disorder (who are often also agoraphobic) also experience high levels of anxiety (often termed "anticipatory" anxiety because it is in anticipation that they may encounter stimuli that will trigger a panic attack), and that this anticipatory anxiety is responsive to treatment with benzodiazepines. Hence all falls into place: Anticipatory anxiety in these patients is accompanied by heightened activity in part of the neural system that is thought to mediate the functions of the BIS.

Panic

What of the panic attacks themselves? Given Graeff's (1987) observations, mentioned earlier, that electrical stimulation of the central gray in animals elicits autonomic responses that resemble those observed in human panic, and that these responses are under serotonergic inhibitory control, one can plausibly suggest: (a) that heightened activity in the central gray portion of the FFS underlies the symptoms seen in a panic attack, and (b) that it is in this region that the antipanic effects of serotonin-uptake blocking drugs are exerted. Limitations on the spatial resolution of *in vivo* neuroimaging techniques preclude direct assessment in human subjects of the role of the central gray in panic. The studies carried out by Reiman's (1990) group have, however, demonstrated increased blood flow during lactate-induced panic (in patients with panic disorder) in the temporopolar cortex, a region that is connected with, on the one hand, the hippocampal formation and parahippocampal gyrus (implicated in the BIS) and, on the other, the amygdala (implicated in the FFS). On the hypothesis being developed here, it is the latter relationship that we would expect to be involved in panic attacks.

Deakin and Graeff (1991) provided an illuminating discussion of the significance of these proposed interactions between panic, mediated by the central gray, and anticipatory anxiety. They pointed out that the inhibitory control exercised over the central gray by serotonergic afferents (regarded as forming part of the BIS) implies not merely that in panic disorder anticipatory anxiety alternates with panic attacks, but that anxiety actively inhibits panic. This capacity to inhibit panic may provide at least part of the explanation for the gradual spread of anticipatory anxiety, with a concomitant reduction in the frequency of panics, noted by Klein and Klein (1989). Deakin and Graeff (1991) suggested, furthermore, that similar mechanisms may be involved in the otherwise puzzling phenomena of relaxation-induced (Adler et al., 1987) and nocturnal panic attacks: The restraint on such attacks normally exercised by anticipatory anxiety, according to their hypothesis, is lost during relaxation and sleep. This framework of explanation may also be applicable to patients whose anticipatory anxiety focuses not on panic attacks but on outbursts of anger and aggression; and also to the negative relationships between anxiety and aggression noted in studies of childhood conduct disorder by Lahey, McBurnett and Loeber (in press), and between fear and pain sensitivity in animal experiments (Bolles & Fanselow, 1980; Fanselow, in press). Recall that, as illustrated in Fig. 2.5, the outputs of the FFS include both escape behavior (which is perhaps equivalent to panic) and defensive aggression (perhaps equivalent to anger), and that painful stimuli constitute a major class of inputs to the FFS. This model therefore implies that anxiety and anger should interact in similar manners to anxiety and panic, because both equate to interactions between the BIS and FFS; and, similarly, anxiety and pain. The same general analysis may apply, finally, to at least some kinds of suicide, especially if this is construed as self-directed aggression: There have been a number of observations on postmortem material from the brains of suicides that imply reduced serotonergic transmission, although to date these observations implicate the frontal lobes (Stanley, Virgilio, & Gershon, 1982) rather than the structures we are considering here.

The Addictions

So far we have discussed emotional behavior related to the BIS and FFS; let us turn now to the BAS. Many of our insights into the activity of this system in human life stem from studies of the neurotransmitter, dopamine. This (Fig. 2.7) provides the transmission both from the substantia nigra to the caudate-putamen and from nucleus A 10 in the ventral tegmental area to the nucleus accumbens. As outlined in detail by Gray, Feldon et al. (1991) and Gray, Hemsley et al. (1991), the release of dopamine in the caudate and accumbens can be regarded as playing the role, within the general conception of the BAS, of switching motor programs from one step to the next.

Behaviorally, much evidence implicates such dopamine release in the normal processes of reinforcement (Fibiger & Phillips, 1988), leading to the establishment, maintenance, and running-off of chains of instrumental responding that lead to food, water, and so on. It is of particular interest in the present context that virtually all drugs of major recreational use or abuse have been shown to cause the release of dopamine in the nucleus accumbens, and in some cases rather selectively in this region: heroin, amphetamine, and cocaine (Stewart, De Wit, & Eikelboom, 1984), alcohol (Di Chiara & Imperato, 1985), and nicotine (Imperato, Mulas, & Di Chiara, 1986; Mitchell, Brazell, Joseph, Alavijeh, & Gray, 1989). One can speculate, therefore, that dopamine release in the nucleus accumbens is closely related to the emotional "high" caused by these compounds, and that this is perhaps an exaggerated version of the pleasure occasioned by more conventional forms of reinforcement. Functionally, one can also speculate that drugs of this kind pervert the normal manner in which instrumental reinforcers act. According to the model developed by Gray, Feldon et al. (1991) and Gray, Hemsley et al. (1991), different sets of neurons fire sequentially in the accumbens system, triggering coupled sets of neurons to fire sequentially in the caudate system, the sequence corresponding to an ordered set of steps in a motor program that lead the respondent, via a series of subgoals, to the final reinforcer (food, water, etc.); the spatiotemporally patterned release of dopamine in the nucleus accumbens acts to switch firing to the next neuronal set, and is itself a consequence of the firing of the previous set. If, now, dopamine release is provoked by a drug (alcohol, amphetamine, etc.) in a manner that is of longer duration than would normally follow neuronal firing and independent of such firing, switching along the ordered set of steps that make up a motor program would not be able to occur. Instead the respondent would, as it were, get "stuck" in whatever it was doing at the time, namely, ingesting the drug. In this way, one can make some sense of the addictive nature of such drug taking.

Depression

If, as indicated in the previous section, dopamine release in the nucleus accumbens is closely related to pleasurable reactions to reward, one might expect that a reduction or impairment in such release would be related to loss of such reactions. A loss of this kind—anhedonia—is, of course, a central feature of clinical depression. Is it possible, then, that depression reflects reduced dopamine release in the nucleus accumbens? The evidence for this hypothesis was considered in detail by Willner (1985), who however is unable to come to any firm conclusion.

Part of the difficulty in doing so is that "depression" is almost certainly not a unitary diagnosis. Rather, there appears to be a continuum of "depressions" running from (1) a condition ("neurotic depression") that, at one extreme, is strongly mixed with anxiety, is characterized by considerable agitation, occurs in individuals with a type of personality (neurotic and introverted; see the section on Personality and Mood, later) that predisposes also to anxiety disorders, and is responsive to the same drugs that are effective in treating anxiety; to (2) a condition ("psychotic depression") that, at the other extreme, is rather free of anxiety, is characterized by motor retardation, occurs in individuals who tend to be neither neurotic nor introverted, and is responsive to treatments that are relatively ineffective in anxiety (see Gray, 1982a, for a detailed discussion). One way of making sense of these data is to call upon the reciprocal inhibition that is postulated (Gray, 1987) to link the BIS and BAS. Consider, first, an individual responding to threat with anxiety (i.e., heightened activity in the BIS); this will give rise secondarily to inhibition of the BAS, experienced as depression mixed with anxiety. This process can plausibly be seen as giving rise to a depression at the first extreme of the continuum distinguished above. The other extreme, in contrast, would arise from a primary failure of adequate reactions to reward on the part of the BAS; this, by release of reciprocal inhibition of the BIS, might lead secondarily to an increased vulnerability to threat. If this analysis is correct, it would only be depressions close to the second extreme of the continuum that might be due to a primary impairment in dopamine release in the nucleus accumbens. This hypothesis is worthy of experimental attention, perhaps by determining whether antidepressant drugs that increase dopaminergic transmission are particularly effective in depression of this kind.

Schizophrenia

As in the case of depression, considered earlier, some of the most interesting possibilities arise when we consider the *interaction* between the BAS and the BIS. Some kind of interaction between these two systems is a conceptual necessity for the smooth functioning of both. The septohippocampal comparator at the heart of the BIS (Fig. 2.3 and 2.4) is, among other things, charged with the function of monitoring the running of ongoing motor programs to ensure that the expected outcomes of such programs (step by step) do actually occur; if they do not, the outputs of the BIS (Fig. 2.2) are operated, these constituting the phobic avoidance symptoms of anxiety (Gray, 1982a, 1982b). For the septohippocampal comparator to be able to function in this way, it must receive information from the BAS about the current step in the motor program. This information is postulated to enter the septohippocampal system via the projections from the prefrontal and entorhinal cortices, after relay to the prefrontal cortex from the nucleus accumbens via the dorsomedial nucleus of the thalamus (Fig. 2.7). However, the monitoring of the success of motor programs is of equal importance to the smooth running of the BAS; hence, it is postulated (Gray, Feldon et al., 1991; Gray, Hemsley et al., 1991) that the septohippocampal comparator passes the relevant information to the BAS via the projection from the subiculum to the nucleus accumbens (Fig. 2.7). This projection is provided with two functions. If there is a "mismatch," that is the appropriate outcome of a step in a motor program does not occur but is replaced by some other event, the ongoing motor program is halted (the "behavioral inhibition" output of Fig. 2.2); if there is a "match" between the expected outcome and the actual event, on the other hand, this message from the subiculum forms part of the information (along with information from the amygdala to the same region of the nucleus accumbens specifying which is the *next* step in the motor program) that permits switching from one step to the next.

A disturbance in these interactions between the BAS and BIS appears to be fundamental to the cognitive dysfunction that gives rise to the positive symptoms of acute schizophrenia (Hemsley, 1987; Gray, Feldon et al., 1991; Gray, Hemsley et al. 1991). Two specific and complementary hypotheses have been proposed, each consistent with the known pathology observed in postmortem schizophrenic brain.

Frith (1987) proposed a dysfunctional input from the prefrontal cortex to the septohippocampal system; psychologically, he suggested, this would have the consequence that the patient would fail to recognize things he does or experiences as his own willed acts, when in fact they are. That is to say, in terms of the analysis of the BAS and BIS developed above, the septohippocampal comparator would not be provided with the information it requires from the BAS for effective monitoring of motor programs; in consequence, outcomes of these programs that should generate "match" messages would in fact generate a "mismatch," that is, would seem novel or alien. Experientially, this would give rise to auditory hallucinations (arising from internally generated speech episodes), thought insertion, and feelings of alien control.

In a complementary fashion, Gray, Feldon et al. (1991) and Gray, Hemsley et al. (1991) proposed a dysfunctional input from the subiculum to the nucleus accumbens, with the consequence that the smooth running of motor programs (including the perceptual programs mediated by the output from the substantia nigra to the superior colliculus; see Fig. 2.7) would be interrupted by events that should have generated "match" messages but are not in fact accompanied by such a message. Gray, Feldon et al. (1991) and Gray, Hemsley et al.'s (1991) model links the disruption of the subicular projection to the nucleus accumbens with the leading current neurochemical hypothesis of schizophrenia, namely, that this reflects functional overactivity in dopaminergic transmission in the latter structure. This linkage between (a) the structural damage in temporal lobe structures, including the hippocampal formation, known to be present in the schizophrenic brain, and (b) dopaminergic transmission is seen as being a consequence of a disturbance in the normal balance between the inputs to the nucleus accumbens from the subiculum and nucleus A 10 respectively. Experientially, the disrupted subicular input to the nucleus accumbens would be expected to give rise to apparently novel, and therefore attention-capturing, percepts, accounting for the bizarre perceptual symptoms reported by schizophrenic patients (Hemsley, 1987); and also to delusional causal associations that, in the normal individual, would be blocked (Jones, 1989; Jones, Hemsley, & Gray, 1990) by prior experience of the event that is, for the schizophrenic, apparently novel (Hemsley, 1990). Although these symptoms, and those for which Frith's (1987) model attempts to account, are not themselves prototypically "emotional," but rather "cognitive," it is instructive to see how the emotion-system framework can be applied to them; applied, furthermore, in a manner that yields experimentally testable, and indeed tested (e.g., Baruch, Hemsley, & Gray, 1988; Gray, Hemsley et al., 1991; N. S. Gray, Pickering, Hemsley, Dawling & Gray, 1992) predictions. Of course, schizophrenia also includes more obviously "emotional" symptoms, some of which can be analyzed reasonably easily within this framework. An example is the high level of anxiety that is often a feature of the early stages of schizophrenia (Chapman, 1966), and that is precisely what would be expected from a malfunction of the interactions between the BIS and the BAS leading to the labelling of many stimuli, wrongly, as "novel" (see the "novelty" input to the BIS in Fig. 2.2).

A second condition that may involve dysfunctional interactions between the BIS and BAS is obsessive–compulsive disorder. The most widely accepted account of the sometimes bizarre behavioral symptoms characteristic of this condition (e.g., compulsive repetitive hand-washing) is that they reflect active avoidance behavior, that is, behavior aimed at preventing the occurrence of a real or imagined aversive event (Gray, 1971; Rachman & Hodgson, 1978). According to the approach adopted here (following Mowrer, 1960, and Gray, 1971), such behavior is accomplished by the BAS (see the feedback loop between "approach" and "signals of nonpunishment" in Fig. 2.6). On the other hand, active avoidance behavior can be carried out only if there are conditioned stimuli associated with the aversive event able to activate such behavior; and stimuli of this kind (a) are thought to be initially established by way of the amygdala (part of the FFS) and (b) also to activate the BIS (see Fig. 2.2). The role of the amygdala can perhaps be neglected, because it is transient, involved only in the establishment of the relevant conditioned stimuli. But, of its nature, active avoidance behavior must include repeated activation of both the BIS and the BAS.

Clinically, the role of the BIS in obsessive–compulsive disorder can be demonstrated by the increase in anxiety that reliably follows upon experimental prevention of the compulsive behavior (Rachman & Hodgson, 1978). The BIS has also been proposed as the system that produces the cognitive phenomena that are equally characteristic of obsessive–compulsive disorder, that is, frequent rumination upon potential threats and checking on whether or not they have occurred or may occur. It has been suggested by Gray (1982a, 1982b) that this kind of excessive cognitive checking is due to overactivity in the septohippocampal comparator system (Figs. 2.3 and 2.4), whose major function is precisely that of detecting events that are threatening, either because they are unpredicted ("mismatch") and therefore indicate environmental uncertainty, or because they are already associated with aversive events.

The role of the BAS in obsessive–compulsive disorder has been given much less consideration. But there is indirect evidence implicating the basal ganglia in this condition. This evidence comes from studies showing a familial association between obsessive–compulsive disorder and Tourette's syndrome (Pauls, Leckman, Towbin, Zahner, & Cohen, 1986), a disorder in which tics and other disturbances of motor behavior figure prominently and that probably involves dysfunction in the dopaminergic innervation of the basal ganglia. The observed association is sex dependent, obsessive–compulsive disorder being relatively more common in females and Tourette's syndrome, in males. The common behavioral elements that link these two conditions may lie in the repetitive and compulsive nature of the symptoms that characterize them (tics in Tourette's syndrome, rituals and ruminations in obsessive–compulsive disorder). These features suggest overactivity in the ascending dopaminergic pathways in the basal ganglia; the dopamine-releasing drug, amphetamine, can produce similarly repetitive and apparently compulsive behavior in animals (Kelly, Seviour, & Iversen, 1975). At least part of the behavior patterns involved in compulsive rituals may be related to grooming behavior observed in animals (Gray, 1982a, p. 443), and perhaps mediated by striatal mechanisms that could become dysfunctional in obsessive–compulsive disorder (Rapoport, 1990; Wise & Rapoport, 1988). This analysis is particularly plausible for that most common of rituals, hand-washing.

This line of argument brings obsessive–compulsive disorder rather close to schizophrenia, a condition that is also thought to reflect in part dopaminergic overactivity in the basal ganglia and that can be provoked or mimicked by the administration of amphetamine (Gray, Feldon et al., 1991; Gray, Hemsley et al., 1991); and there is indeed a long tradition within psychiatric nosology that puts these two conditions together (e.g. Robinson, Winnik, & Weiss, 1976). As noted earlier, one way of thinking about schizophrenia is that it reflects an abnormal input from the subiculum to the nucleus accumbens (Gray, Feldon et al., 1991). At the same time, it appears possible to regard obsessive–compulsive disorder as reflecting a simultaneous overactivity in the BIS and BAS, the former underlying the cognitive phenomena that characterize this condition and the latter, the behavioral outputs. The latter role, played by the BAS, is perhaps in part based on a genetic predisposition to heightened dopaminergic transmission in the basal ganglia, this giving rise to the familial association between obsessive–compulsive disorder and Tourette's syndrome.

The Amygdala

The amygdala appears to play such an important part in emotion that it requires a section all to itself, even though this interrupts the logic, dictated by psychiatric condition rather than neural structure, that we have so far followed. Within the emotion-system framework adopted here, we can distinguish between at least three separate roles played by this structure.

First, the amygdala plays a key role in the formation of cue-reinforcement associations (Rolls & Williams, 1987). Because both the BIS and the BAS respond to conditioned reinforcing events, it is clear that any dysfunction in the neural substrate by which such associations are formed would be expected to have widely ramified effects on emotional life. This expectation is borne out by the well-known Klüver-Bucy syndrome, in which animals after amygdalectomy display inappropriate affective behavior.

Second, by transferring information about proximity to goal objects, based on such cue-reinforcement associations, to the BAS (via the projection to the nucleus accumbens), the amygdala plays an important role in the establishment and maintenance of motor programs (Gray, Feldon et al., 1991). This role is complementary to the input from the subiculum to the nucleus accumbens (see the section on schizophrenia, earlier): This input informs the BAS whether the last step in the motor program has been successfully accomplished, while that from the amygdala helps to select the next step in the program. Although the model we have proposed for the cognitive dysfunctions of acute schizophrenia (Gray, Feldon et al., 1991) has emphasized the subiculo-accumbens projection, it is likely that the amygdalo-accumbens projection also plays a major part; it is noteworthy that the pathology observed in the schizophrenic brain extends to the amygdala as well as the hippocampal formation. Functionally, a disturbance in the sequence with which successive steps follow one another in a motor program could plausibly give rise to the characteristic schizophrenic symptom of thought disorder. (A second such symptom, that of inappropriate affect, may be the human equivalent of the Klüver-Bucy syndrome, noted earlier, and result directly from difficulties in forming cue-reinforcement associations.)

Third, the amygdala is the highest limbic center in the FFS, controlling the outputs of this system by way of its descending projections to the medial hypothalamus and thence to the central gray. Thus, excessive activity in the amygdala is likely to be involved in both terror/panic and extreme anger. Conversely, loss of function in the amygdala would be expected to lead to low reactivity to the unconditioned aversive stimuli that elicit panic and/or defensive aggression; just such a taming effect is a well-known consequence of amygdalectomy in animals (Gray, 1987).

It is as yet unclear whether these three separate functions are discharged by a single neuronal system, or whether different systems are merely located close to one another in the general area of the amygdala. The anatomy of this region of the brain is complex and as yet not fully understood; furthermore, its functional anatomy appears to differ more substantially between different species than does, say, that of the hippocampal formation. Thus, study of this problem remains difficult. Functionally, there is an obvious connection between the first two roles, that of forming cue-reinforcement associations and that of transmitting the resulting information to other structures in the brain. The third role, that of responding to unconditioned aversive stimuli with flight/fight behavior, however, seems rather different; though information about such stimuli is clearly also required for the formation of associative links to them.

Personality and Mood

I have so far concentrated on emotions and emotional disorders. I shall conclude, however, with a brief consideration of the relations between this analysis of emotion systems, on the one hand, and personality dimensions, on the other.

I have previously proposed (Gray, 1970) that individual differences in the reactivity of the BIS to its adequate stimuli, as defined by Fig. 2.2, may underlie a dimension of personality ("trait anxiety") that, in terms of H. J. Eysenck's well-known three-dimensional scheme (Eysenck & Eysenck, 1985), is approximately a 30-degree rotation of his neuroticism dimension in the two-dimensional space defined also by introversion–extraversion; high trait anxiety is thus a mixture of high neuroticism and high introversion, the former being the more important component (by a factor of approximately two) in the mix. Similarly, I have proposed (Gray, 1970) that individual differences in the reactivity of the BAS to its adequate stimuli (Fig. 2.6) underlie a dimension of "impulsivity" that is a 30-degree rotation of Eysenck's introversion–extraversion dimension; so that high impulsivity would be a mixture of high neuroticism and high extraversion, the latter being the more important component. Tellegen (1985) and Eysenck and Eysenck (1985) preferred the only slightly different hypothesis that neuroticism directly reflects the reactivity of the BIS and extraversion, that of the BAS. Given the emotions that we have attributed to state activation of these two systems, it can be predicted from these hypotheses that neurotic (the Tellegen-Eysenck version) or neurotic-introverted (Gray's version) individuals should experience more negative affect, and that extraverted or neurotic-extraverted individuals should experience more positive affect (happiness).

The available data are consistent with these predictions (Argyle & Lu, 1990; Costa & McCrae, 1980; Tellegen, 1985). It is naturally harder, however, to distinguish between the Eysenck and Gray versions of the hypotheses. A recent study by Larsen and Ketelaar (1991) illustrates this difficulty. These authors used two mood-induction procedures, involving affective imagery, aimed at creating negative or positive affect respectively; the effects of the procedures were assessed by having the participants rate their moods on a series of adjectives. For negative affect, these were: "distressed, fearful, nervous, jittery, anxious, annoyed"; and for positive affect, "enthusiastic, excited, elated, peppy, euphoric, lively." The major results of the study are presented in Table 2.1. As predicted by both versions of the hypothesis under test, the effects of the mood-induction procedure were significantly greater in neurotic than stable participants for negative affect; and significantly greater in extraverted than introverted participants for positive affect.

In addition to these findings, however, Gray's (1970) hypothesis predicts that, for negative affect, the effectiveness of mood induction should be enhanced by introversion to a degree about half that of the enhancement produced by neuroticism. This prediction is confirmed by the data shown in Table 2.1 (bottom line, significant correlations between personality and mood of $-.18$ for extraversion versus .34 for neuroticism). But Gray's (1970) hypothesis also predicts that for positive affect the effectiveness of mood induction should be enhanced by neuroticism about half as much as by extraversion. The top line of Table 2.1 shows that, contrary to this prediction (and also not as predicted by the Tellegen-Eysenck hypothesis, though not clearly contradictory to it), there is indeed a significant correlation between neuroticism and induced positive affect about half

TABLE 2.1
Correlations Between Personality Scores
and Mood Within Mood-Induction
Conditions

Induction	Extraversion	Neuroticism
Positive		
PA	.32**	−.19*
NA	.02	.10
Neutral		
PA	.10	−.03
NA	−.12	.29**
Negative		
PA	.00	.13
NA	−.18*	.34**

Note. PA = positive affect; NA = negative affect
* $< .05$ **$p < .01$
Data from Larsen and Ketelaar (1991).

the size of the correlation with extraversion ($-.19$ vs. $.32$); but this correlation is in the wrong direction, *high* neuroticism being associated with *low* positive affect. Thus, the significant subsidiary correlations (between extraversion and negative affect, and between neuroticism and positive affect) pose a problem for both the Tellegen-Eysenck and the Gray versions of the hypothesis: The former predicts zero correlations in both cases, whereas the latter correctly predicts the size and direction of one but is flatly contradicted by the direction of the other. So the jury is still out on the fine details. But in general terms, this approach to understanding the personality correlates of negative and positive affect appears to be on the right lines.

Personality and Reinforcement

In the light of these difficulties in distinguishing between the Tellegen-Eysenck and Gray hypotheses, it might seem reasonable to choose the former. This has the major virtues of simplicity and of consistency with the vast amount of factor-analytic data that has gone into the making of Eysenck's two dimensions of personality, neuroticism and extraversion–introversion. However, there is a problem, posed by other data sets, in adopting the Tellegen-Eysenck view.

Eysenck's (1981) general theory of introversion–extraversion supposes that, under conditions of low arousal, introverts will show learning and performance that is superior to those of extraverts; and that, under conditions of high arousal, these relationships will be reversed. His model has no natural place for reward and punishment as such (though these are relevant variables in setting the level of arousal). Thus the hypothesis that extraverts will show greater positive affect than introverts, even though Eysenck has adopted it (Eysenck & Eysenck, 1985, p. 141), sits rather separately from the rest of his theory. In Gray's (1970) approach, in contrast, the variables of reward and punishment (acting via the BAS and BIS, respectively, as outlined above) are central concepts. Based on these concepts, the specific hypotheses (a) that trait anxiety reflects individual differences in the reactivity of the BIS, (b) that trait impulsivity reflects individual differences in the reactivity of the BAS, and (c) that trait anxiety and impulsivity are 30-degree rotations of neuroticism and introversion–extraversion, respectively (see above), jointly predict that, other things being equal, introverts will learn and perform better than extraverts if punishment is used, whereas extraverts will do better than introverts with reward.

Consider now what predictions one might try to derive about the roles of reward and punishment from the Tellegen-Eysenck hypothesis concerning positive and negative affect. If we preserve the conceptual link (central to the present approach, but surely not immune to question) between affect and reinforcement, it must follow from this hypothesis that extraverts relative to introverts will learn and perform better with reward (neuroticism having no influence), and that neurotic relative to stable individuals will learn and perform better with punishment (introversion–extraversion having no influence). There are at least two major problems with this position.

The first problem is a logical one: It is virtually impossible to combine this position with the alternative already derived from Eysenck's overall theory above, namely, that, whether reward or punishment is used, introverts should do better than extraverts under low arousal and extraverts better than introverts under high arousal, neuroticism being unimportant in either event. Thus, in its current state, Eysenck's overall theory appears to contradict itself.

The second problem for the Tellegen-Eysenck approach lies in the existing data on the influence of reward and punishment on performance as a function of introversion–extraversion. These appear to converge on the conclusion that, irrespective of level of arousal, introverts are superior to extraverts if punishment is used, whereas extraverts are superior to introverts if reward is used (Boddy et al., 1986; Gray, 1981; Lahey, McBurnett, Loeber, & Hart, in press; Newman, 1987; Quay, 1988). This outcome is incompatible both with Eysenck's (1981; Eysenck & Eysenck, 1985) overall model and with the Tellegen-Eysenck hypothesis. For the former, it is an embarrassment (Gray, 1981) that extraverts do better than introverts with reward (unless the experimental conditions are highly arousing, which has not typically been the case in the relevant experiments); for the latter, it is an embarrassment that introverts and extraverts differ when punishment is used (because the effects of this variable should be influenced by the neuroticism dimension only).

Thus, if either the overall Eysenckian or the Tellegen-Eysenck view is correct, the conclusions drawn above from the existing data on interactions between personality and reinforcement must be incorrect. Given the importance, therefore, of this issue, we have embarked on a substantial program of experimental research to examine it afresh; but so far with only inconclusive results (Gray, Hernaiz, Corr, Diaz, & Pickering, 1991).

CONCLUSION

The extension of the emotion-system approach into the field of personality, as in the last two sections, is of course closely related to the analysis of emotion and emotional disorder by which these were preceded. Emotional disorders do not occur randomly in the population. Even when there is a major disaster, those of the victims who develop posttraumatic stress disorder are more likely to be of a neurotic-introverted personality than those who do not; and this kind of predisposing effect of personality is much stronger in the absence of major trauma. Similarly, as noted in the section on depression, those of a neurotic-introverted disposition are more likely to develop neurotic depression, whereas stable-extraverted individuals are more likely to develop psychotic depression. Thus, any complete analysis of psychiatric disorder needs to take into account predisposing personality factors, as well as the phenomenology of emotion itself. One of the advantages of the approach followed here is that it lends itself naturally to this joint attack. Anxiety, for example, is seen as deriving from a currently high level of anxiety in the BIS. Correspondingly, the trait of high susceptibility to anxiety (neurotic introversion) is seen to reflect a BIS that is chronically reactive to its adequate inputs; and the trait of low susceptibility to anxiety, a probable contributing factor in the development of primary psychopathy (Gray, 1981), is seen to reflect a BIS of chronically low reactivity.

Just as the emotion-system approach is able to encompass emotion and personality with equal ease, so the reader will perhaps be convinced that it can move with similar ease between the poles of brain and behavior. The data bases upon which this approach rests have been gathered from experimental studies in both psychology and neuroscience; the arguments we have deployed depend in nearly all cases on both types of data base; and the terminology we have developed straddles the two fields of study in a way which—or so I hope—leaves open few cracks for infiltration by even the thinnest of Cartesian ghosts: There is no hyphen in the "neuropsychology" of emotion.

REFERENCES

Adams, D. B. (1979). Brain mechanisms for offence, defense, and submission. *Behavioral and Brain Sciences, 2,* 201–241.

Adler, C. M., Crafke, M. G., & Barlow, D. H. (1987). Relaxation-induced panic (RIP): When resting isn't peaceful. *Integrative Psychiatry, 2,* 94–112.

Amsel, A. (1962). Frustrative non-reward in partial reinforcement and discrimination learning: Some recent history and a theoretical extension. *Psychological Review, 69,* 306–328.

Argyle, M., & Lu, L. (1990). The happiness of extraverts. *Personality and Individual Differences, 11,* 1011–1017.

Baruch, I., Hemsley, D. R., & Gray, J. A. (1988). Differential performance of acute and chronic schizophrenics in a latent inhibition task. *Journal of Nervous and Mental Diseases, 176,* 598–606.

Berlyne, D. E. (1960). *Conflict, arousal and curiosity.* New York: McGraw-Hill.

Boddy, J., Carver, A., & Rowley, K. (1986). Effect of positive and negative reinforcement on performance as a function of extraversion–intraversion: Some tests of Gray's theory. *Personality and Individual Differences, 7,* 81–88.

Bolles, R. C., & Fanselow, M. S. (1980). A perceptual defensive-recuperative model of fear and pain. *Behavioral and Brain Sciences, 3,* 291–323.

Chapman, J. (1966). The early symptoms of schizophrenia. *British Journal of Psychiatry, 112,* 225–251.

Costa, P. T., & McCrae, R. R. (1980). Influence of extraversion and neuroticism on subjective well-being: Happy and unhappy people. *Journal of Personality and Social Psychology, 38,* 668–678.

Deakin, J. F. W., & Graeff, F. G. (1991). 5-HT and mechanisms of defence. *Journal of Psychopharmacology, 5,* 305–315.

Deutsch, J. A. (1964). *The structural basis of behaviour.* Cambridge: Cambridge University Press.

Di Chiara, G., & Imperato, A. (1985). Ethanol preferentially stimulates dopamine release in the nucleus accumbens of freely moving rats. *European Journal of Pharmacology, 80*, 67–73.

Eysenck, H. J. (Ed.). (1981). *A model for personality.* New York: Springer.

Eysenck, H. J., & Eysenck, M. W. (1985). *Personality and individual differences: A natural science approach.* New York: Plenum Press.

Fanselow, M. S. (in press). The midbrain periaqueductal gray as a coordinator of action in response to fear and anxiety. In A. Depaulis & R. Bandler (Eds.), *The midbrain periaqueductal grey matter: Functional, anatomical and immunohistochemical organization.* New York: Plenum Press.

Fibiger, H. C., & Philips, A. G. (1988). Mesocorticolimbic dopamine systems and reward. In P. W. Kalivas & C. B. Nemeroff (Eds.), *The mesolimbic dopamine system* (pp. 206–215). Bethesda: New York Academy of Sciences.

Fowles, D. (1980). The three arousal model: Implications of Gray's two-factor learning theory for heart rate, electrodermal activity and psychopathy. *Psychophysiology, 17*, 87–104.

Frijda, N. H. (1986). *The emotions.* Cambridge: Cambridge University Press.

Frith, C. D. (1987). The positive and negative symptoms of schizophrenia reflect impairments in the perception and initiation of action. *Psychological Medicine, 17*, 631–648.

Graeff, F. G. (1987). The anti-aversive action of drugs. In T. Thompson, P. B. Dews, & J. Barrett (Eds.), *advances in behavioural pharmacology* (Vol. 6, pp. 129–156). Hillsdale, NJ: Lawrence Erlbaum Associates.

Gray, J. A. (1970). The psychophysiological basis of introversion–extraversion. *Behaviour Research and Therapy, 8*, 249–266.

Gray, J. A. (1971). *The psychology of fear and stress.* London: Weidenfeld & Nicolson; New York: McGraw Hill.

Gray, J. A. (1975). *Elements of a two-process theory of learning.* London: Academic Press.

Gray, J. A. (1977). Drug effects on fear and frustration: Possible limbic site of action of minor tranquilizers. In L. L. Iversen, S. D. Iversen, & S. H. Snyder (Eds.), *Handbook of psychopharmacology* (Vol. 8, pp. 433–529). New York: Plenum.

Gray, J. A. (1981). A critique of Eysenck's theory of personality. In H. J. Eysenck (Ed.), *A model for personality* (pp. 246–276). Berlin: Springer.

Gray, J. A. (1982a). *The neuropsychology of anxiety: An enquiry into the functions of the septo-hippocampal system.* Oxford: Oxford University Press.

Gray, J. A. (1982b). Précis of "The neuropsychology of anxiety: An enquiry into the functions of the septo-hippocampal system." *Behavioural and Brain Sciences, 5*, 469–484.

Gray, J. A. (1984). The hippocampus as an interface between cognition and emotion. In H. L. Roitblat, T. G. Bever, & H. S. Terrace (Eds.), *Animal cognition* (pp. 607–626). Hillsdale, NJ: Lawrence Erlbaum Associates.

Gray, J. A. (1985). Anxiety and the brain: Pigments aren't colour names. *Bulletin of the British Psychological Society, 38*, 299–300.

Gray, J. A. (1987). *The psychology of fear and stress* (2nd ed.). Cambridge: Cambridge University Press.

Gray, J. A. (Ed.). (1990). Psychological aspects of relationships between emotion and cognition (pp. 305–315). Special issue. *Cognition and Emotion, 4*, 161–308). Hove, England: Lawrence Erlbaum Associates.

Gray, J. A. (1991). Fear, panic, and anxiety: What's in a name? *Psychological Inquiry, 2*, 77–78.

Gray, J. A., Feldon, J., Rawlins, J. N. P., Hemsley, D. R., & Smith, A. D. (1991). The neuropsychology of schizophrenia. *Behavioral and Brain Sciences, 14*, 1–20.

Gray, J. A., Hemsley, D. R. Feldon, J., Gray, N. S., & Rawlins, J. N. P. (1991). Schiz bits: Misses, mysteries and hits. *Behavioral and Brain Sciences, 14*, 56–84.

Gray, J. A., Hernaiz, H. S., Corr, P., Diaz, A., & Pickering, A. D. (1991, July). *Can Eysenck's and Gray's factors co-exist in the same personality space?* Paper presented at the Fifth Conference of the International Society for the Study of Individual Differences, Oxford, England.

Gray, J. A., & McNaughton, N. (1983). Comparison between the behavioural effects of septal and hippocampal lesions: A review. *Neuroscience and Biobehavioural Reviews, 5,* 109–132.

Gray, N. S., Pickering, A. D., Hemsley, D. R., Dawling, S., & Gray, J. A. (1992). Abolition of latent inhibition by a single 5 mg dose of d-amphetamine in man. *Psychopharmacology, 107,* 425–430.

Groves, P. M. (1983). A theory of the functional organization of the neostriatum and the neostriatal control of voluntary movement. *Brain Research Reviews, 5,* 109–132.

Hemsley, D. R. (1987). An experimental psychological model for schizophrenia. In H. Hafner, W. F. Gattaz, & W. Janzavik (Eds.), *Search for the causes of schizophrenia* (pp. 179–188). New York: Springer-Verlag.

Hemsley, D. R. (1990). What have cognitive deficits to do with schizophrenia? In G. Huber (Ed.), *Idiopathische Psychosen,* (pp. 111–127). Stuttgart: Schatlauer.

Imperato, A., Mulas, A., & Di Chiara, G. (1986). Nicotine preferentially stimulates dopamine release in the limbic system of freely moving rats. *European Journal of Pharmacology, 132,* 337–338.

Jones, S. H. (1989). *The Kamin blocking effect, incidental learning and choice reaction time in acute and chronic schizophrenia.* Unpublished doctoral dissertation, University of London.

Jones, S. H., Hemsley, D. R., & Gray, J. A. (1990). The Kamin blocking effect, incidental learning and psychoticism. *British Journal of Psychology, 81,* 95–109.

Kelly, P. K., Seviour, P. W., & Iversen, S. D. (1975). Amphetamine and apomorphine responses in the rat following 6-OHDA lesions of the nucleus accumbens septi and corpus striatum. *Brain Research, 94,* 507–522.

Klein, D. F. (1981). Anxiety reconceptualized. In D. F. Klein & J. Rabkin (Eds.), *Anxiety: New research and changing concepts* (pp. 235–263). New York: Raven Press.

Klein, D. F., & Klein, H. M. (1989). The definition and psychopharmacology of spontaneous panic and phobia. In P. Tyrer (Ed.). *Psychopharmacology of Anxiety* (pp. 135–162). Oxford, England: Oxford University Press.

Lahey, B. B., McBurnett, K., Loeber, R., & Hart, E. L. (in press). Psychobiology of conduct disorder. In G. P. Sholevar (Ed.), *Conduct disorders in children and adolescents: Assessments and interventions.* Washington D.C.: American Psychiatric Press.

Larsen, R. J., & Ketelaar, T. (1991). Personality and susceptibility to positive and negative emotional states. *Journal of Personality and Social Psychology, 61,* 132–140.

Lazarus, R. S., & Folkman, S. (1984). *Stress, appraisal and coping.* New York: Springer-Verlag.

LeDoux, J. E. (1987). Emotion. In F. Plum & V. Mountcastle (Eds.), *Handbook of physiology, nervous system V. Higher function* (pp. 419–459). Washington, DC: American Physiological Society.

Lyons, W. (1980). *Emotion.* Cambridge, England: Cambridge University Press.

Mathews, A. (1988). Anxiety and the processing of threatening information. In V. Hamilton, G. H. Bower, & N. Frijda (Eds.), *Cognitive perspectives on emotion and motivation* (pp. 265–284). Dordrecht: Kluwer Academic Publishers.

Miller, N. E. (1951). Learnable drives and rewards. In S. S. Stevens (Ed.), *Handbook of experimental psychology* (pp. 435–472). New York: Wiley.

Mitchell, S. N., Brazell, M. P., Joseph, M. H., Alavijeh, M. S., & Gray, J. A. (1989). Regionally specific effects of acute and chronic nicotine on rates of catecholamine and indoleamine synthesis in rat brain. *European Journal of Pharmacology, 167,* 311–322.

Mowrer, O. H. (1947). On the dual nature of learning: A re-interpretation of "conditioning" and "problem-solving." *Harvard Education Review, 17,* 102–148.

Mowrer, O. H. (1960). *Learning theory and behavior.* New York: Wiley.

Newman, J. P. (1987). Reaction to punishment in extraverts and psychopaths: Implications for the impulsive behavior of disinhibited individuals. *Journal of Research in Personality, 21,* 464–480.

Olds, J., & Olds, M. (1965). Drives, rewards and the brain. In F. Barron, W. C. Dement, W. Edwards, H. Lindmann, L. D. Phillips, J. Olds, & M. Olds (Eds.), *New directions in psychology* (Vol. 2, pp. 329–410). New York: Holt, Rinehart & Winston.

Panksepp, J. (1982). Towards a general psychobiological theory of emotions. *Behavioral & Brain Sciences, 5,* 407–422.

Panksepp, J. (1990). Gray zones at the emotion/cognition interface: A commentary. In J. A. Gray (Ed.), *Psychobiological aspects of relationships between emotion and cognition.* Special edition of *Cognition and Emotion, 4,* 289–302. Hove, England: Lawrence Erlbaum Associates.

Pauls, D. L., Leckman, J. F., Towbin, K. E., Zahner, G. E. P., & Cohen, D. J. (1986). A possible genetic relationship exists between Tourette's syndrome and obsessive–compulsive disorder. *Psychopharmacology Bulletin, 22,* 730–733.

Penney, J. B., & Young, A. B. (1981). GABA as the pallidothalamic neuro-transmitter: Implications for basal ganglia function. *Brain Research, 207,* 195–199.

Quay, H. C. (1988). The behavioral reward and inhibition system in childhood behavior disorders. In L. M. Bloomingdale (Ed.), *Attention deficit disorder* (Vol. 3, pp. 176–186). New York: Pergamon.

Rachman, S., & Hodgson, R. (1978). *Obsessions and compulsions.* Englewood Cliffs, NJ: Prentice Hall.

Rapoport, S. I. (1990). Integrated phylogeny of the primate brain, with special reference to humans and their diseases. *Brain Research Reviews, 15,* 267–294.

Reiman, E. M. (1990). Positron emission topography in the study of panic disorder and anticipatory anxiety. In G. D. Burrows, M. Roth, & R. Noyes Jr. (Eds.), *Handbook of anxiety: Vol. 3. The neurobiology of anxiety* (pp. 289–305). Amsterdam: Elsevier.

Reiman, E. M., Raichle, M. E., Butler, F. K., Hersovitch, P., & Robins, E. (1984). A focal brain abnormality in panic disorder, a severe form of anxiety. *Nature, 310,* 683–685.

Rickels, K. (1978). Use of anti-anxiety agents in anxious outpatients. *Psychopharmacology, 58,* 1–17.

Robinson, M. M., Winnik, H. Z., & Weiss, A. A. (1976). "Obsessive psychosis," justification for a separate clinical entity. *Isr. Ann. Psychiatry, 14,* 39–48.

Rolls, E. T., & Williams, G. V. (1987). Sensory and movement-related neuronal activity in different regions of the primate striatum. In J. S. Schneider & T. I. Kidsky (Eds.), *Basal ganglia and behaviour: Sensory aspects and motor functioning* (pp. 37–59). Toronto: Hans Huber.

Spence, J. T., & Spence, K. W. (1966). The motivational components of manifest anxiety: Drive and drive stimuli. In C. D. Spielberger (Ed.), *Anxiety and behavior* (pp. 291–326). New York: Academic Press.

Stanley, M., Virgilio, J., & Gershon, S. (1982). Tritiated imipramine binding sites are decreased in the frontal cortex of suicides. *Science, 216,* 1337–1339.

Stewart, J., De Wit, H., & Eikelboom, R. (1984). Role of unconditioned and conditioned drug effects in the self-administration of opiates and stimulants. *Psychological Review, 91,* 251–268.

Swerdlow, N. R., & Koob, G. F. (1987). Dopamine, schizophrenia, mania and depression: Toward a unified hypothesis of cortico-striato-palido-thalamic function. *Behavioral and Brain Sciences, 10,* 215–217.

Tellegen, A. (1985). Structures of mood and personality and their relevance to assessing anxiety, with an emphasis on self-report. In A. H. Tuma & J. Mason (Eds.), *Anxiety and the anxiety disorders* (pp. 681–706). Hillsdale, NJ: Lawrence Erlbaum Associates.

Willner, P. (1985). *Depression: A psychobiological synthesis.* New York: Wiley.

Wise, S. P., & Rapoport, J. L. (1988). Obsessive–compulsive disorders: Is it basal ganglia dysfunction? In J. L. Rapoport (Ed.), *Obsessive-compulsive disorder in children and adolescents* (pp. 327–346). Washington, DC: American Psychiatric Press.

Zuckerman, M. (1982). Leaping up the phylogenetic scale in explaining anxiety: Perils and possibilities. *Behavioral and Brain Sciences, 5,* 505–506.

3 The Motivational Organization of Emotion: Affect-Reflex Connections

Peter J. Lang
University of Florida

There is a tendency in contemporary psychology for the field to divide into smaller and smaller independent subspecialties. Given the sheer volume and diversity of research, investigators are ever more inclined to limit the enterprise, by employing a short list of basic paradigms, reading and writing for a restricted set of journals, and interacting with and responding to a small club of investigators. The problem areas of greatest interest, on the other hand, show little respect for these self-protective barriers. They casually penetrate the formal division of science, depositing new intellectual spores, and thus, even the most parochial researcher runs the risk of being surprised by a larger vision. This danger is now acute among students of emotion, as the research area explodes across disciplines. Emotion is currently a central topic for psychopathologists and social psychologists—it has more recently been addressed by cognitive psychologists—and defines a major research effort in animal behavior, neurology, and the neurosciences.

In the early stages of an investigation, Voltaire's admonition to *cultivate our own gardens* is indeed excellent advice. We risk losing our way in a data base that is too large, becoming confused in a multidisciplinary Babel. As a research problem matures, however, cross-pollination from other fields can be positive, stimulating a new growth of ideas and deepening understanding. Emotion research may now be at this stage of broader effort. In this decade of the brain, it may be time to look across the fences that divide areas of study, and begin a serious search for communalities that link diverse data and promise theoretical integration.

It is in this ecumenical spirit (which always illuminates the work of Nico Frijda) that the following commentary is offered. It begins with our own early work on fear imagery and clinical behavior change, highlighting insights gained through psychophysiological measurement. We subsequently describe efforts to conceptualize these data, using the information processing models of an emerging cognitive science. Finally, we relate this analysis to recent findings in neuroscience—first, by delineating some of the subcortical circuitry that appears to drive emotional processing, and second, by showing how methods adapted from animal research on the startle reflex advance our understanding of interactions between emotional states (potentiation or inhibition) in human participants.

FEAR BEHAVIOR AND FEAR CHANGE

Our study of emotion began with clinical experiments on fear and phobia (e.g., Lang & Lazovik, 1963; Lang, Lazovik, & Reynolds, 1965). The focus was on explaining the mechanism of the then new behavioral therapies: desensitization, flooding, exposure, implosive therapy, and the like. The common factor in all these treatments, as in earlier cathartic methods, is the therapist's insistence that during treatment sessions clients repeatedly reexperience their primary fear.

Although this is sometimes accomplished through direct confrontation with actual phobic objects, the client is often simply instructed to image the emotional event, prompted only by the therapist's guiding description of the fear context. In clinical trials, this approach has generally yielded positive results (e.g., Paul, 1969): Repeated presentation in imagination reduces fear in most simple phobic patients. The client's emotional images appear to act in a way similar to actual fear stimuli, and repeated exposure prompts a "working through"—habituation or counter conditioning in the animal laboratory—of the fear response. Of course, not all patients so instructed show fear change. Indeed, some clients go through the entire procedure without appreciable therapeutic gain.

These treatment failures prompted us, some years ago, to analyze carefully individual differences in imaginal responses (e.g., Lang, Melamed, & Hart, 1970). It was soon clear that successful clients could not be distinguished from the unsuccessful on the basis of their reported fear. With few exceptions, phobic patients *all* describe similar, intense fear reactions when imagining fearful events. There were, however, significant differences in physiological reactions. Clients who responded well to treatment (the majority of the sample) showed concordance between heart rate change and fear reports, that is, more frightening images were associated with greater autonomic response increases than less frightening images. This close association between language and autonomic output was not found for the few therapy failures. In addition, successful respondents were more likely to report images to be highly fearful during sessions in which their base heart rate, and presumably physiological arousal, was high. Again, no such effect was apparent in those failing to respond to treatment.

These results affirmed that there were basic differences in participants' fear patterns—physiology, behavior, and language responses (Lang, 1968, 1978). From a treatment perspective, fear images were either functional, that is, they were associated with an arousal physiology and prompted behavior change, or they were verbal epiphenomena. This provocative distinction shifted the focus of our experimental program from the behavioral to the cognitive phenomena of fear, that is, to the internal psychological events that mediate forms of emotional expression.

EMOTION AS INFORMATION PROCESSING

Subjective experience has traditionally defied scientific analysis and, at the outset, the fear image appeared to this researcher like a smooth-sided black box—mysterious and impenetrable. Fortunately, theoretical developments in another field suggested a way inside. Cognitive psychologists had begun to conceive mentation as analogous to the operations of the digital computer. In this view, the brain is an organ for storing and processing information. Reports of thoughts, images, and feelings reflect, however imperfectly, computational events in the brain. The analytic problem is to define information structures and processing programs that link stimulus input and behavior.

Two lines of inquiry were relevant. Firstly, researchers were attempting to understand the information structure of narrative text: How is it represented in the brain? What are the brain's underlying programs for its comprehension. For example, Anderson and Bower (1974; see also Kintsch, 1974) proposed that knowledge was represented as a network of concept units, linked by laws of association. Text became meaningful when input statements (propositions) activated subunits of a particular knowledge network. Activation spread to the entire structure through its associative links, bringing fresh, relevant information from long-term memory into the brain's currently active workspace.

Secondly, several cognitive scientists had proposed that mental images were not unitary, iconic representations, but were also complex knowledge structures, made up of many conceptual (information) subunits. As Pylyshyn (1973) said, an image "is much closer to being a description of the scene than a picture of it. . . . it contains a finite amount of information, it may contain abstract as well as concrete aspects . . . it contains terms (symbols for objects, attributes and relations) which are the results of—not inputs to—perceptual processes" (p. 11). This analysis seemed particularly appropriate for the emotional images of therapy, which, furthermore, have a narrative quality, and generally include action (behavioral) elements.

Armed with this perspective, we reexamined the fear experience in therapy, and discovered not only a way to understand fear, but that "other emotional states (e.g., anger, sexual arousal) [could] be analyzed from a similar conceptual framework," and furthermore, that it provided "a method for examining the interaction of emotional states" (Lang, 1977, p. 884). This view was developed in a series of theory papers over the subsequent decade (e.g., Lang, 1977, 1978, 1979, 1984, 1985, 1987), and in its current form, is briefly described here.

THE BIOINFORMATIONAL THEORY OF EMOTION

Emotions are action dispositions (see also Frijda, 1986, 1987). They are instantiated when specific memory episodes (about context and behavior) are retrieved. Emotional episodes are coded in memory as networks of mutually activating information units. In processing the network, activity in one unit is transmitted to adjacent units, and depending on the strength of activation, the entire structure may be engaged. The probability of whole network processing is increased with the number of units initially stimulated.

We presume that the fundamental network is neural. The network form is, however, an equally useful description at the conceptual level. In this case, the emotion is made up of associated concept units (which, in turn, might be individual neural subnetworks). The higher level concepts are of three basic types: stimulus, response, and meaning. Stimulus units are representations of perceptual events; response units code the three basic response systems or output procedures—behavioral acts, physiological mobilization, and expressive language (Lang, 1978); meaning units refer to associated declarative (semantic) knowledge. This taxonomy is descriptively convenient; however, the actual neural subunits may well cut across the proposed categories. For example, Hebb (1949) early described how visual stimulus representations might be based on the neural patterns instigated by eye movement responses.

Emotion networks can be described in natural language (e.g., Dutch, French, English) as linked set of propositions.[1] The contents of possible fear (phobia) and anger networks are listed below:

FEAR EPISODE—*Stimulus:* You are alone in the woods. A large diamond-backed snake slithers onto the path, right in front of you. Its spade shaped head darts forward; *Meaning:* Snakes are unpredictable. People can die of snakebite; *Response:* Scream, "I'm afraid! (verbal); heart rate increase, face goes pale (visceral); Muscles tense. You run away (behavioral).
ANGER EPISODE—*Stimulus:* A car cuts you off and takes your parking space; the driver laughs; the offending driver is small in stature; *Meaning:* There are no

---

[1]Influenced by the cognitive psychology of the time, earlier formulations of bioinformational theory (Lang, 1977, 1979) suggested that networks should be construed as having a basic propositional suborganization. We are now less convinced of its generality. "Given the connectionist arguments (McClelland & Rumelhart, 1985), all elements, including the lowest order concepts in our model, might be viewed as distributed patterns of values in some hypothetical general brain code" (Lang, 1987, p. 410).

more parking spaces; the same thing happened the day before; small people can be attacked with impunity; *Response:* "That pisses me off!" (verbal); vasodilation in facial tissue, blood pressure, heart rate and palmar sweating increase (visceral); Corrugator and masseter muscles tense, fist clenched and raised (behavioral).

The above rendering, as a set of statements, should not be construed to mean that the information in an emotion network is solely, or even primarily, linguistic. That is, stimulus and response events have more fundamental—ontogenetic and phylogenetic—neuroconceptual representation in memory. In all organisms, they are activated primarily by the external events and actions they represent. In man, these primary representations are more broadly cued, that is, by language descriptions, moving and still pictures, diagrams, and other symbolic stimuli remote from the natural context.

It is important to emphasize, furthermore, that the basic connection between concepts is simple association. Thus, the emotional output of network processing does not depend on narrative structure or apprehended causal connectedness. We do not presume that the information from, for example, the ANGER EPISODE is necessarially processed as an internal, rational monologue, that is, "This person is frustrating my efforts; its unjustified; he doesn't care about me; also, he's not very big, and can't retaliate effectively. Therefore, I will punish him." Indeed, it is held that simple emotion networks mediate affective behavior in organisms with scant, if any, narrative capacity.

On the other hand, we do not suggest that human emotion is never accompanied by causal schemas (e.g., see Leventhal, 1980) or that such stories are unimportant in life. An emotion's story (an *a priori* if–then schema, consistent with activated network concepts) might well be in memory before the affective event; alternatively, the story may develop after the act, to satisfy rationalist demands for explanation. Given the historical and cultural ubiquity of narrative (see Jaynes, 1976), it may even be a basic human need—one founded on a significant survival value in organizing and planning behavior, and in facilitating social cooperation. In the bioinformational view, however, the story is not the quiddity of emotional action.

Imagery and Action Memory

In a previous article (Lang, 1985, see Fig. 3.1), I attempted to capture the layered nature of the emotion network in a three dimensional graphic. From this perspective, an upper, language layer contains, for example, the FEAR EPISODE data as a network of verbal representations. This language data can be processed as narrative, according to stored rules of style, syntax, and grammar. A normal respondent could also, based on associated knowledge, define the words used, tell the story in different words, and explain the background and probable consequences of the event. That is, the respondent would "understand"

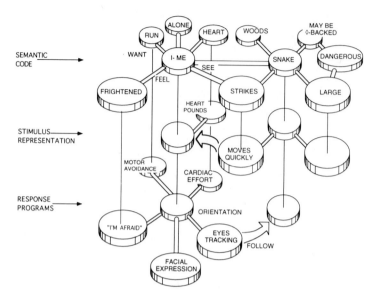

FIG. 3.1. The figure is taken from Lang (1985, p. 160). It is only one of a variety of possible useful models. The same data would currently be rendered very differently, for example, from the perspective of parallel distributed processing (McClelland & Rumelhart, 1988).

A fear prototype is represented here as a conceptual network of propositionally coded information. Subunits are related by association, and the functional output is a visceral and somato-motor program. The prototype may be activated by instructional, media, or objective sensory input, which contains information matching that in the network. The conceptual content is essentially the same as that listed in the test for the FEAR EPISODE (with an additional eye movement component).

Propositions in the network are represented by the round discs, containing the concept name, and the labeled stems that show the links between concepts. In the notation proposed by Kintsch (1974), the stems indicate predicators and the round nodes are their arguments (e.g., Is, Snake, Large). No attempt is made here to indicate all propositions or all possible connections. However, it is suggested that certain propositions are strongly bonded to others, and may thus be keys to the representation. For example, as a basic stimulus representation, (Moves, Snake, Quickly) may have a primitive, high-probability connection to (Pounds, I-Me, Heart), which in turn unlocks the other fear-response propositions, prompting rapid prototype activation.

The model is presented here in Tinkertoy form to illustrate three basic levels in the brain code. The semantic code is the high-level language, which includes three broad classes of information—stimulus, meaning, and response propositions. Stimulus information may also enjoy a more fundamental representation as primary, action-defined, input concepts. The base representation of the entire network

66

the network information as text in a natural language, and in theory, this could be accomplished without activating any imaginal or affective experience. Indeed, researchers in artificial intelligence have tried to build this sort of "understanding" into actual computers (e.g., Schank, 1982), and we recently witnessed a "Turing test" of current achievements on public television (with Daniel C. Dennett as moderator; Markoff, 1991).

The computer is a convenient metaphor for the human brain, and as suggested above, software can be written to emulate some of its computational functions. Unlike the computer, however, the brain's computational machinery is wedded to a biological chassis. Thus, as language input or retrieved text, emotion relevant information is seldom processed in this hypothetically restrictive fashion, that is, only as language. Words that symbolize perceptual events and actions automatically activate more fundamental representations of specific stimuli and responses. Furthermore, these more primitive network layers are connected to brain centers for afferent and efferent processing. Thus, through simple association, a text input can prompt the same action programs for muscles and glands that are cued by real events.

A respondent may say after reading a persuasive text (or hearing a dramatic reading) that it is "as if," or it "feels" something like, the described events were really happening. We propose that it is the associative spread of activation beyond the network's language level, engaging stimulus and response processors in the brain, that underlies such reports of media prompted imagery and affective experience. Considerable neurophysiological and psychophysiological evidence supports this hypothesis. On the sensory side, for example, recent EEG studies (Farah, 1988) have shown that visual images activate the same occipital area of the brain known to be involved in visual perception. From the efferent perspective, beginning with the classic research of Jacobson (1931), there is a vast research literature (see Cuthbert, Vrana, & Bradley, 1991; McGuigan, 1973) showing that instructionally evoked action images—from eye tracking to shooting baskets—prompt potentials in the appropriate muscle systems.

In general, of course, the efferent effects of response information processing

---

is the efferent code that organizes responding. Concepts may or may not be represented across levels. Network activation can theoretically begin with any set of concepts and move within or between structural levels. Similarly, mediation between different emotion networks (as in state-dependent learning) could be carried by concepts of any type—stimulus, response, meaning—or at any of the three levels of the structure.

The view taken here is that the deep structure of the prototype is an action set. Although the prototype can be described in a natural language, and the semantic level may be processed with some degree of independence from the rest of the memory architecture, an affective network is functionally organized to generate efferent output. Thus, the processing of conceptual emotional information (*in imago* or *in vivo*) always involved some degree of visceral and motor outflow.

are so minute, a kind of "efferent leakage," that they can be measured only by the bioelectric amplifier. The respondent's experience of an action context is only "feeling," that is, a disposition to behave that may have no overt sequelae (Frijda, 1986). Thus, effector systems are activated by the network, but the final instruction for overt behavior is "gated out", presumably by context driven inhibitory information (e.g., "the savage polar bears that he's talking about aren't really here in Amsterdam."). The barriers to action, however, can be fragile. Thus, responses move beyond the covert in good hypnotic participants, whose eyes close automatically when they think about "how their eyes are heavy, how weights are attached to the lids, how they are moving inexorably down . . . down."

The associative processes described here are automatic and not controlled, to use Schneider & Shiffrin's distinction (1977). In fact, they may defy intentionality. In the same way that Dostoyevski's brother, once told by the noted author not to think about "a white bear," could not stop thinking ursine thoughts (see Wegner, Schneider, Carter, & White, 1987), we have difficulty suppressing ideomotor connections. Furthermore, although language descriptions were used here to illustrate these effects, there are normally many input paths to an action network, including other media, such as pictures, films, plays, sound, and music. Thus, a televised Olympic jump may elicit an empathic, covert muscle action, though the viewer never leaves the comfort of his armchair.

Processing the Network

An important way that affects differ from other memories is that the former are always based on action networks. They are not declarative knowledge or specific emotion nodes (Bower, 1981) stored in some semantic catalogue, but memories of behavioral episodes (Tulving, 1983). Thus, they include action procedures. More specifically, emotion networks contain response information and activate associated efference (muscles, organ systems, glands).

During the 1970s and 1980s we examined the above view in a series of experiments, evaluating psychophysiological responses to emotionally evocative texts. Our specific aim was to determine the conditions under which a verbal description of events is processed as affect, that is, not solely as "understood" language. Emotional processing was defined as the generation of a pattern of autonomic and somatic activity in the respondent, behaviorally consistent with the emotional context being described.

As we suggest above, this broader, affective processing is normal in human beings. That is, efferent output is expected to occur when an emotional network structure is activated. Furthermore, reported affective intensity is roughly correlated with the magnitude of physiological reactance. Thus, when snake fear information is presented as a narrative, snake phobics (defined by questionnaire or interview) respond strongly—more strongly than participants who report that snakes only make them uncomfortable, and much more than participants with no history of snake fear. In short, although incidents of discordance are not infrequent (i.e., individual respondents who profess strong affect, but whose effector systems are silent), on average, report and behavioral measures of fear intensity are significant predictors of physiological expressivity.

Matching Concepts in Memory

Working with normal college participants (who respond to appropriate text with anger, fear, and the like, but are not pathologically primed), we were subsequently able to specify several other factors that enhance or diminish emotional processing. Firstly, it is an assumption of the model that the network is activated by inputs that match representations in the memory network, and that the more matches, the greater the probability of efferent activation. Consistent with this view, we discovered that adding to the text information about responses ("fist clenched"; "heart racing"), and furthermore, training respondents to attend to this action content, enhanced physiological reactivity (Lang, Kozak, Miller, Levin, & McLean, 1980). We found that autonomic reactions were also facilitated if the verisimilitude of the match was enhanced (Lang, 1984; McLean, 1982), that is, by having the emotional scenario actually acted out before the participant (even though participants "knew" the events were staged).

To some extent, network activation is responsive to processing instructions. That is, when college participants are told to attend to and articulate the specific words in affective text, rather than to image the text as a personal experience, the affective physiological response is reduced (e.g., Vrana, Cuthbert, & Lang, 1989). Significantly, however, the autonomic reactance is not wholly eliminated, that is, despite a verbal orientation, the average participants still responds slightly more to descriptions of emotional situations (a car crash) than neutral situations (sitting at home). As expected, individual differences among respondents are also important. In general, respondents who report a greater prevalence of "vivid" sensory imagery (as measured by questionnaire, Sheehan, 1967) respond to emotional texts (Miller, Levin, Kozak, Cook, McLean, & Lang, 1987) or emotionally evocative pictures (Lang, Greenwald, Bradley, & Hamm, in press) with greater increases in heart rate and skin conductance. Thus, it is possible that an imagery deficit may have contributed to the desensitization failures that we discussed earlier (Lang, Melamed, & Hart, 1970).[2]

When emotional content is well learned, however, the variables considered above are reduced in importance. Thus, although it was shown that an imagistic

---

[2]Although basic differences in cognitive style (e.g., the prevalence or accessibility of images) may determine the therapeutic malleability of emotional memories, much may also depend on the specific procedures employed by the therapist. Foa and Kozak (1986) offer a reasoned response to these issues, based on a novel interpretation of bioinformational theory.

cognitive style facilitated autonomic reactance to text in simple phobics, general fearfulness accounted for substantial, independent variance (McNeil, Vrana, Melamed, Cuthbert, & Lang, in press). Furthermore, when anxiety patients remembered emotional text under alternative imagery and verbal processing instructions, both conditions, unlike for college students, prompted similar, substantial autonomic activity (Patrick, Cuthbert, & Lang, 1989). Thus, in well-established emotion networks, the connections to behavior are not readily deflected by intentional modulation or alternative processing styles. When the cues match, emotion happens.

NEUROPHYSIOLOGICAL FOUNDATIONS OF EMOTIONAL PROCESSING

What Powers the Emotion Network?

The evidence is strong that the retrieval of affective memories is associated with increased autonomic and somatic activity. Furthermore, the evidence suggests that the "functional" consequences of retrieved emotional experience (e.g., as in traumatic sensitization or, alternatively, diminution through therapeutic habituation) depend on some degree of efferent mobilization. In effect, there is no emotion without efference. This is not to say, however, that peripheral feedback is necessary to affective expression. We presume that emotion is primarily a feed-forward system, and that emotion occurs when the central network in the brain is activated (with its efferent component), and that this could occur despite an inactive effector system, for example, one rendered silent through surgery or the administration of curarae.

Furthermore, physiological responding (or evidence that motor or autonomic centers are active) is clearly not in itself an exclusionary index of emotion. For example, memories of effortful tasks (e.g., running up stairs), which would be difficult to label emotional, are often accompanied by an effector shadow of the original energy output.[3] Affective images, however, appear to be a special class of remembered actions: The efferent activation at retrieval is generally more intense. It also appears to be more persistent, more readily instigated by degraded cues, and more refractory to instructional control. In affective expression, the spread of activation from cognition to effectors appears to be specially facilitated?

---

[3]Over 50 years ago, Shaw (1940) reported an experiment in which participants first lifted a series of small lead weights and subsequently imagined this same task. Bioelectric potentials were recorded from the lifting muscles of the forearm. He noted that there was a linear relationship between the amplitude of electromyographic activity during imagery, and the original heft (calibrated in grams) of the remembered lead weight. The intervening years have added considerably to this general literature.

What Makes an Emotional Network Different from other Knowledge Structures in the Brain? The basic answer to this question is that emotion networks include direct connections to the brain's primary motivational system. These are the same subcortical motivational circuits activated by unconditioned appetitive and aversive stimuli. They direct the general mobilization of the organism and the deployment of primitive approach and withdrawal behaviors. Furthermore, it is the same system that mediates the formation of conditioned associations based on primary reinforcement.

We assume that other memory structures do not include these direct links to primary motivational circuits. Thus, if we ask a teenager from a western country to name a population center in southern Vietnam, the memory network activated by the question may yield a specific verbal response, "Ho Chi Minh City," but it does not normally prompt a broad affective, action disposition. If the query is posed to a veteran of the Vietnam war, however, this same input could match content in a network that includes subcortical motivational connections. If the veteran suffers from posttraumatic stress syndrome these connections are high-priority pathways to neural structures that mediate strong autonomic arousal and defensive (fearful or aggressive) behavior. Many of the associated responses are similar to those occasioned by the original trauma. They occur because the same subcortical circuits are reactivated that were motivationally relevant in the original aversive learning context.

The Subcortical Subtext

What is currently known about connections between representations of events and subcortical motivational structures comes from animal research, particularly from studies of aversive learning in the rat. In this species, as in man, massive defensive reactions (autonomic and behavioral) are readily evoked by painful stimuli (e.g., electric shock). If such stimuli reliably occur contiguous with or immediately following a previously innocuous stimulus (e.g., an auditory tone), features of the defensive behavior come to be evoked by the previously neutral stimulus when presented alone. That is, the new stimulus comes to activate a pattern of emotional responses we call fear.

Neurophysiological investigators are beginning to describe the neural basis of conditioning phenomena in information processing terms, for example, "As a result of its association with the US, the CS thus gains access to a network that the US activates. Since the stereotyped emotional responses are coupled to the affective network, they result when that network is activated by either the CS or the US" (LeDoux, 1990, p. 28). For LeDoux (1989), the primary affect network is subcortical, the bottom layer of the larger network structure that we described earlier.

Considerable information is now available about this network's specific neurophysiology (see Fig. 3.2). In the current view, learning (e.g., of an emotional reaction) does not involve the formation of new neural pathways in the brain. Rather, local changes are induced in existing circuits, by altering the neurochemistry of cells and changing the probabilities of synaptic firing. Using anatomical and electrophysiological tools, this chain of probable neural activation can be traced, starting from the input end in the sensory system—proceeding through the necessary connecting structures, defining the links least prodigal in synaptic connections—to the autonomic and motor effectors.

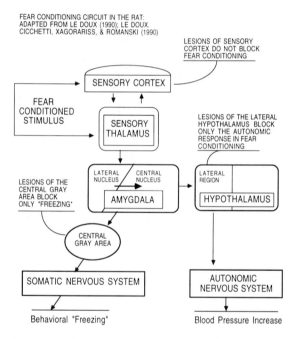

FIG. 3.2.   Schematic representation of a part of the neural network involved in the transformation of an insignificant acoustic tone into a conditioned aversive input. The conditional stimulus is transmitted to the acoustic thalamus (through the auditory system and shell regions of the inferior colliculus [not shown]). The critical thalamic neurons are in the medical geniculate body of the nearby posterior intralaminar nucleus. "The lateral nucleus of the amygdala receives the acoustic signal from the thalamus and transmits to the central amygdala. Efferent to the amygdala the pathway bifurcates. Projections from the central amygdala to the lateral hypothalamic area mediate the autonomic conditioned emotional response, whereas projections to the midbrain central gray region mediate the behavioral conditioned response" (LeDoux, 1990, p. 31).

It was learned early in these investigations that, contrary to Pavlov's view (1927), the activation of simple emotional associations does not depend on prior cortical analysis of the conditioned cue (e.g., DiCara, Braun, & Pappas, 1970). Aversive learning to a simple tone will occur despite extensive lesions to sensory cortex. That is, the higher centers that accomplish "appraisal" or complex pattern recognition are not necessarily in the loop. Information about a stimulus, sufficient to the acquisition of a conditioned emotional response, requires processing only by the acoustically more primitive thalamus.

The next critical connection in this neural network is from the medial geniculate body of the thalamus to the lateral, and then the central nucleus of the amygdala (LeDoux, 1990). The bilateral amygdala, located within the temporal lobes of the brain, has long been known as a critical structure in the mediation of emotional expression (see the edited volume by Ben-Ari, 1981). Both stimulation and ablation of this site reliably produce changes in a variety of affective/motivational behaviors in both animals and man, particularly in autonomic arousal and in fear and aggressive behaviors (Aggleton & Mishkin, 1986; Ursin, Jellestad, & Cabrera, 1981).

Systems and Patterns: Amygdala Connections. In LeDoux's animal model of aversive learning, two dependent variables are assessed, one autonomic (mean blood pressure increase) and one somatic ("freezing," or immobility in the face of threat). By lesioning structures efferent to the central amygdala he has determined that these two conditioned emotional responses are mediated by different structures, with the autonomic response dependent on an intact lateral hypothalamus, and the somatic component requiring an intact midbrain central gray area (see Fig. 3.2). Thus, it might be presumed that, despite a similar system activation, considerable variation in the pattern of affective output could be expected (depending on the weighting of these local pathways).

As the above implies, there is considerable neural plasticity in these subcortical circuits. That is, the brain "learns" at many levels of its anatomy and functioning. The amygdaloid complex is clearly a critical structure in this learning. Furthermore, it appears to be of particular relevance for negative affect and aversion-driven behavior. For example, Cahill and McGaugh (1990) showed that its destruction does not affect appetitively based conditioning; however, lesioning of the amygdala clearly blocks the acquisition of fear responses.

The amygdala circuit appears to be a general mediator of aversive responses, that is, a key site in the general aversive motivational system. Consistent with this role, activation of the amygdala does not define a specific emotional response pattern. Indeed, as indicated above for "freezing" behavior and cardiovascular arousal, there are independent routes from the central nucleus to different response systems, and presumably they can be modulated to produce highly varied outputs. Furthermore, the amygdala circuit has been implicated in a variety of other aversively motivated responses, that is, in escape and avoidance learning (Ursin, 1965); in defensive/aggressive behavior (Blanchard & Blanchard, 1977; Roldan, Alvarez–Pelaez, & Fernandez de Molina, 1974), and, as we will examine in more detail later, in augmenting startle reactions (e.g., Davis, 1989).

This same aversive system also prompts varied hormonal and autonomic responses. For example, Iwata and LeDoux (1988) noted that heart rate and blood pressure decrease in response to a conditioned tone (previously accompanied by shock) when animals are physically restrained; on the other hand, these same autonomic responses increase when the conditional signal is presented to freely behaving animals. These data recall similarly diverse context effects in human participants, who show heart rate acceleration while imaging or thinking about unpleasant events (e.g., Vrana & Lang, 1990), but show significant deceleration when shown unpleasant pictures (e.g., Lang et al., in press).

Cortical Connections:
Unpacking Affective "Appraisal"

In addition to activating descending motor circuits, output from the amygdala system projects to sensory cortex, association cortex, and the hippocampus—structures involved in complex pattern recognition and conceptual information processing. Furthermore, reciprocal circuits from these sites send information back to the lateral amygdala. Thus, the hypothesis that the higher order (semantic or conceptual) network is linked to the subcortical motivation circuit has, at the least, a clear anatomical base. Furthermore, given this two-way traffic lane, it is reasonable to assume that an affect might be initiated at either terminus. That is to say, crude, conditioned sensory input (e.g., a shadow across the visual field) might initiate thalamic activity, which in turn raises the firing level in the amygdaloid system, which would subsequently be projected to association cortex. This aversive motivational input would potentiate associated knowledge structures in memory (e.g., the snake or anger networks listed earlier). The concept network that would capture the brain's primary workspace (and modulate the action pattern) would be one either already primed by previous input, and/or one showing the closest match to other incoming sensations. In this case, emotion (subcortical activation) could be said to precede cognition (the conceptual network), as argued by Zajonc (1980; see also Öhman, Dimberg, & Esteves, 1989, on the preattentive evocation of emotion).

Given the functional anatomy, however, one can as easily imagine an alternative scenario. It is equally reasonable to assume that the initiating stimulus might require more complex primary processing (e.g., someone makes an insulting or demeaning comment). As a unit in a conceptual network, this percept would prime related higher order network matches. The cortical network would then activate lateral and central amygdala, again with collateral emotional autonomic and behavioral sequelae. Does cognition now precede emotion? Was the stimulus first "appraised" (e.g., Lazarus, 1984), before action was initiated?

Although the above issues are popular, we find on examination that the questions are either begged or mired in qualifications. If by cognition we mean only higher cortical processing (conscious thought and the like), then, in the first case, cognition is a late-comer to the party; in the second case, it could perhaps be said that thought precedes the affect. However, the neurophysiological work just reviewed shows great plasticity in the primitive circuitry, that is, it is capable of considerable flexibility in information processing. Are not these subcortical associations part of the ongoing cognition? There are similar problems with appraisal considering that affective association can be learned despite a lesioned cortex. One solution is to redefine the cognitive work of appraisal, as the associative matching mechanism described here. It then has a fundamental role in much affective expression. We would by this course, however, give up every vestige of the term's origins in reasoned, subjective deliberation.

Motivation and Memory: Potentiation and Inhibition of Affective Behaviors

The view of motivation taken here is similar to that of Konorski (1967; see also Mackintosh, 1983): Emotional behaviors, from complex affects to defensive and appetitive reflexes, are categorized according to two different drive states. That is, behaviors are either approach or withdrawal oriented (pleasant or unpleasant), and both these directional dispositions vary continuously in arousal or intensity of activation.

Elsewhere (Lang, Bradley, & Cuthbert, 1990, 1992), we have referred to these variables—affective valence and arousal—as determining the basic strategic stance of the organism. Arousal is a general intensity dimension (perhaps the same as Frijda's 1987 "impact"). It always has valence—either positive or negative affect; however, both drive circuits share some neural connections and structures (e.g., the reticular formation), and both mediate action. Thus, regardless of whether an output is aversively or appetively motivated, intensity of the activation may result in similar visceral logistics and some parallel behavioral consequences. For example, increasing intensity of either positive or negative affect results in greater activity in the sympathetic chain. Because sweat glands are innervated only by the sympathetic system, palmar and plantar skin conductance increases reliably with any emotional activation. That is, when one recalls a pleasant, exciting event, or remembers a distressing traumatic experience, the same sympathetic activation and associated sweat gland activity occurs. Perhaps more importantly, as will be shown below, the arousal value of a memory, irrespective of its valence, can be the primary determinant of what is remembered.

Memory and Arousal

In general, emotional memories are more readily accessed than other stored information, and this effect is augmented with increased affective intensity. For patients with posttraumatic stress disorder, it is exaggerated to the point that strong, fearful memories appear unbidden, disrupting normal life. Without preamble, in the middle of the working day, vivid flashbacks replay previous affective experience of rape or combat; at night, these same images harry the dreamer. Similarly, even simple cues (words like spider, web) will rapidly activate emotional responses in phobics, disrupting ongoing tasks (Watts, McKenna, Sharrock, & Trezise, 1986). Although treatment can reduce these intense fear behaviors, they often spontaneously reappear, or can be reinstated with exposure to minimal cues.

In animals, fear conditioning produces parallel effects. That is, strong, conditioned affective associations are easily elicited and are disruptive of other ongoing behaviors and highly resistant to extinction. Furthermore, even if eventually extinguished, these responses frequently spontaneously recover, or may be reinstated with nominal relearning trials. The persistence and salience of these responses appear to be related to the intensity of the conditioning experience, that is, the amplitude and generality of reactivity at initial learning. Thus, for example, Garcia (Garcia, Hankins, & Rusiniak, 1974) found that poisoned animals—suffering massive, sustained gastric and cardiovascular changes as a result of the poison—showed particularly strong and persistent fear. In conversation, Garcia reported a dramatic instance in which predator wolves were trained to flee in terror from sheep, their natural prey.

Generalizing from the animal data to man, we can presume that the stimuli most readily recalled are those that are most arousing (see Bradley, Chapter 4, this volume). That is, the probability of verbal or visual memory retrieval is increased if the material is strongly connected to the subcortical motivation circuits, as indexed by the intensity of autonomic and somatic behaviors (i.e., persistent and of high amplitude) at encoding. LeDoux (1990) was persuaded that strong emotional memories are to some extent indelible. In support of this view, he cited the fact that cortical lesions reduce or abolish the habituation of fear conditioning. That is, without an intact cortex, permitting the formation of new, inhibitory associations, fear goes on forever.

Memories linked to the positive affect system (as those linked to the aversion circuit) show a similar, arousal-related memorial salience. Clinical cases of intrusive appetitive thoughts and images are as common as are the aversive, phobic, or traumatic stress disorders. The former diagnoses include the great variety of sexual obsessions and drug dependence, as well as the food obsessions associated with anorexia and bulimia. Again, the animal literature provides instructive data on the mechanism. Gold and McGaugh (1975), for example, intervened in the brains of rat subjects during learning, using electrophysiological and pharmacological techniques. This induced activation resulted in the treated animals showing a similar increased resistance to extinction, relative to controls, for both appetitively and aversively reinforced responses.

In a study of human participants, Bradley, Greenwald, Petry, and Lang (1992) studies short- and long-term picture memory for pictures varying in affective valence and arousal: Pictures rated highly arousing, and also evoking large skin conductance responses at first exposure, were best remembered. This effect was the same for both highly arousing positive (sport scenes, erotica) and negative images (mutilated bodies, threatening weapons). Thus, with recall tested in a neutral laboratory environment, intensity of emotion at encoding—rather than valence—appeared as the primary affective determinant of memorial performance.

Positive and Negative Affect

As indicated above, intensity of affect can modulate behavior independent of any directional imperative. On the other hand, appetitive and aversive drives are, in many important ways, reciprocal in influence. In fact, the specific drive state is assumed to tune the organism generally, either appetively or defensively, priming a general class of drive-specific information and behavior. Thus, when a cortical network is engaged with connections, for example, to the aversive system, other affectively negative information is also potentiated. This occurs because of the common associative connections of many different knowledge structures through the subcortical aversive system. Furthermore, following Konorski (1967), and given an active aversive system, evoked appetitive reactions would be reciprocally inhibited. Of course, assuming a dominant appetitive state, the reverse would occur: Positive responses would be primed, and aversive reactions would show relative inhibition.

Strategy and Tactics.   We previously described arousal and valence as strategic motivational dispositions of the organism, meaning by this that they have broad implications for every behavior, but may not be unambiguously reflected in any specific output. Behavior is powerfully influenced by context, which shapes unique patterns of response. From this perspective, much of the variety in emotional expression is best described as tactical, that is, as specific implementations of the strategic motivational disposition, accommodating the available behavioral repertoire and particular situational demands. Thus, aversive learning that originally prompted "freezing" as a response might subsequently occasion attack or flight in a context that permits these options.

Any time a drive system is activated (aversive or appetitive), all networks connected with that specific system are moved towards the threshold of action. The network that ultimately captures the brain's central workspace, and thus determines a specific pattern of behavioral expression, will presumably be the one containing the greatest number of concept matches to the current stimulus context. This network instability, or probabilistic responsiveness to internal and external input variations, is intrinsic in recent "connectionist" modeling of neural networks (e.g., see McClelland & Rumelhart, 1981). From this perspective, emotions are not fixed programs. Thus, aversive system output, for example, may initially look like fear, change to anger if targets are available, or seem to be a blend of both, with either anxiety or agitated depression as potential dominant affects later as arousal diminishes.[4]

As the above account suggests, the hypothesis that simple activation determines memory performance must be amended. When the retrieval context is motivationally neutral, only arousal appears to have significance. When retrieval occurs during a state of enhanced motivation, however, affective contents of matching valence, either appetitive or aversive, have an advantage.

There is considerable data consistent with the above assumption of affect matching. Thus, Berkowitz (in press) recently showed that hostile behavior has a higher probability of occurrence when participants are already in a negative affective state. Results from studies of mood congruence and verbal behavior also follow this pattern. That is, if a negative mood is evoked in participants, or if they are intrinsically unhappy, there is higher probability that they will attend to and seem to better remember unpleasant than pleasant words (see Blaney, 1986, for a review).[5]

AFFECTIVE PRIMING: EMOTION
AND THE STARTLE REFLEX

In the present view, any behavior that was previously motivated by one of the drive systems (aversive or appetitive) is particularly potentiated, when an evoking stimulus occurs during a subsequent, independent activation of that same

---

[4]The model presented here does not presume there are invariant autonomic and/or somatic patterns associated with specific emotions (fear, anger, joy, etc.) as is still argued, for example, by Levenson (1992). The tactical demands of the specific context, and the participant's unique physiological structure, temperament, and specific learning history, inevitably modulate both the behavioral disposition and the physiological logistics of affective expression.

[5]The bioinformational view differs from Bower's (1981) later development of an emotional network model in that it does not assume the existence of separate emotion nodes. In the case of a well-learned affective pattern, the units of the network are in aggregate the emotion prototype. Its facilitation of, or inhibition by, other affects is determined by the degree of associative match between the network's concept units (see Lang, 1985, p. 144–147), and more fundamentally (as we show here) through mutual or discordant connections to the aversive or appetitive motivational systems. Barnard and Teasdale (1991) more recently addressed the same issues of mood congruence in their cognitive subsystems theory. Their approach is derived from psycholinguistics. They conceive an elaborate organization of data processors (including a truly impressive boxology) that operate primarily in the semantic domain. They do not, however, directly address motivational issues, nor is the approach greatly constrained by psychophysiological or neurophysiological data.

system. In this section, we will present evidence that such affect priming is a fundamental mechanism, a general property of organisms, that can be demonstrated at the level of simple reflexes. Specifically, it will be shown that an aversive/defensive reflex (the startle response) is augmented when an organism is already in an aversive state; and furthermore, the reflex is diminished when the prior state does not match, that is, it is positive and appetitive. Furthermore, the neurophysiological substrata of this phenomenon will be explicated for animal subjects, relating it to the aversive learning circuits just considered. Finally, startle research with human participants will be reviewed, showing reflex modulation in emotion that closely parallels the animal model.

The Startle Potentiation

In all mammals, and in most other species, any abrupt sensory event will prompt a general flexor movement of the body, bringing ongoing activity to a halt (Landis & Hunt, 1939). This startle response appears to be a primitive defensive reflex—perhaps serving an immediate protective function, avoiding organ injury (as in the eyeblink), and in acting as an interrupt (Graham, 1979), clearing processors to deal with possible threat. As we presently show, the neural path mediating this behavior is open to modulation by the same aversive motivational system that we have been considering. And, indeed, when the system is activated—as in a fear state—the startle response is considerably faster and of significantly greater amplitude.

The hypothesis that the startle response would be potentiated (augmented) during states of high motivation was first examined systematically by Brown, Kalish, and Farber (1951). These investigators noted that anxiety patients often show exaggerated startle responses. Presuming this to be a function of a high generalized drive state (Hull, 1943), they reasoned that aversively conditioned animals would show a similar enhanced startle when probes (shots from a toy pistol) were presented during the conditioned stimulus (CS) at extinction. Their experiment used male rats as subjects, a light-buzzer compound conditioned stimulus, and a shock unconditioned stimulus. Results conformed to expectation: Animals did indeed react more forcefully, as measured by a stabilimeter in the floor of the cage, when the startle stimuli were presented during previously fear-conditioned signals (see also Ross, 1961; Spence and Runquist, 1958).

The Brain's Fear-Startle Circuit. Davis and his associates (e.g., Davis, 1989; Davis, Hitchcock, & Rosen, 1987) have extensively investigated the neural circuitry underlying the fear–startle connections. Davis holds that classical CS-shock pairings produce a conditioned state of fear, and that it is specifically the presence of this emotional state that augments the reflexive response to startle probes. His work has defined both the basic startle pathway, and the site linking it to the aversive motivational system.

A diagram of the startle circuit is presented in Fig. 3.3. Startle probe input (e.g., an abrupt noise) first activates the cochlear nuclear, sending impulses to the lateral lemniscus, and then on to the reticular formation; the output path passes through spinal neurons to the reflex effectors. This is the basic obligatory circuit, directly driven by the parameters of the input stimulus (e.g., stimulus intensity, frequency, steepness of the onset ramp). The phenomenon of conditioned startle potentiation implies, however, a secondary circuit that modulates the primary reflex pathway. An important initial step in Davis' program was to locate the neural site at which this priming occurs. Their method of investigation

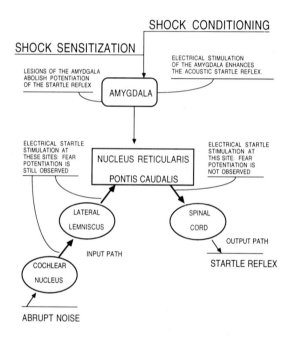

FIG. 3.3. Schematic representation of the primary neural path between a startle stimulus input and its effector output. Locations along this path are shown where stimulation with microelectrodes will, or will not, produce a potentiated startle response. This procedure isolated the neural structure (nucleus reticularis pontis caudalis) where the modulating influence of previous aversive learning impacts on the obligatory startle circuit. The central nucleus of the amygdala (the same central structure in LeDoux's aversive learning network) has monosynaptic projections to this reticular site. The fact that lesioning of the amygdala blocks potentiation, and stimulation with microelectrodes potentiates the reflex (in the absence of prior fear conditioning), prompts the conclusion that this structure is a primary component of the aversive motivational system (see Davis, 1989 for an overview of the neurophysiology).

was to intervene directly in the neural pathway, applying an electrical stimulus with a microelectrode to evoke the startle response (see Berg & Davis, 1985). Although obligatory reflexes were obtained all along the circuit path, the further augmentation of the response due to fear conditioning only occurred if the point of electrical startle stimulation was earlier in the circuit than the nucleus reticularis pontis caudalis. It was thereby deduced that this reticular site is the point at which the modulatory (i.e., motivational) and obligatory circuits intersect.

Considerable evidence suggests that the modulatory circuit that potentiates the startle response is the same subcortical aversive system that has already been discussed. Specifically, it is clear that the central nucleus of the amygdala figures significantly in startle potentiation. Firstly, there are direct, monosynaptic projections from the amygdala to the key reticular site, that is, to the structure in the basic circuit on which modulation of the reflex depends; secondly, electrical stimulation of the amygdala (below the level for kindling) directly enhances startle reflex amplitude; and finally and most important, lesions of the amygdala abolish fear conditioned startle potentiation.

Startle Inhibition

Reward and Drive.   The hypothesis that startle reflex potentiation indexes Hull's generalized Drive (D) factor prompted investigators to examine appetitively as well as aversively determined motivational states. Merryman (1952, described in Brown, 1961) recorded startle probe responses in fear-shock conditioned rats, following food deprivation. Rats who were both fearful *and* hungry reacted more strongly than fear-only or hungry-only animals. Brown interpreted these results as supporting the concept of generalized drive. This effect may have been, however, a unique phenomenon of the shock context. Subsequent investigation of the startle response during food or water deprivation that did not include fear conditioning failed to find reflex increases (Trapold, 1962), failed to replicate initial signs of increased reactivity (Mellgren, 1969), or more often, reported significant startle attenuation (Fechter & Ison, 1972; Ison & Krauter, 1975; Szabo, 1967).

Contrary to the expectations of drive theorists, startle reflex probes were not found to be augmented when presented in the context of conditioned positive incentives. Indeed, several studies have found significantly smaller responses during presentation of cues that signaled food (Armus, Carlson, Guinan, & Crowell, 1964; Armus & Sniadowski–Dolinsky, 1966) or water (Mellgren, 1969). Thus, pairing a CS with an appetitive UCS appears to have an effect opposite to that of pairing it with an aversive, shock UCS: In the appetitive case, probe responses tend to be inhibited during posttraining CS presentations. On the other hand, when the appetitive context is then rendered aversive, that is, cues are presented that are associated with the withholding of rewards and frustration

(Hoffman & Stitt, 1969; Wagner, 1963), startle amplitude may be augmented, as with a punitive shock.

As we have already noted, the amygdala circuit that supports aversive learning does not appear to mediate the acquisition of appetitive associations (Cahill & McGaugh, 1990). Study of the subcortical positive motivation system emphasizes different neural structures and connecting pathways (e.g., Olds, 1960). The rat's smaller startle response in the context of appetitive stimuli suggests, furthermore, that there may be reciprocal, inhibitory connections between motive systems that diminish responses to stimuli that are not affective matches.

Attention and Emotion.   Most human experimentation on the startle probe methodology has not previously been driven by motivational theories; the focus of investigation has been the study of attention and the sensory system (e.g., see Anthony, 1985, and Graham, 1979, for reviews). Various stimuli, tasks, and/or instructional manipulations are used to guide participants' attentional focus. While participants are thus engaged, brief non-task-relevant startling stimuli are presented, with the expectation that the eyeblink component of the reflex will be attenuated to the degree that attentional resources are already allocated to the primary task. Taking this approach, Simons and Zelson (1985) studied differences in probe reflex inhibition as participants processed foregrounds varying in interest value. Participants viewed two content classes of photographic slides as a foreground task: (a) Interesting content—a varying series of attractive nude males and females, and (b) dull content—a picture of a small wicker basket, repeatedly presented, to which it was presumed less attention would be allocated. Unpredictable auditory startle probes were administered during both slide contents. As expected, the blink reflex was significantly smaller for interesting than for dull slide content.

Although the investigators' focus was a sensory hypothesis, it is clear that the stimuli employed were not motivationally neutral. Pictures of attractive nudes are reasonably classified as pleasant and arousing stimuli. Furthermore, as the animal research suggests, cues associated with positive incentives can prompt inhibition of probe startle responses. Thus, the effects observed by these investigators are open not only to an attentional explanation, but could equally be explained by the mismatch between motivational systems activated by foreground and probe stimuli.

Probing Human Emotion

Based on the above laboratory findings, Lang, Bradley, and Cuthbert (1990) hypothesized that the startle reflex probe could be used to test fundamental postulates of the theory of human emotion that is here under consideration. In brief, it was suggested that evoked reflexes would be differentially modulated, depending on the affective valence of the individual's current motivational state. Thus, when the aversive system is activated (i.e., the brain is processing negative affective information and contacting the relevant subcortical, aversive system circuitry) the reflex will be augmented. This hypothesis presumes that (a) the startle response is an aversive/defensive reflex, and that (b) behaviors are synergistically amplified if an "affective match" exists between reflex and motive state. Furthermore, appetitive and aversive/defensive dispositions are held to be opponent states, reciprocally inhibiting nonmatching behaviors. Thus, when appetitive information is the focus of processing, the startle reflex will show relative inhibition.

Looking at Pictures.   Vrana, Spence, and Lang (1988) undertook the first general test of this affect-startle hypothesis in the context of emotional perception. An adaptation of Simons and Zelson's (1985) paradigm was used, in which the respondent viewed a series of photographic slides while acoustic probes were randomly presented, and the amplitude of the startle component of the eyeblink was measured. The slide stimuli were selected from the International Affective Picture System (IAPS; Lang, Ohman, & Vaitl, 1988) on the basis of normative affective ratings, and organized into three affective classes—unpleasant (e.g., poisonous snakes, aimed guns, pictures of violent death), pleasant (e.g., happy babies, appetizing food, attractive nudes), and neutral (e.g., umbrellas, hair dryer, and other common household objects). A significant linear trend was observed over slide valence categories, with the largest startle blink responses occurring during unpleasant content and the smallest during the pleasant pictures.

This phenomenon has since been replicated in several independent experiments: Both Bradley, Lang, & Cuthbert (1990) and Greenwald, Bradley, Cuthbert, and Lang (1990) confirmed that, relative to neutral content, the phenomenon involves *both* a significant potentiation of responding during unpleasant slides, and a significant inhibition during pleasant picture. Bradley, Cuthbert, and Lang (1991) replicated the phenomenon using monaural, rather than binaural acoustic probes and, furthermore, obtained evidence that this affect-startle effect may be lateralized (i.e., left ear probes, presumably conferring an advantage in right brain processing, showed the strongest relationship with affective valence). Jansen and Frijda (1991), using evocative video film clips, and Hamm, Stark, and Vaitl (1990), using IAPS slides, obtained the affect-startle effect in European respondents. Finally, Bradley, Cuthbert, and Lang (1990) found the same pattern of affective modulation using visual rather than acoustic startle probes, disconfirming an alternative hypothesis that affective differences were secondary to differences in modality-directed attention (Anthony & Graham, 1985).

Other data from the above research (Bradley et al., 1990, 1991) further support the view that the affect-startle effect is specific to emotional valence.

Thus, both pleasant and unpleasant slides elicited similar reports of greater arousal and interest value, and furthermore, participants spent more time looking at *both* types of affective slides than neutral pictures, when allowed to control viewing time. Only the startle blink varied linearly over slide valence categories, increasing monotonically in magnitude from pleasant, to neutral, to unpleasant contents.

Recent results (Cuthbert, Bradley, & Lang, 1990) showed an interesting interaction between arousal and valence in these startle data. That is, the affect-startle effect appears to be accentuated for highly arousing stimuli: As unpleasant slides increased in rated arousal, both skin conductance and probe startle augmentation increased. Similarly, as pleasant slides increased in rated arousal, skin conductance (indexing sympathetic activation) also increased. For startle magnitude, however, increasing arousal of pleasant foreground slides prompted an opposite effect: greater reflex inhibition. The finding is, of course, consistent with the motivational matching hypothesis proposed earlier. Furthermore, for such emotional perception, the probe startle response appears to differentially track the dimensions of positive and negative affect, as described by Tellegen (e.g., see Watson & Tellegen, 1985).[6]

Emotional Imagery: The Network Modulates the Reflex.   It was previously suggested that different media potentially activate the same affective networks in the brain. Thus, if startle modulation is driven by the emotional state itself (i.e., it is not exclusively a phenomenon of emotional perception), these effects should be observed under other conditions of network activation. In the first investigation of this hypothesis, Vrana and Lang (1990) studied probe responses to emotional memories. In this case, there was no proximal affective stimulus. At the beginning of the experiment respondents learned pairs of sentences; one was

---

[6]These data are consonant with Konorski's conception of opponent aversive and appetitive arousal systems, in that the different reflex modulation patterns are enhanced by increases in excitation of either affective type. They also follow Watson and Tellegen's (1985) positive and negative affect dimensions, defined by a 45° rotation of the valence-arousal circumplex. This model suggests that magnitude might increase for action affects such as fear and anger, but would be less influenced by sadness, helplessness, or depression, which are equally unpleasant, but may involve low activation. Similarly, little reflex inhibition would be found in contented relaxation, whereas sexual pleasure, elation, or enthusiasm should produce clear reflex attenuation (see Lang et al., 1992).

These results have a broader implication—for mood congruence and other modulatory influences between emotions. They imply that these effects depend on the intensity as well as the valence of emotion. That is, for congruent affects their is a "transfer of excitation" (Zillman, Katcher, & Milavsky, 1972) and associated behaviors, but with incongruence, the incompatible behaviors will be surpressed. Finally, although we have speculated about activation and startle modulation, and the apparent stability of the affect-startle effect with variation in tactical affective physiologies (e.g., see Vrana & Lang, 1990, p. 195), there is as yet little data on the effects of specific behavioral dispositions on probe response, for example, during overt approach or withdrawal, in states of inhibition or restraint, with active or passive coping—all of which have interesting theoretical implications.

neutral in content, and one described a fearful event. Recall of the sentences was subsequently cued by tone signals, and probe stimuli were presented during memory processing. Larger reflex responses were observed when respondents remembered sentences with fearful content than when neutral sentences were recalled. Furthermore, this differential effect varied with the processing task. Probe responses were smaller when participants were told just to articulate the sentences silently than when they were instructed to vividly imagine the sentence content.

Cook, Hawk, Davis, and Stevenson (1991) also studied probe responses during emotional imagery. On the basis of a prior testing, sentences were created that tapped a variety of common emotional episodes (i.e., situations associated with fear, anger, sadness, happiness, etc.). Probe responses during imagery of unpleasant emotions were systematically larger than during pleasant affects. Other studies of emotional imagery have also found this same affect-startle effect (e.g., Bradley, Lang, & Cuthbert, 1991; Cuthbert, Bradley, York, & Lang, 1990).

Psychopathology and Aversion.   Recent findings suggest that individuals with a pathologically exaggerated aversive reaction, or alternatively, with an apparent aversive emotion deficit, show a parallel potentiation or attenuation of the reflex response. Patrick, Bradley, & Lang (1993) recently studied picture probe reactivity in a prison population, including a group of diagnosed psychopaths. [These latter participants are held to have diminished affect (Cleckley, 1976), or specifically, a reduced reaction to aversive stimuli (Lykken, 1957).] Like nonpsychopathic prisoners, the psychopathic group showed normal startle *inhibition* while attending to pleasant pictures; however, psychopaths failed to show a normal reflex *potentiation* during fearful or otherwise unpleasant picture content. These results encourage the hypothesis that psychopathy involves a basic deficit in the subcortical aversive affect system.

Conversely, respondents with particularly strong negative affect show more marked startle potentiation in an aversive context. Thus, individuals with many fears (as defined by questionnaire) show a greater reflex potentiation in fear imagery than participants with fewer fears (Cook et al., 1991); similarly, Hamm, Globisch, Cuthbert, and Vaitl (1991) reported larger probe responses in phobic respondents (looking at phobic pictures) than in nonphobics; furthermore, Vrana (see Bradley & Vrana, 1993) observed a systematic reduction in phobic imagery-potentiated blink reflexes after desensitization therapy.

The association between startle and negative affect is further supported by studies of laboratory induced fear. That is, college participants respond to electric shock sensitization (Greenwald et al., 1990), threat of shock (Grillon, Ameli, Woods, Merikangas, & Davis, 1991), and classical shock conditioning (Hamm, Greenwald, Bradley, & Lang, in press; Hamm et al., 1990) with the same systematic increases in startle reflex response found in animals (Davis, 1989).

Thus, a fear state imposed in human respondents, whether by shock conditioning, visual media, or memory imagery, augments the startle reflex in the same way as does a classical conditioned stimulus in rodents. These results are consistent with the view that, in human beings, the processing of conceptual information with emotional content activates subcortical neural circuitry similar to that explicated by animal models of emotional associative learning.

CONNECTIONS AND CONCLUSIONS

This chapter has been a search for connections—connections that might advance our understanding of human emotion. We asked questions about the bridges between disciplines. How are animal models linked to human affects? What are the connections between neural circuits and cognitive networks? How do complex emotional experiences relate to simple reflexes?

We began with early studies of fear imagery, as used in behavior modification. In this context, the proximal stimulus is a verbal description of a fearful event, which prompts a "fear experience" in phobic patients. Our research suggested, however, that such reported emotional experience had implications for behavior (i.e., could mediate substantive change in avoidance or fear distress) only to the extent that these reports were associated with measurable efference, that is, coincident output patterns of somatic and autonomic activity. Subsequent studies focused on determining the cognitive processes that generated these functional action dispositions (as opposed to merely "understanding" text content).

Our early analysis suggested that affects can be meaningfully construed as networks of information that define an episode in memory. This hypothesized memory network includes representations of relevant stimuli, of patterns of responding, and of related declarative knowledge. Because of the associative connections between these representations, the network as a whole can be activated by input that matches only some of the network concepts. Furthermore, this conceptual response information is linked to action programs for the efferent system. Thus, general network activation results in measurable effector output.

The conceptual content of an affect network is highly idiosyncratic: Stimulus information that one respondent processes as emotion may not affect another, and because affects are basically episodes, response output will also vary greatly depending on the contextual imperatives of the original learning. We suggested, however, that these affective memories are, from the perspective of motivational strategy, much simpler. The network's coherence, its associative strength, derives from its connections to one of only two motive systems—appetitive or aversive. These systems are based on subcortical circuits that determine associative reinforcement learning.

Affective networks differ from other memory structures in that they have direct associative links to these circuits. Both motive systems mediate a broad arousal reaction, hormonal and cardiovascular, that can support strong, rapid reactions. The evidence suggests, however, that aversive and appetitive systems are in other ways independent, facilitating, in the first case, defensive, withdrawal behaviors (negative affects), and in the second case consummatory, nurturant, approach behaviors (positive affects). To some extent, these systems may operate reciprocally; that is, engagement of one system inhibits responses linked to the other.

Neuroscientists are now able to tell us much about this subcortical motivation system, at least as it is organized in lower mammals. We know that the subcortical circuitry is itself plastic. Simple affective associations are learned and retained in the absence of cortical sensory processing. Without benefit of appraisal, connections are established between sensory thalamus and the aversive learning circuits in the amygdala that mediate defensive responding. On the other hand, in intact animals, connections go back and forth between the amygdaloid complex and higher centers. Thus, associated information at the cortical level can influence (enhance, modulate, reduce) activity in the motivation circuit.

The assumption of general motivation circuits—priming a variety of aversive affects, or alternatively, a spectrum of appetitive dispositions—is consonant with the animal research. In this report we have emphasized neurophysiological studies of the startle response, showing that this simple defensive reflex is reliably enhanced when the amygdaloid aversive system is activated (e.g., by prior conditioning). This same startle potentiation effect has now also been shown in human beings. As for the rat, human participants trained to fear stimuli that augur shock show larger startle probe responses to conditioned than control stimuli. Furthermore, the research suggests that activation of any aversive network—via pictures, imagery—has the same effect of enhancing startle reactions. That is, if the aversive motivational circuitry is engaged, other aversive connections are facilitated. These same studies suggest a broader affective congruence. That is, startle reflexes appear to be diminished when participants process appetitive information. Unfortunately, this reciprocal phenomenon has not yet been a subject for neurophysiological exploration, and a foundation for the hypothesized inhibitory appetitive system connection has not been established.

In summary, this presentation has tried to stretch our conception of emotion. In so doing, we are aware that the picture may be distorted. All the phenomena of one discipline cannot be rendered in the operations of another. It is useful, nevertheless, to sometimes force the fit, pressing the boundaries of theoretical generalization. In any event, more powerful theories will not be developed without attending to findings in adjacent fields, noting both the constraints they place on our hypotheses and the new avenues they open to exploration. The startle probe research is a productive example of such heuristic cross fertilization, because the paradigm functions similarly for different organisms, at different levels of analysis, linking mentation to mechanism and behavior. We need more such methods that encourage dialogue between disciplines—clinical and social psychology, neuroscience, cognitive studies. Significant advance in the scientific study of emotion depends on such connections.

ACKNOWLEDGMENTS

Preparation of this chapter was supported in part by National Institute of Mental Health Grants MH37757, MH41950, and MH43975, and Grant AG09779 from the National Institute of Aging. The help of Dr. Margaret M. Bradley and Dr. Bruce N. Cuthbert is much appreciated. They not only helped shape and improve this specific manuscript, but have contributed importantly at every level in the development of these ideas and in their experimental evaluation. Some of the material considered in this chapter is also discussed in P. J. Lang, The Network model of emotion: Motivational connections. In R. Wyer & T. Srull, (Eds.), *Advances in Social Cognition, Volume VI* (pp. 109–133). Hillsdale, NJ: Lawrence Erlbaum Associate 1993.

REFERENCES

Aggleton, J. P., & Mishkin, M. (1986). The amygdala: Sensory gateway to the emotions. In R. Plutchik & H. Kellerman (Eds.), *Emotion theory, research, and experience* (Vol. 3, pp. 281–299). New York: Academic Press.

Anderson, J. R., & Bower, G. H. (1974). A propositional theory of recognition memory. *Memory and Cognition, 2,* 406–412.

Anthony, B. J. (1985). In the blink of an eye: Implications of reflex modification for information processing. In P. K. Ackles, J. R. Jennings, & M. G. H. Coles (Eds.), *Advances in psychophysiology* (Vol. 1, pp. 167–218). Greenwich, CT: JAI Press.

Anthony, B. J., & Graham, F. (1985). Blink reflex modification by selective attention: Evidence for the modulation of "automatic" processing. *Biological Psychology, 21,* 43–59.

Armus, H. L., Carlson, K. R., Guinan, J. F., & Crowell, R. A. (1964). Effect of a secondary reinforcement stimulus on the auditory startle response. *Psychological Reports, 14,* 535–540.

Armus, H. L., & Sniadowsky-Dolinsky, D. (1966). Startle decrement and secondary reinforcement stimulation. *Psychonomic Science, 4,* 175–176.

Barnard, P. J., & Teasdale, J. D. (1991). Interacting cognitive subsystems: A systemic approach to cognitive-affective interaction and change. *Cognition and Emotion, 5,* 1–39.

Ben-Ari, Y. (1981). *The amygdaloid complex.* Elsevier North Holland.

Berg, W. K. & Davis, M. (1985). Associative learning modifies startle reflexes at the lateral lemniscus. *Behavioral Neuroscience, 99,* 191–199.

Berkowitz, L. (1993). Toward a general theory of anger and emotional aggression: Implication of the cognitive-neoassociationistic perspective for the analysis of anger and other emotions. In R. Wyer & T. Srull, (Eds.), *Advances in social cognition* (Vol. VI, pp. 1–46). Hillsdale, NJ: Lawrence Erlbaum Associates.

Blanchard, R. J., & Blanchard, D. C. (1977). Aggression behavior in the rat. *Behavioral Biology, 21,* 197–224.

Blaney, P. H. (1986). Affect and memory: A review. *Psychological Bulletin, 99,* 229–246.

Bower, G. H. (1981). Mood and memory. *American Psychologist, 36,* 129–148.

Bradley, M. M., Cuthbert, B. N., & Lang, P. J. (1990). Startle reflex modification: Emotion or attention? *Psychophysiology, 27,* 513–523.

Bradley, M. M., Cuthbert, B. N., & Lang, P. J. (1991). Startle and emotion: Lateral acoustic stimuli and the bilateral blink. *Psychophysiology, 28,* 285–295.

Bradley, M. M., Greenwald, M. K., Petry, M., & Lang, P. J. (1992). Remembering pictures: Pleasure and arousal in memory. *Journal of Experimental Psychology: Learning, Memory, & Cognition, 18,* 379–390.

Bradley, M. M., Lang, P. J., & Cuthbert, B. N. (1990). Habituation and the affect-startle effect. *Psychophysiology, 27,* S18. [Abstract]

Bradley, M. M., Lang, P. J., & Cuthbert, B. N. (1991). The Gainesville murders: Imagining the worst. *Psychophysiology, 28,* S14. [Abstract]

Bradley, M. M., & Vrana, S. R. (1993). The startle probe in emotion and emotional disorders. In N. Birbaumer & A. Ohman (Eds.), *The organization of emotion* (pp. 270–287). Toronto Hogrefe-Huber.

Brown, J. S. (1961). *The motivation of behavior.* New York: McGraw-Hill.

Brown, J. S., Kalish, H. I., & Farber, I. E. (1951). Conditioned fear as revealed by magnitude of startle response to an auditory stimulus. *Journal of Experimental Psychology, 32,* 317–328.

Cahill, L., & McGaugh, J. L. (1990). Amygdaloid complex lesions differentially affect retention of tasks using appetitive and aversive reinforcement. *Behavioral Neuroscience, 104* (4), 532–543.

Cleckley, H. (1976). *The mask of sanity* (5th ed.). St. Louis, MO: C. V. Mosby.

Cook, E. W., III, Hawk, L. H., Davis, T. L., & Stevenson, V. E. (1991). Affective individual differences and startle reflex modulation. *Journal of Abnormal Psychology, 100,* 5–13.

Cuthbert, B. N., Bradley, M. M., & Lang, P. J. (1990). Valence and arousal in startle modulation. *Psychophysiology, 27*(4a), S24.

Cuthbert, B. N., Bradley, M. M., York, D., & Lang, P. J. (1990). Affective imagery and startle modulation. *Psychophysiology, 27,* S24.

Cuthbert, B. N., Vrana, S. R., & Bradley, M. M. (1991). Imagery: Function and physiology. In P. K. Ackles, J. R. Jennings, & M. G. H. Coles (Eds.), *Advances in psychophysiology IV* (pp. 1–42). Greenwich, CT: JAI Press.

Davis, M. (1989). Neural systems involved in fear-potentiated startle. *Annals of the New York Academy of Sciences, 563,* 165–183.

Davis, M., Hitchcock, J., & Rosen, J. (1987). Anxiety and the amygdala: Pharmacological and anatomical analysis of the fear potentiated startle paradigm. *Psychology of Learning and Motivation* (Vol. 21, pp. 264–306). New York: Academic Press.

DiCara, L., Braun, J. J., & Pappas, B. (1970). Classical conditioning and instrumental learning of cardiac and gastrointestinal responses following removal of neocortex in the rat. *Journal of Comparative and Physiological Psychology, 73,* 208–216.

Farah, M. (1988). Is visual imagery really visual? Overlooked evidence from neuropsychology. *Psychological Review, 95,* 307–318.

Fechter, L. D., & Ison, J. R. (1972). The inhibition of the acoustic startle reaction in rats by food and water deprivation. *Learning and Motivation, 3,* 109–124.

Frijda, N. H. (1986). *The emotions.* New York: Cambridge.

Frijda, N. H. (1987). Emotion, cognitive structure, and action tendency. *Cognition and Emotion, 1,* 115–143.

Garcia, J., Hankins, W. G., & Rusiniak, K. W. (1974). Behavioral regulation of the milieu interne in man and rat. *Science, 185,* 824–831.

Gold, P. E., & McGaugh, J. L. (1975). A single-trace, dual-process view of memory storage processes. In D. Deutsch & J. A. Deutsch (Eds.), *Short-term memory* (pp. 355–378). New York: Academic Press.

Graham, F. K. (1979). Distinguishing among orienting, defense, and startle reflexes. In H. D.

Kimmel, E. H. van Olst, & J. F. Orlebeke (Eds.), *The Orienting Reflex in Humans* (pp. 137–167). Hillsdale, NJ: Lawrence Erlbaum Associates.

Greenwald, M. K., Bradley, M. M., Cuthbert, B. N., & Lang, P. J. (1990). The acoustic startle response indexes aversive learning. *Psychophysiology, 27,* 36 (Abstract).

Grillion, C., Ameli, R., Woods, S. W., Merikangas, K., & Davis, M. (1991). Fear-potentiated startle in humans: Effects of anticipatory anxiety on the acoustic blink reflex. *Psychophysiology, 28,* 588–595.

Hamm, A. O., Globisch, J., Cuthbert, B. N., & Vaitl, D. (1991). Startle reflex modulation in simple phobics and normals. *Psychophysiology.* [Abstract]

Hamm, A. O., Greenwald, M. K., Bradley, M. M., & Lang, P. J. (in press). Emotional learning, hedonic change, and the startle probe. *Journal of Abnormal Psychology.*

Hamm, A. O., Stark, R., & Vaitl, D. (1990). Startle reflex potentiation and electrodermal response differentiation: Two indicators of two different processes in Pavalovian conditioning. *Psychophysiology, 27,* S37. [Abstract]

Hebb, D. O. (1949). *The organization of behavior: A neuropsychological theory.* New York: Wiley.

Hoffman, H. S. & Stitt, C. (1969). Behavioral factors in habituation of acoustic startle reactions. *Journal of Comparative Physiological Psychology, 68,* 276–279.

Hull, C. L. (1943). *Principles of behavior.* New York: Appleton-Century.

Ison, J. R., & Krauter, E. E. (1975). Acoustic startle reflexes in the rat during consummatory behavior. *Journal of Comparative and Physiological Psychology, 89,* 39–49.

Iwata, J., & LeDoux, J. E. (1988). Dissociation of associative and nonassociative concomitants of classical fear conditioning in the freely behaving rat. *Behavioral Neuroscience, 102,* 66–76.

Jacobson, E. (1931). Electrical measurements of neuromuscular states during mental activities. Variation of specific muscles contracting during imagination. *American Journal of Psychology, 96,* 115–121.

Jansen, D. M., & Frijda, N. (in press). Modulation of acoustic startle response by film-induced fear and sexual arousal. *Psychophysiology.*

Jaynes, J. (1976). *The origin of consciousness in the breakdown of the bicameral mind.* Boston: Houghton Mifflin.

Kintsch, W. (1974). *The representation of meaning in memory.* Hillsdale, NJ: Lawrence Erlbaum Associates.

Konorski, J. (1967). *Integrative activity of the brain: An interdisciplinary approach.* Chicago: University of Chicago Press.

Landis, C., & Hunt, W. (1939). *The startle pattern.* New York: Farrar.

Lang, P. J. (1968). Fear reduction and fear behavior: Problems in treating a construct. In J. M. Schlien (Ed.), *Research in psychotherapy, 3* (pp. 90–103). Washington, DC: American Psychological Association.

Lang, P. J. (1977). Imagery in therapy: An information processing analysis of fear. *Behavior Therapy, 8,* 862–886.

Lang, P. J. (1978). Anxiety: Toward a psychophysiological definition. In H. S. Akiskal & W. L. Webb (Eds.), *Psychiatric diagnosis: Exploration of biological predictors* (pp. 365–389). New York: Spectrum.

Lang, P. J. (1979). Presidential address, 1978: A bio-informational theory of emotional imagery. *Psychophysiology, 16,* 495–512.

Lang, P. J. (1984). Cognition in emotion: Concept and action. In C. E. Izard, J. Kagan, & R. B. Zajonc (Eds.), *Emotions, cognitions, and behavior* (pp. 192–228). New York: Cambridge.

Lang, P. J. (1985). The cognitive psychophysiology of emotion: Fear and anxiety. In A. H. Tuma & J. D. Maser (Eds.), *Anxiety and the anxiety disorders* (pp. 131–170). Hillsdale, NJ: Lawrence Erlbaum Associates.

Lang, P. J. (1987). Image as action: A reply to Watts and Blackstock. *Cognition and Emotion, 1*(4), 407–426.

Lang, P. J., Bradley, M. M., & Cuthbert, B. N. (1990). Emotion, attention, and the startle reflex. *Psychological Review, 97,* 377–395.

Lang, P. J., Bradley, M. M., & Cuthbert, B. N. (1992). A motivational analysis of emotion: Reflex-cortex connections. *Psychological Science, 3,* 44–49.

Lang, P. J., Greenwald, M. K., Bradley, M. M., & Hamm, A. O. (1993). Looking at pictures: Affective, facial, visceral, and behavioral reactions. *Psychophysiology, 30,* 261–273.

Lang, P. J., Kozak, M. J., Miller, G. A., Levin, D. N., & McLean, A. Jr. (1980). Emotional imagery: Conceptual structure and pattern of somato-visceral response. *Psychophysiology, 17*(2), 179–192.

Lang, P. J., & Lazovik, A. D. (1963). Experimental desensitization of a phobia. *Journal of Abnormal and Social Psychology, 66,* 519–525.

Lang, P. J., Lazovik, A. D., & Reynolds, D. J. (1965). Desensitization, suggestibility and pseudotherapy. *Journal of Abnormal Psychology, 70,* 395–402.

Lang, P. J., Melamed, B. G., & Hart, J. D. (1970). A psychophysiological analysis of fear modification using an automated desensitization procedure. *Journal of Abnormal Psychology, 76,* 220–234.

Lang, P. J., Öhman, A., & Vaitl, D. (1988). *The international affective picture system* [photographic slides]. Gainesville, FL: The Center for Research in Psychophysiology, University of Florida.

Lazarus, R. S. (1984). On the primacy of cognition. *American Psychologist, 39,* 124–129.

LeDoux, J. E. (1989). Cognitive-emotional interactions in the brain. *Cognition and Emotion, 3,* 267–289.

LeDoux, J. E. (1990). Information flow from sensation to emotion plasticity in the neural computation of stimulus value. In M. Gabriel & J. Moore (Eds.), *Learning and computational neuroscience: Foundations of adaptive networks* (pp. 3–52). Cambridge, MA: Bradford Books/MIT Press.

LeDoux, J. E., Cicchetti, P., Xagoraris, A., & Romanski, L. M. (1990). The lateral amygaloid nucleus: Sensory interface of the amygdala in fear conditioning. *The Journal of Neuroscience, 10*(4), 1062–1069.

Levenson, R. W. (1992). Autonomic nervous system differences among emotions. *Psychological Science, 3,* 23–27.

Leventhal, H. (1980). Toward a comprehensive theory of emotion. In L. Berkowitz (Ed.), *Advances in Experimental Social Psychology* (Vol. 13, pp. 140–208). New York: Academic Press.

Lykken, D. T. (1957). A study of anxiety in the sociopathic personality. *Journal of Abnormal and Clinical Psychology, 55,* 6–10.

Mackintosh, N. J. (1983). *Conditioning and associative learning.* New York: Oxford.

Markoff, J. (1991, November). Man or machine? *The New York Times,* pp. 1, 10.

McClelland, J. L., & Rumelhart, D. E. (1981). An interactive activation model of context effects in letter perception: Part 1. An account of basic findings. *Psychological Review, 88,* 375–407.

McGuigan, F. J. (1973). Electrical measurement of covert processes as an explication of "higher mental events." In F. J. McGuigan & R. A. Schoonover (Eds.), *The psychophysiology of thinking* (pp. 343–376). New York: Academic Press.

McLean, A., Jr. (1982). Emotional imagery: Stimulus information, imagery ability and patterns of physiological response. *Dissertation Abstracts International, 42,* 11, 4884-B.

McNeil, D. W., Vrana, S. R., Melamed, B. G., Cuthbert, B. N., & Lang, P. J. (1993). Emotional imagery in simple and social phobia: "Normal" fear and pathological anxiety. *Journal of Abnormal Psychology, 102,* 212–225.

Mellgren, R. L. (1969). Magnitude of the startle response and drive level. *Psychology Reports, 25,* 187–193.

Miller, G. A., Levin, D. N., Kozak, M. J., Cook, E. W., III, McLean, A., & Lang, P. J. (1987). Individual differences in emotional imagery. *Cognition and Emotion, 1,* 367–390.

Öhman, A., Dimberg, U., & Esteves, F. (1989). Preattentive activation of aversive emotions. In T. Archer & L. G. Nilsson (Eds.), *Aversion, avoidance and anxiety* (pp. 169–193). Hillsdale, NJ: Lawrence Erlbaum Associates.

Olds, J. (1960). Approach–avoidance dissociations in rat brain. *American Journal of Physiology, 199,* 965–968.

Patrick, C. J., Bradley, M. M., & Lang, P. J. (1993). Emotion in the criminal psychopath: Startle reflex modulation. *Journal of Abnormal Psychology, 102,* 82–92.

Patrick, C. J., Cuthbert, B. N., & Lang, P. J. (1989). Automaticity of emotional processing in anxious and non-anxious patients. *Psychophysiology, 26,* S47. [Abstract]

Paul, G. L. (1969). *Insight vs. desensitization in psychotherapy.* Stanford, CA: Stanford University Press.

Pavlov, I. P. (1927). *Conditioned reflexes.* Oxford: Oxford University Press.

Pylyshyn, Z. W. (1973). What the mind's eye tells the mind's brain: A critique of mental imagery. *Psychological Bulletin, 80,* 1–24.

Roldan, E., Alvarez-Pelaez, R., & Fernandez de Molina, A. (1974). Electrographic study of the amygdaloid defense response. *Physiology and Behavior, 13,* 779–787.

Ross, L. E. (1961). Conditioned fear as a function of CS-UCS and probe stimulus intervals. *Journal of Experimental Psychology, 61,* 265–273.

Schank, R. C. (1982). *Dynamic memory: A theory of reminding and learning in computers and people.* Cambridge Press: New York.

Schneider, W., & Shiffrin, R. M. (1977). Controlled and automatic human information processing. *Psychological Review, 84,* 1–66.

Shaw, W. A. (1940). The relation of muscular action potentials to imaginal weight lifting. *Archives of Psychology, 247,* 50.

Sheehan, P. W. (1967). A shortened form of Betts' questionnaire upon mental imagery. *Journal of Clinical Psychology, 223,* 380–389.

Simons, R. F., & Zelson, M. F. (1985). Engaging visual stimuli and reflex blink modification. *Psychophysiology, 22,* 44–49.

Spence, K. W., & Runquist, W. N. (1958). Temporal effects of conditioned fear on the eyelid reflex. *Journal of Experimental Psychology, 55,* 613–616.

Szabo, I. (1967). Analysis of the muscular action potentials accompanying the acoustic startle reaction. *Acta Physiol. Acad. Sci. Hung., 27,* 167–178.

Trapold, M. A. (1962). The effect of incentive motivation on an unrelated reflex response. *Journal of Comparative Physiological Psychology, 55,* 1034–1039.

Tulving, E. (1983). *Elements of episodic memory.* Oxford: Oxford University Press.

Ursin, H. (1965). Effect of amygdaloid lesions on avoidance behavior and visual discrimination in cats. *Experimental Neurology, 11,* 298–317.

Ursin, H., Jellestad, F., & Cabrera, I. G. (1981). The amygdala, exploration and fear. In Y. Ben-Ari (Ed.), *The amygdaloid complex* (pp. 317–329). Amsterdam: Elsevier North Holland.

Vrana, S. R., Cuthbert, B. N., & Lang, P. J. (1989). Processing fearful and neutral sentences: Memory and heart rate change. *Cognition and Emotion, 3,* 179–195.

Vrana, S. R., & Lang, P. J. (1990). Fear imagery and the startle probe reflex. *Journal of Abnormal Psychology, 99,* 189–197.

Vrana, S. R., Spence, E. L., & Lang, P. J. (1988). The startle probe response: A new measure of emotion? *Journal of Abnormal Psychology, 97,* 487–491.

Wagner, A. R. (1963). Conditioned frustration as a learned driver. *Journal of Experimental Psychology, 66,* 142–148.

Watson, D., & Tellegen, A. (1985). Toward a consensual structure of mood. *Psychological Bulletin, 98,* 219–235.

Watts, F. N., McKenna, F. P., Sharrock, R., & Trezise, L. (1986). Colour naming of phobia-related words. *British Journal of Psychology, 77,* 97–108.

Wegner, D. N., Schneider, D. J., Carter, S. R., & White. T. L. (1987). Paradoxical effects of thought suppression. *Journal of Personality and Social Psychology, 53,* 5–13.

Zajonc, R. B. (1980). Feeling and thinking. *American Psychologist, 35,* 151–175.

Zillman, D., Katcher, A., & Milavsky, B. (1972). Excitation transfer from physical exercise to subsequent aggressive behavior. *Journal of Experimental Social Psychology, 8,* 247–259.

II EXPRESSION AND CONSEQUENCES OF EMOTIONS

4 Emotional Memory: A Dimensional Analysis

Margaret M. Bradley
University of Florida

If psychological inquiry were like a crossword puzzle, then, despite differences in origin, procedure, or sequence of moves, one could be assured of ultimately reaching a correct solution. Instead, the study of emotion is typically approached from many different angles without the security of a guaranteed outcome. Final conclusions with respect to mechanism will rely intimately on the questions originally asked, the variables manipulated, and the responses that are measured. Current approaches in the study of emotion include those in which emotion is considered to be primarily organized as a set of specific, discrete affective states (e.g., happiness, sadness, disgust, etc.), and those that view emotion as varying continuously along some limited number of affective dimensions (e.g., pleasure, arousal, etc.). The emotion puzzle looks very different depending on which metatheoretical position launches the search, due to differences in both the nature of the questions asked and the data base to which attention is directed.

Each view is potentially useful, in the sense that it can intelligently inform the debate. Nonetheless, it is likely that the more fundamental organization of emotion is dimensional. Bolstering this viewpoint is the widespread finding that dimensions of affective valence (i.e., pleasantness or quality), arousal (i.e., intensity or impact), and, to a lesser extent, dominance are consistently found to organize judgments for stimuli as diverse as words (Osgood, Suci, & Tannenbaum, 1957), narrative text (Mehrabian & Russell, 1974), pictures (Greenwald, Cook, & Lang, 1989; Lang, Greenwald, Bradley, & Hamm, 1993), advertisements (Morris, Bradley, Waine, & Lang, in press), alcohol effects (Rather, Goldman, Roehrich, & Brannick, 1992), mood states (Frijda, 1987), and more.

Theoretically, any object or event can be mapped into affective space defined by its placement along these emotional dimensions, making location in space one operational method for defining emotion and differentiating among affective categories. According to this conceptualization, even specific emotional states can be distinguished on the basis of their placement in affective space. One might consider, in fact, that the linguistic repertoire of emotion (which is quite vast in English) developed precisely in order to provide a set of verbal labels for identifying, addressing, and referring to different points in affective space. Regardless of whether this "single solution" rapprochement is ultimately supported, dimensional organization is clearly pervasive in emotional judgments.

In this chapter, a dimensional view of emotion is exploited in order to explore the nature of emotional reactions, ranging from psychophysiological responses elicited at encoding to those underlying short- and long-term memory performance. One goal of this work is to determine whether variations in pleasure and arousal are systematically related to changes in emotional reactivity across a wide range of relevant affective response systems. Of particular interest in this chapter is the extent to which this approach aids in determining parameters salient to emotional memory. Throughout, it will be seen that inclusion of psychophysiological measurement in the experimental setting provides a useful window onto the extent and nature of emotional engagement.

To begin the discussion, an extensive set of standardized stimuli that vary systematically along the dimensions of pleasure, arousal, and dominance are introduced (Lang & Bradley, 1990; Lang, Ohman, & Vaitl, 1988). These materials provide the fuel for subsequent investigations of the effects of pleasure and arousal on emotional reactivity, including physiological responses in cardiovascular, electrodermal, and somatic systems, as well as behavioral choice responses, reaction times, and numerous judgments of evaluative reactions to the stimuli.

Working backward in a sense, the first questions focus on memorial consequences of processing these affective stimuli. Prior experiments addressing the effects of pleasure or arousal in memory are briefly reviewed, with an eye towards determining the current status of the relationship between emotion and memory. Earlier studies tended to vary either one or the other affective dimension; these are followed by the presentation of a series of recent experiments that systematically assess the contribution of *each* dimension to memory performance. The resulting data base indicates a strong role of arousal in memory performance. In interpreting these mnemonic effects, effects of variations in pleasure and arousal at encoding are evaluated for specific physiological responses, as well as for reports of affective and cognitive experience. Highly arousing stimuli are found to produce a wide range of reactive responses that presumably work to elaborate and modify the mnemonic representation, ultimately leading to facilitation in both short- and long-term memory performance.

Together, the data reviewed in this chapter suggest that a dimensional approach is quite useful for organizing and describing affective reactions, and that the measurement of psychophysiological indices during emotional engagement—at encoding and retrieval—provides a real-time measure of affective response. Such measurement allows one to not only index elicited emotional responses, but also provides an important source of information with regard to the mechanisms responsible for effects of such reactivity on later memory performance.

DIMENSIONS OF EMOTION

It is significant that Osgood's original characterization of a three-dimensional organizational space based on pleasure, arousal, and dominance arose from his investigations into the nature of meaning, rather than of emotion. That the basic structure underlying language may be fundamentally organized by what appear to be affective parameters points to the primacy of emotion in cognitive life. Whereas Osgood's (1952) early focus was on English words, he later found that the same dimensional structure held equally well for linguistic stimuli in non-English speaking cultures, and was useful in organizing judgments for stimuli as different as sonar signals and aesthetic paintings (Osgood, Suci, & Tannenbaum, 1957). Mehrabian (1970) extended the analysis to nonverbal communication behavior, finding similar dimensions to arise in factor analyses of judgments concerning facial expressions, hand and body movements, and postural positions. Finally, Mehrabian and Russell (1974; Russell, 1980) related these dimensions specifically to affective stimuli by constructing a set of emotionally descriptive texts and a new semantic differential scale for rating them. Not surprisingly, when applied to primarily affective stimuli, pleasure, arousal, and dominance again were clearly the factors underlying subjective judgments.

If human symbolic experience—verbal and nonverbal, semantic and emotional—can be organized by a limited number of fundamental dimensions, an ideal starting place for investigating the nature of mental processes, including emotion, is suggested. Important questions concern the extent to which other indices of affective experience, such as physiological response, behavioral output, or memory performance, are systematically related to these fundamental dimensions. Are there lawful changes in affective response that vary consistently along these organizational dimensions? And, are different dimensions more or less dominant in organizing different aspects of emotional expression and experience? Finally, how do dimensional variations illuminate the nature of the mechanism underlying emotional expression and experience?

DEFINING AFFECTIVE SPACE

Clearly, a first step in addressing these questions requires materials that systematically sample different points in affective space. The task of providing a standardized set of evocative emotional stimuli was undertaken recently by Lang and his colleagues (e.g., Lang & Bradley, 1990; Lang, Greenwald, Bradley, &

Hamm, 1993; Lang, Ohman, & Vaitl, 1988). In this work, a large collection of visual and acoustic affective stimuli—pictures and sounds—were collected from a variety of sources, including books, magazines, tapes, compact discs, and records, as well as stimuli created expressly for this purpose by actors and actresses from the University of Florida. One goal of this work is to provide a set of standardized, language-free stimuli that can be used cross-culturally in investigations (and replications) across individual laboratories.[1]

The color, photographic pictures comprising this collection—called the International Affective Picture System (IAPS; Lang et al., 1988)—depict a wide variety of emotional objects and events, including landscapes, erotica, children, food, sports scenes, household objects, weapons, pollution, injured and dead people, and more. A comparable collection of environmental sounds, including people laughing, crying, screaming, and coughing, as well as sounds from animals, machines, sports events, household objects, and so forth, have been arrayed together in a system of International Affective Digitized Sounds (IADS; Lang and Bradley, 1990), which is currently digitized and stored on computer media.

Stimuli from each type of affective set were presented to subjects who rated each picture or sound for its pleasantness, arousal, and dominance. Figure 4.1 illustrates the placement of each stimulus in the two-dimensional affective space defined by its mean valence and arousal rating. There are two reasons for confining the present analysis to these two dimensions. First, with regard to affective stimuli, the majority of variance in human judgments is accounted for by these two factors (Mehrabian & Russell, 1974) and the interpretive labels assigned to these dimensions (i.e., pleasure, arousal) show remarkable consistency across investigations. The dominance factor typically accounts for less variance, is less consistently labelled across investigations, and sometimes covaries with another dimension. For example, when rating the visual stimuli comprising the IAPS, dominance tends to be positively correlated with pleasure, suggesting redundancy across dimensions for these stimuli (Lang et al., 1993). On the other hand, when Osgood (1952) used nonaffective words as the judged stimuli, potency (his label for dominance) and arousal were positively related. Finally, when stimuli clearly involve some aspect of social interaction (e.g., narrative or actual events described by text or film), the dominance dimension—sometimes construed as social control or aggression—accounts for significant variability (Miller, Levin, Kozak, Cook, McLean, & Lang, 1987).

Focusing on the two-dimensional space defined by pleasure and arousal (Fig. 4.1), it is clear that the picture and sound stimuli evoke a wide range of emotional responses, spanning the affective valence dimension from extremely pleasant to extremely unpleasant, and varying broadly in arousal. The four major quadrants

---

[1]International Affective Picture System (*IAPS*) slides and technical manuals can be obtained from the author or Peter J. Lang, Center for Research in Psychophysiology, Box 100165 H.S.C., University of Florida, Gainesville, 32610.

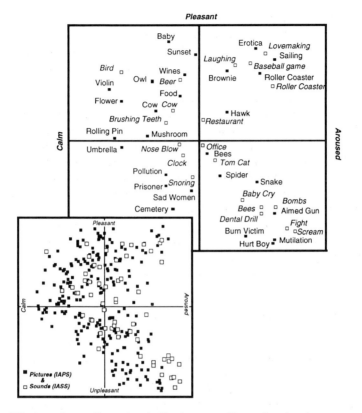

FIG. 4.1.   A two-dimensional affective space illustrating the placement of pictures (filled boxes; from the IAPS, Lang et al., 1988) and sounds (open boxes; from the IADS, Bradley & Lang, 1991) as a function of the mean ratings of pleasantness and arousal for each stimulus. The inset depicts the full affective space for all currently rated stimuli; the larger space presents examples of the locations of specific contents from the full stimulus set.

in the picture space delimit rough boundaries for stimuli that are (a) pleasant and calm, such as babies, flowers, and scenery, (b) pleasant and arousing, including sports, food, and erotica, (c) unpleasant and calm, such as cemeteries, pollution and soldiers, and (d) unpleasant and arousing, including guns, snakes, and mutilated persons. The number of stimuli occurring in each quadrant of space is roughly equivalent, with, perhaps, the exception of the unpleasant, calm portion of space. Whether this is a limitation of the current collection or of this type of media is not yet clear.

Sound stimuli appear to be slightly more activating than the static photographic materials, with the entire affective space shifted a bit towards the high-arousal pole. This is due perhaps to the dynamic nature of the acoustic stimuli, which can develop and change across the presentation interval; this is obviously not the case for pictures. On the other hand, the IADS is not yet as extensive in number as the IAPS, and stimuli may be found in the future that naturally occupy the calmer portions of space.

Nonetheless, the sounds that appear in each quadrant are similar to the categories found in these locations for pictures. Interestingly, a sound or picture that cues the same concept is rated almost identically: For example, the picture of a cow and its "moo" overlap in practically the same location in affective space; similarly, a picture of a downward racing roller coaster and its stomach-turning sound fall identically in the positive/arousing quadrant. Differences in placement occur when the same semantic concept conveys different affective information, however: Whereas the picture of a baby is pleasant, its persistent crying is not. Reminiscent of Osgood's early data, many of the stimuli that are close in affective space (whether pictures or sounds) are exemplars from a variety of different semantic categories, suggesting that the common linking feature is the similarity in their affective, rather than denotative, meaning.

Individual Differences in Affective Space

The normative data on which the IAPS is based were collected from students at the University of Florida in the United States, and comparison studies utilizing the same pictures, but with subjects from Germany, Italy, Sweden,[2] and other countries, have been conducted. Generally speaking, the positive correlations between the dimensional ratings from each country are consistent with the idea that these stimuli evoke a common human emotional reaction, at least in western cultures.

Differences that arise between countries, however, suggest that this methodology may tap cultural variety, with, for instance, Italian respondents rating the pictures as generally higher in arousal than Swedish participants, consistent with common stereotype. Comparing the nature of affective space for normal college-aged subjects and other populations suggests further differences in emotional expression. For instance, compared to young college women, older women (45 to 65 years) showed a high negative correlation between pleasure and arousal such that the most pleasant stimuli were those rated as highly relaxing, rather than arousing (Cuthbert, Bradley, & Lang, 1988). Not surprisingly, phobic subjects report higher unpleasantness and higher arousal for materials related to their specific fears, relative to both nonfearful subjects, and to nonfeared, but unpleasant stimuli (Hamm, Globisch, Cuthbert, & Vaitl, 1991). Finally, a patient who had

---

[2]Investigators contributing to this effort are Alfons Hamm and Dieter Vaitl (University of Giesson, Germany), Daniela Palomba and Luciano Stegnano (University of Padua, Italy), Arne Öhman (Sweden), and others.

previously undergone a right temporal lobectomy (including the amygdala) reported that normally aversive pictures (such as mutilated bodies) were highly unpleasant, but, unlike normal subjects, rated them as extremely low in arousal (Morris, Bradley, Bowers, Lang, & Heilman, 1991). These data suggest that the experimental measurement of affective space—as defined by verbal judgments of pleasure and arousal—may well lead to precise characterization of differences in emotional response due to cultural, ontogenetic, neurological, or other relevant factors.

A DIMENSIONAL APPROACH
TO AFFECTIVE MEMORY

Clinical, anecdotal, and empirical evidence supports practically the entire range of possible relationships relating emotion to memory. Because of this diversity, a dimensional approach might prove helpful in clarifying the mnemonic effects of processing intensely affective experiences. To date, contrasting views have typically concentrated on either one affective dimension (i.e., pleasantness) or the other (i.e., arousal), rather than considering both simultaneously. Thus, it has been proposed that unpleasant events are better remembered than pleasant, or vice versa, and that high arousal affects memory differently than low arousal, sometimes in complex ways.

To the extent that affective space is organized by variations in at least two dimensions, however, explorations that ignore one or the other dimension will necessarily be incomplete. Below, a brief review of studies that are relevant to the issues of whether differences in pleasure or arousal affect memory is presented. Then, a series of studies that covary pleasure and arousal by using the pictures and sounds from the IAPS and IADS as affective stimuli are discussed that test various predictions derived from this earlier work. Finally, the resulting pattern of relationships between dimensional variation and memory performance is interpreted in the context of physiological differences that occur during initial encoding of these materials. This method of measuring emotional engagement at encoding will be found to provide plausible hypotheses regarding the mechanisms underlying emotional memory performance.

Pleasure and Memory I: Good Memory for Bad Things

Brown and Kulik (1977) proposed that a special memory mechanism takes "snapshots" of significant, emotionally evocative events, based on evidence that people seem to remember the personal circumstances surrounding an emotional event (e.g., where one was, how one found out, etc.) vividly (perhaps veridically) and for a long time. Whereas their general description suggests that flashbulb memories might occur for highly arousing events in either the pleasant or unpleasant sectors of affective space, the analysis has typically been restricted to events involving trauma and aversion. This specific focus on the fate of *unpleasant* events in memory is historically well-documented, and continues to be a source of interest in recent investigations.

Theoretical interpretations of flashbulb memory emphasize that a situation must be both highly emotional and significant to produce vivid memories, leading to a search for emotionally evocative events that are important for a large sample of people. Naturally occurring stimuli that meet these criteria are culturally shared, well-publicized events, so when the Challenger space shuttle exploded in the United States in 1987, a number of researchers took the opportunity to determine the role of various factors in affecting flashbulb memories. Bohannon (1988) investigated the role of rehearsal by asking subjects to indicate the number of times they had recounted the circumstances surrounding their discovery of the disaster, as well as the emotional impact of the event. Multiple rehearsals in the absence of strong emotion resulted in high memory performance, which is consistent with known effects of rehearsal on memory. In support of a specific facilitation in memory for traumatic events, however, a strong emotional reaction alone (i.e., accompanied by reports of few rehearsals) produced equivalently high memory performance.

When investigating flashbulb memories, however, it is crucial to ascertain the veracity of subjects' memorial reports (Neisser, 1982), because it is possible that strong emotional responses simply bias the subject to produce a narrative describing personal involvement in the event. Indeed, when assessing the stability and accuracy of subjects' reports of where they were at the time of the Challenger disaster, McCloskey, Wible, and Cohen (1988) found that, over time, considerable forgetting and inaccuracy occurred for events that could be characterized as having flashbulb properties. In addition, despite inconsistencies between reports obtained immediately after the tragedy and those collected months later, subjects were often highly confident that their changed memories were completely accurate.

Clearly, the role of emotionality—specifically unpleasantness—in memory performance is difficult to ascertain using stimuli over which so little experimental control exists. If a mechanism for veridically recording unpleasant events is part of the cognitive armamentarium, however, its facilitatory effects should be detectable even when unpleasant stimuli are presented in a laboratory context. Christianson and his associates pursued this question, assessing memory performance after exposing subjects to either traumatic or neutral versions of similar situations. In one study, Christianson and Loftus (1987) demonstrated that subjects viewing a film of a bank robbery remembered the thematic content better 6 months later if its ending was violent, rather than nonviolent. Similarly, subjects viewing a slide sequence in which a boy was hit by a car were better at recalling the main features of the episode than respondents viewing a version in which the boy was not struck by the car. In these studies, memory for an unpleasant (and presumably arousing) event was better than for one lacking these affective properties.

Pleasure and Memory II:
Poor Memory for Bad Things

Despite the relatively recent emphasis on good memory for bad things (i.e., "flashbulb memory"), there is also a long tradition linking traumatic events to amnesia and repression, propelled first by classic psychodynamic thought, and fueled more recently by a slew of anecdotal evidence. For instance, the American public has recently been inundated with people's reports of repressed memories for sexual and other trauma supposedly suffered as children. In a celebrated legal case, a woman claimed to have forgotten seeing her father murder her 6-year-old friend until she was cued years later by a particular look in her own child's eyes. The case was eventually brought to trial and the man convicted of murder, decades after the crime. Subsequent media discussions concerning whether traumatic childhood events can be repressed in this manner were disheartening in that opinion and theory—and only rarely, convincing data—were the main factors informing the debate.

In fact, reviewing the literature on repression, Holmes (1974) concluded that there is no consistent evidence linking selective forgetting to events that involve threatening personal events (i.e., "ego threat"), despite the use of a variety of different paradigms and procedures. The same conclusion is reached in a more recent study in which Bradley and Baddeley (1990) measured memory for associations that subjects had generated to pleasant, unpleasant, or nonemotional words, either immediately after the generation task or a month later. At the short delay, although associations to nonemotional materials were remembered better than those related to emotional materials, unpleasant associations were no worse remembered than pleasant. A month later, more forgetting had occurred for the neutral stimuli, which resulted in slightly *better* memory for emotional stimuli— both pleasant and unpleasant. Whereas these data do not support the notion of repression, some might hesitate to compare memory for words associated with unpleasant stimuli (e.g., "torture") to the highly traumatic, sometimes violent, personal events that are typically thought to lead to repression (Holmes, 1974).

Although repression is not invoked as the theoretical mechanism, evidence of poor memory after processing unpleasant stimuli in the laboratory has been obtained in a number of different investigations (e.g., Christianson & Loftus, 1987, 1991; Clifford & Hollin, 1981; Loftus & Burns, 1982). In some of these studies, subjects shown different versions of an event (e.g., traumatic or neutral) were subsequently tested for detailed information portrayed in a photographic slide. Although, as discussed above, central elements were better remembered in traumatic versions, peripheral or background elements were remembered more poorly when the situation was traumatic. Thus, Loftus and Burns reported better memory for the number on a boy's shirt if the boy had not been shot in the slide sequence; similarly, recognition of the correct color of a car was better if a woman had not just been struck by it. Similarly degraded detail memory was obtained by Clifford and Hollin (1981), who found that the recall of details associated with the perpetrator of a violent crime was lower than for subjects viewing a nonviolent version. One hypothesis emerging from this work is that trauma leads to a focusing of attention on the central events, with fewer resources allocated to processing the periphery (Christianson & Loftus, 1991). This mechanism, however, is much different from the notion of repression, in that attributing mnemonic effects to differences in attentional allocation suggests a deficiency at the encoding stage, rather than inhibition at retrieval.

A final instance in which trauma has been linked to impoverished memory is when physical injury to the brain produces proactive and/or retroactive amnesia for events that preceded or followed the trauma. One laboratory analog of this phenomenon provokes mental shock by using perceptual stimuli, rather than brain injury, as the trauma-inducing element, and assesses memory for materials that precede, follow, or accompany the target. Typically, whereas the shocking stimulus itself usually is well remembered (unlike the situation where physical trauma is the amnestic agent), poorer memory (i.e., amnesia) is found for the surrounding stimuli. Similar results have been obtained when the shocking event was an unpleasant picture (Christianson & Nilsson, 1984), a word shouted in a loud voice, (Detterman, 1975) or a line drawing of a nude (Detterman & Ellis, 1972). Although one goal in this research is to understand the parameters of organic memory dysfunction, it is, of course, possible that similarities in memory malfunction arising from brain trauma and emotional trauma are merely descriptive.

Pleasure and Memory III:
Good Memory for Good Things

The converse of maintaining that memory for unpleasant events is poor is to emphasize that memory for pleasant events is good, and this approach too has its adherents. From the popular adage that one views the past through "rose-colored glasses" to empirical demonstrations of better memory for pleasant stimuli (Matlin & Stang, 1978), it is clear that some choose to emphasize the primacy of the positive over the repression of the negative. Berlyne's (1960) initial proposal of a Pollyanna hypothesis, which was subsequently elevated to the status of the Pollyanna principle by Matlin and Stang (1978), subscribes to the notion that cognition, including memory, demonstrates a general bias toward pleasant stimuli. This preference for the pleasant is held to extend from simple perceptual processing to the content of thought, and beyond to memory for information regarding the self and others. In reviewing the relevant memory data (which consists predominantly of studies conducted prior to the 1950), Matlin and Stang

(1978) concluded that approximately 60% of the surveyed studies obtained better memory for pleasant, compared to unpleasant or neutral stimuli. Their meta-analysis suggested that selective positive memory was more likely when the materials were well learned and performance was assessed after a delay (Matlin & Stang, 1978).

More current work has failed to provide much evidence that pleasant stimuli lead to better memory performance than unpleasant. Part of the problem is that few recent studies include both pleasant and unpleasant stimuli within the context of the same investigation. When materials from both extremes of the valence dimension are included in the stimulus set, the more general finding is that there is no significant difference in memory for pleasant and unpleasant materials. For instance, Turner and Barlow (1951) found no difference for recall of pleasant and unpleasant recent experiences, when order of output and intensity were controlled. Similarly, Thompson (1985) found no effect of pleasantness when assessing memory for naturally occurring personal events—pleasant and unpleasant— that subjects had recorded in personal diaries. Finally, as mentioned earlier, Bradley and Baddeley (1990) found no difference in memory for pleasant and unpleasant words equated for concreteness and frequency.

Arousal and Memory

Referring to the affective space illustrated in Fig. 4.1, it is clear that highly arousing stimuli can be either very pleasant or very unpleasant; arousal is not linearly correlated with affective valence. In order to determine the role of arousal in memory, then, it is necessary to sample from both extremes of the valence dimension to avoid confounding pleasantness with arousal. In fact, it is not uncommon for studies exploring arousal effects in memory to ignore the affective valence element in the stimuli, which renders conclusions somewhat equivocal.

For instance, studies of arousal and memory that have been spurred by an interest in eyewitness testimony have tended to concentrate solely on unpleasant events. Thus, mirroring presumably the difference between crimes and everyday events, typical comparisons are between an arousing (unpleasant) event and an unarousing (neutral) event. Reviewing some of this material, Deffenbacher (1983) described several studies that found better memory performance as the severity of a staged crime (and presumably arousal) increased, although, of course, it is possible that unpleasantness varied as well. Presentation of faces in the context of loud noise has also been found to improve recognition performance, consistent with an arousal interpretation (Majcher, 1974, as cited in Deffenbacher, 1983), although again loud noise might be experienced as unpleasant, relative to a situation without this property. The results of studies of eyewitness testimony, therefore, predominantly indicate that memory for emotional events—those that are unpleasant and arousing—differs from neutral.

When emotional stimuli that include both pleasant and unpleasant words were compared to nonemotional stimuli in paired-associate learning tasks, one widespread finding in the 1960s was that the high arousal (i.e., emotional) stimuli inhibited the immediate recall of their response terms, but facilitated their long term recall (see Craik & Blankstein, 1975; Eysenck, 1976, and Kleinsmith & Kaplan, 1963, for reviews). Walker's (1958) action decrement theory accounted for this pattern by maintaining that high arousal produced a longer consolidation period (in the brain) during which time the information was not accessible. Short-term unavailability was thought to produce the poor immediate memory performance, whereas the longer consolidation period was held to benefit delayed performance. In reviewing this work, Craik and Blankstein (1975) concluded that if there is any evidence for such a relationship, it exists mainly in this paired-associate paradigm. When stimulus arousal is manipulated using verbal materials in a free recall or recognition procedure, high arousal consistently facilitates later memory performance (Bock & Klinger, 1986; Corteen, 1969; Maltzman, Kantor, & Langdon, 1966).

Consistent with this conclusion, and despite their preference for the Pollyanna principle in explaining affective memory performance, Matlin and Stang (1978) found it necessary to add a secondary Intensity Principle to account for the common finding that arousing stimuli—both pleasant and unpleasant—were often remembered better than those that were low in arousal. Kanungo and Dutta (1966) found in several studies that the rated intensity of adjectives was a more potent factor in determining memory performance than whether the adjectives were perceived as pleasant or unpleasant. Finally, as mentioned earlier, although Turner and Barlow (1951) found no differences in memory between pleasant and unpleasant experiences, both types were remembered better than those that were neutral.

Pleasure and Arousal in Memory

If pleasure and arousal are important in the organization of emotional stimuli, both need to be simultaneously manipulated in order to assess emotional effects in memory. In fact, as discussed earlier, sometimes experimental comparisons are clearly confounded because stimuli simultaneously vary in both dimensions. Observed differences between a neutral and traumatic event, for example, are difficult to interpret because they differ in both pleasantness and arousal. Finally, even when critical comparisons include stimuli from both extremes of the valence dimension (e.g., pleasant and unpleasant), efforts are seldom made to equate (or experimentally vary) the stimuli in terms of levels of arousal.

A necessary ingredient in such experimentation, of course, is the presence of emotionally evocative stimuli that are widely distributed in affective space. Clearly, the stimuli comprising the IAPS and the IADS are suitable for this purpose and afford an opportunity to assess the contribution of the pleasantness dimension, the arousal dimension, and their interaction to memory performance. Using these stimuli, one can begin to determine the nature of emotional memory, and to address additional issues such as the fate of details in affective memory, as well as the role of context, individual differences, mood states, and more. Some of the initial work from our laboratory that utilizes these stimuli to assess affective memory is presented here, much of it for the first time.

Recalling Affective Pictures

To begin these investigations, stimuli that covaried systematically in pleasure and arousal were used to determine dimensional effects on memory performance. Bradley, Greenwald, Petry, and Lang (1992) presented 60 affective pictures to college subjects, and asked them to rate each picture along the dimensions of pleasure, arousal, and dominance, without indicating there would be a later memory test. After a short (15-minute) retention interval, an immediate free recall task was conducted, in which the subject was instructed to write a word or brief phrase describing each picture that the subject could remember seeing in the experiment. A year later, the same subjects were contacted by telephone and again asked to recall as many pictures seen in the study the year before. Recall performance was assessed as a function of the pleasantness and the arousal level of the slide.

The predictions for memory performance, based on past research, are relatively clear. Unpleasant pictures should be remembered best if a bias exists for negative events; conversely, memory for pleasant pictures should exceed that of unpleasant if the Pollyanna principle holds, or if repression is operating at retrieval. Furthermore, if the results from Matlin and Stang's (1978) meta-analysis are correct, pleasant pictures should show the greatest bias in memory at the long test delay. If the "flashbulb" memory hypothesis is correct, memory should be best for materials in the unpleasant, highly arousing cell, since these are most comparable to a naturally occurring "traumatic" event. Based on the arousal literature, one might predict poorer memory for high arousal pictures on the immediate test, but better memory on the delayed test. Or, if delay is only a factor in paired-associate paradigms, highly arousing pictures—either pleasant or unpleasant—should result in greater recall than low arousal materials of either type.

Figure 4.2, top left panel, illustrates the proportion of slides recalled as a function of pleasantness rating. Interestingly, both highly pleasant and highly unpleasant pictures were equally well remembered: There was no significant effect of affective valence in these recall data, suggesting no bias towards stimuli at either extreme of the valence dimension. Clearly, both types of affective pictures were better remembered than more neutral stimuli, as the U-shaped curve relating affective valence to recall performance indicates. Because both the extremely pleasant and the extremely unpleasant stimuli tend to be rated as

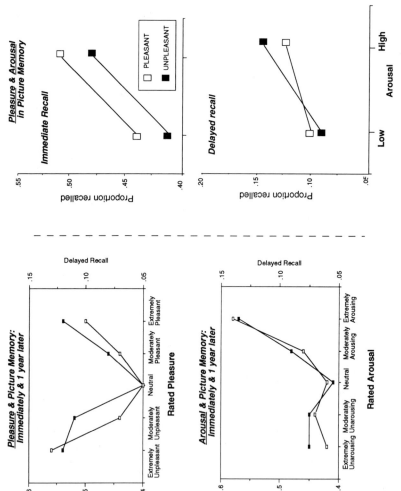

FIG. 4.2. The left panel illustrates that free recall performance for affective pictures (both immediate and delayed) systematically varies as a function of both rated pleasantness (top panel) and rated arousal (bottom panel). The right panel illustrates that, whereas pleasantness has only a small, marginal effect on immediate recall, high stimulus arousal significantly facilitates both immediate (upper panel) and delayed recall (lower panel). (From Bradley et al., 1992)

highly arousing, these data suggest that memory performance in this context is predominantly sensitive to the arousal dimension. Figure 4.2, bottom left panel, illustrates that this hypothesis is supported, in that arousal level had a highly significant effect on memory performance, with highly arousing materials better recalled than those rated lower in arousal.

Despite the lack of a pleasantness effect in memory performance, it may be the case that, if level of arousal were equated, some effect of pleasantness on memory performance might be seen. To address this question, the 60-stimulus picture set was divided into two halves for each subject by ordering the pictures according to the subject's judgments of pleasantness. Each subset of pleasant and unpleasant pictures was further divided into low and high arousal categories by ordering each subset by the subject's own arousal ratings. A manipulation check indicated the success of this procedure in producing categories differing in affective valence but equivalent in arousal, in that the mean arousal ratings for pleasant and unpleasant pictures in the high (or low) arousal cells were highly similar.

Figure 4.2 (right top and bottom panels) illustrates the proportion of pictures recalled both immediately and after a 1-year retention interval as a function of the pleasure and arousal dimensions. At both immediate and delayed free recall, highly arousing slides were remembered better than low arousal slides, regardless of whether they were pleasant or unpleasant in affective direction. A small, marginally significant effect of valence was seen on the immediate recall test, such that pleasant slides showed a slight advantage in memory over unpleasant slides. However, a year later there was no advantage of pleasant stimuli in memory. Rather, arousal continued to exert a strong influence on memory performance. These data are not consistent with either the prediction that high arousal should impair short-term memory or the prediction that selective memory for pleasant stimuli should be strongest after a delay. Rather, high arousal shows a consistent facilitatory effect on memory at all times, with a weak selective memory effect for pleasant pictures only at the immediate test.

Recalling Affective Sounds

A second study investigated dimensional properties of free recall using the sound stimuli from the IADS. The methodology and procedure used was identical to that described above for pictures, except that short acoustic segments of affective sounds (i.e., 6-second clips) were presented to the subject instead of pictures. An incidental free-recall task was administered after a short (15-minute) retention interval; Figure 4.3 illustrates free recall for these affective stimuli as a function of the pleasure and arousal dimensions, respectively. Similar trends in memory performance were obtained for sounds as those obtained with pictures: Unpleasant and pleasant sounds were equally well remembered (with a slight, nonsignificant advantage for pleasant sounds on this immediate memory test), whereas

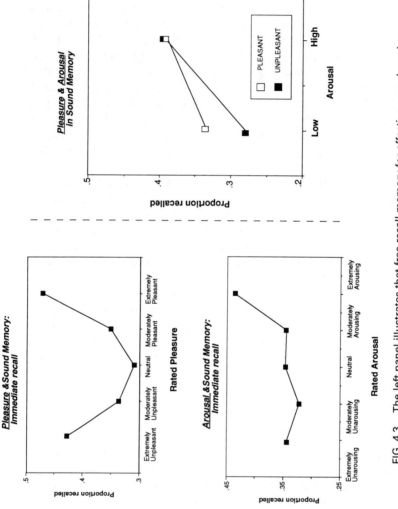

FIG. 4.3. The left panel illustrates that free recall memory for affective sounds varies as a function of rated pleasantness (top panel) and arousal (bottom panel) in ways identical to that found for pictures (see Fig. 4.2). The right panel corroborates that when these variables are covaried, arousal level has the greatest impact on memory performance.

highly arousing stimuli were always remembered better than their low arousal counterparts. Regardless of the specific perceptual properties of the affective stimuli, then, both studies indicate that high arousal facilitates memory for affective events, whereas pleasantness does not appear to exert strong effects, especially on long-term recall.

Recognizing Affective Pictures

Free recall is a particular type of mnemonic adventure: Memory is typically accessed on the basis of a few global cues, which, in the studies presented here, consist of a specification of a particular type of stimulus (i.e., a picture or a sound) processed at a particular point in time (i.e., presented in the context of this psychology experiment). The role of stimulus arousal in this memory process may be related to some specific component of this relatively impoverished (and possibly, quite unnatural) recall task, rather than reflecting a general property of memory retrieval for emotional information. In fact, as discussed above, earlier studies suggested that the role of arousal in memory may be task-related: The differential effects of delay on arousal and memory were related to the specific use of a paired-associate learning task. At the least, this suggests that a memory task that includes more specific information, perhaps even the stimulus itself, should be used when assessing emotional memory. Recognition memory procedures satisfactorily serve this purpose.

Recognition of previously presented pictures is notoriously good: Early studies of picture memory demonstrated people's apparently amazing accuracy in recognizing large numbers of pictures at long retention intervals, especially when compared to memory for isolated words even at short delays (e.g., Shepard, 1967; Standing, 1973). Although more recent studies have indicated that picture recognition performance can be degraded if foils similar to the targets are included among the test items, in the absence of such foils, respondents should be able to accurately recognize IAPS materials presented in an experimental session.

To investigate this, Bradley et al. (1992) compiled two sets of slides from the IAPS that were matched for pleasure, arousal, and semantic content. Each set contained, for example, a baby, a sports scene, a cemetery, a mutilated body, and so forth; the particular set presented at encoding was counterbalanced across subjects. During encoding, the subject rated each picture on the dimensions of pleasure, arousal, and dominance. After a 15-minute retention interval, both sets of pictures—one "old" (seen in the encoding phase) and one "new" (never seen before)—were presented in an episodic recognition task. Assuming high recognition accuracy, the speed of memory retrieval for pictures of different valence and arousal can be assessed. Based on the pattern of effects obtained in free recall, recognition speed should be primarily sensitive to the arousal dimension: Faster recognition speed (and thus, memory retrieval) is predicted for high arousal pictures.

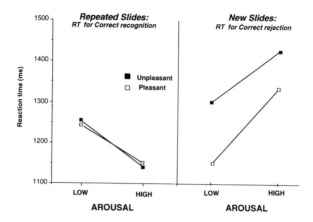

FIG. 4.4.   Mean reaction time for recognizing old pictures (i.e., pre-sented earlier) and new pictures (i.e., not presented earlier) that varied by pleasure and arousal. (From Bradley et al., 1992)

Figure 4.4 illustrates the results from this RT study: Level of arousal again was the central factor affecting memory performance. Mirroring the effect found in recall, pictures that were high in arousal led to better memory performance—in this case, faster recognition decisions. Recognition speed of old pictures was equivalent for unpleasant and pleasant pictures, again showing no effect of valence in memory performance. Because the "old" pictures in this recognition task were the only stimuli that had been previously encoded and stored in memo-ry, it is reasonable to assess *memorial* effects only for these stimuli. The retrieval pattern is identical to that found in free recall: Affective valence does not show a strong effect on memory performance, whereas higher levels of arousal clearly facilitate memory.

Reaction time data for pictures never been seen before, however, provide an opportunity to assess the influence of pleasantness and arousal at initial process-ing. These "new" pictures were functionally undergoing an encoding episode during the recognition task, and, interestingly, both affective dimensions were apparent in performance. One provocative finding was that level of arousal now *inhibited* the speed of the subject's decision, with significantly slower reaction times for high arousal pictures. In addition, affective valence also significantly affected speed, with decisions for pleasant pictures—whether low or high in arousal—faster than for unpleasant pictures.

The advantage of pleasant materials over unpleasant at encoding is consistent with Matlin and Stang's (1978) suggestion that pleasant materials are identified more quickly than unpleasant stimuli. In another study, Bradley and Lang (1991) found that reaction time responses were also significantly faster when subject's encoded and responded to pleasant, compared to unpleasant, words. Frequency is one hypothesis for these effects, in that pleasant words are more frequent in the language (Matlin & Stang, 1978), and it is possible that the stimuli represented in pleasant pictures are more frequent as well. If one considers that, in western culture at least, positive images are mass produced for use in a variety of media contexts including television, film, and advertising, then pictures similar to pleasant IAPS stimuli may appear more frequently than those involving unpleasant or aversive events. In fact, when the affective space for advertisements was recently assessed (Morris, Bradley, Waine, & Lang, in press), overrepresentation in the pleasant half of space, relative to unpleasant, was clear.

On the basis of this hypothesis, however, one might expect that the fastest encoding times would be obtained for pleasant, arousing stimuli. In fact, however, high arousal pictures—whether pleasant or unpleasant—resulted in significantly longer rejection times than low arousal pictures that were pleasant. Other possible explanations for this pattern of differences at encoding, include: (a) the degree of similarity between the targets (i.e., "old" pictures) and foils (i.e., "new" pictures), (b) response competition or interference, and (c) stimulus complexity. Controlled experimentation will be necessary to test between these alternatives. Easiest to assess, perhaps, is the stimulus complexity hypothesis, which suggests that affective pictures contain more information, requiring more time for resolution at encoding. Recent data fail to support this hypothesis in that highly arousing pleasant and unpleasant pictures were rated as equally complex, even though high arousal pictures were rated as more complex than low arousal stimuli (Bradley & Lang, 1993). Thus, only part of the reaction time pattern was reproduced in complexity ratings. However, more direct tests of this (and other) hypotheses are underway, including determining the speed of stimulus identification and evaluation in the absence of a memory task.

Recognizing Details in Affective Pictures

With respect to *memory* performance, these data point firmly to the fact that high arousal facilitates memory retrieval, whether it's measured by free recall or speed of recognition. Both of these mnemonic procedures, however, probe memory for general or global information concerning the presentation of an affective stimulus. Will memory for specific details of these pictures also show improvement with increased arousal? Or, as discussed previously (e.g., Christianson & Loftus, 1991), will detail memory suffer, at least for traumatic (e.g., unpleasant and arousing) stimuli? Bradley and Lang (1993) recently tested this hypothesis by selecting 50 pictures from the IAPS that varied in pleasure and arousal. Subjects viewed each slide, and rated its pleasantness, arousal, and dominance immediately after viewing. A Yes-No recognition test probing memory for details of these pictures was administered after a 2-day retention interval; the subjects (n = 138) were not informed of the memory test prior to its administration.

The recognition test queried the subject regarding a single detail of each picture presented, after ascertaining that the picture in question was, in fact, remembered. The details probed were varied in terms of the type of information sought (e.g., color, number, location, etc.), and the type of question was roughly balanced across the different affective contents. Two forms of the detail test were constructed and counterbalanced across subjects, such that if the correct answer on one form was affirmative, the correct answer on the other form was negative.

Pictures were assigned to one of four cells defined by the factorial combination of pleasure (high, low) and arousal (high, low) based on each subject's individual ratings. Thus, as explained previously, pictures ranked in the top and bottom half of each subject's valence distribution were categorized as pleasant and unpleasant, respectively; within these categories, low- and high-arousal materials were determined by ranking on arousal ratings. Correct responses on the detail question were expressed as a proportion of the number of pictures the subject remembered seeing in each category; Fig. 4.5 illustrates these data. Recognition performance is above chance (i.e., greater than 50%) for all affective categories. Rather than resulting in poor memory performance, however, high arousal again facilitated memory compared to low arousal materials. And, contrary to the prediction that unpleasant pictures should result in especially poor detail memory, details of unpleasant stimuli—either low or high in arousal— were remembered significantly better than their similarly arousing but more pleasant counterparts. Confidence ratings in these recognition judgments mirrored performance exactly: Respondents were significantly more confident of their responses to questions probing high-arousal pictures, as well as to questions concerning unpleasant pictures.

These data are consistent with those obtained in free recall and recognition: High-arousal stimuli consistently produced better memory performance. In addi-

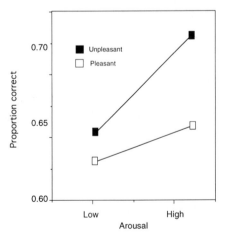

FIG. 4.5.   Mean correct recognition of details for pictures that vary in terms of both pleasantness and arousal.

tion, for the first time a bias towards better memory for unpleasant stimuli was obtained, in direct contradiction to predictions both from earlier work on detail memory as well as those implied by the Pollyanna principle. There are a number of possible reasons for the discrepancies, not least of which concern differences in materials and procedures. Perhaps most importantly, the current study sampled detail memories across a much wider range of materials than in the past, where memory for a single detail in a single picture was often assessed. Probing memory for multiple stimuli in each affective category minimizes the influence of idiosyncratic differences due to individual pictures. On the other hand, this procedure does not equate for the specific details probed in each affective category, which may also be contributing to the pattern obtained here. Future studies in our lab will use digitized forms of the IAPS stimuli, allowing us more precise experimental control over the placement of detail information in the pictures.

AFFECT, AROUSAL, AND ASSOCIATIVE MEMORY

The experiments discussed earlier consistently indicate that increases in rated arousal were associated with better memory, regardless of whether performance was measured by recall or recognition, or whether memory for global or detailed information was probed. Although no systematic differences as a function of pleasantness were obtained across procedures, free recall showed a slight bias towards pleasant stimuli on immediate tests, and recognition memory for details was better for unpleasant pictures.

Encoding "3-System" Responses

How are we to interpret this pattern of effects? One approach is to back up and determine what is going on, emotionally speaking, when these materials are first perceived. To the extent that differences in emotional engagement are obtained at encoding, hypotheses concerning subsequent mnemonic effects might become apparent. Such a methodology raises interesting questions regarding first, the meaning of *emotional response,* and second, its measurement. Thus far, we have assumed that the stimuli in the IAPS and IADS are emotionally evocative on the basis of subjects' verbal reports. Now, the time has come to further substantiate this claim by investigating two of the remaining "3-system" responses (Lang, 1978): measurement of physiology and behavior. That is, Lang (1978, 1989) outlined a 3-systems approach in which emotion is defined as a confluence of responding in subjective report, behavioral, and physiological systems, with measurement in all three important for exhaustively tapping the data base of emotion. We have already determined that subjects' reports of pleasure and arousal vary for the affective stimuli in the IAPS; the next question concerns the extent to which physiological and behavioral responses covary with these dimensions as well. The goal, again, is to determine the feasibility of dimensional organization in emotional response, this time with the additional goal of understanding the effects of such reactivity on memory performance.

Presentation of affective pictures produces remarkable reactivity in a number of response systems that can be measured and used as a handle onto emotional experience. This encoding activity can be quantified and subsequently related to indices of later memory performance. As a first step in this endeavor, several recent studies have demonstrated reliable covariation between subjective reports of affective experience (i.e., pleasure and arousal) and physiological reactivity when encoding pictures from the IAPS (Bradley, Greenwald, & Hamm, in press; Greenwald et al., 1989, Lang et al., 1993). In these studies, a variety of relevant physiological systems, including facial EMG response, heart rate, and electrodermal reactivity, were continuously measured while subjects were exposed to pictures from the IAPS. Subjects' reports of pleasure, arousal, and dominance were collected either immediately after viewing each picture (e.g., Lang et al., in press), or after viewing an entire set of stimuli (e.g., Bradley, Lang, & Cuthbert, 1990). When these stimuli were subsequently ranked from low to high based on each subject's ratings of pleasure or arousal, differences in physiological response associated with changes along the affective dimension of interest can easily be assessed. Interestingly, different response systems are related to different dimensions; Fig. 4.6 illustrates typical relationships obtained using this methodology.

Expressive behavior—measured as facial electromyographic response in the corrugator (frown) and zygomatic (smile) muscles—reliably covaries with judgments of pleasantness. Corrugator EMG changes increase as pictures are rated more unpleasant, whereas zygomatic changes are greatest for pleasant stimuli. Facial expressions associated with displeasure (e.g., facial grimace) also produce some activity in the zygomatic muscle. A traditional physiological measure of emotional response—heart rate—is not depicted here, but is also typically related to pleasantness, albeit less strongly. Peak heart rate response is usually slightly larger for pleasant materials, or, viewed conversely, greater cardiac deceleration is found for unpleasant materials (Bradley et al., 1990).

Electrodermal responses covary impressively with ratings of arousal: As level of rated arousal increases, the magnitude of the skin conductance response emitted during picture viewing increases as well (see Fig. 4.6). Skin conductance responses can be taken as a direct index of sympathetic activation, which is widely recognized as important in emotional engagement. This relationship, then, appears to index the degree of activation at encoding, regardless of the valence of the stimulus. Several other relationships exist between the arousal dimension and various report measures: Judgments of interest covary almost completely with judgments of arousal (Bradley et al., 1990; Lang et al., 1993), as do judgments of stimulus complexity (Bradley & Lang, 1993).

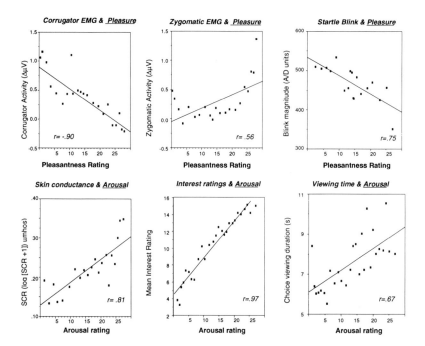

FIG. 4.6. Covariation between reports of pleasure or arousal for affective pictures and various 3-system responses (i.e., physiological, self-report, behavior). These plots were created by first ranking each participant's data by pleasure (or arousal) ratings from low to high; the graphs shown here plot the mean response (across participants) at each rank. Upper panel, from left, illustrates decreasing facial corrugator EMG (i.e., "frown"), increasing facial zygomatic EMG ("smile"), and decreasing startle reflex magnitude as reports of pleasantness increase. Lower panel, from left, illustrates increases in the magnitude of electrodermal responses, interest ratings, and choice viewing duration as rated arousal increases.

Choice viewing duration, defined as the time between stimulus onset and its voluntary termination by the subject, is also predominantly controlled by the arousal dimension: Subjects choose to view stimuli that are highly arousing—both pleasant and unpleasant—for a significantly longer time than for those rated lower in arousal (Bradley et al., 1990). Interestingly, phobic subjects do not show this relationship, instead terminating exposure of feared stimuli significantly earlier than for other aversive, but nonphobic pictures (Hamm et al., 1991).

As of this writing, a physiological investigation involving the sound stimuli from the IADS is not yet completed. However, the same relationships between dimensional judgments and psychophysiological response have been obtained when subjects imagine emotional events, rather than viewing pictures. In this work (Bradley, Lang, & Cuthbert, 1991), sentences describing situations varying in both pleasure and arousal were presented auditorially, followed by a 12-second imagery period. Following all imagery trials, the subject rated each image on the dimensions of pleasure, arousal, and dominance. Similar to the picture studies, the sentences (n = 24) were ranked from low to high on each dimension, and the corresponding physiological response during imagery assessed. Corrugator EMG again showed a strong linear relationship with judgments of pleasure. The electrodermal system was once again differentially sensitive to variations in arousal, with larger responses occurring during imagery of events rated as more arousing. In the context of the internally driven, imagery task, heart rate response covaried more closely with arousal than valence, unlike the picture perception paradigm. Thus, although heart rate is reactive to emotional variables, its direction appears to be quite task dependent (see Lang et al., 1990).

Measurement of the ongoing physiological reaction elicited by an affective stimulus (e.g., a picture or image) is one method for determining the emotional response engendered at encoding. Detecting affective differences at encoding is also possible using the presentation of a probe stimulus that is itself modified by an ongoing affective state (see Lang et al., 1990, 1991). For instance, a startle stimulus—consisting of a sudden burst of noise or light—elicits a reflexive reaction that can be measured electromyographically by recording the magnitude of the reflexive eyeblink. The size of the startle reflex has recently demonstrated remarkable consistency in the manner in which it is modulated by affective response, such that blink reflexes are largest (and fastest) when processing aversive stimuli, including pictures in the IAPS (Bradley et al., 1990), images (Vrana & Lang, 1990), or films (Jansen & Frijda, 1991), and smallest when processing pleasant stimuli. Figure 4.6 illustrates that the covariation of blink magnitude with affective valence in the context of picture processing shows a strong linear relationship, as was previously found for the corrugator EMG facial response.[3] A similarly strong relationship was obtained in imagery when startle probe responses were arrayed in order of increasing fear (Vrana & Lang, 1990). Dimensionally speaking then, startle modulation appears to be primarily responsive to the affective valence, rather than the arousal, dimension.

---

[3]There are several reasons why one might prefer the startle probe response over facial EMG responses, including its fast, reflexive properties (making it less susceptible to voluntary or demand characteristics), its existence in a variety of species (making phylogenetic comparisons possible), and its early onset ontogenetically. In addition, Bradley, Lang, and Cuthbert (in press) determined that with repeated presentation of the same affective pictures, corrugator EMG differentiation between pleasant and unpleasant materials ceased after a few viewings, whereas startle blink differences were observed throughout the entire series. Thus, expressive facial behavior can be turned on (raising demand problems) and turned off (due to habituation), but the startle reflex is a mandatory response that continuously indexes the affective valence dimension.

Encoding Affect and Associative Memory

It is clear that encoding the affective stimuli in the IAPS generates a response set consistent with emotional involvement, including facial displays of frowning, grimacing, or smiling, directional heart rate changes, increased skin conductance magnitude, and, consistently, modulation of the blink reflex by affective valence. Response systems clearly differ with respect to whether they show sensitivity to the affective valence (i.e., pleasantness) or arousal dimensions, and these empirical relationships can be used to constrain subsequent theorizing. That is, response profiles generated at encoding for pleasant and unpleasant pictures differ markedly from those that are neutral, and it is precisely in determining the ramifications of such output for memory that explanation for the mnemonic effects may lie.

As discussed elsewhere in this volume (see Lang, chapter 3), the activation of response information during perceptual encoding of a stimulus can be described at both a cognitive and a neurophysiological level. At a cognitive level, the encoding situation can be characterized as one in which the pictorial stimulus acts as a cue to related information in memory, including past personal experiences and abstract conceptual knowledge. Importantly, memory is considered to include associations to response information, such as appropriate actions (perhaps those taken in the past), which are in turn connected to effector and output systems. The constellation of represented information in memory includes aspects regarding both the current stimulus configuration (i.e., "What is it?") as well as appropriate responses (i.e., "What do I do?"). Based on an overlap between the information available in the cue and that represented in memory, neural units are excited, activating associatively related units at all levels. With respect to efferent information, physiological output measured concomitantly with mentation acts as an index of activated response information. As discussed earlier, both picture perception and imaginal processing evince systematic responding that is measurable as subovert activity in relevant systems.

Based sheerly on the measured output, then, it is possible to conclude that the information network of an affective stimulus is more elaborate and more extensive—by virtue of its connections to efferent outflow—than that representing a neutral stimulus. The fact that subjects' judgments of complexity increase for emotional stimuli—both pleasant and unpleasant—may be indexing the greater elaboration of these stimuli in memory (Bradley & Lang, 1993). To the extent that both intensely pleasant and unpleasant stimuli involve increases in responding, either in the same system (e.g., both produce increases in skin conductance magnitude) or different systems (e.g., activity in different facial muscles), it is understandable that free recall does not differentially favor either type of stimulus. Rather, both types of stimuli appear to have strong associative relations to relevant response information, even at the time of initial coding in the experimental context.

Acquiring Affective Associations

How are associations between perceptual stimuli and emotional reactions made in the first place? Preparedness theory (Ohman, 1986) argues that for some stimuli, such as snakes and spiders, strong links between stimulus and response are hard wired at birth, due to long-standing associations with danger and death throughout evolutionary development. Although such a hypothesis may be appropriate for some stimuli, the preparedness hypothesis does not attempt to account for stimulus–response relationships involving more contemporary objects of threat (e.g., guns or bombs), or for the vast number of idiosyncratic affective associations accruing across individual experience.

Rather, studies of associative learning, conducted under the rubric of "conditioning," point clearly to the role of ongoing emotional response in association formation (see Mackintosh, 1983, for a review). These "unconditioned" affective reactions—elicited by the presence of either naturally unpleasant (e.g., shock) or pleasant (e.g., food) reinforcers in the experimental context—appear to be powerful ingredients in the basic learning process. If reinforcers, either appetitive and aversive, are primary components in associative learning, then clearly the foundations of learning (and memory) are rooted in affective processes. Systematic relationships between emotion and memory will probably be well informed by a close look at the vast data base produced by conditioning experiments, as well as careful scrutiny of the mechanisms proposed to account for these data.

Arousal and Associative Strength

In fact, abundant theoretical and empirical evidence exists linking better learning to increases in arousal. Pavlov's (1927) law of strength formalized the relationship by stating that an increase in the intensity of the unconditioned stimulus was related to the strength of the learned response. Numerous studies have subsequently confirmed this relationship, using either appetitive or aversive reinforcers in a wide variety of conditioning tasks. For instance, Kamin and Bruner (1963) and Gold (1984) both demonstrated facilitation in performance with increases in shock intensity during training. Increases in the intensity of an appetitive reinforcer, often defined in terms of the number of food pellets provided, has similarly been found to facilitate test performance (Kesner & Andrus, 1982; Wagner, Siegel, Thomas, & Ellison, 1964).

In Hull-Spence learning theory, drive was considered to have a multiplicative effect on learning, systematically strengthening associations as drive state increased. If operationalized as long-term food or water deprivation, the concept of drive is more similar to *activation*—defined as a general state of readiness that motivates all subsequent behavior—than to *arousal,* which is often used to refer to specific effects resulting from a particular episode (Pribram & McGuiness, 1975; see Frijda, 1986, pp. 90–94 for a discussion of these differences). Nonetheless, a number of experiments clearly confirm that variations in drive state (i.e., "activation") affect performance in ways almost identical to those produced by magnitude of reinforcement (i.e., "arousal"; see D'Amato, 1970), suggesting that, at least with respect to learning, the underlying mechanism is similar. Here, the common link is held to be that these experimental manipulations similarly modify the motivational strategy of the organism towards high levels of arousal and, in the case of deprivation, unpleasantness (Lang et al., 1990). And, despite the obvious paradigmatic differences between conditioning procedures and those studied here, the results are almost parallel: Higher amounts of arousal at learning, regardless of valence, prompt better performance.

Emotional Learning and Subcortical Involvement

Neuroanatomical explorations of associative learning have long centered on the involvement of subcortical centers in mediating affective responses to perceptual stimuli, and particular attention to aversive learning has more recently focused on amygdaloid involvement (e.g., Davis, Hitchcock, & Rosen, 1987; LeDoux, 1987; Pribram, 1992). As discussed elsewhere in this volume (Lang, chapter 3), current models hypothesize that subcortical processing, either with or without prior cortical involvement, codes affective attributes of a sensory stimulus (see also Sarter & Markovitsch, 1985). Neuroanatomical connections between the amygdala, the hypothalamus, and the autonomic nervous system have been outlined (e.g., Davis, Hitchcock & Rosen, 1987; Sarter & Markovitsch, 1985), providing a strong link between activity in such centers and the production of responses habitually measured in both the picture perception and conditioning paradigms. From the perspective presented here, widespread subcortical processing is assumed to imbue objects with affective value (and intensity) primarily by engaging and initiating relevant action systems. This position clearly echoes that of Frijda (1986), who stated that "action tendency would seem to be the most critical attribute for identifying an experience as emotional" (p. 249).

Extensive response production has a number of ramifications, including the presence of measurable output at encoding, and a clear advantage in memory, relative to events that do not engage these systems. Therefore, to the extent that the fuel propelling associative memory is generated by subcortical involvement, events and stimuli prompting such processing will be those that are well remembered. The fact that the more primitive centers of the brain are central in emotional processing is consistent with the observation that even organisms less well developed cortically must learn about and remember both threatening (e.g., snakes) and appetitive (e.g., food) stimuli if survival is the primary goal. Interestingly, cortical damage, especially frontal, appears to primarily result in affective deficits that are social in nature, including problems in social interactions, preferences, vocalizations, and dominance, which might be considered a later development ontogenetically (Kolb & Taylor, 1990) than the emotional responses elicited by threat or appetitive stimuli.

AROUSAL AND MEMORY: FURTHER ISSUES

To summarize, memory in the picture perception paradigm is considered here to be similar to associative learning in the conditioning paradigm, in that performance in both appears to be primarily affected by the degree of affective responding, or arousal, engendered at input. The central hypothesis is that motivationally relevant events receive widespread subcortical and cortical processing that results in the activation of action-related information pertinent to strategic and tactical levels of response (Lang et al., 1990; Lang, chapter 3, this volume). This information activation forms the basis of a neural network that is considerably more elaborate than the representation of an event that lacks affective engagement, with the obvious ramifications for memory performance. Of course, other factors may be responsible as well, and some of these are briefly discussed below. Finally, this account raises several unanswered questions, which are also discussed below.

Attention and Arousal

In addition to extensive reactive output, highly arousing pictures are rated as more interesting and are voluntarily viewed for a longer period of time, suggesting that mnemonic effects due to arousal may be mediated by differences in attention, interest, or effort that are in effect at encoding as well. Attributing arousal differences to attention raises the difficult issue of conceptually and, more importantly, operationally distinguishing the two. Berlyne (1960) suggested that attention could be differentiated into intensive and selective aspects, with arousal corresponding to the energizing function, and attention to the selection process, although measurement of each aspect was not emphasized. To the extent that increases in arousal facilitate the amount of "effort" or "energy" devoted to the input task, the involvement of such a process at encoding might benefit later memory. Nonetheless, even if effects are due to these mediating factors, the question remains as to why highly arousing stimuli control attentional or effort related processes in this manner. Easterbrook (1959) combined the two aspects of attention by relating increases in arousal to decreases in the breadth of attention (i.e., it became more selective). By this account, however, one would have expected to find that detail memory was poorest for highly arousing stimuli, which was not the case.

Rehearsal and Arousal

Another mechanism that might contribute to better memory for high arousal materials may be that highly arousing stimuli receive greater amounts of rehearsal postencoding, with the obvious facilitatory effect on memory. Because the memory tasks in the studies reviewed above were largely incidental, however, voluntary, spontaneous rehearsal of picture stimuli serves no apparent function. In addition, given the constant presentation of picture stimuli, ratings, and retention interval tasks, such as in the Bradley et al. (1992) experiments, it is not clear precisely when such rehearsal processes were able to operate. If, on the other hand, rehearsal processes are naturally engaged by such stimuli, we return to the question of why high arousal should produce this cognitive bias.

Aspects of Arousal

Taking a measurement-oriented stance, Lacey (1967), argued against a unidimensional arousal construct, outlining instead differences in cerebral, autonomic, and behavioral indices of arousal and highlighting discordances among systems. In the studies reported in this chapter, however, concordance in arousal systems (e.g., verbal reports of arousal and electrodermal reactivity) was consistently obtained, which supports the existence of such an organizing dimension in emotion. At least with regard to affective stimuli, then, it is clear that a unidimensional construct labelled variously as arousal, intensity, or activation is fundamentally related to emotional reactivity, and, in this case, to memory performance.

Memory Stages and Neurochemical Effects

The data reviewed above do not localize the effects of arousal on memory with respect to whether they are operating at encoding, storage, or retrieval. Explanations that attribute the effects to a more extensive information structure arising from activation of relevant response information at encoding (as well as ancillary hypotheses involving attention or effort) clearly hypothesize that the effect of arousal on memory occurs during the initial *encoding* process. In contrast, Walker's (1958) action-decrement theory hypothesized that arousal differences were due to (consolidation) processes occurring after encoding, during memory *storage*.

Interestingly, recent studies from animal laboratories also focus on differences at storage in explaining effects of arousal. Gold and McGaugh and their associates have demonstrated that increasing an animal's arousal level by electrical or chemical intervention *after* training facilitates later performance (Gold & McGaugh, 1975; McGaugh, Gold, Handwerker, Jensen, Martinez, Meligeni, & Vasquez, 1979). Thus, an *identical* learning experience is modified by a postencoding increase in arousal. Storage—rather than retrieval—is hypothesized as the locus of the effect because memory modulation is only obtained within a relatively narrow temporal window after training. Posttraining arousal facilitation has been obtained in both aversive (Gold & Zornetzer, 1983) and appetitive training tasks (Sternberg, Isaacs, Gold, & McGaugh, 1985), suggesting that a factor sensitive to the intensity or arousal of the event, rather than affective valence, is the controlling variable.

In assessing whether these arousal manipulations relate to naturally occurring consequences of arousing events, Gold and van Buskirk (1976) determined that increases in the amount of foot shock used during training produced an increase in the level of circulating epinephrine (as well as better learning, up to a point). Using posttraining injections of epinephrine to mimic the effects of greater shock, they demonstrated improved memory performance for animals given epinephrine, relative to animals not receiving the drug. Interestingly, administration of an adrenergic receptor antagonist (phenoxybenzamine) *prior* to learning inhibited both facilitation of memory performance (Sternberg et al., 1985) and the amnesia that can be obtained with higher doses (Gold and Sternberg, 1978), suggesting that both mnenomic effects are mediated by a common mechanism. Taken together, these data suggest that the natural physiological consequences of arousing experiences can affect memory performance.

Applied to the picture perception paradigm reviewed above, one ramification from these data is that the arousal reaction engendered during viewing of highly pleasant and unpleasant slides results in the circulation of brain chemicals that have a direct, facilitatory effect on memory. Within the context of the response-related hypothesis developed above, such an additional concomitant of affective processing is eminently reasonable. That is, a relevant affective "response" to stimuli involving subcortical coding may be the output of circulating hormones that directly modulate memory strength. Whether these neurochemical responses are best attributed to an encoding or storage stage of memorial processing, or whether the two can be operationally distinguished, awaits further research. Answers to these questions will depend on the resolution of issues such as the temporal parameters of peripheral (e.g., skin conductance, etc.) and neurochemical responses, the specificity of arousal responses with respect to a particular stimulus, the effects of sequencing arousing and nonarousing events on memory performance, and others.

In addition, the presence of arousal at *retrieval* needs closer scrutiny in order to determine what, if any, effects it has on memory performance. According to a cue-matching retrieval process (e.g., Bower, 1981; Lang, 1979, 1985), high arousal at retrieval should only facilitate memory to the extent that high arousal was present at encoding. Memory data confirming such a context dependency are rare, but do exist (e.g., Clark, Milberg, & Ross, 1983). More often than not, however, context-dependent effects regarding affective state in recall are unstable and difficult to replicate (Bower & Mayer, 1985). The data presented above (e.g., Bradley et al., 1992) clearly indicate an advantage for high arousal stimuli at retrieval even when the affective state at recall was presumably neutral, in that no attempt was made to vary the subject's affective state at retrieval. This assumption is even more reasonable when the recall task occurred a year after the encoding episode (Bradley et al., 1992) in which it is extremely unlikely that residual effects of the arousing input were still operating. Even in this case, however, high arousal stimuli were better recalled. Clearly, many questions remain regarding the effects of affective variables at retrieval and their interaction with the affective nature of the encoded stimuli.

Mood and Memory

In fact, the studies reviewed above, in which memory for emotional stimuli in the absence of a controlled, persistent mood state was assessed (e.g., Bradley et al., 1992; Christianson & Loftus, 1987), are actually somewhat atypical. The focus of much current research is on the investigation of interactions between mood states at encoding and retrieval, or interactions between mood states and the valence of encoding materials (see Blaney, 1986, for a review). In both mood-congruent and mood-dependent work, however, it is again relatively uncommon to find studies that covary or control mood states in terms of both valence and arousal; rather, the prototypical comparison is between a happy and sad mood (Blaney, 1986). This choice is somewhat unfortunate, in that arousal is clearly confounded with valence: Sadness is characterized by low valence and relatively low arousal, whereas happiness tends to be high on both dimensions (Bradley et al., in press; Lang et al., in press). This difficulty renders interpretations of the resulting data somewhat difficult. A recent, preliminary investigation in our laboratory used blocks of IAPS slides to induce a persistent emotional state and was encouraging in that physiological and performance indices were consistent with the proposed mood manipulation (Bradley & Lang, 1991). Such results suggest that the influence of mood states—characterized by systematic differences in valence and arousal, and induced experimentally using a stream of IAPS (or IADS) stimuli—on memory may be profitably explored using this methodology.

Individual Differences and Emotional Memory

Effects of stable individual differences in emotionality might also be expected to influence the pattern of obtained effects of emotion in memory. Studies demonstrating selective memory performance as a function of clinically diagnosed affective disorders have recently been conducted (e.g., Matthews & MacLeod, 1985; Watts, McKenna, Sharrock, & Trezise, 1986; Watts & Sharrock, 1987). In this research, priming effects, indicating faster or more accurate processing of stimuli related to a subject's emotional disorder, have been obtained as a function of clinical or temperamental variables. Such relationships can easily be pursued using the wide range of stimuli available in the IAPS (or IADS), and additionally, one can localize effects with respect to dimensional differences (i.e., pleasure, arousal, or dominance), specific contents (e.g., phobic objects), or both. For instance, to the extent that a clinical sample such as anhedonics or depressives find it difficult to mobilize for emotional engagement, memory performance might generally be poorer for these populations, relative to normal participants.

Specific deficits in arousal-related effects might also be postulated, and it is likely that heretofore unseen effects of affective valence (i.e., pleasure) in memory performance may occur when groups are isolated on the basis of differences in emotional disposition or temperament.

It is in the realm of individual differences in emotionality that physiological measurement of affective engagement at encoding and retrieval becomes quite relevant. For instance, whereas all subjects report that scenes of mutilation and death are unpleasant and highly arousing, those diagnosed as psychopathic fail to produce palpable reflex modulation when viewing these materials, although normal respondents evince large startle reflexes (Patrick, Bradley, & Lang, 1993). Similarly, phobic subjects produce heart rate acceleration (e.g., perceptual rejection) when viewing pictures of feared objects, whereas nonphobic subjects consistently demonstrate large cardiac deceleration (i.e., perceptual intake) to the same materials (Klorman, Weissberg, Wiesenfeld, 1977). In addition, a patient who had undergone right temporal lobectomy not only reported that unpleasant materials were unarousing, but also failed to produce an electrodermal reaction of arousal when viewing aversive materials (Morris et al., 1991). Finally, even within a large sample of normal college students, differences in emotional reactivity across a wide range of response systems have recently been obtained as a function of temperament (Bradley & Lang, 1992). Taken together, these data encourage further explorations of individual differences using IAPS and IADS materials, guided by a dimensional view that relies on a "3-system" measurement to determine the range and vicissitudes in emotional reactivity.

Functional Memory?

Regardless of the ultimate resolution of issues involving memory, affect, and individual differences discussed above, current hypotheses clearly focus on events during or shortly following encoding as underlying arousal differences in memory, and pinpoint the important elements as those related to affective output in behavioral, autonomic, and perhaps neurochemical systems. The fundamental hypothesis presented here is that arousal responses result in the production of a more extensively elaborated memory representation, involving associations to information on numerous levels, from stimulus to response related. Additionally, it is possible that release of endogenous neurochemicals directly acts to strengthen connections in this neural network. Interestingly, conclusions regarding the function of a memory system sensitive primarily to arousal level are identical whether animals or humans are the subjects: Motivationally significant events— those that are high in arousal, regardless of whether they are aversive or appetitive—are probably more relevant to future environmental transactions than those that are redundant, mundane, and not able to mobilize the organism for action (e.g., Bradley et al., 1992; Gold & McGaugh, 1975).

AFTERWORD:
DIMENSIONAL ORGANIZATION
IN LANGUAGE AND ACTION

The heavy emphasis here on the importance of pleasure and arousal in affective life may seem so obvious as to be a truism: Even Wundt was clear in identifying these dimensions as central in differentiating among specific emotions. A simple trip through the literature on emotion and learning confirms the centrality of this concept, revealing a plethora of synonyms labelling dimensions like these as fundamental. For pleasure, for instance, one finds the terms quality, direction, evaluation, and valence; for arousal—activation, intensity, vigor, impact, and magnitude, to name a few. In what might appear to be a regressive step, here we have focused solely on this low-level affective organization in order to determine the extent to which such dimensional variations relate to affective responses ranging from online psychophysiological reactions to long-term memory performance. The resulting relationships suggest this approach is fruitful with regard to description, and potentially informative with respect to mechanism.

If pleasure and arousal are pervasive organizers of human judgments, almost parallel dimensions of *direction* and *vigor* were earlier advocated as fundamental in organizing behavior (e.g., Hebb, 1949; Konorski, 1967). To the extent that language has developed to describe the basic parameters of behavior, it is reasonable that its primary dimensions are related to those that control action. Both ontogenetically and phylogenetically, emotional response is clearly action oriented (Frijda, 1986), its trajectory dictated by the motivational parameters of direction (toward or away) and vigor prompted by the stimulus context (Lang et al., 1990).

Thus, the data obtained here suggest that judgments of pleasantness reflect the degree to which a person is disposed to approach or withdraw from a stimulus. Interestingly, physiological systems differentially sensitive to this valence dimension include motor responses, such as facial expressions (both corrugator and zygomatic EMG) and startle reflex magnitude, as well as heart rate change, which has often been directly linked to preparation for action (Obrist, 1981). On the other hand, the dimension of vigor is clearly paralleled in judgments of arousal, which covaried closely with degree of sympathetic mobilization as measured by skin conductance magnitude. General activation of this sort is presumably necessary to support actions that are either appetitive or aversive in direction.

It would be difficult to obtain systematic variations in these response systems if the dimensions of direction/valence and vigor/arousal were not intrinsic to the organization of emotion. The dominance dimension, which received little attention here, is likely to reemerge as important when organizing emotional responses that are elicited in a context involving social or interactive elements (unlike the picture viewing paradigm, for example). Differences in dominance have been found to discriminate between anger and fear situations, which both tend to be similarly high in arousal and low in pleasure (Miller et al., 1987). Stimuli in which dominance accounts for independent variance—including, perhaps, materials that involve a narrative, as opposed to an object-oriented, description—can be used to map the relations between emotional response and the dimension of control.

Whatever the ultimate outcome of such an investigation, the existence of the lawful relationships between pleasure, arousal, and affective response obtained here encourages the formulation of additional questions regarding emotion in dimensional terms. Importantly, the nature of emotional responses engendered at encoding appear to not only index the on-line affective reaction, but also have clear implications for later memory performance. Because memory performance was primarily sensitive to level of arousal, it suggests that intense stimuli of either direction (i.e., appetitive or aversive) prompt extensive processing at the time of encoding, and perhaps beyond.

One clear prediction from this work is that memory should be strongly and positively related to a statistic that summarizes response engagement during affective encoding. Clearly, 3-system measurement of physiological, behavioral, and self-report data will be necessary in accurately assessing emotional engagement during encoding. Variables identifying differences in temperament or clinical disorder can be assessed within the same context, as can those investigating developmental or neuropsychological aspects. Because the organizing framework provided by the dimensional view simply specifies two or three major dimensions along which affect varies, it provides an obvious starting point, a clear methodology and, hopefully, an ultimate solution regarding the puzzle that is emotion.

ACKNOWLEDGMENTS

Preparation of this article and much of the research described was supported in part by National Institute of Mental Health (NIMH) Grants MH37757, MH41950 and MH43975, and Grant AG09779 from the National Institute of Aging to Peter J. Lang.

Thanks to Peter Lang for his many contributions to the research discussed in this chapter.

Address correspondence concerning this article to: Margaret Bradley, Box 100165, H.S.C., University of Florida, Gainesville, FL, 32610.

REFERENCES

Berlyne, D. E. (1960). *Conflict, arousal, and curiosity.* New York: McGraw-Hill.
Blaney, P. H. (1986). Affect and memory: A review. *Psychological Bulletin, 99,* 229–246.
Bock, M., & Klinger, E. (1986). Interaction of emotion and cognition in word recall. *Psychological Research, 48,* 99–106.

Bohannon, J. N., III. (1988). Flashbulb memories for the space shuttle disaster: A tale of two theories. *Cognition, 29,* 179–196.

Bower, G. H. (1981). Mood and memory. *American Psychologist, 36,* 129–148.

Bower, G. H., & Mayer, J. D. (1985). Failure to replicate mood-dependent retrieval. *Bulletin of the Psychonomic Society, 23,* 30–42.

Bradley, B. P., & Baddeley, A. D. (1990). Emotional factors in forgetting. *Psychological Medicine, 20,* 351–355.

Bradley, M. M., Greenwald, M. K., & Hamm, A. O. (in press). Affective picture processing. In N. Birbaumer & A. Öhman (Eds.), *The organization of emotion.* Toronto: Hogrefe-Huber.

Bradley, M. M., Greenwald, M. K., Petry, M., & Lang, P. J. (1992). Remembering pictures: Pleasure and arousal in memory. *Journal of Experimental Psychology: Learning, Memory, & Cognition, 18,* 379–390.

Bradley, M. M., & Lang, P. J. (1991). Probing resource allocation in mood states: Startle and reaction time measures. *Psychophysiology, 28,* S13.

Bradley, M. M., & Lang, P. J. (1993). [*Emotional memory: Individual differences, recall task, and effects of context.*] Unpublished raw data.

Bradley, M. M., & Lang, P. J. (1992). Temperament and emotional reactivity: Sociability, fear, and restraint. *Psychophysiology, 29,* 522.

Bradley, M. M., Lang, P. J., & Cuthbert, B. N. (in press). Startle reflex habituation in human beings: Emotion, novelty, and content. *Behavioral Neuroscience.*

Bradley, M. M., Lang, P. J., & Cuthbert, B. N. (1991). The Gainesville murders: Imagining the worst. *Psychophysiology, 28,* S14.

Brown, R., & Kulik, J. (1977). Flashbulb memories. *Cognition, 5,* 73–99.

Christianson, S.-Å., & Loftus, E. F. (1987). Memory for traumatic events. *Applied Cognitive Psychology, 1,* 225–239.

Christianson, S.-Å., & Loftus, E. F. (1991). Remembering emotional events: The fate of detailed information. *Cognition and Emotion, 5,* 81–108.

Christianson, S.-Å., & Nilsson, L.-G. (1984). Functional amnesia as induced by a psychological trauma. *Memory & Cognition, 12,* 142–155.

Clark, M. S., Milberg, S., & Ross, J. (1983). Arousal cues arousal-related material in memory: Implications for understanding the effects of mood on memory. *Journal of Verbal Learning and Verbal Behavior, 22,* 633–649.

Clifford, B. R., & Hollin, C. R. (1981). Effects of the type of incident and number of perpetrators on eyewitness memory. *Journal of Applied Psychology, 66,* 364–370.

Corteen, R. S. (1969). Skin conductance changes and word recall. *British Journal of Psychology, 60,* 81–84.

Craik, F. I. M., & Blankstein, K. R. (1975). Psychophysiology and human memory. In P. H. Venables & M. J. Christie (Eds.), *Research in psychophysiology* (pp. 388–417). Chichester, UK: Wiley.

Cuthbert, B. N., Bradley, M. M., & Lang, P. J. (1988). Psychophysiological responses to affective slides across the life span. *Psychophysiology, 25,* 441. [Abstract]

D'Amato, M. R. (1970). *Experimental psychology.* New York: McGraw-Hill.

Davis, M., Hitchcock, J., & Rosen, J. (1987). Anxiety and the amygdala: Pharmacological and anatomical analysis of the fear potentiated startle paradigm. In G. H. Bower (Ed.), *Psychology of learning and motivation.* (Vol. 21, pp. 263–305). New York: Academic Press.

Deffenbacher, K. A. (1983). The influence of arousal on reliability of testimony. In S. M. A. Lloyd-Bostock & B. R. Clifford (Eds.), *Evaluating witness evidence* (pp. 235–251). UK: Wiley.

Detterman, D. K. (1975). The Von Restorff effect and induced amnesia: Production by manipulation of sound intensity. *Journal of Experimental Psychology: Human Learning and Memory, 1,* 614–628.

Detterman, D. K., & Ellis, N. R. (1972). Determinants of induced amnesia in short-term memory. *Journal of Experimental Psychology, 95,* 308–316.

Easterbrook, J. A. (1959). The effect of emotion on cue utilization and the organization of behavior. *Psychological Review, 66,* 183–201.

Eysenck, M. W. (1976). Arousal, learning and memory. *Psychological Bulletin, 83,* 389–404.

Frijda, N. H. (1986). *The emotions.* New York: Cambridge.

Frijda, N. H. (1987). Emotion, cognitive structure, and action tendency. *Cognition and Emotion, 1,* 115–143.

Gold, P. E. (1984). Memory modulation: Roles of peripheral catacholamines. In L. R. Squire & N. Butters (Eds.), *Neuropsychology of memory.* New York: Guilford Press.

Gold, P. E., & McGaugh, J. L. (1975). A single-trace, dual-process view of memory storage processes. In D. Deutsch & J. A. Deutsch (Eds.), *Short-term memory* (pp. 355–378). New York: Academic Press.

Gold, P. E., & Sternberg, D. B. (1978). Retrograde amnesia produced by several treatments: Evidence for a common neurobiological mechanism. *Science, 201,* 367–369.

Gold, P. E., & van Buskirk, R. (1976). Enhancement and impairment of memory processes with posttrial injections and adrenocorticotrophic hormones. *Behavioral Biology, 16,* 387–400.

Gold, P. E., & Zornetzer, S. F. (1983). The mnemon and its juices: Neuromodulation of memory processes. *Behavioral and Neural Biology, 38,* 151–189.

Greenwald, M. K., Cook, E. W., & Lang, P. J. (1989). Affective judgment and psychophysiological response: Dimensional covariation in the evaluation of pictorial stimuli. *Journal of Psychophysiology, 3,* 51–64.

Hamm, A. O., Globisch, J., Cuthbert, B. N., & Vaitl, D. (1991). Startle reflex modulation in simple phobics and normals. *Psychophysiology.* [Abstract]

Hebb, D. O. (1949). *The organization of behavior: A neuropsychological theory.* New York: Wiley.

Holmes, D. S. (1974). Investigations of repression: Differential recall of material experimentally or naturally associated with ego threat. *Psychological Bulletin, 81,* 632–653.

Jansen, D. M., & Frijda, N. (in press). Modulation of acoustic startle response by film-induced fear and sexual arousal. *Psychophysiology.*

Kamin, L. J., & Bruner, C. J. (1963). The effects of intensity of conditioned and unconditioned stimuli on a conditioned emotional response. *Canadian Journal of Psychology, 17,* 194–198.

Kanungo, R. N., & Dutta, S. (1966). Retention of affective material: Frame of reference or intensity? *Journal of Personality and Social Psychology, 4,* 27–35.

Kesner, R. P., & Andrus, R. G. (1982). Amygdala stimulation disrupts the magnitude of reinforcement contribution to long-term memory. *Physiological Psychology, 10,* 55–59.

Kleinsmith, L. J., & Kaplan, S. (1963). Paired associate learning as a function of arousal and interpolated interval. *Journal of Experimental Psychology, 65,* 190–193.

Klorman, R., Weissberg, R., & Wiesenfeld, A. (1977). Individual differences in fear and autonomic reactions to affective stimulation. *Psychophysiology, 14,* 45–51.

Kolb, B., & Taylor, L. (1990). Neocortical substrates of emotional behavior. In N. Stein, B. Leventhal, & T. Trabasso (Eds.), *Psychological and biological approaches to emotion* (pp. 115–144). Hillsdale, NJ: Lawrence Erlbaum Associates.

Konorski, J. (1967). *Integrative activity of the brain: An interdisciplinary approach.* Chicago: University of Chicago Press.

Lacey, J. I. (1967). Somatic response patterning and stress: Some revisions for activation theory. In M. M. Appley & R. Trumbull (Eds.), *Psychological stress.* New York: Appleton-Century-Crofts.

Lang, P. J. (1978). Anxiety: Toward a psychophysiological definition. In H. S. Akiskal & W. L. Webb (Eds.), *Psychiatric diagnosis: Exploration of biological predictors* (pp. 365–389). New York: Spectrum.

Lang, P. J. (1979). A bio-informational theory of emotional imagery. *Psychophysiology, 16,* 495–512.

Lang, P. J. (1985). The cognitive psychophysiology of emotion: Fear and anxiety. In A. Tuma & J. Maser (Eds.), *Anxiety and the anxiety disorders* (pp. 131–170). Hillsdale, NJ: Lawrence Erlbaum Associates.

Lang, P. J. (1989). What are the data of emotion? In V. Hamilton, G. H. Bower, & N. Frijda (Eds.), *Cognitive perspectives on emotion and motivation* (pp. 173–191). Boston: Martinus Nijhoff.

Lang, P. J., & Bradley, M. M. (1990). International affective digitized sounds. [Digitized affective sounds for the MacIntosh]. Gainesville, FL: The Center for Research in Psychophysiology, University of Florida.

Lang, P. J., Bradley, M. M., & Cuthbert, B. N. (1990). Emotion, attention, and the startle reflex. *Psychological Review, 97*, 377–398.

Lang, P. J., Bradley, M. M., & Cuthbert, B. N. (1992). A motivational analysis of emotion: Reflex-cortex connections. *Psychological Science, 3*, 44–49.

Lang, P. J., Greenwald, M. K., Bradley, M. M., & Hamm, A. O. (1993). Looking at pictures: Evaluative, facial, visceral, and behavioral responses. *Psychophysiology, 30*, 261–274.

Lang, P. J., Öhman, A., & Vaitl, D. (1988). *The international affective picture system* [Slides]. Gainesville, FL: The Center for Research in Psychophysiology, University of Florida.

LeDoux, J. E. (1987). Emotion. In F. Plum (Ed.), *Handbook of physiology: Section 1. The nervous system: Vol. V. Higher functions of the brain* (pp. 419–460). Bethesda, MD: American Psychological Society.

Loftus, E. F., & Burns, T. E. (1982). Mental shock can produce retrograde amnesia. *Memory & Cognition, 10*, 318–323.

Mackintosh, N. J. (1983). *Conditioning and associative learning.* New York: Oxford.

Maltzman, I., Kantor, W., & Langdon, B. (1966). Immediate and delayed retention, arousal and defensive reflexes. *Psychonomic Science, 6*, 445–446.

Mathews, A., & MacLeod, C. (1985). Selective processing of threat cues in anxiety states. *Behavior Research & Therapy, 23*, 563–569.

Matlin, M., & Stang, D. (1978). *The Pollyanna principle: Selectivity in language, memory and thought.* Cambridge, MA: Schenkman.

McCloskey, M., Wible, C. G., & Cohen, N. J. (1988). Is there a special flashbulb-memory mechanism? *Journal of Experimental Psychology: General, 117*, 171–181.

McGaugh, J. L., Gold, P. E., Handwerker, M. J., Jensen, R. A., Martinez, J. L., Meligeni, J. A., & Vasquez, B. J. (1979). Altering memory by electrical and chemical stimulation of the brain. In M. A. B. Brazier (Ed.), *Brain mechanisms in memory and learning: From the single neuron to man* (pp. 151–164). New York: Raven Press.

Mehrabian, A. (1970). A semantic space for nonverbal behavior. *Journal of Consulting and Clinical Psychology, 35*, 248–257.

Mehrabian, A., & Russell, J. A. (1974). *An approach to environmental psychology.* Cambridge, MA: MIT Press.

Miller, G. A., Levin, D. N., Kozak, M. J., Cook, E. W., III, McLean, A., & Lang, P. J. (1987). Individual differences in emotional imagery. *Cognition and Emotion 1*, 367–390.

Morris, J. D., Bradley, M. M., Waine, C. A., & Lang, J. B. (in press). Assessing affective reactions to advertisements with SAM (the self-assessment manikin). *Proceedings of the Southeastern Marketing Society.*

Morris, M., Bradley, M., Bowers, D., Lang, P., & Heilman, K. (1991). Valence-specific hypo-arousal following right temporal lobectomy. *Journal of Clinical and Experimental Neuropsychology, 13*, 42. [Abstract]

Neisser, U. (1982). Snapshots or benchmarks? In U. Neisser (Ed.), *Memory observed: Remembering in natural contexts* (pp. 43–48). San Francisco: W. H. Freeman.

Obrist, P. (1981). *Cardiovascular psychophysiology: A perspective.* New York: Plenum Press.

Öhman, A. (1986). Face the beast and fear the face: Animal and social fears as prototypes for evolutionary analyses of emotion. *Psychophysiology, 23*, 123–145.

Osgood, C. (1952). The nature and measurement of meaning. *Psychological Bulletin, 49*, 172–237.

Osgood, C., Suci, G., & Tannenbaum, P. (1957). *The measurement of meaning*. Urbana, IL: University of Illinois.

Patrick, C. J., Bradley, M. M., & Lang, P. J. (1993). Emotion in the criminal psychopath: Startle reflex modification. *Journal of Abnormal Psychology, 102*, 82–92.

Pavlov, I. P. (1927). *Conditioned reflexes*. Oxford: Oxford University Press.

Pribram, K. (1992). Familiarity and novelty: The contributions of the limbic forebrain to valuation and the processing of relevance. In D. S. Levine & S. J. Leven, (Eds.), *Motivation, emotion, and goal direction in neural networks* (pp. 337–365). Hillsdale, NJ: Lawrence Erlbaum Associates.

Pribram, K., & McGuiness, D. (1975). Arousal, activation, and effort in the control of attention. *Psychological Review, 82*, 116–149.

Rather, B. C., Goldman, M. S., Roehrich, L., & Brannick, M. (1992). Empirical modeling of an alcohol expectancy memory network using multidimensional scaling. *Journal of Abnormal Psychology, 101*, 3–17.

Russell, J. (1980). A circumplex model of affect. *Journal of Personality and Social Psychology, 39*, 1161–1178.

Sarter, M., & Markovitch, H. J. (1985). Involvement of the amygdala in learning and memory: A critical review, with emphasis on anatomical relations. *Behavioral Neuroscience, 99*, 342–380.

Shepard, R. (1967). Recognition memory for words, sentences, and pictures. *Journal of Verbal Learning and Verbal Behavior, 6*, 156–163.

Standing, L. (1973). Learning 10,000 pictures. *Quarterly Journal of Experimental Psychology, 25*, 207–222.

Sternberg, D. B., Isaacs, K. R., Gold, P. E., & McGaugh, J. L. (1985). Epinephrine facilitation of appetitive learning: Attenuation with adrenergic receptor antagonists. *Behavioral and Neural Biology, 44*, 447–453.

Thompson, C. P. (1985). Memory for unique personal events: Effects of pleasantness. *Motivation & Emotion, 9*, 277–289.

Turner, R. H., & Barlow, J. A. (1951). Memory for pleasant and unpleasant experiences: Some methodological considerations. *Journal of Experimental Psychology, 52*, 189–196.

Vrana, S. R., & Lang, P. J. (1990). Fear imagery and the startle probe reflex. *Journal of Abnormal Psychology, 99*, 189–197.

Wagner, A. R., Siegel, S., Thomas, E., & Ellison, G. D. (1964). Reinforcement history and the extinction of a conditioned salivary response. *Journal of Comparative Physiological Psychology, 58*, 354–358.

Walker, E. L. (1958). Action decrement and its relation to learning. *Psychological Review, 65*, 129–142.

Watts, F. N., McKenna, F. P., Sharrock, R., & Trezise, L. (1986). Colour naming of phobia-related words. *British Journal of Psychology, 77*, 97–108.

Watts, F. N., & Sharrock, R. (1987). Cued recall in depression. *British Journal of Clinical Psychology, 26*, 149–150.

5 Personality and the Structure of Affective Responses

Eva Gilboa
William Revelle
Northwestern University

A common observation about people in emotional situations is the great variability of their reactions. For example, faced with rude service in a restaurant, one person may get extremely upset, brooding about the episode for hours, another might get momentarily furious, whereas a third might just be slightly irritated for a minute or two. Even if these people construe the situation in essentially similar terms, the magnitude and the duration of their reactions can vary significantly. Moreover, the structure of their reactions seems to transcend any particular situation. Thus, if the restaurant incident had occurred to our friend, we could make an "educated guess" as to his probable reaction. In other words, it appears that the structure of individuals' responses to emotion-inducing events is to some extent a consistent and coherent feature of personality.

The obvious questions arising from these everyday observations have led to the investigation of the relationship between personality and affect, or more specifically between personality and emotional responses. It is our contention that the examination of discrete emotional episodes can enrich our understanding of both personality and emotions. In particular, we believe that the comparison of positive and negative emotional responses may shed some light on emotional mechanisms per se, as well as on individual differences in affective reactions. However, before examining these claims in more detail, it will be helpful to review briefly relevant aspects of personality theory and emotion theory, as well as some of the more recent research on the relation between personality and affect.

A consistent conclusion from the growing body of literature on the structure of personality is the identification of five main dimensions (Digman, 1990).

Although the five dimensions have been given different labels by different researchers, the bulk of literature refers to extraversion (or surgency), agreeableness, conscientiousness, neuroticism, and culture or openness to experience (Costa & McCrae, 1985). One can order individuals along the introversion–extraversion dimension, where individuals scoring high on this dimension (i.e., extraverts) tend to experience positive emotions, to behave in a more dominant and active way, and to be socially active. On standard personality questionnaires, extraverts are more likely than introverts to endorse items such as "I love going to lively parties." Agreeableness refers to cooperation, trust, and altruism, as exhibited by the endorsement of items having to do with such humane activities as nurturing, caring, and providing emotional support. Conscientiousness encompasses organization, dependability, achievement motivation, and prudence. Individuals scoring high on the emotional stability–neuroticism dimension (i.e., neurotics) tend to experience negative emotions, especially anxiety, and are predisposed towards emotional instability. For example, neurotics are more likely than emotionally stable individuals to report worrying about things that they should have done or said, to be troubled by aches and pains, and to endorse items such as "Sometimes I feel miserable for no good reason." The culture, or openness dimension is seen as a broad dimension of intellect and refinement, aesthetic sensitivity, curiosity, the need for variety of experience, flexibility of thought, and so on.

In spite of the general agreement regarding the "what" of these five dimensions (i.e., their descriptive content), there is frequently a sense of discontent about their ability to provide a causal account with respect to the "how and why" of behavior (Revelle, 1987). Some of the most intriguing attempts to provide a causal theory of individual differences were made by H. J. Eysenck (1967, 1981, 1991) and Gray (1972, 1981). These attempts usually concentrated on a subset of the "Big Five," namely, extraversion and neuroticism for Eysenck, and anxiety and impulsivity for Gray. These two dimensions, albeit somewhat differently conceptualized, form what some researchers consider the "Big Two" primary personality dimensions (Wiggins, 1968). The primacy of these dimensions refers to their consistent and interpretable pattern of relationships with measures of cognitive, behavioral, and affective responses. Of particular interest in the current context are the findings of Tellegen (1985), who related these dimensions to one of the typical categories of affective states, namely mood. In what follows, we attempt to broaden the relationship between the "Big Two" personality dimensions (specifically, extraversion and neuroticism) and another category of affective phenomena, namely, emotions.

Emotions can be analyzed from many different perspectives: neurological, physiological, phenomenological, cognitive, and sociological, to name some of the more prominent ones. One of the common denominators of all these approaches is the attempt to find a classification scheme for emotions. Attempts to differentiate amongst discrete emotions have been based on cognitive appraisal patterns (e.g., Arnold, 1960; Lazarus, 1991; Lazarus & Folkman, 1984; Ortony, Clore, & Collins, 1988; Roseman, 1984; Smith & Ellsworth, 1985), action tendencies (Frijda, 1986; Frijda, Kuipers, & Terschure, 1989), facial expressions (e.g., Ekman, 1984; Ekman & Friesen, 1975; Izard, 1977), as well as physiological responses (e.g., Ekman, Levenson, & Friesen, 1983).

However, the bulk of this and other emotion research has dealt primarily with *qualitative* distinctions (such as differentiating between various affective states), and has paid little attention to *quantitative* dimensions of emotional experience. Yet in the real world, people tend to describe their emotional experiences as "intense," "prolonged," and "deep," which are quantitative rather than qualitative descriptions. The failure of current emotion research to seriously consider quantitative aspects of emotions might be viewed as one of a number of simplifying assumptions made to facilitate research. A related assumption is the view of an emotion as a unimodal burst of activity of relatively brief duration. In fact, however, research conducted by Frijda and his colleagues (Frijda, Mesquita, Sonnemans, & van Goozen, 1991; Frijda, Ortony, Sonnemans, & Clore, 1992) indicates that more than half of the emotions studied lasted over an hour. This suggests that it may be unwise to restrict oneself to a single measure of emotion intensity over a narrow time interval, because emotions take place in time, and the quality of the overall emotional experience is related not only to its initial magnitude, but also to its temporal characteristics. Thus, we think it useful to think of the overall impact of an emotion not only in terms of its magnitude (which we shall sometimes refer to as *peak intensity*) but also in terms of its temporal aspects.

Another tacit assumption in most emotion research is that discrete emotions occur in isolation. In fact, emotional reactions frequently involve more than one discrete emotion. While describing an argument with a close friend, one of our participants reported getting angry, feeling hurt, and becoming increasingly upset over the possibility of losing the friend's affection and support. Another reported having a whole gamut of emotions regarding her sorority rush, ranging from extreme anxiety to elation intermingled with feelings of guilt. In view of such data it seems unlikely that one can capture the richness and complexity of an emotional episode by simply classifying it as "anger," "joy," or whatever.

We should perhaps think of an emotional experience as being like a piece of music: It has a certain structure, tempo, and duration. Several concurrent emotions, like instruments, can be involved, each playing its own melodic line. Musicologists go beyond the key, the tempo, and the leading instrument to study themes and variations as well as the interplay among the instruments in the piece. Similarly, psychologists should not restrict themselves to studying only the type and magnitude of emotional reactions, but should also consider their constituents, their duration, and their overall structure.

EMOTIONS: A BASIS FOR PERSONALITY?

Recent years have witnessed a growing interest in the relations among emotions, personality, and mood (e.g., Costa & McCrae, 1980; Larsen & Diener, 1987; Meyer & Shack 1989; Thayer, 1989). Several goals may be served by this endeavor. First, as we have already mentioned, the incorporation of considerations relating to emotional experience might lead to improved theories of personality. When viewed from the perspective of emotion theory, a theory of personality acquires many desirable characteristics, such as a link to the temporal ebb and flow of human actions, appraisals, and cognitions (Larsen, 1988; Larsen & Ketelaar, 1991). Moreover, because emotions have a long evolutionary history, they might provide an evolutionary basis for the structure of personality and the development of individual differences. Linking personality dimensions to emotional experience could provide a much needed theoretical "anchor," endowing personality models with more than just descriptive flavor (Revelle, 1987). This approach can be viewed as continuing the line of research initiated by Gray and Eysenck, aiming to explain basic personality dimensions in terms of primitive physiological, affective, and cognitive mechanisms.

Second, defining personality in affective terms has both theoretical and methodological advantages. On the theoretical side, recent research indicates that the structure of personality can be meaningfully related to the structure of mood (Meyer & Shack, 1989; Watson & Clark, 1984). In particular, this research indicates that personality dimensions of extraversion and neuroticism can be related to mood dimensions of positive affectivity and negative affectivity, respectively. Other research (e.g., Diener & Iran-Nejad, 1986; Diener, Larsen, Levine, & Emmons, 1985) has attempted to link personality to the characteristic intensity with which individuals respond to emotion-inducing events. These studies have consistently uncovered wide individual differences in emotional response as measured by the affect intensity measure (AIM, Larsen, Diener, & Emmons, 1986), a measure that assesses the characteristic overall intensity with which individuals typically experience their emotions. However, because both personality and emotional experiences are multidimensional constructs, it seems that a more informative relationship could be established if one could relate individual differences to more than one index of emotional experience. For example, in addition to looking at individual differences with regards to average or overall intensity, the relationship between personality and the temporal structure of emotional experience is likely to provide valuable theoretical insights.

On the methodological side, the link between personality and emotion research provides a new paradigm for the experimental study of personality, such as the one described in Larsen and Ketelaar (1991). In that study, a standard mood induction technique was used to induce positive and negative affect. This manipulation was used to test the hypothesis that the efficacy of negative mood induction would be better predicted by neuroticism scores than by extraversion scores, whereas the efficacy of positive mood induction would be better predicted by extraversion than by neuroticism scores. If additional relationships between affect and personality can be established, it might be possible to manipulate various parameters of emotion-inducing situations and to use the data so derived to draw conclusions regarding personality.

Third, the study of emotional episodes could provide a link between the "fixed" and the "fluid" (Larsen, 1988) approaches to personality. The former approach concentrates on uncovering consistencies of acts, with a view to determining the nature and number of basic personality tendencies, whereas the latter approach is concerned with understanding adjustment patterns. These approaches differ radically along the time dimension: whereas the "fixed" approach focuses on discrete behavioral acts, the "fluid" one pays attention to the unfolding of behavioral patterns over extended time periods (e.g., a life time). Because emotions can last from a few seconds to years, they provide a meaningful and manageable way of unifying these two approaches. In other words, emotional episodes, replete with actions, cognitive changes, and phenomenological experiences, provide a fertile ground for examining stable traits and tendencies (such as the magnitude of emotional responses) as well as the changes and adaptations that occur over time.

Finally, one might view research concerning individual differences in emotion responsivity as a way to deepen our understanding of emotion mechanisms. Just as the primary way of studying the nature of intelligence has been to study individual differences, attempting to uncover the common factors that underlie cognitive abilities, so too, the study of individual differences in emotional responses might help us to better understand some of the rudimentary mechanisms of emotions.

Personality and Emotion

Two lines of research predominate attempts to relate the personality and emotion domains: One links personality to differently valenced affective responses, whereas the other concentrates on individual differences in emotion intensity, regardless of hedonic value.

Personality and Valence.   The basic theoretical premise in the work of Gray (1972, 1981, 1987) and of H. J. Eysenck and colleagues (1967, 1981; H. J. Eysenck & M. W. Eysenck, 1985) is that personality dimensions are best understood as biologically based constructs. In addition to the biological fight-flight system, Gray has proposed two neurologically based motivational systems with differential sensitivity to cues of reward and punishment: the behavioral approach system, which is postulated to control behavior when signals of reward are encountered, and the behavioral inhibition system, which is postulated to control behavior when signals of punishment or nonreward are encountered. Whether these systems can be conceptualized as directly causing (M. Eysenck, 1987; Fowles, 1987; Newman, 1987; Tellegen, 1985), or as only indirectly related to (Emmons & Diener, 1986) different personality dimensions, and how these systems relate to the dimensions of extraversion and neuroticism (or some other personality dimensions) remain open research questions. However, whatever these relations might be, there is considerable evidence from the biological perspective for the existence of *two systems,* each sensitive to differently valenced stimuli.

In addition to biologically based models, mood research (e.g., Thayer, 1989) has provided additional support for the existence (and relative independence) of two affective systems. Mood studies have indicated that personality dimensions correlate differentially with affect dimensions. Specifically, neuroticism tends to correlate with negative affectivity, that is, the predisposition to experience relatively excessive negative affect, but does not correlate with positive affectivity (Costa & McCrae, 1980; Meyer & Shack, 1989; Thayer, 1989). In contrast, extraversion tends to correlate with positive affectivity, but not with negative affectivity. These correspondences have been extensively validated using various measurement scales, time scales, and report types (Mayer & Gaschke, 1988; Meyer & Shack, 1989; Tellegen, 1985; Watson & Clark, 1991; Watson & Tellegen, 1985; Zevon & Tellegen, 1982).

As a part of an effort to understand the working of the two affective systems, Watson and Clark (1984) sought to specify the nature of negative affectivity, which they define as the "sensitivity to minor failures, frustrations, and irritations of daily life, as evidenced by the likelihood, magnitude and duration of . . . reactions." (p. 466). However, whereas the likelihood and the magnitude of emotional response have been heavily investigated, the temporal aspects have not. Furthermore, although all three aspects are easily separable from a conceptual viewpoint, existing research provides little in the way of constraining the set of possible interrelations between them and personality dimensions. More general hypotheses (e.g., postulating independent responsivity characteristics to each) need to be examined before all three can be tied together to form a unified notion of "sensitivity." Furthermore, one may ask whether the structure of positive affectivity mirrors that of negative affectivity, or is it the case that positive and negative affectivity relate differentially to the likelihood, magnitude, and duration parameters?

Personality and Intensity.   That people differ in terms of the intensity with which they experience various emotions is an undeniable truth confirmed by everyday experience. In line with this intuition, Diener, Larsen, and their colleagues conducted extensive research regarding individual differences in emotion intensity (e.g., Diener, Larsen, Levine, & Emmons, 1985; Diener & Larsen, 1987). The main findings of their studies are that differences in affect intensity are highly stable over time and consistent across situations with different hedonic values; that is, people who tend to have extreme reactions to positive events, tend to exhibit extreme reaction to negative events as well. Their research also suggests that the construct of affect intensity is related in a meaningful way to a variety of indices—physiological, behavioral, and cognitive. For instance, individuals scoring high on the affect intensity measure (AIM, Larsen, Diener, & Emmons, 1986) tend to be less physiologically aroused. On the other hand, behaviorally, they tend to be more sociable, more impulsive, and more extraverted. Finally, from the cognitive viewpoint, these individuals tend to interpret their emotional experiences in a more personally relevant way, to overgeneralize the consequences of both positive and negative events, and to selectively focus their attention on emotion-inducing events (Larsen, Diener, & Cropanzano, 1986).

Larsen and Diener (1987) attempted to explain such findings in terms of the modulation-of-arousal theory. This theory postulates a common optimal level of arousal for all individuals. However, individuals differ in their base level of arousal, and attempt to modulate their level of arousal at any particular time so as to keep that level close to the optimal level. According to this theory, affect intensity, extraversion, and sensation-seeking (i.e., attempting to increase sensory stimulation levels) originate from individual differences in the base level of arousal and exemplify various adjustment mechanisms designed to modulate the arousal level. Underaroused individuals might attempt to modulate arousal in different ways: Sensation-seeking activities raise the arousal level by providing intense sensory experiences (Zuckerman, 1979, 1987), whereas extravert activities increase arousal through social stimulation (M. Eysenck, 1987). On this view, emotional responsivity can be viewed as a manifestation of an (unconscious) heuristic designed to compensate for a low level of base arousal.

Hedonic Value: One Dimension or Two? Different lines of research agree in suggesting that a two-dimensional space adequately describes the structure of affect. However, there is much disagreement as to what the coordinates of this space are (Meyer & Shack, 1989). The mood literature (e.g., Costa & McCrae, 1980; Zevon & Tellegen, 1982) and biologically based models (e.g., Gray, 1987) suggest differential and partially independent systems of positive and negative affect, implying a need for two *unipolar* dimensions, one positive and one negative, as an adequate way to describe affective space. However, such a representation appears to be inconsistent with the emotion literature, in which theorists tend to assume one *bipolar* dimension of pleasantness–unpleasantness and another, orthogonal dimension of arousal (e.g., Russell, 1979, 1980). In addition, the view offered by Diener, Larsen and their colleagues (Diener et al., 1985) seems to suggest that they too embrace a view of emotional affectivity in which positive and negative affect form a single continuum. In short, the problem is the following: On the one hand, the two dimensions of affect, positive and negative, appear to vary independently, and to correlate differentially with various personality dimensions; on the other hand, positive and negative affect have been found to correlate within individuals, consistent with a bipolar dimension of affect intensity.

Diener, Larsen, and their colleagues (e.g., Diener et al., 1985; Larsen & Diener, 1987) attempted to resolve this controversy by proposing two alternative dimensions of affect—intensity and frequency. In their view, intensity is the degree to which emotions are experienced regardless of valence, whereas frequency is the amount of time during which individuals experience *predominantly* positive or *predominantly* negative emotions (Diener et al., 1985). Thus, the dimension of intensity is independent of (and separable from) the dimension of frequency. Guided by this conceptualization, Diener et al. (1985) used a single measure of intensity in their investigation of subjective well-being: They assessed (over a period of several weeks) the degree to which respondents reported feeling various emotions (e.g., "happy," "pleased," "angry," "depressed"). Then, the frequency with which an individual experienced positive affect was measured by the number of units of time (e.g., days) for which he or she experienced predominantly positive or predominantly negative emotions. A day was designated as "predominantly positive" if the mean positive intensity score exceeded the mean negative intensity score. Intensity was computed as the mean strength with which individuals experienced their *dominant* affect.

In our view, this approach is still biased toward a bipolar view. The definition of frequency used by Diener, Larsen, and their colleagues, relying as it does on their notion of "predominant affect," involves an implicit assumption of bipolarity. Moreover, this kind of approach might overestimate the consistency with which people evaluate emotion intensity as they move from making judgments about one type of emotion to making judgments about another. This is because the approach assumes that emotion intensity is a unitary construct rather than one involving multiple, relatively independent components. However, Frijda and colleagues (Frijda et al., 1991; Frijda et al., 1992) identified dimensions such as peak intensity, duration and rumination, amount of felt arousal, strength of cognitive change, and strength of felt action readiness as being relatively independent dimensions of affect intensity. To the extent that emotion intensity is indeed a complex construct involving independent or partially independent components such as these, one should be cautious in assuming that participants use a stable criterion in making intensity judgments. Given that such judgments might implicate a multitude of somatic, behavioral, and cognitive features, a respondent in an experiment is likely to focus on the most salient feature of the particular emotional experience being judged—perhaps the strength of the initial reaction, or an unusually strong tendency to act, or (given time for it to occur) an abnormally long rumination time. It seems quite plausible that in evaluating the intensity, for example, of sadness, people will tend to focus primarily on duration, whereas when making the same judgment for anger they will focus mostly on peak intensity. Thus, a rating of 4 on some 7-point "intensity" scale might as easily represent a 3-hour long sadness episode, as a 5-minute anger episode. We suspect that this problem is likely to be exacerbated with respect to judgments of intensity of emotions differing in valence. For these reasons we are skeptical about the validity of Diener et al.'s (1985) construct of "dominant affect." So far, researchers have been rather vague about which aspect of emotion intensity they are using as their measure, although most appear to use peak intensity almost by default. It seems to us that when studies necessitate asking participants to indicate the intensity of their emotions, it is preferable to be quite explicit as to which feature or features of emotion intensity they should focus on.

Having discussed the relationship between personality and emotion intensity on the one hand, and the multidimensionality of intensity on the other, a natural question is whether there exist meaningful relationships between the duration dimension of intensity and personality. Perhaps individual differences in emotional responses are related not only to differential susceptibility or vulnerability to positive and negative events, but also to the duration and the degree of recurrence and elaboration of various experiences. In a recent article, Larsen and Ketelaar (1991) sought to specify the concept of "sensitivity," which until now has been only loosely defined. They asked "whether the obtained effects [of differential hedonic capacity] are due to stimulus sensitivity or the response magnitude side of the stimulus–response equation" (p. 139). We think there is yet another possibility; hedonic capacity may be due to the length of the impact, or the rate of decay of the affective experience. By considering the duration of emotions, we might be able to examine and refine the nature of differential sensitivity of neurotics and extraverts to positively and negatively evaluated events.

AN EMPIRICAL INVESTIGATION
OF THE PERSONALITY-EMOTION CONNECTION

In an attempt to explore some of the issues we have discussed, especially the relation between the temporal structure of emotional experience and different personality dimensions, we conducted a simple study to examine two main hypotheses. First, we hypothesized that the independence of positive and negative affect could be demonstrated not only in the structure of mood (e.g., Tellegen, 1985; Watson & Clark, 1984), but also in the temporal pattern of emotional responses. Second, we examined the possibility that personality characteristics would predict the temporal structure of emotional response. In particular, following the models of Watson and Clark (1984), and Gray (1972, 1981, 1987), we attempted to determine whether negative affectivity (linked to neuroticism) as well as positive affectivity (linked to extraversion and impulsivity) can be characterized as the susceptibility to intense and *protracted* reactions to events inducing negative and positive emotions, respectively. We predicted that neurotics would report greater magnitudes and longer durations for negative, but not for positive emotions, and that extraverts would report greater magnitudes and longer durations for positive, but not for negative emotions.

Participants in the study were undergraduate students who completed the Eysenck Personality Inventory (EPI, Eysenck & Eysenck, 1964) several weeks before the study, providing neuroticism, impulsivity, sociability, and extraversion scores.[1] During the study proper, the participants completed a 70-item emotion questionnaire. Each item consisted of a short description of an event that a college undergraduate might experience. Event descriptions were designed to vary widely in their emotional significance from being extremely significant to slightly significant on both positive and negative dimensions. Importantly, some events had the potential to elicit both positive and negative responses simultaneously, representing instances of mixed emotions. In addition, some of the questionnaire items were classified according to the type of emotion they were likely to elicit. Sample events in the questionnaire included, "You are late to an interview with a prospective summer job employer," "You got back the wallet you forgot in a restaurant," "You bought something you could not afford," and "Your boyfriend/girlfriend tells you that you should stop seeing each other."

The introductory paragraphs of the questionnaire made clear that each event described might elicit either positive, negative, or mixed (i.e., both positive and negative) emotions. Each event description was followed by a response sheet on which respondents were instructed to indicate the peak intensity and the time-course parameters of their imagined reaction on one or both hedonic dimensions as appropriate (i.e., the person might indicate that he or she experienced some positive reaction *but also* some negative reaction after, say, buying an expensive item).

Several 8-point scales were selected to represent different facets of the temporal structure of emotional responses (Frijda et al., 1992). They included: (a) *peak-intensity,* the magnitude of the emotional reaction at its highest, ranging from *you would not be moved by the event* to *extremely pleased/displeased by the event;* (b) *rise-time,* the amount of time between the onset of the emotion and its peak. Response categories were: *Immediately, Few seconds, About a minute, Few minutes, 10–15 minutes, About an hour, Few hours, About a day;* (c) *duration,* the length of time between the peak of the emotional reaction and the return to baseline activity. Responses categories were: *About a minute, A few minutes, 10–15 minutes, About an hour, Few hours, About a day, Few days, About a week;* and, (d) *rumination,* the length of time that thoughts about the emotion-inducing event and/or its consequences would spontaneously arise after having once subsided. Responses were indicated on a scales with anchors: *Same*

---

[1]The extraversion scale of the EPI (Eysenck & Eysenck, 1964) has two subcomponents: impulsivity and sociability, that have been shown to have different effects on a variety of cognitive tasks (Revelle, Humphreys, Simon, & Gilliland, 1980).

as above (i.e., one forgets about the event as soon as the immediate emotional reaction subsides), *Same day, Next day, About a week, About a month, Few months, About a year, Few years.*

The three temporal scales (rise-time, duration, and rumination) were designed to allow a transformation of the temporal anchors into an equal-interval logarithmic time scale. An attempt was made to keep the labels cognitively salient ("A few hours," "About a day," etc.). These temporal scales, when considered as one continuum, form a seconds-based logarithmic scale. So for example, "Immediately" refers to 2^2 seconds, "Few minutes" refers to 2^8 seconds, "10–15 minutes" is roughly 2^{10} seconds, "About a day" refers to approximately 2^{16} seconds, and so on.

Temporal Structure of Emotional Responses

The data revealed that in general the temporal structure of an emotional response[2] involves a swift rise-time, taking less than half a minute in about 80% of the cases, followed by a relatively slow decay. After an emotional response reaches its peak, it can take hours, or even days for a person experiencing an extremely intense negative emotion to get back to his or her "normal" state again. Respondents judged that approximately 50% of the emotion episodes described would last more than an hour. Moreover, thoughts concerning the emotional episode were expected to continue to spontaneously come to mind for a couple of days. The median rumination period associated with the events described in our questionnaire was approximately 11 hours.

Some interesting relationships emerged between magnitude and temporal aspects of emotional experiences. First, it seems that peak intensity and the rise-time of emotions are related by an "inverted-U" function. Mild emotions (i.e., those with low peak intensities) tend to elicit an immediate reaction. As peak intensity increases, it takes longer to reach an emotional peak. However, at high levels of peak intensity rise-time is again shorter. One explanation of this relationship exploits the interplay between cognitive complexity and the urgency with which the event appears to demand a response. Reactions to complex situations are likely to demand the evaluation of many possible consequences, perhaps slowing down the time to reach peak intensity to which these evaluations might be contributing. In contrast, situations inducing intense reactions are likely to be high on the urgency dimension, thus necessitating a more immediate response. So, it might be that situations inducing mild emotional responses, and thus not likely to be very complex or urgent, result in a relatively short rise-time. Situations inducing moderate emotional responses might have considerable com-

---

[2]In most of what follows we sometimes discuss our results as though participants were reporting their actual rather than their imagined reactions to the specified events. Although aware of the issues involved in this distinction, we shall postpone our discussion of it until later.

plexity and moderate urgency, resulting in more time to reach a full-blown emotional state. Finally, high peak-intensity situations might be so high on the urgency dimension, that they necessitate an immediate response, regardless of complexity.

Second, whereas peak intensity was consistently related to the temporal decay measures, the data suggest that given comparable levels of peak intensity, duration can vary dramatically. For example, our participants rated the positive emotion associated with having "someone you find attractive suggest you meet for coffee" as high as 5.7 (on a 0 to 7 scale), which was almost as high as the emotion experienced after "saving your neighbor's child from a car accident." However, the average estimated duration associated with the former was 20 minutes, whereas for the latter it was more than 5 hours. The same pattern emerged with respect to rumination indices—respondents reported that they would stop ruminating about the coffee suggestion after an average of two hours, whereas the car accident experience leads to rumination for about a week. These results indicate that, in general, the overall reaction to an emotion-inducing event cannot be determined from peak intensity alone. It may be that some events elicit mostly somatic and expressive reactions (which are probably most relevant to estimations of peak intensity), whereas for others the attentional resources are claimed by information processing components concerned with examining and reevaluating the current world representation, resulting in longer duration and rumination components.

Positive and Negative Emotions.   The data reveal many differences between positive and negative emotions with respect to their temporal characteristics, the most salient of which is that the duration and the amount of rumination associated with negative events is greater than that associated with positive events. Whereas this fact alone may not be very surprising, the size of the effect is. People expect to ruminate about events inducing strong negative emotions about five times as long as they do about events inducing strong positive ones (44 days and 8 days, respectively). Similarly, the effects of negative events of low intensity seem to outlast their positive counterparts. Mild positive experiences tend to be relatively brief, with their immediate effects dissipating in about 20 minutes, and their long-term effects lasting about 5 hours. However, a mild negative experience (i.e., one of comparable peak intensity), a trivial vexation, is associated with a much longer response period—a typical instance lasting a little less than an hour (almost three times as long as a comparable positive one) with a rumination phase lasting as long as 12 hours. A schematic depiction of these results is presented in Fig. 5.1, which highlights the differential decay rates of positive and negative emotions while illustrating their comparability in terms of peak intensity and rise-time.

Another way to quantify the differences in temporal patterns associated with positive and negative emotions is to consider the rates of change in duration and

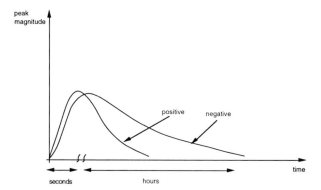

FIG. 5.1. Schematic representation of the duration of positive and negative emotions.

rumination. A one-unit increase in peak intensity was associated with an average increase in duration of approximately 40 minutes for positive emotions, but 110 minutes for negative emotions. A similar pattern of results was obtained with respect to rumination: The increase in rumination per unit of peak intensity was almost four times as large for negative as for positive emotions.

One might attempt to explain this difference by considering the typical consequences of events leading to positive and negative emotions. Negative emotions are often experienced when a goal is blocked. This means that events leading to negative emotions might necessitate the construction of new plans to attain the blocked goal, or the formation of a new goal to compensate for the lost one. Thus, negative emotions require cognitive resources to be allocated to the creation and elaboration of these plans. In contrast, positive emotions are usually experienced when a goal is achieved, so that plan revision and other demanding cognitive operations are less likely to be needed. For this reason alone, one might expect negative emotions to be more prolonged than positive ones (Taylor, 1991).

Mixed Emotions.   Mixed emotions are instances in which both positive and negative affect are experienced. In our study, two thirds of the respondents expected to experience mixed emotions with respect to the possibility of speaking in public and after buying an item they could not afford, and nearly 40% expected to experience both positive emotions and negative emotions after being told that a friend had won a free ticket to Europe. In addition to eliciting expectations of mixed emotions, several items elicited differently valenced reactions in different individuals. For example, receiving a compliment from a stranger elicited expectations of only positive reactions from some participants, only negative reactions from others, and mixed reactions from the rest.

Our findings, as well as those of Diener and Iran-Nejad (1986), suggest that mixed emotions emerge primarily at mild or moderate levels of affect. So, for example, in our study, even such mild everyday experiences as receiving a compliment from a stranger, or having a friend win a vacation tended to elicit both positive and negative reactions. Nevertheless, the scarceness of reports of mixed emotions with high levels of intensity was somewhat surprising, especially given that discussions of mixed emotions (e.g., Zuckerman, 1987) often focus on intense experiences such as skiing and riding on roller coasters. In fact, mixed emotions *can* be experienced (and are reported) at relatively high levels of intensity if tapped at the time of occurrence. For example, reports of mixed emotions were collected at weddings (Revelle, 1991), presumably intensely emotional occasions. Other examples of such occasions include leaving home to go to college, graduations, selling of a house, and so on. One explanation for our failure to detect mixed emotions at high intensity levels might be that memory acts as a natural "dichotomizer," causing mixed emotions to be remembered as purely positive or purely negative. This possibility is consistent with the view that memory-mediated reports of emotional experiences are influenced by, and tend to conform to individuals' naive theories of the bipolarity of emotional experience. If this explanation is correct, we might expect more simultaneous occurrences of positive and negative emotions to emerge when experiential sampling, as opposed to memory-mediated techniques, is used.

One of the more intriguing questions in the literature on emotion and affect concerns the relation between positive and negative affect. As already discussed, the well-being literature (e.g., Diener & Emmons, 1984; Zevon & Tellegen, 1982), converging with the mood literature (e.g., Tellegen, 1985), indicates that the two dimensions of affect correlate differentially with various external variables such as personality dimensions. Moreover, recent research (e.g., Diener & Emmons, 1984; Diener & Iran-Nejad, 1986; Watson & Tellegen, 1985) has demonstrated that these dimensions tend to be independent with respect to average levels of positive and negative intensity, especially when assessed over long time periods. Our results provide support for the independence of positive and negative affect from two different perspectives: First, the nature of the relationship among various emotional indices depends on valence. Second, the existence of mixed emotions appears to be more easily accommodated by a view of positive and negative affect as being partially independent.

Distinct Emotions.   Finally, there were stable differences across emotions in terms of their reported duration and rumination. The five emotions examined were joy, pride, anxiety, anger, and sadness.[3] The shortest reactions were those

---

[3]In fact, respondents did not specifically indicate which emotions they expected to experience in response to the different events described. The results we report are based on a preexperimental classification of the event descriptions into the emotions that we, the experimenters, thought they were most likely to elicit.

associated with pride and anger, which respondents rarely expected to last more than half an hour. Joy lasted significantly longer, with almost 60% of the cases lasting over an hour. The emotional state following an anxiety- or sadness-inducing event frequently spanned interruptions due to sleep (Frijda et al., 1991), with 30% of the occurrences lasting more than 18 hours, and the associated rumination lasting days or even weeks. The duration data for anger, sadness, and joy seem to be consistent with those reported in Scherer, Wallbott, and Summerfield (1986). However, in our grouping, the items focusing on negative prospects for the self were mostly pertinent to endangering self-esteem (perhaps best called anxiety), whereas the classification of Scherer et al. included items relevant mostly to physical danger (perhaps most appropriately called fear). This distinction seems to be crucial to the pattern of response: in Scherer et al.'s (1986) research, fear emerged as a relatively brief emotion, whereas in our study, anxiety emerged as a lingering emotion, persisting for hours and even days.

Individual Differences in Emotional Response

So far we have discussed the (partial) independence of positive and negative dimensions of affect, particularly with respect to duration. However, our data also suggest that this independence can be observed in individuals' responses to various life events. Specifically, neurotics seem to respond to emotion-inducing events in an amplified way regardless of the valence of the experience (in a way, "overreacting" to situations). They tend to report not only greater peak intensities, but also more prolonged duration and rumination periods. To give a concrete example, high neurotics (i.e., upper quartile) expected the duration of their affective reaction to "you realize that you've said the wrong thing in an important interview" to last about 18 hours, whereas low neurotics (i.e., lower quartile) expected it to last approximately 3 hours. A similar relationship was found for the associated rumination phase (about 4 days for high neurotics and less than 2 days for low neurotics). In addition, however, our duration data revealed that neurotics react even more strongly to *mild negative* as opposed to *mild positive* events. With respect to specific emotions, neurotics seem to react more strongly than stable individuals to anxiety- and anger-inducing situations.

In contrast, impulsivity and sociability tend to correlate with peak *positive* but not with peak *negative* intensity. Impulsives and respondents who rank high on the sociability dimension seem to be particularly sensitive to positive (in particular, moderate and mild) emotion-inducing events. With respect to specific emotions, impulsives tend to report greater peak intensities of reactions to joy-eliciting situations. In contrast to neuroticism, impulsivity tends to be particularly related to peak intensity, but not to the duration of the emotional response. For instance, individuals who are likely to endorse items such as "I like doing things in which I have to act quickly" (i.e., high impulsives) expect to react more strongly to events such as "you go to a fun party," expecting peak intensity to reach 6.3 (on a scale of 0 to 7), as compared to 5.2 for low impulsives (i.e., the

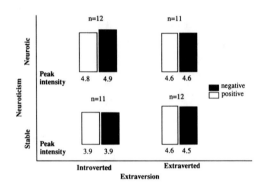

FIG. 5.2. Relations between personality type and peak emotion intensity.

lower quartile). However, no corresponding differences were observed with respect to the duration of positive experiences.

Another way of viewing the data is to consider them with respect to different personality "types" (Gray, 1987). Using a median split technique, we divided the respondents into high and low groups on both extraversion and neuroticism dimensions, artificially creating four personality "types." The data for positive and negative peak intensities for these groups are presented in Fig. 5.2.

Consistent with previous studies (e.g., Wallbott & Ellgring, 1986), participants low on both dimensions reported expecting to experience particularly low levels of peak intensity, whereas participants high on the neuroticism dimension and low on extraversion dimension expected to experience relatively high levels of peak intensity. A statistical analysis of these data revealed that although there were significant differences between respondents in terms of the magnitude of emotional reaction as a function of neuroticism and extraversion, there were no corresponding differences between positive and negative peak intensities within respondents.

Second, we examined the differences in the duration of positive and negative emotions between the same four groups (see Fig. 5.3).

Comparing Fig. 5.2 and Fig. 5.3 reveals that the differences between personality types are much more pronounced for duration than for peak intensity. The

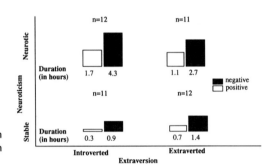

FIG. 5.3. Relationship between personality types and emotion duration.

duration data show that participants high on the neuroticism and low on the extraversion dimension tend to exhibit a "high" emotional profile, apparently "immersing" themselves in their affective experiences for long periods of time (particularly for negative emotions). Respondents low on both dimensions tend to exhibit a "low" emotional profile, devoting relatively little time to their emotional reactions. A statistical analysis of the data revealed significant between-respondent differences in terms of duration as a function of neuroticism, as well as significant within-respondent differences in responses to positive as opposed to negative emotion-eliciting events as a function of extraversion, and an interaction between neuroticism and extraversion. These results suggest that using duration as an index of emotional response enhances our ability to differentiate between various personality types. Our initial hypothesis regarding individual differences in emotional experience postulated that neuroticism is related to intense and protracted negative experiences, whereas extraversion is related to intense and protracted positive experiences. Our data reveal that this hypothesis was too simplistic. A more refined account, postulating differential relationships of neuroticism and extraversion to different indices of emotional response is needed.

It might be objected that the relations between personality dimensions and aspects of emotional experience are not impressive in terms of the magnitude of the observed effects. Indeed, Wallbott and Ellgring (1986) reported a similar pattern of relationships between personality dimensions and affective reactions that they regarded as uninteresting. For example, they found a significant correlation between neuroticism and peak intensity of fear, and between neuroticism and duration of fear ($r = .30$ and $r = .28$ respectively), and a significant correlation between extraversion and the peak intensity of joy ($r = .21$). However, they concluded that individual differences are not very important for the study of emotions, saying, "The personality characteristics discussed above do not seem to be very important predictors of emotional experiences" (p. 209). On the other hand, we think that knowing that somebody is highly neurotic would enable us to predict, for example, that he or she is likely to have a relatively protracted response to a negative emotion-inducing situation. Furthermore, from the perspective of emotion theory, individual differences in intensity and duration might be indicative of different processes underlying similar emotional responses. For example, it is possible that one process is driven by physiological reactivity whereas the other is driven by cognitive activity. Thus, tracing the cause of protracted (or brief) emotional episodes to either physiological or cognitive differences (or, more likely, a combination of the two) might elucidate the structure, as well as the process of emotional responses.

So far, we have concluded that positive and negative events differ in the temporal aspects of the emotional responses they evoke, as well as in their relationships with different personality characteristics. Moreover, we have discussed some possible reasons for differences in duration of positive versus negative emotions and speculated about the imbalance of the consequences of positive and negative events. We now want to consider the possibility that the causes of differences in duration of individuals' responses to emotion-inducing situations might be linked to a variety of physiological and cognitive factors.

DURATION OF EMOTIONS: COGNITIVE AND
PHYSIOLOGICAL FACTORS

Some theories of depression and neuroticism (e.g., Martin, 1985; Nolen-Hoeksema, Morrow, & Fredrickson, 1993; Teasdale, 1988) argue for a cognitive interpretation of the prolonged experience of negative emotions. For example, Teasdale suggests that it is the nature of cognitive processes and representations that determines whether a person's initial depression will be transient or prolonged. Our findings are consistent with this hypothesis, particularly when one takes into account the reciprocal relationship of affect and cognition. Thus, neuroticism is not only associated with a predisposition to experience negative emotions, but also with a predisposition for (relatively) excessive rumination about the events that lead to them. These ruminations have obvious mood and memory consequences (Blaney, 1986), increasing the availability of negatively valenced information, which in turn influences the interpretation of future events, creating an affective-cognitive vicious cycle. We think that our results may help to elucidate the persistence and recurrence of depression episodes associated with individuals who rank high on the neuroticism dimension (Nolen-Hoeksema, 1987; Nolen-Hoeksema et al., 1993; Teasdale, 1988; Weissman, Prusoff, & Klerman, 1978). The duration of the negative affect following an emotion-eliciting event has direct implications for the expectations, experience, and recall of these episodes. With respect to expectations, neurotics might be especially apprehensive about negative experiences because their memories of, and estimates of the consequences of such experiences are more intimidating: They encode these experiences as being prolonged and expect even a mild negative experience to demand considerable cognitive resources. They might also tend to develop ruminative response characteristics (similar to the ones described by Nolen-Hoeksema, et al., 1993) because the protracted duration of the emotional response provides more opportunities for noticing and subsequently focusing on one's emotional state. With respect to experience, the longer the period during which a person is influenced by physiological and cognitive processes activated by the emotion, the higher the probability that this experience will be subjectively perceived as important and meaningful. Finally, with regards to recall, longer events are presumably more likely to be recalled than shorter ones. For all these reasons, it seems plausible to suppose that individual differences in perceived affective duration might play a causal role in individuals' differential susceptibility to depression persistence.

Viewed from a physiological perspective, it is also plausible that cognitive mechanisms of rumination and recall are set in motion by simple differences in biologically determined parameters. Thus, one could postulate the existence of biologically determined decay rates of affective responses (with decay rates of negative responses being typically slower than those of positive ones), which determine the length of impact of an emotional experience. For example, a slow decay rate for negative emotions might be responsible for neurotics' prolonged preoccupation with the inducing event and its implications for the self, whereas impulsives' emotional "forgetfulness" might be associated with a rapid decay rate. Thus conceived, affective decay rate could be likened to the physiological characteristic of base-level arousal (Eysenck, 1967). Like arousal, affective decay rates might affect a variety of cognitive and emotional processes, influencing a wide range of behaviors. On a more global note, it might be that personality traits could be conceived of as rates of change of affective responses (Revelle, 1989), with the associated behaviors being the result of particular decay rates.

However, it is unlikely that individual differences in responses to emotion-inducing events can be attributed to cognitive factors alone or to physiological factors alone. A more accurate account would almost certainly have to consider both. A better understanding of the relative roles of physiological and cognitive components may resolve one of the most important questions in personality research, namely, the direction of influence between affective reactions and personality characteristics. For example, are individuals who rank high on the neuroticism dimension predisposed towards feeling negative affect, or does feeling negative affect lead to the phenomenological experience of dissatisfaction and depression?

Some Caveats

The empirical study of emotions is beset with difficulties. Emotions are a paradigmatic example of private experiences, so the method of choice in the study of emotions is often self-report. There are, of course, undeniable problems and limitations connected with the use of self-report techniques, and there are no definitive answers to or rebuttals of these criticisms (however, see Averill's, 1983, discussion of the subject). People's introspective abilities have been questioned with respect to such "cold," "objective," and "public" phenomena as problem solving and decision making (Nisbett & Wilson, 1977); given that, how can one rely on introspection when people are asked to report details regarding their "hot" emotional experiences? Nevertheless, it remains true that many psychological phenomena, such as preferences, attitudes, moral judgments, and similarity judgments, are routinely studied using self-report techniques. In the case of emotions, one might argue that because they demand attentional resources, they are likely to be relatively accessible to introspection. It is at least encouraging that physiological measures of emotional activity (such as heart rate, galvanic skin response, etc.) tend to correlate higher with self-report data than they do with one another (Thayer, 1970).

Imagining Versus Recollection.   In this chapter we have sometimes discussed the results of our study as though participants were reporting their actual reactions to various life events. In fact, of course, all our conclusions are based on data about respondents' "imagined" reactions to imaginary events. This raises the question of whether these "imagined" reactions are similar to what the corresponding actual reactions would have been. We do not know whether, when faced with a "what if" question pertaining to a hypothetical emotional reaction, respondents employ a mental model of a "typical emotion episode," or whether they try to remember a recent experience that was similar to the one in question. Of course, some of these problems also apply to methodologies using recollections of emotions, even though the use of recollections has more face validity. In any event, we thought it worthwhile to compare some of our results with those obtained using a recall paradigm. Some convergence of the two paradigms could be viewed as lending support to the validity of our "imagination" method.

Table 5.1 compares the distributions of durations using an autobiographical recall method versus our "imagination" method. The first column (entitled "Re-

TABLE 5.1
Distributions of Emotion Durations:
Percentages Using Methods of Recall and Imagination

	Recall Method*	Imagination Method
0 sec–5 sec	0	3
5 sec–1 min	5	12
1 min–10 min	20	16
10 min–1 hour	25	21
>1 hour	50	48

*From Sonnemans (1990), as reported in Frijda, Mesquita, Sonnemans, & van Goozen (1991).

call Method") presents results from Sonnemans' (1990) study (cited in Frijda et al., 1991) and shows the percentage of emotions in each time category. The second column (entitled "Imagination Method") shows the comparable data from our own study. The table shows that the distributions are quite similar.

A comparison of our data to the data reported in Frijda et al. (1991) using an additional index of *total* emotion duration also yields similar distributions.

Our results are also consistent with the rank ordering of emotion duration reported in Ricci-Bitti and Scherer (1986): Sadness lasts longer than joy, which, in turn, lasts longer than anger. However, there is less agreement regarding the percentage of cases falling within a particular time interval. For example, the results differ in the case of joy experiences: Ricci-Bitti and Scherer report 22% of joy experiences lasting less than an hour, as compared to 43% in our study. On the other hand, our results are closer to theirs with respect to anger: Their results indicate that 75% of anger experiences last less than a few hours, whereas our data show approximately 67%.

This mixed pattern of results might be explained by the differences in the task used in the two studies. In the Ricci-Bitti and Scherer study, respondents were asked to report *salient emotional episodes* experienced in the last few weeks (see Scherer et al., 1986, p. 23). Thus, it is likely that participants in that study perceived their task to involve recalling a (relatively) intense emotional experiences, as opposed to the more common mild emotions. Also, one might expect prolonged emotions to be more salient, thus making them more accessible and so more likely to be recalled. By contrast, in our study an effort was made to sample events from diverse intensity levels. Thus, because the typical duration of intense episodes (reported in Scherer et al.) is relatively long, the differences in distributions might be due to differences in tasks.

Whereas the convergence of the two methods (recollection and imagination) is encouraging, it could still be the case that both methods tap individuals' "naive" theories of emotions as opposed to their actual experiences, and that both are based on reconstructive processes. Clearly, only the comparison of these results with data obtained from an "experiential," "on-line" paradigm, providing information on emotional experiences during the period of their occurrence can shed light on this question, but such paradigms make it difficult to collect longer term duration data.

CONCLUSION

Recent research has attempted to create a link between emotion and personality. This research has started to reveal some of the questions that arise in the interaction between these two domains. In this chapter we have attempted to address some of these questions, as well as to raise some new ones. In particular, we have concentrated on the similarities and differences between different types of affect and the structural dimensions of personality. More generally, we have attempted to create a framework within which patterns of relationships between emotions and personality can be examined. Yet we have only scratched the surface of the problem. There is much more that could be done.

Perhaps the most natural first step would be to explore additional parameters of emotional response. Presumably, the temporal dimension is but a single aspect on which individuals exhibit wide variability of emotional responses. The most obvious extension of the present research would be to explore the relationships between personality and additional parameters of emotional response such as action tendencies. Frijda (1986, 1989) defined action tendencies as the "tendencies to establish, maintain, or disrupt a relationship with the environment" (Frijda, 1986, p. 71). Examples include "active" tendencies of getting closer, fleeing, removing obstacles, "passive" tendencies of paying little attention to the outside world, and absence of action readinesses (as in the case of the tendency to rest). Frijda et al. (1989) contended that just like appraisal patterns, action readinesses can be regarded as distinguishing features of emotions, and thus ought to play an important role in emotion research. Granting that the type of action (approach, avoidance, apathy, etc.) as well as the urgency to act are functions of emotions, it is natural to inquire how they are related to personality. For example, do some individuals tend to respond more passively (in terms of the strength or the urgency to act, as well as in terms of the type of action chosen) than others? And if so, how is "action intensity" related to other dimensions of personality, such as neuroticism, extraversion, affect intensity, and so on?

ACKNOWLEDGMENTS

Preparation of this article was supported in part by grant IRI-8812699 awarded to Andrew Ortony by the National Science Foundation, in part by Anderson Consulting through Northwestern University's Institute for the Learning Sciences, and in part by contract MDA903-90-C-0108 from the U.S. Army Research Institute awarded to William Revelle and Kristen Anderson. The views, opinions, and findings contained in this report are those of the authors and should not be construed as an official Department of the Army position, policy, or decision, unless designated so by other official documentation.

We are indebted to Andrew Ortony for many thoughtful comments and suggestions that greatly influenced this work. We also wish to thank Stephanie van Goozen for helpful comments on an earlier version of this chapter.

REFERENCES

Arnold, M. B. (1960). *Emotions and personality*. New York: Columbia University Press.

Averill, J. R. (1983). Studies on anger and aggression: Implications for theories of emotion. *American Psychologist, 38,* 1145–1160.

Blaney, P. H. (1986). Affect and memory: A review. *Psychological Bulletin, 99,* 229–246.

Costa, P. T., & McCrae, R. R. (1980). Influence of extraversion and neuroticism on subjective well-being: Happy and unhappy people. *Journal of Personality and Social Psychology, 38,* 668–678.

Costa, P. T., & McCrae, R. R. (1985). *The NEO personality inventory manual*. Odessa, FL: Psychological Assessment Resources.

Diener, E., & Emmons, R. A. (1984). The independence of positive and negative affect. *Journal of Personality and Social Psychology, 47,* 1105–1117.

Diener, E., & Iran-Nejad, A. (1986). The relationship in experience between different types of affect. *Journal of Personality and Social Psychology, 50,* 1031–1038.

Diener, E., Larsen, R. J., Levine, S., & Emmons, R. A. (1985). Intensity and frequency: Dimensions underlying positive and negative affect. *Journal of Personality and Social Psychology, 48,* 1253–1265.

Digman, J. (1990). Personality structure: The emergence of the five-factor model. *Annual Review of Psychology, 41,* 417–440.

Ekman, P. (1984). Expression and the nature of emotions. In K. Scherer & P. Ekman (Eds.), *Approaches to emotion* (pp. 319–344). Hillsdale, NJ: Lawrence Erlbaum Associates.

Ekman, P., & Friesen, W. V. (1975). *Unmasking the face*. Englewood Cliffs, NJ: Prentice-Hall.

Ekman, P., Levenson, R. W., & Friesen, W. V. (1983). Autonomic nervous system activity distinguishes among emotions. *Science, 221,* 1208–1210.

Emmons, R. A., & Diener, E. (1986). Influence of sociability and impulsivity on positive and negative affect. *Journal of Personality and Social psychology, 50,* 1211–1215.

Eysenck, H. J. (1967). *The biological basis of personality*. Springfield, IL: Thomas.

Eysenck, H. J. (Ed.). (1981). *A model for personality*. New York: Springer-Verlag.

Eysenck, H. J. (1991). Dimensions of personality: 16, 5, or 3? Criteria for a taxonomic paradigm. *Personality and Individual Differences, 12,* 773–790.

Eysenck, H. J., & Eysenck, M. W. (1985). *Personality and individual differences*. London: Plenum Press.

Eysenck, H. J., & Eysenck, S. B. G. (1964). *Manual of the Eysenck personality inventory*. San Diego: Educational and Industrial Testing Service.

Eysenck, M. (1987). Trait theories of anxiety. In J. Strelau & H. J. Eysenck (Eds.), *Personality dimensions and arousal* (pp. 79–97). New York: Plenum Press.

Fowles, D. C. (1987). Application of a behavioral theory of affect to the concepts of anxiety and impulsivity. *Journal of Research in Personality, 21,* 417–435.

Frijda, N. H. (1986). *The emotions*. Cambridge, England: Cambridge University Press.

Frijda, N. H., Kuipers, P., & Terschure, E. (1989). Relations between emotions, appraisal, and emotional action readiness. *Journal of Personality and Social Psychology, 57,* 212–228.

Frijda, N. H., Mesquita, B., Sonnemans, J., & van Goozen, S. (1991). The duration of affective phenomena or emotions, sentiments and passions. In K. T. Strongman (Ed.), *International review of studies on emotion* (Vol. 1, pp. 187–225). New York: Wiley.

Frijda, N. H., Ortony, A., Sonnemans, J., & Clore, J. (1992). The complexity of intensity. In M. Clark (Ed.), *Review of personality and social psychology, 13,* 60–89.

Gray, J. A. (1972). The psychophysiological basis of introversion–extraversion: A modification of Eysenck's theory. In V. D. Nebylitsyn & J. A. Gray (Eds.), *The biological basis of individual behavior* (pp. 182–205). New York: Academic Press.

Gray, J. A. (1981). A critique of Eysenck's theory of personality. In H. J. Eysenck (Ed.), *A model for personality* (pp. 246–276). New York: Springer-Verlag.

Gray, J. A. (1987). *The physiology of fear and stress.* Cambridge, England: Cambridge University Press.

Izard, C. E. (1977). *Human emotions.* New York: Plenum.

Larsen, R. J. (1988). A process approach to personality psychology: Utilizing time as a facet of the data. In D. M. Buss & N. Cantor (Eds.), *Personality psychology: Recent trends and emerging directions* (pp. 160–177). New York: Springer-Verlag.

Larsen, R. J., & Diener, E. (1987). Affect intensity as individual differences characteristic: A review. *Journal of Research in Personality, 21,* 1–39.

Larsen, R. J., Diener, E., & Cropanzano, R. S. (1986). Cognitive operations associated with individual differences in affect intensity. *Journal of Personality and Social Psychology, 53,* 767–774.

Larsen, R. J., Diener, E., & Emmons, R. A. (1986). Affect intensity and the reactions to daily life events. *Journal of Personality and Social Psychology, 51,* 803–814.

Larsen, R. J., & Ketelaar, T. (1991). Personality and susceptibility to positive and negative emotional states. *Journal of Personality and Social Psychology, 61,* 132–140.

Lazarus, R. J. (1991). Cognition and motivation in emotion. *American Psychologist, 46,* 352–367.

Lazarus, R. S., & Folkman, S. (1984). *Stress, appraisal and coping.* New York: Springer-Verlag.

Martin, M. (1985). Neuroticism as a cognitive predisposition toward depression: A cognitive mechanism. *Personality and Individual Differences, 6,* 353–365.

Mayer, J. D., & Gaschke, Y. N. (1988). The experience and the meta-experience of mood. *Journal of Personality and Social Psychology, 55,* 102–111.

Meyer, G. J., & Shack, J. R. (1989). Structural convergence of mood and personality: Evidence for old and new "directions." *Journal of Personality and Social Psychology, 57,* 691–706.

Newman, J. P. (1987). Reaction to punishment in extraverts and psychopaths: Implications for the impulsive behavior of disinhibited individuals. *Journal of Research in Personality, 21,* 464–480.

Nisbett, R. E., & Wilson, T. D. (1977). Telling more than we can know: Verbal reports on mental processes. *Psychological Review, 84,* 231–259.

Nolen-Hoeksema, S. (1987). Sex differences in unipolar depression: Evidence and theory. *Psychological Bulletin, 101,* 256–282.

Nolen-Hoeksema, S., Morrow, J., & Fredrickson, B. L. (1993). Response styles and the duration of episodes of depressed mood. *Journal of Abnormal Psychology, 102,* 20–28.

Ortony, A., Clore, J. L., & Collins, A. (1988). *The cognitive structure of emotions.* New York: Cambridge University Press.

Revelle, W. (1987). Personality and motivation: Sources of inefficiency in cognitive performance. *Journal of Research in Personality, 21,* 436–452.

Revelle, W. (1989, June). *Levels of analysis: The place of impulsivity in trait theories of personality.* Paper presented at the meeting of International Society for the Study of Individual Differences, Heidelberg, Germany.

Revelle, W. (1991, August). The place of mood in a theory of personality and cognition. In R. E. Thayer (Chair), *Theoretical implications and practical application of modern mood theory.* Paper presented at the 99th Annual Convention of the American Psychological Association, San Francisco, CA.

Revelle, W., Humphreys, M. S., Simon, L., & Gilliland, K. (1980). The interactive effects of personality, time of day, and caffeine: A test of the arousal model. *Journal of Experimental psychology: General, 109,* 1–31.

Ricci-Bitti, P., & Scherer, K. R. (1986). Interrelations between antecedents, reactions, and coping responses. In K. R. Scherer, H. G. Wallbott, & A. B. Summerfield (Eds.), *Experiencing emotion: A cross-cultural study* (pp. 129–142). Cambridge, England: Cambridge University Press.

Roseman, I. (1984). Cognitive determinants of emotions: A structural theory. In P. Shaver (Ed.), *Review of personality and social psychology: Vol. 5. Emotions, relationship and health* (pp. 11–36). Beverly Hills, CA: Sage Publications.

Russell, J. A. (1979). Affective space is bipolar. *Journal of Personality and Social Psychology, 37,* 345–356.

Russell, J. A. (1980). A circumplex model of affect. *Journal of Personality and Social Psychology, 39,* 1161–1178.

Scherer, K. R., Wallbott, H. G., & Summerfield, A. B. (Eds.). (1986). *Experiencing emotion: A cross-cultural study.* Cambridge, England: Cambridge University Press.

Smith, C. A., & Ellsworth, P. C. (1985). Patterns of cognitive appraisal in emotions. *Journal of Personality and Social Psychology, 48,* 813–838.

Taylor, S. E. (1991). Asymmetrical effects of positive and negative events: The mobilization-minimization hypothesis. *Psychological Review, 110,* 67–85.

Teasdale, J. D. (1988). Cognitive vulnerability to persistent depression. *Cognition and Emotion, 2,* 247–274.

Tellegen, A. (1985). Structure of mood and personality and their relevance to assessing anxiety, with an emphasis of self-report. In A. H. Tuma & J. Mason (Eds.), *Anxiety and anxiety disorders* (pp. 681–706). Hillsdale, NJ: Lawrence Erlbaum Associates.

Thayer, R. E. (1970). Activation states as assessed by verbal report and four psychophysiological variables. *Psychophysiology, 7,* 86–94.

Thayer, R. E. (1989). *The biopsychology of mood and arousal.* New York: Oxford University Press.

Wallbott, H. G., & Ellgring, H. (1986). The German case: Personality correlates of emotional reactivity. In K. R. Scherer, H. G. Wallbott, & A. B. Summerfield (Eds.), *Experiencing emotion: A cross-cultural study* (pp. 205–210). Cambridge, England: Cambridge University Press.

Watson, D., & Clark, L. A. (1984). Negative affectivity: The disposition to experience aversive emotional states. *Psychological Bulletin, 96,* 465–490.

Watson, D., & Clark, L. A. (1991). Self- versus peer ratings of specific emotional traits: Evidence of convergent and discriminant validity. *Journal of Personality and Social Psychology, 60,* 927–940.

Watson, D., & Tellegen, A. (1985). Towards a consensual structure of mood. *Psychological Bulletin, 98,* 219–235.

Weissman, M. M., Prusoff, B. A., & Klerman, G. L. (1978). Personality and the prediction of long-term outcome of depression. *American Journal of Psychiatry, 135,* 797–800.

Wiggins, J. S. (1968). Personality structure. *Annual Review of Psychology, 19,* 119–138.

Zevon, M. A., & Tellegen, A. (1982). The structure of mood change: An idiographic/nomothetic analysis. *Journal of Personality and Social Psychology, 43,* 111–122.

Zuckerman, M. (1979). *Sensation seeking: Beyond the optimal level of arousal.* Hillsdale, NJ: Lawrence Erlbaum Associates.

Zuckerman, M. (1987). A critical look at three arousal constructs in personality theories: Optimal level of arousal, strength of the nervous system and sensitivities to the signals of reward and punishment. In J. Strelau & H. J. Eysenck (Eds.), *Personality dimensions and arousal* (pp. 217–232). New York: Plenum Press.

6 Affect Bursts

Klaus R. Scherer
University of Geneva

One of the major reasons for the relative lack of advancement in research on emotion is the fragmentation of the phenomenon. Different groups of experts in psychophysiology, facial expression, or verbal labelling tend to study emotion in a rather piecemeal fashion. Although the very complexity of the methodology used in some domains may explain the need for specialization, the consequence seems to be a serious lack of agreement on the definition of emotion (see Scherer, 1993) and a dearth of collaborative efforts to study different facets of emotional experience and behavior. This chapter represents a plea for research integrating the different facets of affective phenomena. First, I consider the relationship between facial and vocal expression and discuss the major differences between these two modes of externalizing internal states. I then introduce a particular piece of behavior, which I shall call "affect burst," as a prime example of integrated facial/vocal expression. After reviewing some of the relevant litera- ture, I try to identify some of the major research issues and suggest possible approaches for the empirical study of affect bursts.

WHAT DOES FACIAL EXPRESSION EXPRESS?

Based on the work of the early pioneers in this area (Darwin, 1872/1965; de Sanctis, 1904; Duchenne, 1876/1990), I claim (Scherer, 1989a, 1992) that spe- cific innervation patterns of the facial musculature index (a) ongoing information processing (reflecting the involvement of the facial musculature in the regulation of sensory input) and (b) adaptive behavior tendencies (reflecting the outcome of event or situation evaluation). Both the pioneers of facial expression research

161

and, more recently, ethologically oriented researchers (Eibl-Eibesfeldt, 1984; van Hooff, 1972) have provided examples for these two classes of functional facial muscle movements. Information processing related expression might consist of an increase in the tension of the muscles in the eye and brow region (to increase visual acuity) or the activation of muscles affecting sensory input to the nose or the mouth (as in the case of shutting out unpleasant stimulation). An expression of an action tendency in the face could be the act of pushing the lower jaw forward or of baring the teeth, the rudiments of preparation for aggressive action such as biting. Most of the authors who have underlined the phylogenetic continuity of facial muscle movements in the service of behavioral adaptation, stress that the occurrence and the characteristics of these facial movements are only partly explained by their functional significance. They are also determined by their role as expressive signals in the communication of reactions and action tendencies of an organism with respect to an event. The selective shaping of functionally based facial movements for the purpose of communicative signalling through processes like ritualization, formalization, or symbolization (Leyhausen, 1967) constitutes a fascinating topic for research on human facial expression (see Chevalier-Skolnikoff, 1973; Eibl-Eibesfeldt, 1984; Redican, 1982; Schneider & Dittrich, 1990; van Hooff, 1972).

How can we reconcile the argument that expressive facial muscle movements, although shaped by the needs of communicative signalling, index information processing and action tendencies with the widely held conviction that facial expression primarily serves to express emotions? The component process model of emotion (Scherer, 1984, 1986a) may help to explain this apparent contradiction: In this model, the prototypical expression of a so-called basic or fundamental emotion (see Ekman, 1972; Izard, 1971, 1977; Tomkins, 1962, 1963, 1984) is seen as the result (in the sense of a frozen time slice) of a sequential cumulative process. It is hypothesized that within this process a number of "stimulus evaluation checks" (see also Scherer, 1988a) successively trigger specific facial muscle movements considered to be adaptive with respect to information processing, appropriate behavior tendency, and communicative intention. Each of these partial facial response patterns (which follow each other in rapid succession, as triggered by the respective stimulus evaluation checks) "adds on" to the prior expression pattern in such a way that the "final" expression consists of an accumulation of the series of facial muscle innervation patterns. Figure 6.1 shows a highly simplified illustration of this theoretically postulated process (see Scherer, 1992, for greater detail).

Clearly, much empirical research will be needed to investigate both the nature of the stipulated process and the detailed predictions concerning the link between particular outcomes of information processing involved in the stimulus evaluation checks (or appraisal in general) and particular facial muscle movements. Because the sequential, cumulative processes involved are likely to occur with very high speed and because some of the facial muscle innervations may not lead

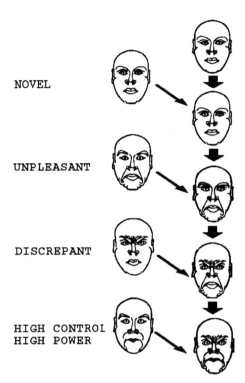

NOVEL

UNPLEASANT

DISCREPANT

FIG. 6.1. Sequential, cumulative changes in facial expression as a result of specific SEC outcomes (as predicted by component process theory).

HIGH CONTROL
HIGH POWER

to visible changes on the facial skin, such research is likely to require a high level of conceptual and technical complexity. However, recent studies using facial electromyography (EMG) or a molecular coding system for facial movement (Facial Action Coding System, FACS, Ekman & Friesen, 1978) demonstrate that the relatively brief and discrete innervations of muscle regions or facial action units can be assessed reliably and with good temporal resolution (Cacioppo, Martzke, Petty, & Tassinary, 1988; Ekman, Friesen, & Ancoli, 1980; Ekman, Friesen, O'Sullivan, & Scherer, 1980; Fridlund, 1991; Fridlund & Izard, 1983; Smith, 1989). If these research paradigms can be improved further, it is possible to envisage running a critical experiment to test the opposing predictions made by component process theory on the one hand and discrete emotion theory on the other; that is, sequential cumulative facial expression changes triggered by stimulus evaluation checks versus triggering of neuromotor programs with simultaneous appearance of the integral facial expression.

Although there may be theoretical dissension as to the dynamic and componential constitution of the facial expression of emotion, most researchers in this area would probably agree that the face functions as a *continuous* read-out (see Buck, 1985) of ongoing cognitive and emotional processes. Although the nature and form of these facial expressions may, in the course of evolution, have been selectively shaped to facilitate their functioning as communicative signals, the origins of these signal characteristics seem to be discrete functional movements in the service of sensory intake and the preparation of action. It is important to note that the continuous read-out of ongoing processes is largely independent of the visibility of the resulting muscle innervation in the face, because facial EMG research has shown continuous changes in facial muscle activity that seem correlated with changes in cognitive and emotional state (cf. the continuous flow model suggested by Cacioppo et al., 1988). Obviously, the continuous read-out process is subject to attempts at regulation or control (see later).

WHAT DOES VOCAL EXPRESSION EXPRESS?

Because I have developed my point of view in much detail elsewhere (Scherer, 1985b, 1986a), I summarize the argument only briefly here. As shown for the facial muscles in Fig. 6.1, component process theory predicts that the organic structures involved in voice production (muscles, cartilages, and mucous skin contributing to the processes of respiration, phonation, and articulation) will be sequentially and cumulatively affected by the outcomes of the series of stimulus evaluation checks (see Table 6.1). Just like the facial musculature as the somatic substrate of facial expression, the organs involved in voice production are assumed to be continuously affected by ongoing cognitive and emotional processes. As for the face, the vocal expression of the prototypical fundamental or basic emotions (which I call "modal" emotions, see Scherer, 1984) are seen as the outcome of a sequential, cumulative process of changes in voice production resulting in a prototypical patterning of the vocalization during the time window of an emotion episode. Table 6.1 shows the modifications in voice quality expected as a result of the outcome of each stimulus evaluation check. On the basis of hypothetical patterns of these outcomes specific for each major modal emotion (see Scherer, 1986a, 1988a), one can attempt to predict the respective prototypical vocal expressions. Table 6.2 shows these predictions, many of which have been empirically confirmed in subsequent studies (Scherer, 1989b; Scherer, Banse, Wallott, & Goldbeck, 1991).

The similarities between vocal and facial expressions do not end here. Based on earlier theorists (Darwin, 1872/1965; Trojan, 1975) and work on animal communication (Marler & Tenaza, 1977; Morton, 1977; Tembrock, 1975), I argued that vocal expression, like facial expression, is phylogenetically continuous and that the origin of many expressive forms can be traced back to clear functional significance with respect to sensory intake (e.g., closing or narrowing of the buccal and nasal passages), behavioral intentions (such as expulsion or effort vocalizations), and, finally, communicative signals (such as threat).

Both the facial and vocal biological markers of the information processing and affective reaction have been subject to selective shaping by the communication

TABLE 6.1
Component Patterning Theory Predictions of Vocal Changes
after Different Stimulus Evaluation Check Outcomes

Novelty Check	
Novel	*Old*
Interruption of phonation Sudden inhalation Silence Ingressive (fricative) sound with a glottal stop (noise-like spectrum)	No change

Intrinsic Pleasantness Check	
Pleasant	*Unpleasant*
Faucal and pharyngeal expansion, relaxation of tract walls Vocal tract shortened by mouth, corners retracted upward More low-frequency energy, F1 falling, slightly broader F1 bandwidth, velopharyngeal nasality Resonances raised *Wide voice*	Faucal and pharyngeal constriction, tensing of tract walls Vocal tract shortened by mouth, corners retracted downward More high-frequency energy, F1 rising, F2 and F3 falling, narrow F1 bandwidth, laryngopharyngeal nasality Resonances raised *Narrow voice*

Goal/need significance check	
Relevant and consistent	*Relevant and discrepant*
Shift toward trophotropic side: overall relaxation of vocal apparatus, increased salivation F_0 at lower end of range, low-to-moderate amplitude, balanced resonance with slight decrease in high-frequency energy	Ergotropic dominance: overall tensing of vocal apparatus and respiratory system, decreased salivation F_0 and amplitude increase, jitter and shimmer, increase in high-frequency energy, narrow F1 bandwidth, pronounced formant frequency differences
Relaxed voice If event conducive to goal: relaxed voice + wide voice If event obstructive to goal: relaxed voice + narrow voice	*Tense voice* If event conducive to goal: tense voice + wide voice If event obstructive to goal: tense voice + narrow voice

Coping Potential Check	
Control	*No Control*
Ergotropic dominance (see tense voice) (See tense voice)	Trophotropic dominance: Hypotension of the musculature in the vocal apparatus and respiratory system Low F_0 and restricted F_0 range, low-amplitude, weak pulses, very low high-frequency energy, spectral

(*continued*)

TABLE 6.1   (*Continued*)

Coping Potential Check	
Control	*No Control*
	noise, formant frequencies tending toward neutral setting, broad F1 bandwidth
Tense voice	*Lax voice*

Power	*No Power*
Deep, forceful respiration; chest register phonation	Rapid, shallow respiration; head register phonation
Low F_0, high amplitude, strong energy in entire frequency range	Raised F_0, widely spaced harmonics with relatively low energy
Full voice	*Thin voice*

Norm/Self Compatibility Check	
Standards Surpassed	*Standards Violated*
Wide voice + full voice	Narrow voice + thin voice
+ Relaxed voice (if expected)	+ Lax voice (if no control)
+ Tense voice (if expected)	+ Tense voice (if control)

Note. The voice types (in italics) are summaries of the detailed changes. F_0 = fundamental frequency. F1 = first formant. F2 = second formant. F3 = third formant. Reproduced with permission from Scherer, 1986a, p. 156.

function with respect to signal clarity, conventionality, and transmission characteristics (Scherer, 1985b). In fact, it is one of the major characteristics of both facial and vocal expression that they are determined by both "push effects" (the biologically determined externalization of naturally occurring internal processes of the organism, particularly information processing and behavioral preparation) and "pull effects" (socioculturally determined norms or moulds concerning the signal characteristics required by the socially shared codes for the communication of internal states and behavioral intentions (see Scherer, 1985b; Scherer, Helfrich, & Scherer, 1980; Scherer & Kappas, 1988).

DIFFERENCES BETWEEN FACIAL AND VOCAL EXPRESSION

Thus far, it seems as though facial and vocal expression are organized both biologically and socioculturally in a highly parallel fashion. If this were the case, one would wonder to what extent these two externalizing and signalling systems are redundant or at least overlapping in the sense of providing the same information to outside observers, in terms of either biological marking or read-out, or

TABLE 6.2

Changes Predicted for Selected Acoustic Parameters on the Basis of the Voice Type Predictions in Table 6.1

	Parameters											
Voice Type	ENJ/ HAP	ELA/ JOY	DISP/ DISG	CON/ SCO	SAD/ DEJ	GRI/ DES	ANX/ WOR	FEAR/ TER	IRR/ COA	RAGE/ HOA	BOR/ IND	SHA/ GUI
F₀												
Perturbation	<=			<>	>	>		≈				
Mean	>	≈	>		<>	>	>	≈	<>	<>	≈	>
Range	<=	≈			<	>		≈	>	≈≈		
Variability	>	≈			<	>		≈	>	≈≈		>
Contour	>	≈			<	>	>	≈	<	=		
Shift regularity	=	>			<	>		>	>			
F1 mean	>	>	>	>	>	>	>	>	>		>	>
F2 mean		<	<	<	<	<	<	<	<		>	<
F1 bandwidth	>	<>	<<	<	<>	<<	<	<<	<<	<<	<	<
Formant precision	>	>	>	>	<	>	>	>	>	>	>	>
Intensity												
Mean	>	≈	>	>>	<<	>		>	≈	≈≈	<>	
Range	<=	>	>	>>	<			>	>	>		
Variability	>	>	>	>	<			>	>	>		
Frequency range	>	>	>	>>	>	>>		>>	>	>	>	
High-frequency energy	>	<>	>	>>	<>	>>	>	≈≈	>>	>>	<>	>
Spectral noise					>							
Speech rate	>	≈			<=	>		≈		≈		
Transition time	>	<			<	<		<		<		

Note. ANX/WOR = anxiety/worry. BOR/IND = boredom/indifference. CON/SCO = contempt/scorn. DISP/DISG = displeasure/disgust. ELA/JOY elation/joy. ENJ/HAP = enjoyment/happiness. FEAR/TER = fear/terror. GRI/DES = grief/desperation. IRR/COA = irritation/cold anger. RAGE/HOA = rage/hot anger. SAD/DEJ = sadness/dejection. SHA/GUI = shame/guilt. F₀ = fundamental frequency. F1 = first formant. F2 = second formant. > = increase, < = decrease. Double symbols indicate increased predicted strength of the change. Two symbols pointing in opposite directions refer to cases in which antecedent voice types exert opposing influences. Symbols that are underlined represent predictions that are supported by empirical findings.
Reproduced with permission from Scherer, 1986a, p. 158

167

sociocultural signalling. To address this fascinating question, we need to examine a number of potential differences between these two expressive systems.

One major difference is the availability of markers or signals from the respective system. The continuous changes in the innervation of the facial musculature do not always produce visible changes on the skin of the face, and the changes in the organs participating in voice production are not always audible. However, there is a major difference. It would seem that the visibility of changes in the tension level of the facial musculature is mainly due to the intensity of the innervation and the communication intention of the expresser, that is, the absence of control or regulation attempts or the amplification of a weak signal for communicative purposes. Conversely, in the case of vocal expression, information processing and/or emotion produced changes in vocal quality are only audible if a sound is uttered—in other words, if the vocal folds are set into vibration to produce a train of glottal pulses that, after having been filtered by the supra-laryngeal tract, will result in the acoustic voice signal that we can hear or record on electromagnetic media. It is only during vocalization that the manifold effects of information processing and/or action tendency on respiration, phonation, and articulation parameters will become externalized and available for scrutiny by observers. For this reason, the audibility of vocal markers is not exclusively determined by the intensity of the underlying arousal but depends also on onset or offset of vocalization as triggered by (conscious or unconscious) motor commands.

For example, a person may be so extremely tense that this tension becomes visible in the face in spite of strong attempts to hide it. However, involuntary manifestation of tension in the voice is impossible as long as the person does not vocalize. Also, whereas the nature and visibility of facial expression is determined by control or amplification efforts in a more or less continuous fashion, communication attempts in the vocal domain, both with respect to suppression or amplification, are all-or-nothing affairs in the sense that vocalization can be voluntarily suppressed or produced as an on–off phenomenon. Only when vocalization is actually occurring, will the changes in the acoustic characteristics of the voice waveform provide a continuous read-out of the differential waxing and waning of biological push and social pull effects.

The situation is complicated by the fact that in the course of human evolution, vocalization has been selected to serve as the carrier signal for the most important code in human communication—language, or more specifically speech. As I have tried to show elsewhere (Scherer, 1979; 1985b), the phylogenetically recent, highly cognitive mode of speech communication is grafted upon a phylogenetically old vocal call system mainly used for affective and social signalling. This has important semiotic implications. For example, because the emotional state of a person continuously affects respiration, phonation, and articulation, all speech activity provides a continuous marking or read-out of the respective state of the speaker, which serves as important context information for the listener.

Obviously, we can turn on vocalization when we want to speak and we can turn it off when we want to shut up. Because speech is one of the most controlled human activities (see Bargh, 1984), the availability of nonverbal vocal signals of information processing, affect, and attitude, which always accompany vocalization, is strongly determined by consciously controlled speech activity.

Whereas facial signals are continuously available, vocal signals are only available when the vocal folds are set in motion. This is of utmost importance for understanding the relationship between facial and vocal expression. The second fundamental difference is related to the functional origins of the respective muscular movements. If we abstract from the selective shaping of the expressive signals for communicative purposes, the functional origins of most facial expressions seem to be relatively brief and *discrete* adaptive behaviors, for example, squinting, frowning, pulling the nose up, baring one's teeth, and so on. Although there is some controversy about the functionality claims made by some of the older authors, for example, with respect to depth of field in vision as depending on the innervation of the orbicularis oculi muscle (cf. Ekman, 1979), it does seem possible to link some facial actions directly to a particular aim. This is not often the case for vocal expression. Here, many of the changes that affect the acoustical waveform seem to be related in a somewhat more undifferentiated way to patterns of physiological arousal, such as ergotropic or trophotropic dominance (cf. Gellhorn, 1970; Scherer, 1979, 1986a).

Another major difference between facial and vocal expression consists in the transmission characteristics of these two signal systems that account for their differential utility in different communication situations. Obviously, for facial expression to have a communicative function, the receiver has to be directly oriented toward the face of the sender and the distance between them has to be relatively small to ensure the correct differentiation of complex facial expression patterns (see Hager & Ekman, 1979). In consequence, facial expression is a short distance, directional communication system. Vocal signals, on the other hand, are omnidirectional. Because we cannot shut our ears (as all those of us who suffer from noise know only too well), we are likely to hear sounds whether we focus on them or not, and even at a rather great distance. Thus, the vocal channel is optimally suited for a nondirectional long distance communication system with no selection or turnoff facility provided. Given these design features, this system is very well adapted for the communication of danger, as in alarm or fear calls, as well as for dominance-related signals, including territorial defence, which imply a threat to a large number of unspecified potential contenders.

These kinds of considerations may be useful in trying to answer questions concerning the relative importance, availability, or decodability of facial versus vocal signals in the expression and impression of different sender states. The interpretation of data on the relative ability of judges to identify personality traits (Scherer, Rosenthal, & Koivumaki, 1972) or emotional states (Scherer, Banse, Wallbott, & Ellgring, in preparation; Wallbott & Scherer, 1986) from studies using multichannel presentation of expression would be greatly facilitated by a better understanding of the phylogenetic origin and the communicative function of the facial and vocal signalling systems. Using this kind of approach, one could attempt, both from a theoretical and empirical vantage point, to answer questions concerning the amount of redundancy or overlap versus independent information contribution of those two major signalling systems in both humans and their closest relatives, the nonhuman primates.

INTRODUCING THE CONCEPT OF AFFECT BURSTS

It would be overly ambitious to attempt to tackle this important issue in the context of the present chapter. Instead, I focus attention on a relatively special case, the spontaneous co-occurrence of facial and vocal expression as triggered by a single event. Contrary to what one might think, these are relatively rare events. Whereas facial and vocal expression co-occur in the act of speaking, the different patterns of expression are determined, as discussed above, by a multitude of push and pull effects related to different types of marking or read-out functions as well as different communicative functions. For example, various parts of the upper face can be shown to have very important paralinguistic or conversational functions (Ekman, 1979). Similarly, many of the vocal changes related to intonation and pausing also carry a large variety of syntactic and pragmatic, and in some languages even semantic functions (see Cutler & Ladd, 1983; Key, 1975). Because of this huge number of determining factors, it has been almost impossible to study the relative role of facial and vocal expression and their interrelation in ongoing social interaction. Early attempts to look at nonverbal behavior in terms of a multichannel partition (see, for example, Scherer & Wallbott, 1985, pp. 218–222) have remained rather sterile demonstrations of the technical feasibility of such an approach without having encouraged any substantial research activity.

In consequence, the vocal/facial integration I focus on here is of a more nonverbal nature. I am referring to what I call "affect bursts," that is, very brief, discrete, nonverbal expressions of affect in both face and voice as triggered by clearly identifiable events.[1] One of my preferred examples of an affect burst (see Scherer, 1988b) is a facial/vocal disgust expression upon seeing a hairy black worm emerging from an oyster shell one is about to bring closer to one's mouth. Although reactions may differ, for most people there will be a brief burst of facial and vocal activity that is directly triggered by the visual information and the

---

[1]Why choose *affect* rather than *emotion* burst? At least in English, *affect* seems to be weaker and more general than *emotion*. In consequence, this term is better suited for the piece of behavior discussed in this paper (which may at times be closer to a strong attitude or a hot cognition than a full-blown emotional episode).

evaluation of the significance of the worm's appearance. With respect to the effect of push and pull effects in this burst, I assume a strong predominance of push effects during the initial appearance of the worm that will probably be quickly superseded by a predominance of pull effects, especially in situations of the communal eating of oysters (particularly in "good" company).

The phenomena I am labelling here as facial/vocal affect bursts are, to my knowledge, not well described in the literature. This is probably due, at least in part, to the difficulty of clearly delimiting the phenomenon in time, especially in the facial domain. These are neither micromomentary expressions (as described by Haggard & Isaacs, 1966), nor necessarily full-blown prototypical expressions of fundamental emotions (the facial phenomenon that has been most intensively treated in the literature), nor conversational markers as described by Ekman (1979). Because of the on/off characteristics of vocal signals, it is easier to isolate and identify these affect bursts in the vocal domain. In fact, the description of the vocal part of these affect bursts goes back to the pioneers in the study of speech and language. The term often used in this literature is "interjection." I will briefly survey some of the earlier literature in this area.

A REVIEW OF WRITINGS ON INTERJECTIONS

Essays dealing with the origins and functions of interjections are frequently found in earlier writings on the psychology of language, particularly in those concerned with speculations about the origins of human language. Kleinpaul (1888/1972), for example, claimed that the reflexive "nature and feeling sounds" belong to the household of the organism, so to speak, and therefore sound very much the same when uttered by speakers in different cultures. He tried to verify this conjecture by citing a number of examples of interjections in diverse languages whose sounds correspond to each other. Kleinpaul also referred to the fact that the same sounds, for example "o," can be used not only as an interjection, but also as a deliberate vocal signal. However, he insisted on a sharp distinction between spontaneously occurring interjections or exclamations expressing an emotional state and calls and shouts intentionally uttered for communicative reasons.

In his ethnopsychology, Wundt (1900) also discussed the "sounds of nature" (*Naturlaute*) and their role in language in great detail, tracing these back to inarticulate screams and cries accompanying very intense feelings of aversion, rage, and fear. Wundt distinguished between (a) primary interjections, defined as nature sounds that, being isolated remnants of a prelinguistic period, only serve to interrupt the continuity of speech, and (b) secondary interjections that become assimilated into the language and eventually, in the course of cultural development, replace the primary interjections. He pointed out that the number of primary interjections found in any one language depends not only on the degree of civilization in a culture, but also on the restraints on affect expression imposed by custom or social norms. For example, one would expect cultures with strong control of emotional expression to develop secondary interjections like "ouch" to replace primary, "raw" pain cries like "aghghgh."

Kainz (1962) also differentiated between primary and secondary interjections and contrasted them with amorphous screams and sighs, which he considered to be sheer reflexive vocalizations serving only to release emotions. Kainz assumed that prelinguistic nature sounds would most likely be uttered in emotionally charged situations. These in turn are presumably intuitively and sympathetically understood by the listener and are therefore of value for communication. He made a distinction between these sounds and true interjections, however, for two reasons: (a) The nature sounds would not be intentionally uttered, and (b) they lacked the required phonetic symbol constancy due to their large intra- and interindividual variance. This constancy is expected for interjections considered to be components of language, due to the stylizing and conventionalizing that has moulded these sounds to correspond to the phonological requirements of a given language. Kainz differentiated between expressive and informative interjections (yuck, oh, ah, aua) and eliciting interjections (he, holla, pst) and assumed a diachronic development from expression to information and finally to elicitation in a process by which reflexive sounds of expression acquire communicative and linguistic significance.

Like Wundt, Kainz claimed that the "civilized individual" expresses emotions less and less frequently by means of pure nature sounds as civilization becomes more advanced. Instead, interjections that have been assimilated into language are used. This progressive transformation and symbolization of reflexive affect symptoms is attributed to increased cortical control of behavior (a view that reminds one of the central role Elias, 1977, assigned to affect control in the process of civilization).

Thus far, I have been focusing on early contributions in the German tradition of "*Psychologie der Sprache*." As one might expect, linguists interested in speech have also discussed these "prelinguistic fragments" in the flow of speech. James (1974) reviewed the respective writings of some of the classic authors in the field (Bloomfield, Fries, Jespersen, Sapir) who all agreed on the affective significance of interjections, their "primitive" and noncommunicative nature, and their lack of grammatical structure. As in the German literature, the emphasis is generally on an evaluation of these vocalizations with respect to the structural criteria of language.

SOCIAL PSYCHOLOGICAL APPROACHES
TO AFFECT VOCALIZATIONS

In my own contribution to this literature (Scherer, 1977), I focused on the *functions* of what I called "affect vocalizations." It seems as if the vocalizations discussed here serve practically all the semantic, syntactic, pragmatic, and dialogical functions of nonverbal behavior in conversation (see Scherer, 1980, for a more detailed discussion of these functions). Some examples of a functional analysis of affect vocalizations may help to illustrate this approach.

The *semantic function* (relation of a specific nonverbal behavior to the meaning of an accompanying verbal utterance) seems to correspond to the communicative or informative aspect of affect vocalizations as emphasized in the literature. *Substitution,* in which a nonverbal symbol takes the place of a verbal symbol, is especially important here. A prerequisite for the quasi-lexical use of nonverbal symbols is clear and invariant coding (at least in the subculture in which these symbols are regularly used as a speech substitute). Based on the work of Efron, Ekman and his collaborators have enumerated some of the features characterizing such nonverbal substitutes with respect to gestural emblems (Efron, 1941/1973; Ekman & Friesen, 1969, 1972). As the vocalizations discussed here can take over functions similar to those of such gestures, I have proposed the term "vocal emblems" for a subset of affect vocalizations that meet the code requirements expected of emblematic signals (see later).

Whereas gestural and vocal emblems seem to be limited mainly to the substitution function, affect vocalizations (similar to nonemblematic gestures, e.g., illustrators, see Ekman & Friesen, 1972) can function in a great number of other ways. Other semantic functions might be the amplification, contradiction, or modification of verbally mediated meanings by the accompanying nonverbal behavior patterns. In contrast not only to gestures and facial expression, but also to intonation, affect vocalizations cannot, by their very nature, appear simultaneously with acoustic phoneme realizations such as words that have a meaning of their own. Therefore, a more elaborate definition of the context units relating verbal and nonverbal utterances in terms of the described functions is required. Unfortunately, linguists have not yet agreed on macrosegmental units that could serve to define the context of meaning in an utterance. We are therefore limited for the time being to the vague concept of "utterance" in order to elucidate the semantic functions of affect vocalizations. (It remains to be seen whether pragmalinguistics will succeed in defining the speech act concept more precisely and in a fashion that allows empirical research; see U. Scherer, 1990, for some of the problems.)

It is generally assumed that the "oh" in the expression "Oh, I'm so glad" serves as an *amplification* representing an extremely high degree of cheerfulness/joyfulness. However, the use of affect vocalizations does not automatically amplify the meaning, especially when vocal emblems that have become fully integrated into the written language are used. Consequently, "Oh, what a pity", spoken indifferently (e.g., with a falling intonation contour), hardly leads us to assume there is reason for greater regret than when only the word "Pity!" with strong emphasis on the first syllable is uttered. This example shows the extent to which the meaning and function of affect vocalizations depend on the type of their acoustic realization. One can assume that they fill the function assigned to them the better, the more their acoustical sound form corresponds to the vocalization uttered spontaneously when a certain emotion is actually present. The degree to which such spontaneous production encourages or allows "intuitive" understanding of nature sounds, perhaps even in the form of the process of *Einfühlung* (empathy via motor mimicry) as suggested by Lipps (1907), remains to be investigated. An example of *contradiction* would be the word "gladly," spoken in compliance to an offer one cannot refuse and accompanied by a deep groan. An apologetic clearing of one's throat or an embarrassed cough exemplify *modification.*

The *syntactical functions* of nonverbal behavior, including the segmentation of behavior in various channels of communication, present great conceptual difficulties. In addition, they have as yet only rarely been subjected to empirical examination. One example is the segmentation of the flow of speech caused by diverse forms of "ah, ahm, em." These sounds, frequently uttered during so-called filled pauses, are considered by a number of psychologists to be important aids in the transformation of cognitive processes into speech production (e.g., Dittman, 1972; Goldman-Eisler, 1968). In addition, they offer the listener important aids to comprehension due to their effect of segmenting running speech. At the same time, they can have affective significance signalling hesitation, uncertainty, or embarrassment.

The *pragmatic function* involves expression of speaker states and traits as well as marking of the reaction toward someone else's behavior. *Expression* refers to the marking of affect, personality, and other idiosyncratic characteristics such as membership in certain social classes and culture groups (see Scherer & Giles, 1979) in speech. The majority of affect vocalizations are to be classified here. The relations between emotional state and vocalizations will be discussed in greater detail below. Affect vocalizations can also mark specific personality types (for example, when certain vocalizations are strongly preferred and frequently uttered by a speaker or when certain acoustic realizations of vocal emblems are used that deviate from the norm).

When an interlocutor's utterance or behavior receives evaluative commentary by gestural and facial expressions such as nodding, shaking one's head, or a doubtful smile, the respective nonverbal behavior is considered a reaction. Affect vocalizations serve this function extremely frequently, as for instance in the affirmative "mhm, mhm," the negative "eh, eh," the disdainful "pah," and "phfui!" signifying aversion or disgust, and so on.

The meaning of affect vocalizations can be modified by paralinguistic phenomena. For example, the reaction "mhm" can express doubt, agreement, surprise, joy, and so on, in response to an utterance. Along with other acoustic variables, the intonation contour is a significant factor here, as are facial expressions accompanying the vocalization. The facial expression not only facilitates the receiver's decoding process, but it can also affect the articulatory formation of the sound itself (see later).

Finally, the *dialogical function* comprises regulation of the interaction and dialogue sequences. An obvious and well-recognized example of this type of function is the role of affect vocalizations in phatic communication, that is, the sheer establishment and maintenance of some kind of link between persons that can potentially interact in a given situation. Goffman (1978, see later) nicely illustrates the way in which interjections can serve as an elegant means of inviting comments or providing license to speak in an otherwise noncommunicative situation (e.g., uttering a loud disparaging "tsk, tsk" while reading the sports pages of a newspaper in a crowded waiting room).

The dialogical function of affect vocalizations also encompasses the designation of the relation between interlocutors, for example, dominance/submission or sympathy/antipathy. This relationship, which is determined by posture and eye contact in particular, deals with a relatively stable attitude prevailing for the entire dialogue or interaction period, as distinguished from the reaction to specific utterances.

Moreover, the dialogical function includes the regulation of interaction, particularly the turn-taking process. There are many well-documented examples of regulatory affect vocalizations, such as the backchannel signals that indicate to the speaker that one is still listening and that encourage him to continue (e.g., "mhm, mhm . . . mhm"), as well as the bridging of speech pauses by means of long drawn "ahhs" to prevent an interruption or to indicate that one plans to continue speaking (Duncan, 1972). Although many of these vocalizations are not highly emotional, they can have affective significance indicating doubt, hesitation, enthusiasm, or similar states.

This last example demonstrates the multifunctionality of affective vocalizations. By preventing premature interruptions, these sounds serve a *dialogical function,* namely regulation. At the same time, by synchronizing the speaker's speech flow with cognitive processes, (e.g., via segmentation) they serve a *syntactical function,* and finally, they serve a *pragmatic function* when they signal insecurity on the part of the speaker (expression).

This example shows the difficulties connected with trying to use the concept of intentionality to define different classes of vocalizations (as is common in the literature on interjections). Thus, a speaker may deliberately prolong his "ah" because his interlocutor has repeatedly tried to interrupt. On the other hand, it is possible that he or she is making use of this "floor-holding" signal because it is a frequently used and, to a great extent, ritualized behavior, without being aware of it. With regard to the expression function, it can hardly be postulated that a speaker is totally at the mercy of an expression that is pushed out automatically: In most cases, as mentioned earlier, the speaker can make an attempt (consciously or unconsciously) to modify, to amplify, or to entirely suppress it.

Just as a sender is able to create a certain effect more or less consciously or intentionally, a receiver is able to make more or less use of the information provided by the sender's vocalizations. Therefore, the functions that vocalizations and nonvocal behavior generally assume are not unequivocally determined by concrete situations or by specific mental processes, physiological arousal, or behavior of sender and receiver.

In consequence, one can argue that nonlinguistic vocalizations can neither be classified on the basis of sender characteristics (e.g., spontaneous expression vs. deliberate, intended communication) nor receiver characteristics (e.g., the type of information processing or causal attribution involved), due to the fact that both can differ from situation to situation, even when the vocalization is exactly the same. Even a categorical classification on the basis of conversational functions hardly seem to make sense, because many vocalizations can serve several functions, often even simultaneously (see Scherer, 1977).

Goffman (1978, reprinted 1979) provided an exquisitely written analysis of interjections from an interactionist view. He defined exclamatory, nonlexicalized, discrete interjections as "response cries," expressions that he sees as "a natural overflowing, a flooding up of previously contained feeling, a bursting of normal restraints, a case of being caught off-guard" (p. 800). He discussed the following standard cries: (1) the transition display (e.g., Brr! upon escaping from adverse weather), (2) the spill cry (e.g., Oops! after having dropped something), (3) the threat startle (e.g., Eek! or Yipe! in response to facing a potentially dangerous situation), (4) revulsion sounds (e.g., Eeuw! upon seeing a disgusting sight), (5) the strain grunt (lifting or pushing something heavy), (6) the pain cry (e.g., Oww! or Ouch!), (7) the sexual moan, (8) floor cues (e.g., a deprecatory sound while reading the newspaper in company), and (9) audible glee (e.g., Oooo! or Wheee!). Goffman insisted that the significance of such response cries does not lie in the expressiveness that they share with most other talk ("Naked feelings can agitate a paragraph of discourse almost as well as they can a solitary imprecation. Indeed, it is impossible to utter a sentence without colouring the utterance with some kind of perceivable affect. . . ." p. 813). Instead, it lies in their social interaction function, which "allows and obliges us momentarily to open up our thoughts and feelings and ourselves, through sound, to whoever is present. Response cries, then, do not mark a flooding of emotion outward, but a flooding of relevance in" (Goffman, 1978, p. 815).

Poggi (1981), in one of the most exhaustive treatments of interjections to date (with mostly Italian examples), approached the topic from the standpoint of a pragmalinguist, focusing on the actual use of different interjections in different contexts. She provided the most systematic and comprehensive effort toward a classification of the different sounds with respect to the underlying state of the speaker, distinguishing between information, interrogation, and request interjections. Because the subcategories proposed and the examples given are of great interest for the analysis of the emotional meaning of affect vocalizations, I reproduce a condensed version of her classification system in Table 6.3.

TABLE 6.3
Poggi's Classification of Italian Interjections

Informative interjections

Cognitive assessment	**Understanding** (acquiring new knowledge): *ah* **Recognition** (Information already potentially available): *già* **Denial or incredulity** (Information is suggested to be false): *macché, sée . . . ,* *affato, bum!, che!, no* **Ignorance** (Information not available): *boh, chissà, mah* **Confirmation** (Information already obtained by other means): *capisca, davvero, diamine, eh, mhm, öh, okay, (sic!)* *appunto, anzi, cacchio!, cavolo!, cazzo!, certo, diavolo, ostia!,* *proprio, sì, sicuro, vero altro che* **Doubt or hesitation** (Indecision between different possibilities): *bah, bèh . . . , èeh . . . , ehm, mhm . . . , mah* *allora . . . , cioé, così, dico, dunque . . .* **Surprise** (violation of expectation): *ah, ih, oh, öh, ölla, tòh, uh, caspita, caspiterina, cribbio, diamine, ul-* *lallà* *accidenti, boia, cacchio, capperi, cavolo, cazzo, cristo, diavolo, dio,* *figli!, gente!, gerusalemme, gesù, madonna, mamma, maria, merda,* *misericordia, ostia, no!, perbacco, però!, ragazzi!, sacripante,sorbe,* *vacca* *la madonna, la vacca!*		

Goal assessment	**Compromised goals**	**Physical discomfort**	**Pain,** : *ahi, ahia, ahio, uhi* **Cold** : *brr* **Disgust** : *bleach, puah* **Fatigue** : *aùff, uffa*
		Psychic suffering	**Boredom or embarrassement:** *uffa, uh* **Contempt** : *puah, pfui, poh* **Displeasure or desperation** : *ahimè, ohimè* no! peccato **Worrying** : *nc* **Repulsion** : *aaah!, no!* **Indignation** : *éeh, ohibò, ööh* **Disappointment** : *acciderba, accipic-chia, alé, caspita, cribbio, diamine* Accidenti, boia, cacchio, cavolo, cazzo, diavolo, dio, gente!, geru-salemme, gesù, mamma, maria,

(continued)

TABLE 6.3 *(Continued)*

			madonna, merda, misericordia, ostia, ragazzi, sacripante, sorbe, vacca la madonna . . . .
Achieved goals		Generic	**Satisfaction** : *aah, òh, òoh* ecco meno male **Triumph** : *evviva, hurrà, iuhù* alleluia, osanna
		Specific	**Different types** : *aah, éureka, ha, iùm, maraméo, mirallegro, tié, uée!, vivaddio* ecco, là, piacere

Interrogative interjections

Confirmation questions : *eh?, neh?, nevvero?*
   davvero?, no?, vero?

Asking for repetition or clarification : *eh?, bèh?,*
   che?, come?, cosa?

Request for explanation : bèh?

Requestive interjections

Generic requests	**Pure incitements** : *alé*
	avanti, coraggio, dài, prego, su
	
	Concerning performative :
	   Prayer : *dèh*
	   Encouragement : *orsù, suvvia, coraggio*
	   Prohibition : no
	
	Concerning aspect :
	   To start : *marsch !*
	   sotto! via!
	   To continue : avanti
	   To stop : alt, basta, stop
	   To repeat : bis

Specific requests	**Attention** : *ahò, ehi, ehilà, ohé, ohilà, pst, uehi, uehilà* **Different types** : *altolà, arri, pardôn, sc . . . , sciô, ss . . . , té té* aiuto, allegria, avanti, calma, cuccia, largo, perdono, permesso, prego, pietà, pista, pronto, scusa, silenzio, soccorso, sveglia, vergogna, via va là

Optative interjections

Ejaculations	**Invocations** : gesù, madonna, mamma, maria, misericordia madonna mia, maria vergine, oddio, san giuseppe . . . . **Imprecations** : *cribbio, perbacco, perbaccolina, perdiana, perdinci, perdindirindina, perdio, porcaloca, accidenti, accipicchia*

TABLE 6.3 (*Continued*)

	boia, cacchio, cavolo, cristo, dannazione, diavolo, dio, maledizione, merda, ostia, sacripante, vacca corpo di mille bombe, la madonna, per la madonna, porco diavolo, porco dinci, porco due, porco giove . . . .
Ceremonial expressions	**Greetings** : *arrivederci, addio, buonanotte, buonasera, buongiorno ciao* saluti, salve **Wishes** : auguri, in bocca al lupo, cento di questi anni . . . . **Politeness expressions** : complimenti, congratulazioni, condoglianze, grazie, rallegramenti, salute!, salve! . . . .

Translated by Grazia Ceschi. Reproduced with permission from Poggi, 1981, pp. 68–73.

FROM AFFECT VOCALIZATIONS
TO AFFECT BURSTS

This brief review of the literature reflects some of the attempts to define and classify interjections or affect vocalizations from the vantage point of language, communication, and social interaction. Two major issues emerge: One of the central problems is the definition of the sign status of the sound pattern in comparison with other phonemic units in language (the issue of raw or brute expression vs. socioculturally and linguistically conventionalized symbols). Another core problem, as for many nonlinguistic phenomena in communication and expression, is the determination of the degree of intentionality with which the signal was uttered (spontaneous expression vs. deliberate production). This problem is particularly troublesome because of the multifunctionality of affect vocalizations.

The authors cited above have approached these issues from the vantage point of their particular approach and disciplinary predilection. The term *interjection*, coined by students of language and speech, emphasizes the way that the nonlexical sounds described here or single words and brief expressions, such as imprecations ("shit!") or exclamations ("good god!"), interrupt the speech flow in an emphatic, forceful fashion. As we have seen, the main interest is in analyzing the role of the interjection in the utterance and its relationship to the surrounding language elements. Goffman's term *response cries*, in line with his interactionist viewpoint, stresses the effects of the sounds on the social environment and the way in which the "crier" situates himself or herself within the situation.

My suggestion of the term *affect vocalizations* is obviously influenced by my agenda as an emotion psychologist, highlighting the affective or emotional state of a speaker (real or deliberately affected) at the moment of uttering an interjection. Clearly, each of these terms corresponds particularly well to the major goal of the respective analysis and we may need to use different terms depending on the context and the nature of the investigation. In what follows, I exclusively focus on the affective nature of these exclamations in the sense of *affect bursts* (directing the reader to the linguistic and interactionist works cited earlier for a more complete coverage of other aspects).

I believe that a major shortcoming of the literature on interjections and affect vocalizations is the fixation on the vocal part of these phenomena. Once one focuses on the underlying affect rather than on linguistic or paralinguistic function, it becomes imperative to include facial expression (but possibly also gestural and postural aspects) in the analysis. The literature cited earlier has mentioned these aspects only in passing, if at all. Yet, it is patently obvious that each of the affect vocalizations commonly encountered is accompanied by a very specific pattern of facial expression. This is partly a direct consequence of the phonation and articulation that produces a particular sound. For example, the upper part of the vocal tract—mouth opening, tongue, position, lip shape, and so on—assumes different positions for the production of different vowel-like sounds such as "aahh!," "oh," "ugh!," or "iii!" (thus producing the characteristic formant structures for these sounds). Similarly, the production of nonvoiced sounds such as "brrr!" or "pe!" requires special actions of the tongue, the jaw, and the lips. All of these articulatory settings involve movements of the musculature in the lower face that often result in highly visible facial patterns. However, facial action during affect vocalization is not limited to the lower face. We have all seen "oh!" accompanied by raised eyebrows (frontalis), or "heh?" by a frown (corrugator innervation). Taking the list of Poggi's (1981) examples in Table 6.3, we would have little difficulty in imagining frequently encountered upper face expressions for almost all of the items. The most important aspect of this co-occurrence of facial and vocal activity in what I call *affect bursts* is the *integration and synchronization* of the two expressive modalities, particularly with respect to onset. How do we account for this powerful coordination?

I propose to study affect bursts from the vantage point of a theory of emotion. This will allow us to engage in a more systematic study of this simple but fundamental case of facial/vocal expression integration. Its special significance lies in the fact that it may be one of the phylogenetically oldest constituents of our communication system and seems to be directly related to the display and call systems in many mammalian species.

In the component process model, *emotion* is defined as a sequence of interrelated synchronized changes in the states of all organismic subsystems (information processing, support, execution, action, monitoring) in response to the evaluation of an external or internal stimulus event as relevant to central concerns of the organism (see Scherer, 1993). I believe that highly emotionally charged affect bursts are one of the best illustrations of this definition, in particular with respect to the strong *synchronization* of various organismic systems, particularly the various expressive channels, over a very brief period of time. Concretely, I argue that the results of the stimulus evaluation checks will produce functionally determined changes in the different organismic subsystems, including the ANS and the SNS, changes that will serve to accommodate the needs of information processing and behavioral adaptation (particularly with respect to specific action tendencies; see Frijda, 1986, for a detailed discussion of the latter point). These push effects will result in specific consequences for facial and vocal expression as reviewed in the first part of this chapter. It is possible, then, to use theoretically derived predictions, as shown above, to formulate specific research questions. The situation is complicated, of course, by the existence of pull effects in the form of social control or emphasis rules. These predictions are clearly related to the two major issues mentioned above. I review each of these in turn.

RAW EXPRESSIONS
VERSUS CONVENTIONALIZED SYMBOLS

The theoretical approach advocated here, coupled with the notion of push versus pull effects in expressive signalling, might help us to advance both conceptually and empirically in the study of affect bursts and their derivatives.[2] As pointed out above, the ritualization and conventionalization of expressive phenomena that originated as externalizations of organismic and psychic states is one of the central features of the evolution of communication. One of the recurring debates in this area concerns the categorization of the observed behavior patterns into discrete classes of raw expressions and conventionalized symbols.

A classification on the basis of the constancy or stability of the phonetic features of the vocalizations, as Kainz (1962) suggested, seems to run into difficulties. Phonetic feature constancy surely cannot be inferred from the mere existence of a transcription for a vocalization in written language, especially in view of the fact that a consensus as to the nature of the transcription exists only for very few sounds. In many cases, the articulation of a particular sound is transcribed by using a combination of letters of the alphabet. Unfortunately, quite frequently there are numerous alternative ways of transcribing a given sound, for instance, the clicking sound of disapproval found in American English has been transcribed in the following manner "tsk, tsk" "tusk, tusk" or "tisk, tisk" (Key, 1975, p. 73).

Even in conventionally transcribed sounds that seem to have a relatively clear

---

[2]By derivatives I mean facial/vocal behavior expression integrations that give the impression of being affect bursts, but that differ in a number of important characteristics from true affect bursts.

definite meaning, like "ouch" or "oh," evidence of the constancy of phonetic features in spoken language can hardly be provided. The acoustic signal of the vocalization must obviously contain some constant structural characteristics if it is to be informative and not random. However, because a few invariant characteristics are usually sufficient to allow stimulus differentiation, as Bühler (1934/1984) emphasized, this aspect does not seem to provide a good basis for differentiation. It is possible that even the "amorphous screams and sighs" for which Kainz (1962) contested phonetic feature constancy and which he therefore distinguished from true interjections, contain such constant structural characteristics. Thus, there might be acoustic characteristics, for example, that differentiate a "sulky groan" from a "painful groan." To test whether such invariant differentiating features exist, one would need to investigate whether receivers are able to make this distinction when hearing the sound out of context. Feature constancy would be even more difficult to establish for facial expressions because there is no reference with respect to a formalized system of communicative signals as constituted by language phonemes and morphemes. In consequence, I suggest that we determine the position of these bursts on a dimension reflecting the relative strength of push versus pull effects rather than attempting to neatly classify affect bursts into raw and conventionalized types.

Pure affect bursts should be almost entirely determined by push effects, (i.e., the functional effects of stimulus evaluation checks pushing the physiological reactions underlying facial and vocal expression into specific directions). However, given facial/vocal integration, one can imagine direct and indirect push effects. For example, to what extent is sound production (or at least the specific acoustic structure of a vocalization) just a by-product of a certain facial expression (i.e., the result of an indirect push effect)? Facial expression has been explained as functional, adaptive behavior that assumed signal character in the course of evolution. For example, it is possible to imagine that the facial expressions characteristically shown in disgust are a residual manifestation of the choking movements occurring prior to vomiting, accompanied by an expulsion of air. Although the occurrence of vocalization would be independent of the facial expression, the acoustic structure might not be. The nature of the acoustic voice signal is determined by the modification of the glottal pulses (produced by phonation) by means of the filter characteristics of the upper vocal tract. These depend on tongue position, mouth opening, lip shape, and so forth, and are thus influenced to a degree as yet unknown by the position of the facial musculature. In consequence, the particular acoustic structure of the vocal part of an affect burst might well be the by-product of the concomitant facial expression.

In a pilot study that I conducted in collaboration with Paul Ekman, we were able to demonstrate this phenomenon empirically. The effects of a systematic innervation of particular facial action units (AUs: in this case, AUs 18 and 20, see Ekman & Friesen, 1978) are clearly visible in the spectrum of the stationary schwa-like vowel that was produced simultaneously. For example, AU 18 (lip pucker) tends to increase the relative energy in the lower frequency range (below 500 Hz), whereas AU 20 (lip stretch) tends to increase relative energy of the upper frequency partials (Scherer, 1985a, p. 14; see Scherer, 1989b, for details concerning the acoustic parameters involved).

However, the reverse can also hold, that is, the signalling function of the vocalization might have shaped the accompanying facial expression. Ohala (1980) argued that the facial features of the smile might have been determined by the requirements of the production of vocalizations with higher pitch and particular spectral characteristics on the shape of the upper vocal tract. In this case the desired acoustic form "pulls" the facial musculature into the required shape. Another example of such pull effects is the possibility that a sound is produced because of its acoustic transmission characteristics. An example of this would be the hiss sound "ssss!" used in a number of cultures to attract the attention of another person without having to be greatly disturbing to others (e.g., to call a waiter in a crowded restaurant). The noise-like hiss has acoustical attributes (e.g., the distribution of energy over the frequency range) that are especially suitable for sound transmission in this situation.

The push–pull distinction implies that biological marking (push) is directly externalized in motor expression, whereas pull effects (based on sociocultural norms or desirable, esteemed reference persons) will require the shaping of the expression to conform to these models. Given that the underlying biological processes are likely to be dependent on both the idiosyncratic nature of the individual and the specific nature of the situation, we would expect relatively strong interindividual differences in the expressive patterns resulting from push effects. This is not the case for pull effects. Here, because of the very nature of the models that pull the expression, we would expect a very high degree of symbolization and conventionalization, in other words comparatively few and small individual differences. With respect to cross-cultural comparison, we would expect the opposite: very few differences between cultures for push effects, large differences for pull effects.

I suggest using the term *affect bursts* for the extreme push pole of the dimension or continuum suggested above, that is, those behavior elements that are almost exclusively determined by the effects of physiological changes and that are therefore highly synchronized (with a graduated onset, following the sequential cumulative model), and barely conventionalized in form. In consequence, their occurrence should be quite universal, but their form should be variable over individuals and situations. I suggest using *affect emblem* (based on Efron, 1941/1973, and Ekman & Friesen, 1969, 1972) as the term for the extreme pull pole, brief facial/vocal expressions that are almost exclusively determined by sociocultural norms or models and that in consequence show a high degree of conventionality (with a simultaneous onset of all components and very little real synchronization among them).

Between these two extremes, we would expect a large number of intermediate cases, that is, nonverbal facial/vocal expressions that are triggered by a particular affect-arousing event and that show at least some degree of componential synchronization, but are at the same time subject to shaping by pull effects, as evident in control and regulation attempts. It is difficult to give examples of these different types on paper. But we can again use the example of the black, hairy worm crawling out of the oyster shell. An affect burst would be the spontaneously triggered production of a nature sound of disgust accompanied by a rapid turning of the head away from it and a facial expression likely to help avoid further visual or olfactory exposure to the stimulus. An affect emblem is most likely to occur in a narrative concerning this event where a person may talk about the black worm by producing a highly culturally standardized vocalization, such as "yuck" in the United States or "igittigitt" in Germany (or "burck" in French) and a conventionalized disgust face. In this case, it is unlikely that the facial, vocal, and gestural modalities are highly integrated or synchronized (with respect to onset, duration, intensity, or covariation of the various components) as predicted by a sequential-cumulative model.

Affect emblems constitute an especially fertile ground for examining how behavior that originated as spontaneous affect bursts acquired shared, symbolic character. Without attempting to deal with the precarious terminological problems in this area, some of the requirements that allow us to designate a brief facial/vocal expression unit as a culturally accepted affect emblem as part of a culturally shared code will be discussed here.

According to Ekman and his collaborators, the following requirements must be met before a particular instance of behavior can be counted as a visual emblem: (a) it must have a verbal "translation" consisting of one or two words or an expression; (b) all or nearly all of the members of a group, class, subculture, or culture must know its meaning; (c) it must be used consciously with the intention of conveying a particular item of information to another person; (d) the receiver must know the meaning of the emblem and generally understand why the sender has used it; and (e) the sender generally assumes responsibility for the production of the emblem.

Unfortunately, these criteria, developed for the definition of visual emblems, cannot be directly applied to facial/vocal affect emblems. The difficulties concerning the postulate of intentionality have already been mentioned. In addition, most affect emblems designate an emotional state that, as such, is extremely difficult to verbalize, whereas gestures signify actions or relatively clear states or intentions. Furthermore, there are many more gradations and varieties to differentiate when designating states of affect (e.g., an "oh" of simulated surprise with a slightly aggressive undertone) than is true of the various meanings of visual emblems, which seem to refer to broader, more unequivocal meanings (e.g., "OK," "I am hungry," "He's crazy," "Give me a lift," etc.). In consequence, the requirements for the precise verbal transcription of a vocal emblem need to be defined differently. Moreover, whereas visual emblems can sometimes even be group specific, one has to assume (in view of the fact that affect emblems are seen to have developed out of universal affect bursts) that all members of a language community—if not perhaps even those outside of this group—are able to understand their meaning.

Ekman's requirement that the producer of an emblem must always acknowledge its production seems to apply to affect emblems only to a limited extent. On the contrary, it seems to be one of the great advantages of using affect emblems, that it is easily possible to deny having intended to convey a particular meaning if challenged to account its production. Thus a slight cough or clearing one's throat (possibly accompanied by a wink or eyebrow flash) for demonstrative purposes (to draw the attention of a third person to one's disbelief in a statement of a speaker) can very easily be explained away (as the beginning of a cold) in order to get out of a sticky situation (such as being accused of derogating the speaker). We have suggested earlier that one of the great advantages of using nonverbal behavior is precisely its "negotiability" (see Scherer & Scherer, 1981). This shows clearly the problems involved in postulating emblematic characteristics of a type of behavior that can represent at the same time physiologically conditioned vocalizations and culturally defined conventional symbols of a nonlinguistic nature (cf. excusing cough).

Another central criterion for identifying a certain instance of behavior as a gestural emblem, the independence of its meaning from a given context, does not seem to apply to affect emblems. On the contrary, the meaning of affect emblems can be modified by the context (which is probably also true for some visual emblems). For example, changes in the facial expression accompanying a specific vocalization can reverse its normally associated meaning into the exact opposite (which may be the information actually intended) or at least give this impression. An example would be the production of a surprise emblem like "oh" inserted in a broad smile that may well communicate that the sender feigns surprise in a mocking fashion—having brought about the effect him/herself.

Similarly, the situational context can change the meaning of affect emblems. The emblematic production of exaggerated groaning, screaming, booing, belching, and yawning in obviously unsuitable situations can convey a message or induce a shift in significance (as could be observed rather frequently in university seminars or meetings during the so-called student revolution).

SPONTANEOUS EXPRESSION
VERSUS INTENTIONAL COMMUNICATION

Earlier I argued that the distinction made in the literature between reflexively uttered nature sounds (*Naturlaute*) in the process of emotional expression and intentionally used interjections for informative and communicative purposes is highly problematic (Scherer, 1977). As in other areas of behavior, it seems impossible to clearly distinguish between spontaneous or reflexive behavior on the one hand and deliberate or intentional behavior on the other. Even if an "aghghgh" is uttered as a reflexive reaction to pain, a person can, in uttering it in the presence of others, either reduce, suppress, or otherwise modify it to hide his suffering or intensify or amplify it to stir up compassion. On the other hand, there are a number of conventionalized affect emblems that are so highly overlearned and clearly attached to certain affect situations that they occur quite spontaneously in the respective situation, without the explicit intention of informing anyone (like "ouch"). Even when there are no listeners present, a speaker's affect burst is not necessarily purely reflexive because his or her behavior can be determined by the character of the self presentation or the role adopted (see Goffman, 1978, for an analysis of the social embedding of self talk).

It is not likely to be disputed that under certain conditions affect bursts are uttered relatively spontaneously and without prior consideration, whereas at other times the production of a facial/vocal expression is obviously planned in advance for definite communicative purposes. However, the distinction between these ideal types constitutes one of the most controversial issues in the field of communication research. It is essential to distinguish between the receiver's information processing and the transmitter's intended communication (see MacKay, 1972). There is little reason to assume, however, that a certain class of expressions is always uttered reflexively, whereas another is always used intentionally. Instead, the majority of human expressions (perhaps with the exception of unbearable pain) is presumably monitored by the central nervous system involving control structures that can suppress, modify, or amplify the behavior. Therefore, it makes little sense to differentiate between reflexive and intentional types of expressions. The problem of intentionality becomes even more complicated if one examines affect bursts or emblems with respect to their occurrence in "repair" situations, that is, in the attempt to cover up or to reassert oneself as a competent social actor after having committed a blunder. Erving Goffman (1978) provided a very perceptive analysis of the use of affect vocalizations in such situations. For example, uttering the pitch-drop "oh-oh" with an apologetic facial expression after having unwittingly insulted a member of the company, at least reestablishes one as a person able to recognize blunders after having committed them.

How can the anchoring of affect bursts in a theory of emotion help to investigate the difference between the spontaneous and the deliberate production of an affect burst? One of the fundamental characteristics of an emotional episode in the definition I propose is the synchronization of the different components in the organism's effort to recruit as much energy as possible to master a major crisis situation (in a positive or negative sense). Such a synchronization, which detracts from the normal functioning of the subsystems, is costly and would only occur in situations that justify this expenditure.[3]

---

[3]This is why I have suggested to define *stress* as an abnormally long and intense emotion synchronization (see Scherer, 1986b; Wallbott & Scherer, 1991).

A direct consequence of this assumption is that the symbolic representation of an emotion—which is basically what happens in an affect emblem—is unlikely to involve a complete synchronization of all important systems (because that would be too costly). More likely, only the activation of some of the more visible markers of bona fide emotion synchronizations, particularly the motor expression channels will be observed. Thus, we would expect little synchronization between expressive and physiological change for feigned, faked, or symbolically represented emotions, including affect emblems.[4]

A second corollary of this position would be that even when there is an attempt to fake synchronization and integration of different components, it will be artificial and less perfect than real synchronization. For example, one might assume that the attempt to synchronize facial and vocal expression intentionally will be different from natural synchronization with respect to onset duration, intensity, and other dynamic characteristics (see also the role of symmetry in facial expression, Ekman, Hager, & Friesen, 1981). This also concerns the sequential and cumulative nature of the synchronization process as predicted by the component process model (see Scherer, 1993). If the model is correct, one would expect a sequential cumulation of individual features of the respective expression patterns in the process of synchronization. If the expression is faked, one would expect a simultaneous onset of all subparts of the total pattern in terms of an integrated motor command.

A PLEA FOR EMPIRICAL RESEARCH
ON AFFECT BURSTS

I end this chapter with a plea for increased research activity on affect bursts and affect emblems as different types of brief, discrete, integrated, nonverbal facial/vocal expressions. I am convinced that a better understanding of these phenomena would greatly help in tackling the much more complicated issues we face in trying to understand facial/vocal expression integration in interactive speech behavior. Before starting extensive empirical projects, we need to better understand the functions of such affect bursts. In this, we might be aided by a comparative approach, looking at similar affect displays across many different species. Of particular importance is a better understanding of their functional origins, as mentioned above. What we would need, for example, is a more satisfactory understanding of the links between sensory intake and stimulus processing and the activity of the striated musculature involved in facial and

---

[4]The acting out of emotion in the theater is a fascinating issue in this respect; one might argue that Stanislavski tried to push his actors to an extremely costly form of emotion faking by asking them to produce as much synchronization as possible of the various subsystems in the sense of actually experiencing the emotion to be portrayed on stage.

vocal expression. Similarly, we need to have a clearer notion of the relationship between expressive patterns and action tendencies or rudimentary behavior patterns as adaptive reactions to specific event evaluations (see Frijda, 1987).

It would also be helpful to have a better understanding of the neurophysiological substratum of both push and pull effects. For example, with respect to vocal phenomena, it would be important to investigate some of the speculations concerning the relationship between physiological arousal and respiratory, phonatory, and articulatory phenomena. In the past (Scherer, 1986a), I have attempted to piece together the evidence from many different sources in the literature. Many of the difficulties I had in doing this stem from the rather wide differences in the interests of the disciplines concerned with this truly interdisciplinary phenomenon. For example, many physiologically oriented phoneticians are exclusively interested in vocal pathology. Researchers in acoustic phonetics are mostly interested in speech comprehension and production by computers or in the phonemic structure of the language system. Most emotion psychologists limit their interest to expression in the face. Without truly interdisciplinary work in this area, we have little hope of making progress. In a similar vein, the study of pull effects based on sociocultural models for appropriate affect vocalizations should be one of the concerns in the field of semiotics. So far, few attempts have been made in this direction (but see Poggi, 1981). Given the social significance of affect emblems in social interaction, one would also expect contributions from anthropology, sociology, and social psychology. However, apart from the major contribution by Goffman (1978), little of relevance can be found.

The lack of pertinent research on the type of expressive behavior described here may be explicable in part by one of the fundamental problems of research on emotion: the difficulty of having access to naturally occurring emotion situations, including affect bursts. However, following the examples from studies on emotional expression in general (see Frijda, 1969; Scherer, Banse, Wallbott, & Goldbeck, 1991; Wallbott & Scherer, 1986), one might modestly start with portrayals of affect bursts and affect emblems. Although this would be the natural production condition for affect emblems that one should be able to study perfectly in a laboratory setting, the demand to produce spontaneous affect bursts can only be an approximation to realistic recording of such events. However, it might be possible to obtain some first insight into the differences by manipulating the eliciting conditions and the context given to participants.

With respect to the methodology for studying the patterns, the intensity, and the synchronization of the behaviors produced in such a way, we are now in good shape. Appropriate and affordable techniques for the analysis of facial expression by facial electromyography (EMG, see Cacioppo et al., 1988; Fridlund & Izard, 1983) or coding from videotape (via FACS, Ekman & Friesen, 1978) and vocal expression (see Scherer, 1988b) are now available, accessible, and feasible.

I have started to conduct pilot studies on affect vocalizations (e.g., by interviewing members of many different cultures and by asking for the systematic portrayal of major types of affect bursts and affect emblems). The experience gained from these pilot studies has strongly impressed on me the need to tackle this research area in a cross-culturally comparative fashion. For example, learning that in some African tribes the affect emblems used vary depending on the sex or the age of the addressee, demonstrated the enormous complexity of this signalling system. A comprehensive cross-culturally comparative approach is imperative if we want to even begin to understand the complex interrelationship between push and pull factors in the production of vocal/facial affect expressions.

In conclusion, I want to stress the positive effect that growing concern with the empirical investigation of affect bursts could have on the field of emotion research. To begin with, the very nature of the phenomenon requires integrative research approaches involving the assessment of all components of emotion. Even though this paper emphasized facial and vocal expression, one should also assess antecedent cognitive or subcognitive appraisal, autonomic response patterning, motivational or action tendencies, and subjective feeling state. In line with the definition of emotion as a synchronization of all organismic subsystems (as presented earlier), all response modalities need to be studied to understand the special nature of affect bursts as an interruption of normal functioning, however brief. The clear temporal delimitation or bondedness of affect bursts make them easier to study in comparison to longer emotional states where the endings are often difficult to determine (see Frijda, Mesquita, Sonnemans, & van Goozen, 1991). The need to study simultaneously all components of an emotional episode, which requires collaboration of researchers specialized in the study of different response modalities, could help to break up the splendid isolation with which much emotion research is confined to a single aspect of the multicomponential phenomenon of emotion.

Such collaboration would greatly advance the development of emotion theory, which is currently endangered by somewhat pointless controversies between theorists whose outlook is at times too much affected by the respective response domain their empirical work specializes in. Research on affect bursts could also combat a tendency in some psychological subdisciplines, like social psychology, where emotion research is increasingly limited to studies on rather general positive or negative affect states or moods. While defying measurement with semantic differential scales, affect bursts illustrate the nature of emotion as characteristic biological, psychological, and social adaptations—marked and differentiated by appropriate action tendencies, as Nico Frijda's (1986, 1987) seminal work has so cogently shown.

ACKNOWLEDGMENTS

This chapter is dedicated to Nico Frijda, whose mostly spontaneous affect bursts in our many interactions have been a constant source of delight. More importantly, Nico Frijda has strongly influenced many of the views expressed in this chapter and has contributed valuable advice to my attempt at developing the notion that the face expresses emotion and cognition.

I gratefully acknowledge major contributions to the preparation of this chapter by Ursula Scherer.

REFERENCES

Bargh, J. A. (1984). Automatic and conscious processing of social information. In R. S. Wyer, Jr. & T. K. Srull (Eds.), *Handbook of social cognition* (Vol. 3, pp. 1–44). Hillsdale, NJ: Lawrence Erlbaum Associates.

Buck, R. (1985). Prime theory: An integrated view of motivation and emotion. *Psychological Review, 92,* 389–413.

Bühler, K. (1984). *Sprachtheorie* [Theory of language]. Jena: Germany. Fischer. (Original work published in 1934)

Cacioppo, J. T., Martzke, J. S., Petty, R. E., & Tassinary, L. G. (1988). Specific forms of facial EMG response index emotions during an interview: From Darwin to the continuous flow hypothesis of affect-laden information processing. *Journal of Personality and Social Psychology, 54,* 592–604.

Chevalier-Skolnikoff, S. (1973). Facial expression of emotion in nonhuman primates. In P. Ekman (Ed.), *Darwin and facial expression* (pp. 11–89). New York: Academic Press.

Cutler, A., & Ladd, D. R. (Eds.) (1983). *Prosody: Models and measurements.* Berlin: Springer.

Darwin, C. (1965). *The expression of the emotions in man and animals.* Chicago: University of Chicago Press. (Original work published in 1872)

de Sanctis, S. (1904). *La mimica del pensiero* [Facial expression of thought processes]. Milano: Sandron.

Dittman, A. T. (1972). The body movement-speech rhythm relationship as a cue to speech encoding. In A. Siegman & B. Pope (Eds.), *Studies in dyadic communication* (pp. 135–151). New York: Pergamon.

Duchenne, G. B. (1876). *Méchanisme de la physionomie humaine Ou Analyse électrophysiologique de l'expression des passions.* Paris: Baillière (English edition: The mechanism of human facial expression. Edited and translated by R. A. Cuthbertson. Cambridge and New York: Cambridge University Press, 1990).

Duncan, S. D., Jr. (1972). Some signals and rules for taking turns in conversations. *Journal of Personality and Social Psychology, 23,* 283–292.

Efron, D. (1973). *Gesture, race, and culture.* The Hague: Mouton. (Original work published 1941)

Eibl-Eibesfeldt, I. (1984). *Die Biologie des menschlichen Verhaltens. Grundriss der Humanethologie* [The biology of human behavior. A primer of human ethology]. Munich: Piper.

Ekman, P. (1972). Universals and cultural differences in facial expression of emotion. In J. R. Cole (Ed.), *Nebraska Symposium on Motivation* (pp. 207–283). Lincoln: University of Nebraska Press.

Ekman, P. (1979). About brows: Emotional and conversational signals. In M. von Cranach, K. Foppa, W. Lepenies, & D. Ploog (Eds.), *Human etthology* (pp. 169–249). Cambridge: Cambridge University Press.

Ekman, P., & Friesen, W. V. (1969). The repertoire of nonverbal behavior: Categories, origins, usage, and coding. *Semiotica, 1,* 49–98.

Ekman, P., & Friesen, M. V. (1972). Hand movements. *Journal of Communication, 22,* 353–374.

Ekman, P., & Friesen, W. V. (1978). *The Facial Action Coding System: A technique for the measurement of facial movement.* Palo Alto, CA: Consulting Psychologists Press.

Ekman, P., Friesen, W. V., & Ancoli, S. (1980). Facial signs of emotional experience. *Journal of Personality and Social Psychology, 39,* 1125–1134.

Ekman, P., Friesen, W. V., O'Sullivan, M., & Scherer, K. R. (1980). Relative importance of face, body, and speech in judgments of personality and affect. *Journal of Personality and Social Psychology, 38,* 270–277.

Ekman, P., Hager, J. C., & Friesen, W. V. (1981). The symmetry of emotional and deliberate facial actions. *Psychophysiology, 18,* 101–106.

Elias, N. (1977). *Der Prozeß der Zivilisation* [The civilizing process]. Frankfurt: Suhrkamp.

Fridlund, A. J. (1991). Sociality of solitary smiling: Potentiation by an implicit audience. *Journal of Personality and Social Psychology, 60,* 229–240.

Fridlund, A. J., & Izard, C. E. (1983). Electromyographic studies of facial expressions of emotions and patterns of emotions. In J. T. Cacioppo & R. E. Petty (Eds.), *Social psychophysiology: A source-book* (pp. 243–286). New York: Plenum.

Frijda, N. H. (1969). Recognition of emotion. In L. Berkowitz (Ed.), *Advances in experimental social psychology. Vol. 4* (pp. 196–223). New York: Academic Press.

Frijda, N. (1986). *The emotions.* Cambridge and New York: Cambridge University Press.

Frijda, N. (1987). Emotion. Cognitive structure and action readiness. *Cognition and Emotion, 1,* 115–143.

Frijda, N., Mesquita, B., Sonnemans, J., & van Goozen, S. (1991). The duration of affective phenomena or emotions, sentiments, and passions. In K. T. Strongman (Ed.), *International Review of Studies on Emotion* (Vol. 1, pp. 187–226). Chichester: Wiley.

Gellhorn, E. (1970). The emotions and the ergotropic and trophotropic systems. *Psychologische Forschung 34,* 48–94.

Goffman, E. (1978). Response cries. *Language, 54,* 787–815.

Goffman, E. (1979). Response cries. In M. von Cranach, K. Foppa, W. Lepenies, & D. Ploog (Eds.), *Human ethology* (pp. 203–240). Cambridge: Cambridge University Press.

Goldman-Eisler, F. (1968). *Psycholinguistics. Experiments in spontaneous speech.* New York:

Hager, J. C., & Ekman, P. (1979). Long distance transmission of facial affect signals. *Ethology and Sociobiology, 1,* 77–82.

Haggard, E. A., & Isaacs, K. S. (1966). Micromomentary facial expressions as indicators of ego mechanisms in psychotherapy. In L. A. Gottschalk, & A. H. Auerbach (Eds.), *Methods of research in psychotherapy* (pp. 154–165). New York: Appleton-Century-Crofts.

Izard, C. E. (1971). *The face of emotion.* New York: Appleton-Century-Crofts.

Izard, C. E. (1977). *Human emotions.* New York: Plenum.

James, D. (1974). *The syntax and semantics of some English interjections.* Papers in Linguistics, Vol. 1, p. 3. University of Michigan, Ann Arbor.

Kainz, F. (1962). *Psychologie der Sprache. I. Band. Grundlagen der allgemeinen Sprachpsychologie* [Psychology of language. Vol. 1. Fundamentals of a general psychology of language] (3rd ed.). Stuttgart: Enke

Key, M. R. (1975). *Paralanguage and kinesics.* Metuchen, NJ: Scarecrow Press.

Kleinpaul, R. (1888). *Sprache ohne Worte. Idee einer allgemeinen Wissenschaft der Sprache* [Language without words. Outline of a general science of language] Leipzig (New printing The Hague: Mouton, 1972).

Leyhausen, P. (1967). Biologie von Ausdruck und Eindruck (Teil 1) [Biology of expression and impression. Part 1]. *Psychologische Forschung, 31,* 113–176.

Lipps, T. (1907). Das Wissen von fremden Ichen. [Knowing other selves]. In T. Lipps (Eds.), *Psychologische Untersuchungen. Band 1* [Psychological investigations. Vol. 1]. Leipzig: Engelmann.

MacKay, D. M. (1972). Formal analysis of communicative processes. In R. A. Hinde (Ed.), *Nonverbal communication* (pp. 3–26). Cambridge, England: Cambridge University Press.

Marler, P., & Tenaza, R. (1977). Signaling behavior of apes with special reference to vocalization. In T. A. Sebeok (Ed.), *How animals communicate* (pp. 965–1033). Bloomington, IN: Indiana University Press.

Morton, E. S. (1977). On the occurrence and significance of motivational-structural rules in some bird and mammal sounds. *American Naturalist, 111,* 855–869.

Ohala, J. J. (1980). The acoustic origin of the smile. *Journal of the Acoustic Society of America, 68,* 33 (Abstract).

Poggi, I. (1981). *Le interiezoni: Studio del linguaggio e analisi della mente* [Interjections: Study of language and analysis of mind]. Torino: Boringhieri.

Redican, W. K. (1982). An evolutionary perspective on human facial displays. In P. Ekman (Ed.), *Emotion in the human face* (2nd ed.). New York: Cambridge University Press.

Scherer, K. R. (1977). Affektlaute und vokale Embleme [Affect vocalizations and vocal emblems]. In R. Posner & H. P. Reinecke (Eds.), *Zeichenprozesse: Semiotische Forschung in den Einzelwissenschaften* [Sign processes: Semiotic research in individual disciplines] (pp. 199–214). Wiesbaden: Athenaion.

Scherer, K. R. (1979). Non-linguistic indicators of emotion and psychopathology. In C. E. Izard (Ed.), *Emotions in personality and psychopathology* (pp. 495–529). New York: Plenum Press.

Scherer, K. R. (1980). The functions of nonverbal signs in conversation. In R. St.Clair & H. Giles (Eds.), *The social and the psychological contexts of language* (pp. 225–244). Hillsdale, NJ: Lawrence Erlbaum Associates.

Scherer, K. R. (1984). On the nature and function of emotion: A component process approach. In K. R. Scherer & P. Ekman (Hrsg.), *Approaches to emotion* (pp. 293–318). Hillsdale, NJ: Lawrence Erlbaum Associates.

Scherer, K. R. (1985a). Pragmatische Bedeutungskomponenten von Intonationskonturen. [Pragmatic components of meaning in intonation] Arbeitsbericht an die Deutsche Forschungsgemeinschaft. Unpublished Research Report, University of Giessen.

Scherer, K. R. (1985b). Vocal affect signalling: A comparative approach. In J. Rosenblatt, C. Beer, M.-C. Busnel, & P.J.B. Slater (Eds.), *Advances in the study of behavior: Vol. 15.* (pp. 189–244). New York: Academic Press.

Scherer, K. R. (1986a). Vocal affect expression: A review and a model for future research. *Psychological Bulletin, 99,* 143–165.

Scherer, K. R. (1986b). Voice, stress, and emotion. In M. H. Appley & R. Trumbull (Eds.), *Dynamics of stress* (pp. 159–181). New York: Plenum.

Scherer, K. R. (1988a). Criteria for emotion-antecedent appraisal: A review. In V. Hamilton, G. H. Bower, & N. H. Frijda (Eds.), *Cognitive perspectives on emotion and motivation* (pp. 89–126). Dordrecht: Kluwer.

Scherer, K. R. (1988b). On the symbolic functions of vocal affect expression. *Journal of Language and Social Psychology, 7,* 79–100.

Scherer, K. R. (1989a). Affektausdruck als Indiz mentaler Prozese: Ein neues Paradigma für die Kognitionsforschung [Affect expression as index of mental processes: A new paradigm for cognitive research]. In W. Schönpflug (Eds.), *Bericht über den 36. Kongreß der Deutschen Gesellschaft für Psychologie in Berlin 1988* [Proceedings of the 36th Congress of the German Society for Psychology] Volume 2, (pp. 344–353). Göttingen: Hogrefe.

Scherer, K. R. (1989b). Vocal correlates of emotion. In H. Wagner & A. Manstead (Eds.), *Handbook of psychophysiology: Emotion and social behavior* (pp. 165–197). London: Wiley.

Scherer, K. R. (1992). What does facial expression express? In K. Strongman (Ed.), *International Review of Studies on Emotion* (Vol. 2, pp. 139–165). Chichester: Wiley.

Scherer, K. R. (1993). Neuroscience projections to current debates in emotion psychology. *Cognition and Emotion, 7,* 1–41.

Scherer, K. R., Banse, R., Wallbott, H. G., & Ellgring, H. (in prep.). The facial and vocal expression of emotion in actors. Manuscript in preparation.

Scherer, K. R., Banse, R., Wallbott, H. G., & Goldbeck, T. (1991). Vocal cues in emotion encoding and decoding. *Motivation and Emotion, 15,* 123–148.

Scherer, K. R., & Giles, H. (Eds.). (1979). *Social markers in speech*. Cambridge: Cambridge University Press.

Scherer, K. R., & Kappas, A. (1988). Primate vocal expression of affective state. In D. Todt, P. Goedeking, & D. Symmes (Eds.), *Primate vocal communication* (pp. 171–194). Berlin: Springer.

Scherer, K. R., Rosenthal, R., & Koivumaki, J. (1972). Mediating interpersonal expectancies via vocal cues: Differential speech intensity as a means of social influence. *European Journal of Social Psychology, 2,* 163–176.

Scherer, K. R., & Scherer, U. (1981). Nonverbal behavior and impression formation in naturalistic situations. In H. Hiebsch, H. Brandstätter, & H. H. Kelley (Eds.), *Proceedings of the XXIInd International Congress of Psychology,* Leipzig, 1980, *Social Psychology*. Amsterdam: North Holland.

Scherer, K. R., & Wallbott, H. G. (1985). Analysis of nonverbal behavior. In T. A. van Dijk (Ed.), *Handbook of discourse analysis* (Vol. 2, pp. 199–230). London: Academic Press.

Scherer, U. (1990). *Sprechakte als Interaktionsverhalten* [Speech acts as interaction behavior]. Hamburg: Buske.

Scherer, U., Helfrich, H., & Scherer, K. R. (1980). Internal push or external pull? Determinants of paralinguistic behaviour. In H. Giles, P. Robinson, & P. Smith (Eds.), *Language: Social psychological perspectives* (pp. 279–282). Oxford: Pergamon.

Schneider, K., & Dittrich, W. (1990). Evolution und Funktion von Emotionen [Evolution and function of emotion]. In K. R. Scherer (Ed.), *Encyclopädie der Psychologie. Band Emotion* [Encyclopedia of emotion. Volume Emotion] (pp. 41–114). Göttingen: Hogrefe.

Smith, C. A. (1989). Dimensions of appraisal and physiological response in emotion. *Journal of Personality and Social Psychology, 56,* 339–353.

Tembrock, G. (1975). Die Erforschung des tierlichen Stimmausdrucks (Bioakustik) [The study of animal vocalization. Bioacoustics] In F. Trojan (Ed.), *Biophonetik*. Mannheim: Bibliographisches Institut.

Tomkins, S. S. (1962). *Affect, imagery, consciousness. Vol. 1. The positive affects*. New York: Springer.

Tomkins, S. S. (1963). *Affect, imagery, consciousness. Vol. 2. The negative affects*. New York: Springer.

Tomkins, S. S. (1984). Affect theory. In, K. R. Scherer & P. Ekman (Eds.), *Approaches to emotion* (pp. 163–196). Hillsdale, NJ: Lawrence Erlbaum Associates.

Trojan, F. (1975). *Biophonetik*. Mannheim: Bibliographisches Institut.

van Hooff, J.A.R.A.M. (1972). A comparative approach to the phylogeny of laughter and smiling. In R. A. Hinde (Ed.), *Nonverbal communication* (pp. 209–37). Cambridge, England: Cambridge University Press.

Wallbott, H. G., & Scherer, K. R. (1986). Cues and channels in emotion recognition. *Journal of Personality and Social Psychology, 51,* 690–699.

Wallbott, H . G., & Scherer, K. R. (1991). Stress specificities: Differential effects of coping style, gender, and type of stressor on autonomic arousal, facial expression, and subjective feeling. *Journal of Personality and Social Psychology, 61,* 147–156.

Wundt, W. (1900). *Völkerpsychologie. Eine Untersuchung der Entwicklungsgesetze von Sprache, Mythos and Sitte. Band I. Die Sprache* [Ethnopsychology: A study of the evolutionary principles of language, myth, and norms. Vol. 1. Language]. Leipzig: Kröner.

III

SOCIAL INTERACTION AND EMOTIONS

7 Social Homeostasis and the Regulation of Emotion

Jan A.R.A.M. van Hooff
Filippo Aureli
Universiteit Utrecht

Some titles of books have become classics in their own right. *The expression of emotions in animals and man* of 1872 is one of them. In this ground-breaking work the great evolutionary biologist Charles Darwin categorized emotional expression from a comparative and evolutionary perspective. Since then emotions have figured prominently in human psychology as a subject of interest. By contrast the term has hardly occurred in ethological texts (*cf.* McNaughton, 1989). Students of animal behavior have rarely referred to emotions, obviously because these have traditionally been described in terms of subjective experiences. Ethologists have tended to avoid the use of such intervening variables in attempting to relate behavioral sequential contingencies directly to contextual contingencies. Accordingly characterizations of expressive states have preferably been put in terms of behavioral tendencies and their motivating factors. This is not to imply that there are no behavioral manifestations in nonhuman species that are not analogous or even homologous to emotional expression. It is the great merit of Frijda (1986) that he has presented a perspective on emotions and emotional behavior that integrates the different views and approaches, psychological, comparative and evolutionary, and physiological that have been developed concerning emotional behavior and its underlying mechanisms.

In the comparative study of animal behavior the entrance to the phenomenon of emotional behavior has been the occurrence of so-called displays. These were interpreted as ritualized movements and postures, the form of which has been specialized for a communicative function. In as far as certain movements or postures are informative to conspecifics or even animals of other species, and in as far as such information leads to changes in the behavior of these receivers that benefit the fitness of the sender, natural selection will operate to adapt the

197

informative behavior elements. By the exaggeration of frequency and intensity characteristics, by their stylization, and by development of special supportive structures of form and color, the informative elements are made conspicuous and unambiguous.

As sources of the derivation of displays have been recognized, first, intention movements and intention postures of behaviors near the threshold of actual release; second, ambivalent or compromise movements and postures that are due to a conflict of simultaneously aroused but incompatible behavior tendencies, and, third, the autonomous processes associated with all these. In their non-ritualized form the processes merely are the ethophysiological anticipation of the necessity of certain forms of action. They reflect the way the animal has evaluated its situation, a process that involves cognitive interpretation, in that the animal assesses its actual state and probabilities of the development of the latter on the basis of previous experience. It furthermore involves the appreciation of the situation in terms of the animal's needs and the consequent choices of its behavioral priorities. Roughly speaking, it is at the moment when this evaluation is done, when choices from alternative action courses and coping strategies have to be made, when a choice has to be carried into a decision of action, that an action tendency and the preparatory postural and physiological activation for it take place that we recognize as emotional behavior (cf. Frijda, 1986; Schachter & Singer, 1962; Wiepkema & Koolhaas, 1992).

In most animals an array of ritualized expressions can be distinguished that refer to certain behavioral probabilities. Darwin (1872) already undertook to categorize these. More recent comparative studies of the expression movements of primates and man have confirmed that there is, across these species, a set of basic emotional dimensions, and that there is evolutionary continuity both with respect to this contextual and motivational categorization and the respective behavioral morphology (Frijda, 1986; van Hooff, 1972, 1976). Ethologists have emphasized communicative aspects of expressive behavior. As Frijda pointed out communication can mean different things. In the broadest sense it can mean that processes in one system influence those in another. This includes unintended transmission of information. When, however, the transmission is intended this can be interpreted in two ways that do not exclude one another.

First, the sending system may regulate its display in such a way that it modulates its displaying in interaction with feed-back information concerning its effects; it aims at influencing a receiver in a certain way. Many of the displays we use have this communicative intent. Certainly in higher animals we can recognize the same, namely when displays are emphatically directed at a certain partner and when the reactions of this partner immediately modulate the display. This is likely in many manifestations of threat, submission, courting, and the like. Other forms of emotional communication do not have this form, in particular in those cases where the expression is not directed at any one receiver in particular; in our species we can occasionally notice that the effects generated by emotional displays are embarrassing to the sending subject, for example, when blushing or yawning. Nevertheless some of these may nevertheless be regarded as evolutionarily adaptive displays. That is, natural selection has led to the development of ritualized displays, the particular form and dynamics of which have evolved, because they led to adjustments in the behavior of respondents that benefitted the fitness of the sender.

An interesting example is the behavior of yawning. Analysis of the temporal patterning of yawning has confirmed the folk wisdom that in our own species it is associated, as is stretching (Provine, Hamernik, & Churchak, 1987), with drowsiness and boredom. It differs from stretching in that it occurs both in the pre- and the postsleeping phase, whereas stretching occurs primarily in the postsleeping stage. One of the most curious features of yawning is its high degree of social infectiousness, suggesting that it has been ritualized as a signal, possibly synchronizing states of rest taking (Provine, 1986). Students of primate behavior have reported yawning to occur in states of fatigue, drowsiness, stress, uneasiness, and tension (e.g., Hinde & Rowell, 1962; Redican, 1975). In some cercopithecines, notably in macaques and baboons, exposure of the canines during yawning is assumed to be a signal of threat, because it signals an uneasiness that in dominant animals spells danger (e.g., Bertrand, 1969; see Schino & Aureli, 1989, for a review; Darwin, 1872; Hall & DeVore, 1965). Altmann (1967) distinguished three kinds of yawns: (a) the "true" yawn of drowsiness, (b) the conflict yawn, shown in anxiety-producing situations, and (c) the semantic yawn, as a show of weaponry. Hadidian (1980) analyzed the occurrence and the age–sex distribution of yawning in a macaque species. The situations ranged from drowsiness to tension. In the later there was a temporal association with male aggressiveness, although the display itself did not release immediate responses on the part of recipients. Remarkably, the performance of the display

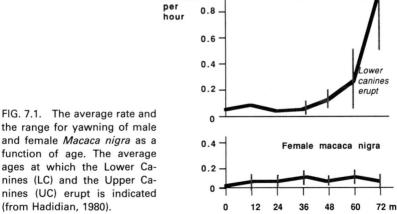

FIG. 7.1. The average rate and the range for yawning of male and female *Macaca nigra* as a function of age. The average ages at which the Lower Canines (LC) and the Upper Canines (UC) erupt is indicated (from Hadidian, 1980).

showed a strong sexual dimorphism (cf. Troisi, Aureli, Schino et al., 1990). When males grew to adults they began to show yawns with a comparatively high frequency (Fig. 7.1). In a chimpanzee community yawning was shown particularly by the dominant group members (te Boekhorst, de Weerth, & van Hooff, 1991). The fact that there is no evidence for a similar sex-age-status differentiation in yawning in the human species (Provine *loc.cit.;* Schino & Aureli, 1989) suggests that there are interspecific differences in the degree of evolutionary ritualization of this response, even though the response itself appears to be unintended and autonomic in probably all species.

In this presentation we focus our attention on behavioral and physiological lindicators of anxious stress and their relation to social processes and social position.

SOCIAL LIVING, DIVERGING
AND CONFLICTING INTERESTS, SOURCES
OF EMOTION

Animals, at least the higher ones, live in communities that vary greatly in the size of their membership, their composition, their cohesion and the patterns of relationships between their members. The organization of such a community, a system of relationships, is the outcome of the interactions of its individual members (Hinde, 1979). With its social behavior each individual tries to shape its social environment in such a way that it can most effectively and efficiently realize the vital functions that determine its fitness. Deductive evolutionary reasoning in combination with socioecological investigations have greatly furthered our insight into the factors that determine the shape of such communities. These show that any given social organization is the result of the interaction of various, sometimes opposed selection pressures and that it necessarily is a compromise in which the benefits of social living are maximized and the unavoidable costs are kept at a minimum (Dunbar, 1988; van Hooff, 1988; van Schaik, 1983).

The benefits and costs of group living, however, differ for different group members. First, animals of different age, sex, and condition often have different needs and run different risks. Correspondingly the importance for them to stay close to conspecifics differs. For a great many species there is now evidence that safety against predators is a major evolutionary reason for social living (e.g., Dunbar, 1988; van Schaik, 1983; van Schaik & van Hooff, 1983). The risks of predation are relatively great for the more vulnerable classes within the society, namely the juveniles that have just about become independent. For these animals it is more important to stay surrounded with conspecifics. By contrast, large adult males may feel more free to attune their group membership at any given time to the likelihood that they will find females there in a reproductive state. These diverging interests exert a centrifugal influence on group life (van Schaik & van Noordwijk, 1986). Similarly there are indications that the sexes differ in their dietary needs in at least some primate species. In wild long-tailed macaques, studied in Sumatra, the males went for carbohydrate loaded fruits more often, whereas the females spent more time on foraging for insects and the like, rich in proteins. This led to temporary separations in the group, because the group members tended to follow their own foraging preferences. Such *diverging interests,* therefore, exerted a centrifugal force on group life (van Schaik & van Noordwijk, 1986).

Second, there are *conflicting interests,* namely when there is competition over scarce resources. If, in addition, such a resource can be monopolized, asymmetries in power will decide who can claim the resource and animals will consequently have an interest in investing in positions of dominance. There are an increasing number of indications that, for instance amongst primate species, the degree to which dominance hierarchies are expressed depends on the degree to which animals of that species can claim exclusive access to important resources such as food. The degree to which such resources can be monopolized depends on their clump size, their quantity, and their pattern of dispersal (van Schaik & van Noordwijk, 1988). Whereas fruits occur often locally concentrated, leafs tend to occur much more evenly dispersed; this might be one reason for the fact that leaf-eating primates tend to have more egalitarian societies than those that subsist to a large extent on fruits.

Both *diverging* and *conflicting* interests exert a dissociating influence on social life. Theoretically such influences should lead to an actual disruption of the social bonds whenever for a certain individual the costs exceed the benefits of its joining or staying in a community. Subordinate animals will suffer *more* from the contests of competition than dominant ones (it is clear that contest is costly in terms of energetics, time budget, and risks of wounding for *both* dominants and subordinates). However, when a subordinate decides that it does not make sense any longer to stay in a group, this might diminish the value of the group also for other members, dominants and other subordinates alike, for instance when such a subordinate contributes to the safety of the group by its vigilance behavior. This means that dominants should restrain their monopolistic and dominating attitudes to prevent that the cost-benefit balance for valued subordinates tips to the negative side. Such balances of mutual interest will undoubtedly determine to what extent a social organization is "despotic" or "egalitarian" (Hand, 1986; van Schaik, 1989; Vehrencamp, 1983). Especially when subordinate group members control commodities that cannot be taken from them by force, or when they can make investments beneficial to others to which they cannot easily be forced, such animals have a power leverage compelling others to make it interesting for such subordinates to stay in the group and render their services by tolerating them or even rewarding them. It is worthwhile to investigate the service and favor systems in animal societies from this point of view (Noë, van Schaik & van Hooff, 1991).

In conclusion, conflicts are part and parcel of animal life. However, it would not be in the interest of the animals concerned if such conflicts were to disrupt bonds that are valuable to these animals in other respects. For instance, individuals in a group may profit from the accumulated safety effect that ensues from each individual's contribution to vigilance behavior (van Schaik, 1983; van Schaik, van Noordwijk, Warsono, & Sutriono, 1983). So it is in the interest of both dominants and subordinates to maintain a social homeostasis. One may, therefore, expect that social mechanisms have evolved by which the social disruption and relational uncertainty caused by these conflicts can be prevented or repaired. We can expect that in particular the loser of a conflict may be in need of such restoration. But also winners may have an interest in convincing losers that they still see the relationship as valuable. In the second part of this paper we will pay attention in particular to the behavior of losers in such a situation.

CONFLICTS AND ANTICIPATORY AROUSAL

In addition to creating a risk for the maintenance of valuable bonds, conflicts of interest are also costly for the contestants in a more direct way. Such conflicts are often settled by agonistic interaction, in the form of actual fighting or the threat of it. Fighting is costly because it involves energetic investment, because it disrupts other maintenance functions, because it detracts from keeping an eye open for dangers, such as predators, and—last but not least—because it may lead to wounding. Since Cannon (1929) we have learned that the energetic investment is shown in certain physiological changes. These comprise an instantaneous activation of the sympathico-adrenomedullar ("SAM") system, leading to the secretion of the catecholamines adrenaline and noradrenaline. The result is a situation of readiness for rapid and energetic action, the so-called fight–flight response. The next step is the activation of the hypophyse-adrenocortical ("HAC") system, leading to the secretion of ACTH and corticosteroids. This inhibits anabolic processes and, instead, mobilizes energetic reserves to become available for catabolic use (Seley, 1946).

Crucial in these processes is the element of anticipation. Since the classical experiments of Weiss (1971, 1972) on rats and those by others (e.g., de Boer, de Beun, Slangen, & van der Gugten, 1990a; de Boer, Koopmans, Slangen & van der Gugten, 1990b; Dess-Beech, Linwick, Patterson, & Overmier 1983) we know that the degree to which an animal is able to predict, and more importantly still, to control the occurrence of events that stimulate the mentioned endocrine systems is of great importance for its general functioning and, eventually, its health and survival. When an animal is able to predict and to control important aspects of its living situation, the animal will be able to regulate the activation of the two systems in an efficient manner; it can tune the responses of alertness preparedness and action more precisely to the challenges (Wiepkema & Koolhaas, 1992). On the other hand, when an animal is expecting threats or challenges, but does not know the nature or the moment of the challenge, then it will be forced to maintain a state of preparedness.

The respective emotional and physiological changes, subsumed under the term *stress* (Levine, 1985), are clearly adaptive. However, if a state of alarm and stress, of catabolic activation, is maintained too long, anabolic restoration will be thwarted and negative consequences may follow. Sustained activation of the SAM system increases the risk of cardiovascular disfunctioning, whereas sustained HAC activation inhibits growth, development, immunity against diseases and reproductive functions, and causes brain damage (Henry, 1982; von Holst, 1985; Kaplan, 1986; van Hooff, 1990; Uno, Tarara, Else, Suleman, & Sapolsky, 1989). There is evidence that in humans emotional states are associated with certain endocrine-physiological states (e.g., Henry & Stephens, 1977) and even with psychiatric disorders (Altemus & Gold, 1990). Thus an increase in the level of noradrenaline is associated especially with aggressive and assertive states (the "fight" response) and with states of irritation and frustration (e.g., Frankenhaeuser, 1979). Fear and an activated flight tendency is associated with increased adrenaline. Anxiety and nervous arousal, eventually leading to a state of apathetic depression has been connected with increased levels of ACTH and cortisol (for reviews see Gray, 1987; McNaughton, 1989). These associations may be complex. Thus an experimental increase of the level of ACTH in itself does not result in a change of mood. The increase, however, does strengthen the emotional response to an appropriate challenge. The same applies to injections of adrenaline, which increased emotional arousal in accordance with the releasing quality of the stimulus situation (Lader & Tyrer, 1975; Schachter & Wheeler, 1962).

Uncertainty due to unpredictability and uncontrollability of situations, then, is the most important psychological factor that causes stress (Levine, 1985). This applies also to social situations. Asymmetries in social control become manifest in the form of dominance hierarchies. High-ranking animals have a greater freedom of conduct and a greater influence on social processes (van den Bercken & Cools, 1980a, 1980b). Low-ranking animals, by contrast, must remain prepared to adjust to the behavior of high-ranking animals. That social functioning has endocrine effects that are in accordance with the controllability model has been well demonstrated for rodents by, for instance, the work of the Groningen etho-physiology group (e.g., Schuurman, 1981; Koolhaas, Fokkema, & Benus, 1985; Bohus et al., 1987; Fokkema, Smit, van der Gugten, & Koolhaas, 1988; Koolhaas & Bohus, 1989). Especially the loser of a conflict is confronted with the requirement to maintain "catabolic anticipation," uncertain as he may be about further harassment (Fig. 7.2).

For insectivores and primates there are similar indications in the laboratory investigations, for instance, of von Holst (1986) and Manogue, Leshner, & Candland (1975). They found that the level of plasma cortisol of dominants is lower than that of subordinates. The studies of von Holst show, that losers may respond in two different ways, as actively coping "subdominants" and as passively coping "subordinates." The first are characterized by high noradrenaline levels, the second by high cortisol levels. When these animals were kept within the territory of a winner or in a separate cage from where they could still see the winner, the condition of the losers deteriorated fatally. However, a reverse rela-

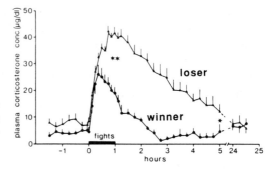

FIG. 7.2. Plasma corticosterone concentration of winners
and losers of an 1-hour agonistic encounter of two male rats.
From Schuurman, 1981.

tion between rank position and associated measures of adrenocortical activation
has also been found. In small captive groups of chimpanzees, studied by Mas-
ataka et al. (1990), dominant males had lower serum levels of immune globulines
than subordinates. The correlation was found only when the respective animals
were kept in groups; the difference disappeared when the same animals were
housed separately. The authors saw this as an indication that the maintenance of
high rank has its physiological costs.

Suitable as studies on animals kept in confinement are for revealing the
mechanisms involved, they have as a disadvantage that the losers of conflicts
may have little opportunity to realize the spatial and behavioral adjustments
perceived as adequate by both winner and loser. In order to judge whether the
endocrine-physiological patterns that have been found in the laboratory occur to
the same extent in natural social equilibrium constellations, field studies are
necessary. Pioneering examples are those of Sapolsky (1982, 1986). The basal
level of plasma cortisol of feral male savanna baboons was found to be related to
the hierarchical position of the males. Amongst dominant males, low levels were
found particularly in those individuals who relatively often took social initiatives
and who, when starting an initiative, were obviously good in predicting the result
of their social involvement. Lower levels were also found in losers that redirected
aggression than in those who did not (Sapolsky & Ray, 1989). However, differences were not always as clear. In feral vervet monkeys there were no rank-
related interindividual differences when social relationships were normal and
stable. Only in phases of rank instability could such differences be found
(Raleigh & McGuire, 1990).

BEHAVIORAL INDICATORS
OF EMOTIONAL AND SOCIAL UNCERTAINTY

The states of high emotional arousal can also be expressed in the behavior. This
is observable in the form of nervous and agitated behaviors. In particular,
scratching has often been mentioned as a signal of emotional arousal. Tinbergen

(1952) regarded it as a displacement activity, characteristic of situations of behavioral conflict. In primates, scratching has been observed in situations of undecidedness and uncertainty (e.g., Diezinger & Anderson, 1986; Kummer, 1957) and of social tension (Aureli & van Schaik, 1991b; Aureli, van Schaik, & van Hooff, 1989; Bertrand, 1969; Easley, Coelho, & Taylor, 1987; Poirier, 1974; Rowell & Hinde, 1963; Schino, Scucchi, Maestripieri, & Turillazzi, 1988), just as body shaking (e.g., Rowell & Hinde, 1963) and autogrooming (e.g., Aureli & van Schaik, 1991b; de Waal & Yoshihara, 1983; Troisi & Schino, 1987); for a review see Maestripieri, Schino, Aureli, & Troisi (in press). Indeed, certain electrophysiological and pharmacological brain stimulation led to an increase both of these behaviors and of the physiological manifestations of stress (Ninan et al., 1982; Redmond & Huang, 1979). Since Darwin (1872) yawning has also been considered as an expression of apprehension, for example, in baboons (*Papio* sp.), where it is has been interpreted as a threat signal (e.g., Coelho & Bramblett, 1981; Hall & DeVore, 1965; Kummer, 1968). Undoubtedly the mentioned behaviors are associated with the states of arousal in different ways. In Chimpanzees (*Pan troglodytes*), both the rates of yawning and scratching were higher in high-ranking individuals, in both males and females (te Boekhorst, deWeerth, & van Hooff, 1991). Aureli and van Schaik (1991b) showed that, in long-tailed macaques (*Macaca fascicularis*), the rates of scratching and body-shaking were increased in victims during the first few minutes after the conflict (provided that the conflict was not followed by an affiliative contact between the opponents during this period or by a redirection of aggression by the victim to a third animal—see later). The rate of yawning was not elevated, which would make sense if the aggressive connotation of the movement would make it a provocation on the part of the victim (see earlier). Also the rate of self-grooming was increased in victims. However, this increase occurred only after the first few minutes, when the rates of body shaking and scratching had returned to control levels (see Fig. 7.3).

This suggests a different role of these behaviors. Whereas scratching and body shaking mark the phase of increased arousal and uncertainty, autogrooming may indicate the phase of return to emotional balance. Scratching and body shaking normally occur in immediate reaction to disarrangement of the pelage and to irritation of the skin. This may be the result of behavioral activity and has been interpreted as a preparatory response of thermoregulation needed in connection with increased activity. Autogrooming seems to be used as a means to achieve relaxation as a desired state after the activity. It may serve to redress a foul-up of the pelage that occurred as part of the activity (for a review, see Spruijt, van Hooff, & Gispen, 1992). The different phasing of these behaviors is also visible in experiments by Meisenberg (1988). In mice injected with vasopressin there was a rather direct release of scratching. Only after the scratching rate had again decreased to normal levels an increase in autogrooming was observed. In a similar vein there are indications that scratching and body shaking are connected more directly with each other than with self-grooming.

FIG. 7.3. The rates of *body shaking, scratching* and *autogrooming* during Post conflict periods (PC) in which no reconciliation or redirection of aggression occurred, and during Matched Control periods (MC) on a subsequent day at the same time, when there had been no conflict between these two animals. For the PC the means over individuals for the consecutive minutes are presented; for the MC the mean and the 95% confidence interval over the individuals during the total 10-minue period are presented. From Aureli & v. Schaik (1991b).

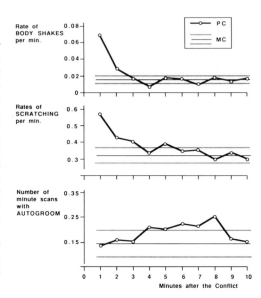

THE RESTORATION OF SOCIAL HOMEOSTASIS

Social conflicts undoubtedly are disruptive and upsetting. When agonistic conflicts arise in relationships that in other respects are of value to the individuals, then mechanisms to repair the disruptive effects may be expected (de Waal, 1989). In the first place one expects these to operate in the relationship of the contestants. Such a restorative function has been called *reconciliation*. In the second place one may expect that outsiders might interfere in the relation between contestants in such a way as to steer that relationship in a direction that is beneficial for the social fabric on which they depend and for their position in this. Such triadic interference can take various forms. The first to attract ethological attention were those in which outsiders participate in conflicts by agonistically supporting one of the contestants. This kind of interference may, if only temporarily, aggravate the conflict. A third individual might also show affiliative behaviors to one of the contestants with effects that might be described as restoration of confidence or consolation of that contestant. Indications for a variety of such functions have been found in a community of chimpanzees (de Waal & van Hooff, 1981; de Waal & van Roosmalen, 1979), but not in macaques (Aureli & van Schaik, 1991a; Judge, 1991). If a third party has an interest in a good relationship between the contestants, one might expect also processes of pacifying mediation (de Waal, 1982).

In 1979, in a study on the chimpanzee community of the Arnhem Zoo, de Waal and van Roosmalen (1979) drew attention to "post-conflict affiliative contacts" (PCACs) occurring between animals that have been involved in aggressive interaction. They supposed that these PCACs functioned as reconciliation behaviors by which the risen uncertainty about the relationship was taken away. Since then, similar PCAC behaviors have been reported for a number of species, with a much refined methodology to detect these behaviors and their effects (Aureli et al., 1989; de Waal & Yoshihara, 1983). The essence of these methods is to score the behavior of two interactants in an aggressive conflict for a given length of time after the conflict, to record their interactions with one another and with other group members. The nature and patterning of these behaviors in this post-conflict period (PC) are then compared with those of the same interactants in a so-called matched control (MC) period, that is, at the same time on a subsequent day when there had been no preceding conflict.

Figure 7.4a demonstrates that the frequency of PCACs is markedly increased during the first 3 minutes in conflicts between long-tailed macaques. By the fourth minute the level has returned to the baseline level of the MC (Aureli et al., 1989). Similar results, although established in most cases with a different analysis, have been obtained in other studies and for a number of other primate species (e.g., *Macaca mulatta,* de Waal & Yoshihara, 1983; *M. arctoides,* de Waal & Ren, 1988; *M. fascicularis,* Cords, 1988, 1992; *M. nemestrina,* Judge, 1991; *M. sylvana,* Aureli et al., in press; *M. fuscata,* Aureli, Veenema, Panthaleon van Eck, & van Hooff, 1993; *Erythrocebus patas,* York & Rowell, 1988; *Rhinopithecus roxellanae* Ren, Yan, Su, Qi, Liang, Bao, & de Waal, 1991; *Cercopithecus aethiops,* Cheney & Seyfarth, 1989, and the bonobo, *Pan paniscus,* de Waal, 1987). Similarly, there is an increased likelihood that after a conflict the victim undertakes aggressive actions against third individuals. This phenomenon, known as *redirection,* will be dealt with below.

The term *reconciliation* for these PCAC behaviors is meaningful if it can be shown that these PCACs indeed function to decrease the likelihood of renewed aggression (i.e., if the frequency of subsequent aggressive acts in reconciled PCs is lower than in unreconciled PCs) and if the tolerance around resources is restored. There was indeed a strong increase, compared to control situations, in the likelihood that new acts of aggression against the victim would take place for a period of at least 10 minutes (Aureli & van Schaik, 1991b); see Fig. 7.5. Such aggression did not come only from the former aggressor, but also from its kin, and even from group members not related to the aggressor. Aureli and v. Schaik

FIG. 7.4.   The frequency of first affiliative contacts between two long-tailed macaques (*Macaca fascicularis*) in the 10-minute period after they had an agonistic interaction (the PC period) and in a Matched Control period (from Aureli et al., 1989).

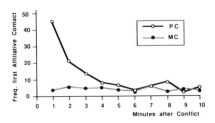

FIG. 7.5. Frequency of aggressive acts against the loser of a previous conflict during Postconflict periods (PC) in which no reconciliation or redirection took place, in Matched Control (MC) periods, and in periods in which reconciliation or redirection took place. From Aureli & v. Schaik (1991b).

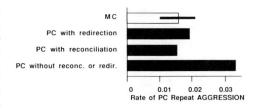

(1991b) showed that this elevation of the level of continued aggression was lower in PCs with reconciliation than in PCs without. The predicted effect has also been demonstrated recently for chimpanzees (*Pan troglodytes;* de Waal, 1992) and for experimental pairs of *Macaca fascicularis* (Cords, 1992). The latter author showed, in addition, that tolerance around a resource in a drinking test decreased when, before the test, a conflict between the pair members had been induced. Tolerance was at the baseline level when the conflict had been followed by a reconciliation (Fig. 7.6).

THE REASSURING EFFECT
OF POSTCONFLICT BEHAVIORS

The decreased probability of a renewed attack and the increased intolerance imply an amelioration of the relationship. This undoubtedly is the relevant psychological factor responsible for a number of changes in behavioral indicators of emotional arousal in victims of aggression that are caused by the PCAC. The effects of reconciliation on emotional responses were studied by Aureli and van Schaik (1991b). They compared the rates of the different measures of arousal in PC periods in which an affiliative contact with the aggressor took place during the

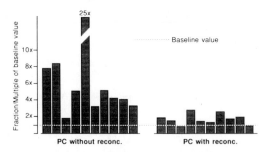

FIG. 7.6. In a series of drinking competition tests, two *Macaca fascicularis* monkeys were given access to a source after having been in one of three conditions: (a) after having been provoked into a conflict that was not followed by reconciliation; (b) after having been in a conflict that was followed by a reconciliation, and (c) after having been in a nonconflict situation. The modal latency with which the subordinate of each of 10 pairs got to drink in conditions (a) and (b) is expressed as a fraction of the latency in condition (c), the baseline value (modified after Cords, 1992).

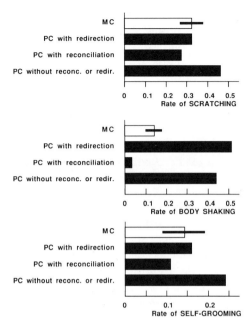

FIG. 7.7. Rates of *scratching, body shaking,* and *autogrooming* during different types of Postconflict epidodes (PCs) and during the Matched Control period (MC) (from Aureli & van Schaik, 1991b).

first 3 PC minutes (i.e., when a reconciliation occurred according to the definition; see above) and in PC periods where there were no affiliative contacts.

Significant effects were found for scratching, body shaking and autogrooming alike, all being lower in PCs with reconciliation than in those without (Fig. 7.7). This means that postconflict affiliative behaviors of the victim do indeed reduce its own emotional expressions of anxious tension.

An interesting differentiation was found when the effects of another form of postconflict behavior was considered. Just as after a conflict the likelihood of affiliative contacts is increased in certain relationships, so is the likelihood that the victim undertakes aggressive actions against third animals. In *Macaca fascicularis* a significant increase was noted in the first PC minute (Aureli & van Schaik, 1991a). Aggressive actions occurring within this time after a conflict may, therefore, justifiably be called aggressive redirections.

Just as the occurrence of reconciliations did, redirection of aggression also led to a reduction of scratching. However this was not so with respect to body shaking. Whereas reconciliation brought about a strong reduction of body shaking, even below the MC level, the level was not reduced after redirection of aggression; there even seemed to be a slight increase (see Fig. 7.7). Much the same was found with respect to autogrooming.

This leads us to two conclusions: First, although body shaking and scratching occur in the same span of time after the conflict, and thus differ from autogrooming, the underlying mechanism must be different: Body shaking may not be taken to indicate anxious uncertainty and tension, as may scratching; perhaps it rather reflects more general catabolic arousal. However, then we should also expect it to occur before stressing events, as is the case in chimpanzees with respect to scratching (Cervi & van Hooff, 1990). This clearly deserves further investigation. Second, the soothing effect of reconciliation cannot be attributed simply to the fact that reconciliation behavior consists of rather calm behaviors, such as touching, muzzle contact, mounting, and, in particular, allogrooming. For we note the same significant reduction in scratching, in comparison with PCs in which no redirection or reconciliation takes place, also after the victim has attacked other group members than its former opponent. This form of behavior hardly qualifies as energetically relaxed. We must, therefore, conclude that it is the regaining of a certain degree of control and certainty in the disturbed relationship that is mediating the effect. This explanation is preferable over the one that sees the return to emotional balance as a relaxing effect of soothing behaviors. In different macaque species the PCAC was found to be specifically directed to the previous opponent, and not to other group members (such as relatives) that might be inclined to direct affiliative behavior to the stressed animal (Aureli et al., in press, 1993). Only in Chimpanzees has the phenomenon of "consolation" has been found (de Waal & van Hooff, 1981).

THE FUNCTION OF REDIRECTION: EVIDENCE FOR REVENGE?

Why should victims of aggression redirect the aggression toward a third party? The simplest explanation is that it is a mere aftereffect of aggressive arousal that finds an outlet in a direction that involves no risk for the actor. However, it might also affect the relation of the victim with the former aggressor. This it could do in two ways. The redirection could serve to divert the attention of the former aggressor and its allies to a new target, thus relieving the pressure from the victim. For such a relief to be successful, the victim is expected to redirect its aggression to targets that most easily release aggression in the opponent(s) of the victim. In other words, the prediction is that the victim will select targets that do not have a friendly relationship with these opponents. Such redirection might even serve to improve the bond between the former opponents, as was suggested already by Lorenz (1966). In agreement with this hypothesis we found that redirection reduces the rate of renewed aggression against the victim (Fig. 7.5).

Victims might also redirect their aggression to weaker relatives or friends of their opponent. At first sight this does not seem to be a sensible option, especially in species, such as macaques, where there is a strong nepotistic support system. Attacking one's opponent's relatives might further aggravate the situation for the victim by activating the opponent's alliance system. Nevertheless Aureli et al (1992) found clear evidence for kin-oriented redirection in a group of

Japanese macaques (see also Aureli & van Schaik, 1991a; Judge, 1982). After being attacked the victim was considerably more likely to direct aggression against relatives of the previous attacker than in control periods, even though the absolute level of such redirections was only about 2%. This preference existed within a period of at least up to 1 hour after the conflict. The authors argue that such redirection may act as a *revenge,* functioning to inhibit aggressors to molest group members that have an opportunity to take it out on their kin. The study reported was not designed, however, to detect such a long-term effect.

Of course the functional interpretations given to redirected aggression are not mutually exclusive. Whether redirection is used to divert an aggressor, to achieve a bond restoring effect, or to intimidate by revenge may depend on the particular context and the overall relationships of the participants in interaction. The different functions may also have their own temporal patterns. The function of diverting may be effectively used especially when following immediately on an attack. Redirection as a revenge may be effective on a much longer time scale. Testing of predictions following from this with respect to differences in target preferences, depending on contextual and temporal factors, has as yet to be done.

CONCLUSION

Postconflict behaviors shown by the victim of an agonistic interaction appear to have two important effects, which are not mutually exclusive. In the first place they may be used to influence the future development of the relationships between animals (de Waal, 1989). In the case of reconciliation, this is indicated by the fact that the occurrence of a reconciliation after a conflict is determined by the overall nature of the relationship between the victim and its opponent. Reconciliations were more likely, independent of the intensity of the preceding conflict, if this relationship in general was important (e.g., kinship relationships) or if it was "good" (i.e., of an affiliative and tolerant character throughout). Both relatives, who as a rule have comparatively strong affiliative and supportive relationships, and nonrelatives with a close bond reconciled after a larger proportion of conflicts than animals lacking this bonding (e.g., Aureli et al., 1989; de Waal & Yoshihara, 1983). In other words the reconciliation acts to restore an obviously valuable bond. Redirection may serve to influence future relationships in other ways. When directed to vulnerable kin of the former aggressor it may act as a revenge system serving to intimidate that aggressor and to make the latter think twice before maltreating the victim again.

In the second place, postconflict behaviors can help in what Frijda (1986) called *secondary coping.* Both reconciliation and redirection led to a reduction of scratching, an indicator of emotional arousal. Such a reduction is justified and meaningful only when the reasons for the victim to remain prepared for action have been removed, that is, when the uncertainty of the victim about the relationship has been reduced. These reasons may be removed when it becomes evident to the loser that the winner accepts the reconciliation. The acceptance of a reconciliation is obviously associated with a restoration of the diminished tolerance and a reduction of the probability of renewed attacks. Such a reduction is also brought about by redirection. Besides bringing about these social effects, these PCACs are a meaningful response of secondary coping in that they allow the animal to return to other functions that had been halted by the agonistic intermezzo. The need to restore arousal in its own right is supported by experiments in which autogrooming was observed after an animal was brought in a situation of arousal by nonsocial stimuli, such as novel stimuli. In these solitary animals, autogrooming is clearly soothing in its own right (for a review on the relation between grooming and tension see Spruijt et al., 1992).

The study of social processes in nonhuman primates has often proved revealing in that it clearly demonstrates certain principles that also apply in the behavior of our own species. An interesting example is the discussion concerning the phenomenon of revenge. Frijda (chapter 10, this volume) considers the question of whether revenge represents a specific emotional category. The comparative approach is enlightening in showing that interactional processes similar in their patterning may occur in nonhuman primates. The studies reviewed in this chapter discuss the contextual and social characteristics of redirection of aggression. Several hypotheses concerning the possible functional significance of this behavior could be tested by investigating specific predictions, namely concerning the selection of opponents for redirection. The data suggest that opponents may be curbed with the threat of being hurt. The advantage of such indirect retaliation, hitting your opponent in his vulnerable kin rather than fighting back directly, is an obvious reduction of risk. Another way in which such a revenge system might work is by reciprocity in contracoalitions, a form of delayed retaliation made comparatively safe if the retaliator joins powerful coalitions. For a number of primates there is evidence that they show positive reciprocity of support namely by intervening in aggressive interactions of other group members by supporting those who also supported them. (de Waal & Luttrell, 1988). A similar *negative reciprocity,* namely that an individual's interventions against a certain partner correlate with that partner's interventions against this individual, has so far been found only in chimpanzees. Such correlations did not exist in macaques (de Waal, 1992). The reasons for this difference remain unclear. It might be due to differences in the cognitive capacities of keeping records for squaring accounts. However, because the dominance hierarchy in macaques is much more strict than in chimpanzees, this simply might make contraintervention too risky in these species. Whatever the reason for the difference, when such retaliatory aggression can hurt an opponent in situations where he cannot prevent this, retribution may be selected as a long-term means of checking antagonistic tendencies. This may have exerted an evolutionary pressure selecting for the emotional structure of revenge and a lust for vindictiveness.

REFERENCES

Altemus, M., & Gold, P. W. (1990). Neuroendocrinology and Psychiatric Illness. *Psychoneuroendocrinology, 11*, 238–265.

Altmann, S. A. (1967). The structure of primate social communication. In S. A. Altmann (Ed.), *Social communication among primates* (pp. 325–362). Chicago: University of Chicago Press.

Aureli, F., Cozzolino, R., Cordischi, C., & Scucchi, S. (1992). Kin-oriented redirection among Japanese Macaques: An expression of a revenge system? *Animal Behaviour, 44*, 283–291.

Aureli, F., Das, M., Verleur, D., & Hooff, J.A.R.A.M. van (in press). Post-conflict social interactions among barbary macaques (*Macaca sylvanus*). *International Journal of Primatology*.

Aureli, F., Cozzolino, R., Cordischi, C., & Scucchi, S. (1992). Kin-oriented redirection among Japanese macaques: An expression of a revenge system? *Animal Behaviour, 44*, 283–291.

Aureli, F., & Schaik, C. P. van. (1991a). Post-conflict behaviour in long-tailed macaques (*Macaca fascicularis*): I. The social events. *Ethology, 89*, 89–100.

Aureli, F., & Schaik, C. P. van. (1991b). Post-conflict behaviour in long-tailed macaques (*Macaca fascicularis*): II. Coping with uncertainty. *Ethology, 89*, 101–114.

Aureli, F., Schaik, C.P. van, & Hooff, J.A.R.A.M. van. (1989). Functional aspects of reconciliation among captive long-tailed macaques (*Macaca fascicularis*). *American Journal of Primatology, 19*, 39–51.

Aureli, F., Veenema, H. C., Panthaleon van Eck, C. J. van, & Hooff, J.A.R.A.M. van. (1993). Reconciliation, consolation and redirection in Japanese macaques (*Maaca fuscata*). *Behaviour, 124*, 1–21.

Bercken, J. van den, & Cools, A. R. (1980a). Information-statistical analysis of factors determining ongoing behaviour and social interaction in Java monkeys (*Macaca fascicularis*). *Animal Behaviour, 28*, 189–200.

Bercken, J. van den, & Cools, A. R. (1980b). Information-statistical analysis of social interaction and communication: An analysis of variance approach. *Animal Behaviour, 28*, 172–188.

Bertrand, M. (1969). *The behavioural repertoire of the stumptail macaque*. Basel: Karger.

Boekhorst, I.J.A. te, Weerth, C. de, & Hooff, J.A.R.A.M. van. (1991) Does scratching signal stress in chimpanzees. In I.J.A. te Boekhorst *Social structure of three ape species: An approach based on field data and individual oriented models* (pp. 157–175). Utrecht: Dissertation Universiteit Utrecht.

Boer, S. F. de, Beun, R. de, Slangen, J. L., & Gugten, J. van der. (1990a). Dynamics of plasma catecholamine and corticosterone concentrations during reinforced and extinguished operant behavior in rats. *Physiology and Behavior, 47*, 691–698.

Boer, S. F. de, Koopmans, S. J., Slangen, J. L., & Gugten, J. van der. (1990b). Plasma catecholamine, corticosterone and glucose responses to repeated stress in rats: Effect of interstressor interval length. *Physiology and Behavior, 47*, 1117–1124.

Bohus, B., Benus, R. F., Fokkema, D. S., Koolhaas, J. M., Nyakas, C., Oortmerssen, G. A. van, Prins, A.J.A., Ruiter, A.J.H. de, Scheurink, A.J.W., & Steffens, A.B. (1987). Neuroendocrine states and behavioural and physiological stress responses. *Progress in Brain Research, 72*, 57–70.

Cannon, W. B. (1929). *Bodily changes in pain, hunger, fear and rage. An account of recent researchers into the functional of emotional excitement*. New York: Appleton.

Cervi, L. M., & Hooff, J.A.R.A.M., van. (1990). Anticipatory pacification in chimpanzees. *International Journal of Primatology, 5*, 171.

Cheney, D. L., & Seyfarth, R. M. (1989). Redirected aggression and reconciliation among vervet monkeys, *Cercopithecus aethiops*. *Behaviour, 110*, 258–275.

Coelho, A. M., & Bramblett, C. A. (1981). Sexual dimorphism in the activity of olive baboons (*Papio cynocephalus anubis*) housed in monosexual groups. *Archives of Sexual Behavior, 10*, 79–91.

213

Cords, M. (1988). Resolution of aggressive conflicts by immature long-tailed macaques, *Macaca fascicularis*. *Animal Behaviour, 36,* 1124–1135.

Cords, M. (1992). Post-conflict reunions and reconciliation in long-tailed macaques. *Animal Behaviour, 44,* 57–61.

Darwin, C. (1872). *The expression of the emotions in man and animals.* London: John Murray.

Dess-Beech, N., Linwick, D., Patterson, J., & Overmier, J. (1983). Immediate and proactive effects of controllability and predictability on plasma cortisol responses to shocks in dogs. *Behavioral Neuroscience, 97,* 1005–1016.

Diezinger, F., & Anderson, J. R. (1986). Starting from scratching: A first look at a "displacement activity" group-living rhesus monkeys. *American Journal of Primatology, 11,* 117–124.

Dunbar, R.I.M. (1988). *Primate social systems.* London: Croom Helm.

Easley, S. P., Coelho, A. M., & Taylor, L. L. (1987). Scratching, dominance, tension, and displacement in male baboons. *American Journal of Primatology, 43,* 397–411.

Fokkema, D. S., Smit, K., Gugten, J. van der, & Koolhaas, J. M. (1988). A coherent pattern among social behaviour, blood pressure, corticosterone and catecholamine measures in individual male rats. *Physiology and Behavior, 42,* 485–489.

Frankenhaeuser, M. (1979). Psychoendocrine approaches to the study of emotion as related to stress and coping. In H. E. Howe & R. A. Dienstbier (Eds.), *Nebraska symposium on motivation* (pp. 123–161). Lincoln: University of Nebraska Press.

Frijda, N. H. (1986). *The emotions.* Cambridge: Cambridge University Press.

Gray, J. E. (1987). *The psychology of fear and stress.* Cambridge: Cambridge University Press.

Hadidian, J. (1980). Yawning in an old world monkey, *Macaca nigra* (Primates: Cercopithecidae). *Behaviour, 75,* 133–147.

Hall, K.R.L., & DeVore, I. (1965). Baboon social behavior. In I. DeVore, (Ed.), *Primate behavior: Field studies of monkeys and apes* (pp. 53–110). New York: Holt, Rinehart & Winston.

Hand, J. L. (1986). Resolution of social conflicts: Dominance, egalitarism, spheres of dominance, and game theory. *Quarterly Review of Biology, 61,* 201–220.

Henry, J. P. (1982). The relation of social to biological processes in disease. *Social Science and Medicine, 16,* 369–380.

Henry, J. P., & Stephens, P. M. (1977). *Stress, health and the social environment: A sociobiologic approach to medicine.* New York: Springer.

Hinde, R. A. (1979). *Towards understanding relationships.* London: Academic Press.

Hinde, R. A., & Rowell, T. E. (1962). Communication by postures and facial expressions in the rhesus monkey (*Macaca mulatta*). *Proceedings of the Zoological Society, London, 138,* 1–21.

Holst, D. von. (1985). Coping behaviour and stress physiology in male tree shrews (*Tupaia belangeri*). *Fortschritte der Zoologie, 31,* 461–469.

Holst, D. von. (1986). Psychosocial stress and its pathophysiological effects in tree shrews (*Tupaia belangeri*). In T. H. Schmidt, T. M. Dembrowski, & G. Blümchen (Eds.), *Biological and psychological factors in cardiovascular disease* (pp. 476–490). Berlin: Springer.

Hooff, J.A.R.A.M. van. (1972). A comparative approach to the phylogeny of laughter and smiling. In R. A. Hinde (Ed.), *Non-verbal communication* (pp. 209–241). Cambridge: Cambridge University Press.

Hooff, J.A.R.A.M. van. (1976). The comparison of facial expression in man and higher primates. In M. von Cranach (Ed.), *Methods of inference from animal to human behaviour* (pp. 165–196). Chicago: Aldine.

Hooff, J.A.R.A.M. van. (1988). Sociality in primates: A compromise of ecological and social adaptation strategies. In A. Tartabini & M. L. Genta (Eds.), *Perspectives in the study of primates* (pp. 9–23). Cosenza: DeRose.

Hooff, J.A.R.A.M. van. (1990). Social behaviour and its influences on reproduction and growth in primates. In A. K. Slob & M. J. Baum (Eds.), *Psychoneuroendocrinology of growth and development* (pp. 187–197). Rotterdam: Medicon.

Judge, P. J. (1982). Redirection of aggression based on kinship in a captive group of pigtail macaques. *International Journal of Primatology, 3,* 301.

Judge, P. J. (1991). Dyadic and triadic reconciliation in pigtail macaques (*Macaca nemestrina*). *American Journal of Primatology, 23,* 225–237.

Kaplan, J. R. (1986). Psychological stress and behavior in nonhuman primates. In G. Mitchell & J. Erwin (Eds.), *Comparative primate biology Vol. 2A: Behavior, conservation and ecology* (pp. 455–492). New York: Alan R. Liss.

Koolhaas, J. M., & Bohus, B. (1989). Social control in relation to neuroendocrine and immunological responses. In A. Steptoe & A. Appels (Eds.), *Stress, personal control and health* (pp. 295–304). Brussel: Wiley.

Koolhaas, J. M., Fokkema, D. S., & Benus, I. (1985). Stresspathologie bij de rat en de muis. *Vakblad voor Biologen, 65,* 356–358.

Kummer, H. (1957). *Soziales Verhalten einer Mantelpavian-Gruppe.* Bern: Hans Huber.

Kummer, H. (1968). Social organization of hamadryas baboons. *Bibiotheca primatologica, 6,* 1–189.

Lader, M., & Tyrer, P. (1975). Vegetative system and emotion. In L. Levi (Ed.), *Emotions, their parameters and measurement* (pp. 65–83). New York: Raven.

Levine, S. (1985). A definition of stress? In G. P. Moberg (Ed.), *Animal stress* (pp. 51–69). Bethesda: American Physiological Society.

Lorenz, K. (1966). *Das sogenannte Böse.* Wien: Borotha Schoeler.

Maestripieri, D., Schino, G., Aureli, F., & Troisi, A. (in press). A modest proposal: Displacement activities as an indicator of emotions in primates. *Animal Behaviour.*

Manogue, K. R., Leshner, A. I., & Candland, D. K. (1975). Dominance status and adrenocortical reactivity to stress in squirrel monkeys (*Saimiri sciureus*). *Primates, 16,* 457–463.

Masakata, N., Ishida, T., Suzuki, J., Matsumura, S., Udono, S., & Sasaoka, S. (1990). Dominance and immunity in chimpanzees (*Pan troglodytes*). *Ethology, 85,* 147–155.

McNaughton, N. (1989). *Biology and emotion.* Cambridge: Cambridge University Press.

Meisenberg, G. (1988). Vasopressin-induced grooming and scratching behavior in mice. *Annals of the New York Academy of Sciences, 525,* 257–269.

Ninan, P. T., Insel, T. M., Cohen, R. M., Cook, J. M., Skolnick, P., & Paul, S. M. (1982). Benzodiazepit receptor-mediated experimental "anxiety" in primates. *Science, 218,* 1332–1334.

Noë, R., van Schaik, C. P., & van Hooff, J.A.R.A.M. (1991). The market effect: An explanation for pay-off asymmetries among collaborating animals. *Ethology, 87,* 97–118.

Poirier, F. E. (1974). Colobine aggression: A review. In R. L. Holloway (Ed.), *Primate aggression, territoriality and xenophobia* (pp. 123–157). New York: Academic Press.

Provine, R. R. (1986). Yawning as a stereotyped action pattern and releasing stimulus. *Ethology, 71,* 109–122.

Provine, R. R., Hamernik, H. B., & Curchack, B. C. (1987). Yawning: Relation to sleeping and stretching in humans. *Ethology, 76,* 152–160.

Raleigh, M. J., & McGuire, M. T. (1990). Social influences on endocrine function in male vervet monkeys. In T. E. Ziegler & F. B. Bercovitch (Eds.), *Socioendocrinology of primate reproduction* (pp. 95–111). New York: Wiley-Liss.

Redican, W. K. (1975). Facial expressions in nonhuman primates. In L. A. Rosenblum (Ed.), *Primate behavior* (pp. 103–194). London: Academic Press.

Redmond, D. E., & Huang, Y. H. (1979). New evidence for a locus coeruleus-norepinephrine connection with anxiety. *Life Sciences, 25,* 2149–2162.

Ren, R. M., Yan, K. H., Su, Y. Y., Qi, H. J., Liang, B., Bao, W. Y., & de Waal, F.B.M. (1991). The reconciliation behavior of golden monkeys (*Rhinopithecus roxellanae roxellanae*) in small breeding groups. *Primates, 32,* 321–327.

Rowell, T. E., & Hinde, R. A. (1963). Responses of rhesus monkeys to mildly stressful situations. *Animal Behaviour, 11,* 235–243.

Sapolsky, R. M. (1982). The endocrine stress-response and social status in the wild baboon. *Hormones and Behavior, 16,* 279–292.

Sapolsky, R. M. (1986). Stress, social status, and reproductive physiology in free-living baboons. In D. Crews (Ed.), *Psychobiology of reproductive behaviour, an evolutionary perspective* (pp. 291–322). Englewood Cliffs: Prentice Hall.

Sapolsky, R. M., & Ray, J. R. (1989). Styles of dominance and their endocrine correlates among wild olive baboons (*Papio anubis*). *American Journal of Primatology, 18,* 1–13.

Schachter, S., & Singer, J. E. (1962). Cognitive, social and physiological determinants of emotional state. *Psychological Review, 69,* 379–399.

Schachter, S., & Wheeler, L. (1962). Epinephrine, chlorpromazine and amusement. *Journal of Abnormal and Social Psychology, 65,* 379–399.

Schaik, C. P. van. (1983). Why are diurnal primates living in groups? *Behaviour, 87,* 120–144.

Schaik, C. P. van. (1989). The ecology of social relationships amongst female primates. In V. Standen & R. Foley (Eds.), *Comparative socioecology of mammals and man* (pp. 195–218). Oxford: Blackwell.

Schaik, C. P. van, & Hooff, J.A.R.A.M. van. (1983). On the ultimate causes of primate social systems. *Behaviour, 85,* 91–117.

Schaik, C. P. van, Noordwijk, M. A. van, Bragt, T. van, & Blankenstein, M. A. (1991). A pilot study of the social correlates of levels of urinary cortisol, prolactin and testosterone in wild long-tailed macaques. *Primates, 32,* 345–356.

Schaik, C. P. van, & Noordwijk, M. A. van (1986). The hidden costs of sociality: Intra-group variation in feeding strategies in Sumatran long-tailed macaques (*Macaca fascicularis*). *Behaviour, 99,* 296–315.

Schaik, C. P. van, & Noordwijk, M. A. van (1988). Scramble and contest among female long-tailed macaques in a Sumatran forest. *Behaviour, 105,* 77–89.

Schaik, C. P. van, & Noordwijk, M. A. van (1989). The special role of male *Cebus* monkeys in predation avoidance, and its effect on group composition. *Behavioral Ecology and Sociobiology, 24,* 265–276.

Schaik, C. P. van, & Noordwijk, M. A. van, Warsono, B., & Sutriono, E. (1983). Party size and early detection of predators in Sumatran forest primates. *Primates, 24,* 211–221.

Schino, G., & Aureli, F. (1989). Do men yawn more than women? *Ethology and Sociobiology, 10,* 375–378.

Schino, G., Scucchi, S., Maestripieri, D., & Turillazzi, P. G. (1988). Allogrooming as a tension-reduction mechanism: A behavioral approach. *American Journal of Primatology, 16,* 43–50.

Schuurman, T. (1981). *Endocrine processes underlying victory and defeat in the male rat.* Groningen. Unpublished doctoral dissertation, Universiteit Groningen.

Scucchi, S., Cordischi, C., Aureli, F., & Cozzolino, R. (1988). The use of redirection in a captive group of Japanese monkeys. *Primates, 29,* 229–236.

Seley, H. (1946). The general adaptation syndrome and the diseases of adaptation. *Journal of Clinical Endocrinology and Metabolism, 6,* 117–231.

Spruijt, B. M., Hooff, J.A.R.A.M. van, & Gispen, W. H. (1992). The ethology and neurobiology of grooming behaviour. *Physiological Reviews, 72,* 825–851.

Tinbergen, N. (1952). "Derived" activities; their causation, biological significance, origin, and emancipation during evolution. *Quarterly Review of Biology, 27,* 1–32.

Troisi, A., Aureli, F., Schino, G., Rinaldi, F., & de Angelis, N. (1990). The influence of age, sex, and rank on yawning behavior in two species of macaques (*Macaca fascicularis* and *M. fuscata*). *Ethology, 86,* 303–310.

Troisi, A., & Schino, G. (1987). Environmental and social influences on autogrooming behaviour in a captive group of Java monkeys. *Behaviour, 100,* 292–303.

Uno, H., Tarara, R., Else, J. G., Suleman, M. A., & Sapolsky, R. M. (1989). Hippocampal damage associated with prolonged and fatal stress in primates. *Journal of Neuroscience, 9,* 1705–1711.

Vehrencamp, S. (1983). A model for the evolution of despotic versus egalitarian societies. *Animal Behaviour, 31,* 667–682.

Waal, F.B.M. de. (1982). *Chimpanzee politics,* London: Jonathan Cape.

Waal, F.B.M. de. (1987). Tension regulation and nonreproductive functions of sex among captive bonobos (*Pan paniscus*). *National Geographic Research, 3,* 318–335.

Waal, F.B.M. de. (1989). *Peacemaking among primates.* Cambridge, MA: Harvard University Press.

Waal, F.B.M. de. (1992). Coalitions as part of reciprocal relations in the Arnhem chimpanzee colony. In A. H. Harcourt & F.B.M. de Waal (Eds.), *Coalitions and alliances in humans and other animals* (pp. 233–258). Oxford, Oxford University Press.

Waal, F.B.M. de, & Hooff, J.A.R.A.M., van, (1981). Side-directed communication and agonistic interactions in chimpanzees. *Behaviour, 77,* 164–198.

Waal, F.B.M. de, & Luttrell, L. (1988). Mechanisms of social reciprocity in three primate species: Symmetrical relationship characteristics or cognition? *Ethology and Sociobiology, 9,* 101–118.

Waal, F.B.M. de, & Ren, R. M. (1988). Comparison of the reconciliation behavior of stumptail and rhesus macaques. *Ethology, 78,* 129–142.

Waal, F.B.M. de, & Roosmalen, A. van (1979). Reconciliation and consolation among chimpanzees. *Behavioural Ecology and Sociobiology, 5,* 55–66.

Waal, F.B.M. de, & Yoshihara, D. (1983). Reconciliation and redirected affection in rhesus monkeys. *Behaviour, 85,* 224–241.

Weiss, J. M. (1971). Effects of coping behavior in different warning signal conditions on stress pathology. *Journal of Comparative and Physiological Psychology, 77,* 1–13.

Weiss, J. M. (1972). Psychological factors in stress and disease. *Scientific American, 226,* 104–112.

Wiepkema, P. R., & Koolhaas, J. M. (1992). The emotional brain. *Animal Welfare, 1,* 13–18.

York, A. D., & Rowell, T. E. (1988). Reconciliation following aggression in patas monkeys, *Erythrocebus patas. Animal Behaviour, 36,* 502–509.

8 Emotions as Psychological Achievements

Shelley E. Taylor
University of California, Los Angeles

Lisa G. Aspinwall
University of Maryland, College Park

Traci A. Giuliano
University of California, Los Angeles

Recent years have witnessed substantial progress in understanding the cognitive underpinnings of emotional states. Research on the cognitive appraisal of emotion has had substantial theoretical and heuristic value (e.g., Frijda, 1986, 1987; Frijda, Kuipers, & Ter Schure, 1989). Building on these ideas, the present chapter maintains that, under some circumstances, emotions may be thought of as psychological achievements, the end states of goal-directed activity. That is, we suggest that augmenting positive emotions and avoiding negative ones can be the goals of cognitive appraisals, and that events are interpreted and distorted in ways that enable people to maintain or enhance their emotional well-being. We review a variety of literature indicating that people have available to them positive illusions about themselves, the world, and the future that enable them to experience positive emotions in a world that might otherwise be filled with disappointment, sadness, and frustration.

All things considered, people prefer to experience positive rather than negative emotions. This assertion is hardly controversial. Generally speaking, people also report positive emotional states, at least more often than negative ones (e.g., Kanouse & Hanson, 1972). Researchers have sometimes interpreted these findings as consequences of the objective distribution of outcomes (e.g., Kanouse & Hanson). That is, given that positive outcomes are more likely than negative outcomes, one anticipates a corresponding emotional skew in the direction of positive emotions. We suggest instead that the tendency to experience a preponderance of positive emotions, both across people and within a given individual, should also be thought of as a goal-directed achievement, the product of an active construal of experience in a manner that produces positive emotions.

The theoretical basis for this argument comes from our work on positive illusions (Taylor, 1989; Taylor & Brown, 1988). A substantial literature attests to the existence of cognitive illusions, modest biases in the construal of personally relevant information that have the effect of representing one's situation and oneself somewhat more favorably than may be justified. Specifically, we have found that among those coping with the normal hassles of daily life, as well as those coping with more intensely stressful events, there is a tendency to view the future more optimistically than objective circumstances can justify, to maintain that one has a higher degree of personal control over one's situation than might be justified by objective facts, and to modestly inflate one's attributes and characteristics in a self-enhancing direction. These mild, positive biases have been observed across a variety of populations in a variety of settings and appear to characterize the majority of individuals going through these experiences.

In this chapter, we briefly review the literature that leads us to these conclusions and extend them in several directions. We first examine evidence to suggest that when people undergo intensely threatening events they often, paradoxically, report at least as many benefits from those events as harm. We next consider evidence that people's decision-making processes are constructed and reconstructed in ways that minimize the aversive consequences of decisions with poor outcomes. We then report research that explores how people use information about others and compare themselves with others in ways that are designed to enhance their emotional functioning. Finally, we discuss the consequences of positive illusions, highlighting their role in mood enhancement and psychological self-regulation.

POSITIVE ILLUSIONS
AND THE MANAGEMENT OF DAILY EXPERIENCES

In a 1988 article, Taylor and Brown argued that most people interpret themselves, their world, and the future in ways that are mildly biased in a positive direction. These positive illusions, as we call them, are thought to help people cope with the ebb and flow of daily experience. In other words, they may help to protect people from the negative implications of minor negative events, such as personal rebuffs and hassles. We argue here that one of the central goals of this process is the maintenance or achievement of positive affect.

A first domain in which illusion predominates concerns positively biased views of the self. When asked to indicate how accurately positive and negative personality traits describe them, most people judge positive traits to be more characteristic of themselves than negative ones (e.g., Alicke, 1985; Brown, 1986). In addition, positive information about the self is more efficiently processed and recalled than negative information (e.g., Kuiper & Derry, 1982; Kuiper & MacDonald, 1982; Kuiper, Olinger, MacDonald, & Shaw, 1985). People tend to have poor recall for their failures and recall their task performance as better than it actually was (Crary, 1966; Silverman, 1964). Research on the self-serving bias suggests that people are more likely to take credit for positive than negative outcomes (see, for a recent review, Ross & Fletcher, 1985). Finally, negative aspects of the self tend to be ignored or dismissed as inconsequential or widely shared (Campbell, 1986; Marks, 1984).

Evidence that these self-perceptions are unrealistic or illusory comes from several sources. First, there is a pervasive tendency to see the self as better than others on a variety of attributes and talents (Alicke, 1985; Brown, 1986; Campbell, 1986; Larwood & Whittaker, 1977). Individuals' self-ratings also appear to have an inflated positive quality when compared with judgments made by observers (Lewinsohn, Mischel, Chaplin, & Barton, 1980). It appears, then, that people think better of themselves than others think of them.

A second domain in which most people's perceptions about themselves are somewhat unrealistic concerns their degree of personal control over environmental outcomes. People often act as if they have personal control over situations that are entirely determined by chance (Langer, 1975; Langer & Roth, 1975). A large literature on covariation indicates that people substantially overestimate their degree of control over heavily chance-determined events (see Crocker, 1982). When people expect to produce a particular outcome and the outcome then occurs, they often overestimate the degree to which they were instrumental in bringing it about (Miller & Ross, 1975).

Research also suggests a general unrealistic optimism about the future. Although most people are optimistic about most aspects of the future, they are particularly so about their own. People estimate the likelihood that they will experience a wide range of positive events and avoid a wide range of negative events as much higher than that of their peers (e.g., Kuiper, MacDonald, & Derry, 1983; Perloff & Fetzer, 1986; Weinstein, 1980; Robertson, 1977). Because not everyone's future can be better than that of their peers, the extreme optimism that people display about their own future appears to contain a degree of illusion. Across a wide variety of tasks, people's predictions of what will occur correspond more closely to what they would like to see happen than to what is objectively likely (Cantril, 1938; Lund, 1975; McGuire, 1960; Pruitt & Hoge, 1965; Sherman, 1980).

There is substantial evidence that these positive illusions—self-aggrandizing self-perceptions, the illusion of control and unrealistic optimism—are tied to the maintenance or creation of a positive mood. People in a positive mood, whether natural or manipulated, have higher opinions of themselves (e.g., Beck, 1967; Kuiper & Derry, 1982; Kuiper & MacDonald, 1982; Kuiper et al., 1985; Lewinsohn et al., 1980; Shrauger & Terbovic, 1976), they are more likely to demonstrate the self-serving attributional bias (Kuiper, 1978; Rizley, 1978), they have exaggerated beliefs in their ability to control what goes on around them (Abramson & Alloy, 1981; Golin, Terrell, & Johnson, 1977; Golin, Terrell, Weitz, & Drost, 1979), and they are more likely to be unrealistically optimistic (Alloy & Ahrens, 1987). Although positive mood appears to augment these illusions, at least some research demonstrates the reverse causal relationship between illusions and mood, indicating that when people see themselves as better off than others, their mood improves (Gibbons, 1986; see also MacFarland & Ross, 1982).

Conversely, individuals who are low in self-esteem, moderately depressed, or under threat, are more balanced in their self-perceptions (e.g., Coyne & Gotlieb, 1983; Rhuehleman, West, & Pasahow, 1985; Watson & Clark, 1984). Mildly and severely depressed individuals also appear to be less vulnerable to the illusion of control (e.g., Alloy, Abramson, & Viscusi, 1981; see also Shrauger & Terbovic, 1976). Mildly depressed people, those with low self-esteem, and those under threat appear to entertain more balanced assessments of their likely future circumstances (see, for a review, Rhuehleman et al., 1985).

COPING WITH INTENSELY THREATENING EVENTS

Perhaps the most stringent test of the ability to construe positive affect from one's personal circumstances involves reactions to intensely stressful, traumatic, or life-threatening events. A large body of previous research has emphasized the mental anguish and intense feelings of vulnerability that may result in the wake of events such as assaults, natural disasters, and life-threatening diseases (e.g., Janoff-Bulman & Frieze, 1983; Silver, Boon, & Stones, 1983). Yet an amassing body of literature indicates that sometimes people construe as many, if not more, benefits from these experiences as harm (Taylor & Aspinwall, 1990).

Our research has focused on the paradoxical positive effects that threatening events can have (Taylor, 1983; Taylor, Wood, & Lichtman, 1983). For example, in studies with cancer patients (Collins, Taylor, & Skokan, 1990; Taylor, Lichtman, & Wood, 1984), we found that over 90% of these patients reported positive changes in their lives as a result of the cancer experience. They reported such beneficial effects as an increased ability to appreciate each day, the willingness to put more effort into their relationships, and feelings that as individuals they were stronger, more self-assured, and more compassionate. Similar findings have been uncovered among gay men living with AIDS (Taylor, Kemeny, Reed, & Aspinwall, in press), spinal cord-injury victims (Janoff-Bulman & Wortman, 1977), parents of children with perinatal health problems or diabetes (Affleck, Allen, Tennen, McGrade, & Ratzan, 1985; Affleck, Tennen, & Gershman, 1985), and burn patients (Andreasen & Norris, 1972). In fact, two studies that have compared the quality of life experienced by cancer patients with that of a sample free of chronic disease have found the quality of life experienced by the cancer patients to be higher than that of the healthy sample (Danoff, Kramer, Irwin, & Gottlieb, 1983; Tempelaar et al., 1989).

Such findings have not been confined solely to individuals suffering from serious or life-threatening disease. Although the degree to which benefits are experienced is sometimes lower than that associated with chronic or life-threatening illness, similar findings have been found among adults reacting to the death of a parent (Malinak, Hoyt, & Patterson, 1979), among victims of incest (Silver, Boon, & Stones, 1983), among rape victims (Veronen & Kilpatrick, 1983), and among the bereaved (Miles & Crandall, 1983).

Although many of these perceived benefits are based on actual experiences, most depend to a degree on how individuals view or interpret their circumstances and distort threatening events in a positive, perhaps even self-deceptive direction. For example, many of the cancer patients in one study (Taylor, Lichtman, & Wood, 1984) reported that they could now exert personal control over the course of their cancer and prevent a recurrence; yet their medical charts indicated that they had metastatic disease and were virtually certain to die eventually of the cancer. Despite the illusionary nature of these positive reconstructions of negative events, research shows perceived benefits to be associated with positive adjustment to traumatic events (Collins et al., 1990). Similar findings have been uncovered in studies among men at risk for AIDS (Taylor, Kemeny et al. 1991) and among men already diagnosed with AIDS (Taylor, Helgeson, Reed, & Skokan, 1991).

The ability to derive benefits from highly stressful and life-threatening events is predicted by the same variables as is true of the normal illusions of everyday life. Those under continuous threat, those low in self-esteem, and those suffering from depression are less able to experience these benefits. Moreover, there appear to be constraints imposed by the nature of the events themselves, such that some events are more conducive to positive reconstruction than others. Sudden losses and assaultive events, in particular, do not appear to foster positive reconstruction to the same degree as is true of impersonal threatening events, such as life-threatening illness (Taylor, 1989).

Nonetheless, the fact that positive illusions reduce not only the experience of daily stress, but also the experience of more extreme trauma, illustrates an important consistency between the psychological management of the major and minor events of daily life. Moreover, this consistency suggests that the dynamics of the two are quite similar. Perhaps most important is the fact that positive emotional states appear to be the goal of these positive reconstructions of adverse events. Very few of the benefits reported by individuals in the wake of intensely threatening events involve dramatic life changes, recharting the course of one's activities, or changing one's daily behavior in dramatic ways. Rather, most of them appear to be changes in how people think about these events, thoughts that appear in turn to reduce distress and enhance emotional well-being.

ILLUSIONS, DECISION-MAKING,
AND POSITIVE AFFECT

The fact that positive illusions appear to be associated with positive psychological outcomes (see Taylor & Brown, 1988, for a review) flies in the face of much psychological wisdom. Traditional models of mental health have argued that people need to see reality objectively in order to function effectively in the world. The truly mentally healthy person has been regarded as one who sees things as they really are, rather than as he or she might wish them to be (e.g., Allport, 1943; Erikson, 1950; Fromm, 1955; Jahoda, 1958; Jourard & Landsman, 1980; Maslow, 1950; Menninger, 1930; Schulz, 1977). Among the primary justifications for this position is the belief that if illusions are subsequently disconfirmed, the discovery of their falsity will be devastating psychologically, overcoming any psychological advantages that might have initially been experienced. Accordingly, our research program has attempted to identify circumstances in which illusions might have adverse psychological effects.

One such situation is when individuals are actively involved in making decisions about stressful circumstances, and the decisions turn out to be wrong or to have major adverse consequences. Often when people are faced with intensely stressful events, they are forced to make decisions that have long-term implications for their own or others' welfare. Sometimes these decisions must be made under time pressure or on the basis of incomplete information, increasing the likelihood that a wrong decision will be made. If the outcome of such a decision is unsuccessful, the decision-maker is faced with potential feelings of responsibility for the poor outcome, as well as the possibility of feelings of regret and psychological distress. Moreover, even decisions made under the best of circumstances can still have adverse outcomes to which the decision-maker must often adjust. As with the illusions described in previous sections, we argue that similar processes may buffer individuals against the negative outcomes of decisions that they choose or for which they assume responsibility. That is, the same adaptive powers that appear to help individuals adjust to stressful events more generally may also apply when they are attempting to adjust to the adverse outcomes of their decisions.

In the medical arena, the question of patient participation in decision-making has assumed substantial medical, ethical, and legal proportions (Brock & Wartman, 1990; President's Commission for the Study of Ethical Problems in Medicine and Biomedical and Behavioral Research, 1983). As patients have increasingly adopted a consumer orientation toward their health care (Taylor, 1991) and as the dictates of informed consent have increasingly provided patients with information and options (e.g., Stockwell, 1983), even patients who do not desire a role in the decisions affecting their medical care have often been thrust into this role. A controversy around this issue has consequently assumed sharp focus in recent years.

224

Some have argued that such increases in responsibility give patients feelings of control. For the most part, researchers have found such "decision control" (Thompson, 1981) to be adaptive. When people feel that they have chosen to undergo an aversive event, they often adapt better to that event (for a review, see Thompson, 1981; Fiske & Taylor, 1984). As yet, however, there has been little systematic analysis of the psychological consequences of participation in decisions that lead to unsuccessful outcomes. For example, when patients are involved in decisions regarding surgeries and other often experimental treatments and those treatments are unsuccessful, are patients worse off or better off for having been involved in the decision-making process? Are they buffered against feelings of responsibility, self-blame, and regret that might have been generated by active participation in such decision-making? Or does self-blame, attributions of responsibility, and regret lead to poor adjustment when participative decision-making leads to unsuccessful outcomes (see Clements & Sider, 1983; Crile, 1972, for discussions of these issues)?

We examined this issue in the context of renal transplantation (Wagener & Taylor, 1986). Patients who had received cadaver-donor kidney transplants participated in an interview concerning their retrospective perceptions of the decision to undergo the transplantation. For 13 of the 29 patients, the transplant procedure had been successful, whereas for 16 of the patients, the transplant had failed. At the time they decided to undergo kidney transplantation, patients in the two groups were equivalent in terms of the factors that predict transplant success or failure. That is, there were no risk factors known either to the physicians or to the patients that could have systematically influenced the likelihood of transplantation success at the time the decision to undergo the transplant was made. All patients had been told in advance that the expected success rate for a cadaver transplant procedure is approximately 60%.

The question of interest, then, is how the failed transplantation patients come to terms with a decision that has often left them in a worsened state, vulnerable to infectious disease and life-threatening malignancies. Consistent with the work on positive illusions, our interviews revealed that these people reconstructed the circumstances surrounding the decision-making in ways that buffered them against the regret and negative affect that they might have experienced in response to the failed transplant. Relative to the successfully transplanted patients, failed transplant patients recalled the circumstances of the initial decision in a manner that lessened personal responsibility and regret regarding that decision. In essence, they indicated that they had little choice but to make the decision they had made. More specifically, the failed transplantation patients reported that the decision had been significantly less difficult to make than was the case for patients whose transplants succeeded. They were also more likely than successfully transplanted patients to perceive the decision as their only course of action, and they reported that they would have accepted lower minimum odds for the renal transplant than did successfully transplanted patients. They were less likely to indicate that they seriously considered staying on dialysis, and they were somewhat more likely to believe that they could not have stayed on dialysis any longer. They were also more likely to report that dialysis was not working for them, compared to successfully transplanted patients.

Whether the transplant was successful or not also influenced retrospective perceptions of the initial chances of success. Despite the fact that all patients had received the same statistics about the likely success of a renal transplant, those whose transplants had failed indicated that the physician had given them lower odds initially for the success of the transplant than did the successfully transplanted patients. Patients had also been asked their private odds for success, and the results again differed between the two groups, with failed transplantation patients reporting lower subjective odds.

A risk of participative decision-making that has received attention in the medical literature concerns the possibility that patients will project responsibility for failed decisions onto others. We did not find any evidence for this potential problem. When patients were asked to allocate responsibility for the transplant decision to themselves, their family members, or the physician, there were no differences between the successful and failed transplantation groups. Most saw the decision as a joint one between themselves and the physician, with the self holding a slightly greater decision-making role.

In short, rather than projecting responsibility onto others or manifesting psychological distress following the failed transplant, the failed renal transplantation patients were more likely than the successful ones to see the transplant as their only course of action. These findings suggest tentatively that patients may be at least somewhat buffered against the negative outcomes of decisions in which they have participated. They may have available to them cognitive "escape routes" that minimize the negative affect that might otherwise occur when they bear some personal responsibility for a decision that leads to unsuccessful outcomes.

One caveat regarding the generalizability of these results concerns the extent to which patients are actively involved in the initial decision-making circumstances. In the renal transplantation situation, all of the patients were actively involved, and so it was not possible to examine differences in perceived control or choice as moderators of the postdecision or posttreatment reconstruals of the initial decision-making circumstances. However, it appears that active control and participation may be important in the ability to construe decisions in a positive manner. The decision control literature cited earlier refers only to circumstances in which individuals have been actively involved in choosing conditions that produce adverse circumstances. Research on cognitive dissonance theory, likewise, suggests that people are buffered against the adverse consequences of decisions that they choose, but not against the adverse consequences of decisions that others make for them (Brehm, 1956; Brehm & Cohen, 1962; Collins & Hoyt, 1972; Festinger, 1957; Festinger & Carlsmith, 1959; Wicklund

& Brehm, 1976). People who experience the adverse effects of a decision for which they feel personally responsible alter their cognitions to minimize the adverse psychological outcomes of that decision. The process may be considerably more muted when they have not been actively involved.

To summarize, then, we suggest that when people are involved in decisions that affect them, they may be cognitively buffered, at least to a degree, against the adverse outcomes of those decisions. Self-protective illusions that appear to arise in response to stress more generally may also be engaged when people see themselves as bearing some responsibility for or as having had control over the decisions and circumstances that led to the adverse outcomes.

So far, we have discussed illusions largely in intrapsychic terms. We have considered the stable, overly-positive perceptions that people hold of themselves, their circumstances, and their future, and we have inferred that incoming information may be accommodated to those beliefs in the interest of maintaining mood and coping effectively. We now suggest that similar processes may occur on an interactive level, leading people to seek out and actively construe social information in ways that are self-enhancing. Evidence for these points comes from our recent program of research on social comparison activity.

SOCIAL COMPARISON AND EMOTIONAL RESPONSES TO INFORMATION ABOUT OTHER PEOPLE

Other people and their situations are often a powerful source of emotions. Upon encountering a highly successful classmate at a school reunion, one may experience a rush of envy, or upon seeing a person who is disabled, one may experience a sense of relief that one is not similarly afflicted and experience gratitude for one's good fortunes. The traditional framework for interpreting such emotional responses has been social comparison theory. Conventional wisdom and a substantial amount of research maintains that when one encounters another person who is better off than the self, negative emotions can be expected. One may feel diminished or inferior and react with unhappiness or envy (Diener, 1984; Marsh & Parker, 1984; Morse & Gergen, 1970; Salovey & Rodin, 1984; Tesser, Millar, & Moore, 1988; Testa & Major, 1988). Despite these adverse reactions, people are thought to want information about better-off-others, because it is a useful source of information for self-evaluation or self-improvement; emotional responses are thought to be sacrificed to these goals (see Nosanchuk & Erickson, 1985; Wheeler et al., 1969).

Correspondingly, it has been assumed that comparisons with others worse off than the self, so-called downward comparisons, make people feel better (e.g., Wills, 1981). Indeed, a substantial amount of research suggests that downward comparisons to less fortunate others boost self-esteem, increase the experience of positive emotion, and reduce anxiety (Amoroso & Walters, 1969; Crocker &

Gallo, 1985; Gibbons, 1986; Hakmiller, 1966; Kiesler, 1966; Lemyre & Smith, 1985; Morse & Gergen, 1970).

We propose that this view of affective responses to comparison information is too simple. We maintain instead that because individuals actively seek positive emotional states, they will, on balance, construe information about others in ways that make themselves feel good. We argue that, although information about others' opinions, abilities, and outcomes may serve a variety of informational and emotional purposes, that people will generally seek to experience positive emotions as a consequence of their contact with others, and thus construe these contacts in ways that are positive. Doing so involves focusing on particular aspects of comparison information.

Learning that another person is better off than yourself suggests two conclusions: that you are not as well off as that other, or that it may be possible for you to be better than you are at present. Learning that another is worse off than yourself also suggests at least two conclusions: that you are not as badly off as you could be, or that it might be possible for you to get worse. Which part of the information one focuses on may predict the nature of the emotional response.

Consistent with our prior work on positive illusions, we suggest that social comparisons may be another context in which people are able to construe information in a manner favorable to themselves. This general point translates into the specific prediction that when individuals are confronted with either upward or downward comparison information, positive affective outcomes should be the rule, regardless of comparison direction. We have confirmed this prediction in three separate investigations.

First, in an interview study of 55 cancer patients (Buunk, Collins, Taylor, VanYperen, & Dakof, 1990, Study One), respondents were asked to indicate their emotional responses, when they encountered cancer patients who were doing better or not as well as they were. They were also asked to indicate how often they felt frustrated or depressed, when reacting to better off others, and how often they felt inspired or comforted when reacting to better off others. Specifically, they were asked how often they felt lucky or grateful when they reacted to worse off others, and how often they felt fearful or anxious when reacting to worse off others. (The specific emotions cued in the questions were derived from pretesting indicating that these were the most common affective outcomes of upward and downward comparisons). Overall, positive affective responses were reported to be significantly more common than negative reactions in response to both upward and downward comparison information.

Second, in a study of 632 married residents of a middle-sized Dutch town (Buunk et al., 1990, Study Two), individuals were asked questions about their marital relationships, including items designed to assess responses to upward and downward comparisons to other married couples. Participants were asked how often they felt happy and pleased when comparing their own marital relationship to that of others who had a relationship better or worse then their own, and how often they felt unhappy or displeased when comparing their marital relationship with that of others who had a relationship either better or worse than their own. Positive emotional responses were again significantly more likely to be reported in reaction to both upward and downward comparisons.

In a third study with 60 adults enrolled in a cardiac rehabilitation program, respondents were asked to indicate their emotional responses in reaction to other patients who were worse off or better off than themselves. As in the other two studies, positive emotional responses were reported to be significantly more frequent than negative emotional responses, regardless of comparison direction (Helgeson & Taylor, 1991).

Previous research on positive illusions has suggested that certain people are less able to develop these illusions than others (Taylor & Brown, 1988). Specifically, as previously noted, individuals who are depressed, under threat, or low in self-esteem appear to have more difficulty construing information about themselves, their circumstances, and their futures in ways that are self-enhancing. Consequently, we predicted that these same variables might moderate whether or not people are able to construe social comparison information in a self-enhancing manner. We predicted that those low in self-esteem or those experiencing distress might focus on the negative information inherent in upward and downward social comparisons, rather than on the positive information.

These predictions were generally upheld in two of the investigations just reported. (We were unable to test them in the third study.) The low and high self-esteem groups did not differ in the frequency with which they reported positive affect in response to the two different types of comparisons. However, there were striking differences in the negative affect they reported experiencing after social comparisons. In the study of cancer patients, those with high self-esteem were less likely to feel bad when comparing in an upward direction and were also less likely to feel bad when comparing in a downward direction, compared to those with low self-esteem.

In the study of marital satisfaction, those uncertain about their marital situation or who were experiencing marital distress were more likely to experience negative affect from upward and downward comparisons. The ability to derive positive affective outcomes from upward and downward comparisons, however, was not moderated by marital satisfaction or uncertainty about the marital relationships.

Overall, the results from these investigations suggest that people successfully avoid negative affect that might derive from social comparison information. Instead, they report a preponderance of positive emotional consequences. Although comparisons with less fortunate others have the potential to make people feel frightened or depressed, most people seem to be able to avoid this possibility by focusing on the fact that they are better off. Similarly, although upward comparisons have the capacity to make people feel bad because they are not doing as well by comparison, most people seem to be able to avoid this potential pitfall by focusing on the positive aspect of these comparisons. Consistent with previous work on positive illusions, those low in self-esteem or dissatisfied or uncertain with respect to the dimension under evaluation are less able to avoid the negative implications of social comparisons than others. Their states of low self-esteem, negative affect, or psychological distress appear to sensitize them to the negative implications of social comparison information. This capacity to avoid negative information extends to informational preferences more generally, as we next consider.

THE PREFERENCE FOR POSITIVE STORIES

Recently, our investigations have examined the type of information that people prefer to have about other people. Current theorizing and research in social comparison has maintained that downward comparisons to others who are doing less well than the self are particularly helpful to individuals undergoing stressful events. In particular, Wills' (1981) downward comparison theory suggests that people often feel better about their own circumstances when they are exposed to others worse off, or when they have the opportunity to derogate others. Specifically, Wills predicted that these responses are especially characteristic of people undergoing stressful or threatening experiences or people low in self-esteem.

As previously noted, traditional social comparison theory has argued that upward comparisons may threaten self-esteem by underscoring the fact that one is not doing as well as others. Yet our previous work, suggesting that individuals are able to derive positive affect from both upward and downward comparisons, clearly indicates that these hypothesized affective responses are not inevitable. In a series of field and laboratory investigations, we examined people's responses to positive and negative stories.

In the first study (Taylor, Aspinwall, Giuliano, Dakof, & Reardon, 1991, Study One), cancer patients were interviewed about the information they encountered about other patients. We inquired about information that they had either sought out on their own or that other people had provided to them. Overwhelmingly, cancer patients reported that positive stories about other patients were preferable to and more helpful than negative stories. This preference for positive stories was obtained even though negative stories were more commonly told to them by others.

In a second study, we pursued this issue further by manipulating the valence and source of stories told to college students facing midterm examinations (Taylor, Aspinwall et al., 1991). These stories contained information about a fellow college student who was either doing quite well in college or struggling, with the likelihood of dismissal. Across all measures, stories with positive endings were regarded more favorably than stories with negative endings. In Study Three, we manipulated the valence and informativeness of stories in a similar college sample. Again, positive stories were rated more favorably than negative stories.

Each of the experimental studies included variables designed to address the limiting conditions under which positive stories might be preferred. Thus, for example, we had hypothesized that positive stories are helpful only when they are informative, or that positive stories are helpful only when they are relayed by experts whose opinions can presumably be trusted. We found that stories relayed by experts were regarded more positively than stories told by nonexperts, and that informative stories were rated more positively than less informative stories. However, these findings were independent of the robust preference for positive stories overall. The preference for positive information about others did not, then, depend on that information being useful or on its coming from an expert source. Rather, the preference for positive stories appeared to be purely affective. Indeed, the most robust effects we encountered concerned mood. Positive stories made people feel significantly better than studies about average individuals or individuals struggling in college, despite the fact that most of these respondents acknowledged that these students were doing better than they were.

This pattern of effects is important to the current argument for several reasons. We have argued that positive emotional states are an important reason why people develop and maintain positive illusions about themselves, the world, and the future. However, to date, our argument has focused largely on the self-serving aspects of positive illusions. That is, most of the evidence for positive illusions concerns beliefs that have a self-aggrandizing quality. Such findings appear to speak to the emotional experiences of pride, self-satisfaction, and personal happiness, but not to the more social emotions of empathy and concern for others. The research just reviewed, then, is significant, in part for extending the range of emotions experienced to those involving vicarious positive emotional states. If the goal of illusions were simply the maintenance of a personally rewarding affective state, individuals might prefer stories about less fortunate others, because it reminds them of their own advantaged and superior position. Yet the robust preference for positive information about others means that people are willing to set aside whatever short-term self-satisfaction they might experience at the expense of others in favor of stories that convey positive information about others.

This is not to suggest that the emotions experienced in response to upward comparisons are entirely selfless. Indeed, upward comparisons can confer a number of benefits on the perceiver, such as a sense of motivation and inspiration. Yet recall that the impact of positive stories is independent of their informativeness or the source of the stories. These findings imply that it is the affective experiences themselves, rather than their informational byproducts, that prompt the preference for upward comparisons. Consequently, these findings extend the range of emotional responses that may be engendered by the ability to construe information in a positive manner beyond a relatively limited self-serving purpose to include the ability to feel good about the positive experiences of others.

How do we reconcile these results with downward comparison theory and

Wills' hypothesized preference for information about worse off others? There do appear to be limited circumstances under which people derive positive affect from downward comparisons. That is, there does appear to be a set of conditions that fosters comfort in one's own situation when one encounters someone who is worse off. In an experimental study (Aspinwall & Taylor, 1991), we manipulated mood (positive or negative) and measured self-esteem to see how these variables determine affective responses to upward and downward social comparison information. The participants were college students who completed a mood induction task and then read and responded to a description of a college student who was doing either better than they were or worse than they were. For most participants, upward comparisons produced increased positive mood, greater hope, and less frustration than did downward comparisons. However, low self-esteem participants, in whom a negative mood had been induced, were the only respondents to report improved mood only after exposure to downward social comparison information. We then examined responses to comparison information as a function of whether or not the participant had experienced an academic setback and how recent that setback was. Respondents who had experienced a recent academic setback reported less favorable self-evaluations and greater frustration in response to upward comparisons, and greater hope in response to downward comparisons than respondents whose setbacks were less recent. In a second study (Aspinwall, 1991), the responses of 198 college freshmen to upward and downward social comparison information about other students were examined as a function of naturally occurring academic threats and dispositional self-esteem. As in the previous study, the only participants to profit emotionally from exposure to downward social comparisons were low self-esteem individuals under threat.

Thus, individuals under stress, low in self-esteem, and experiencing negative affect were less likely than other individuals to prefer positive information. Instead, they derived comfort from information about worse off others. It is important to note the parallels between these findings and our previous work on illusions. Recall that these are the same individuals who appear habitually to have difficulty construing information in a personally beneficial way. In this case, although they derived some comfort from downward comparisons, they derived less comfort from comparison information overall and they were less able to benefit emotionally from the positive stories about others.

POSITIVE EMOTIONS
AS GOALS OF ILLUSIONS

What is the role that emotions play in the dynamic interplay of positive illusions and personal experience? In our initial paper (Taylor & Brown, 1988), we argued that positive illusions are psychologically adaptive because they are consistently associated with traditional criteria of mental health. These include the ability to be happy or contented, the ability to care for and about others, and the capacity for creative and productive work. We here make an argument for the primacy of mood improvement in this pattern of effects. Mood is the most quickly and directly affected outcome of these positive illusions. The ability to care for and about others may occur eventually, but it requires, at a minimum, the presence of others and conducive situations to evoke relevant behavior. The facilitation of intellectual functioning and the impact of illusions on motivation, persistence, and performance are long-term outcomes. Indeed the payoffs of striving after difficult goals may be months, years, or even decades away. In contrast, the impact that positive illusions have on happiness or contentment occurs instantly, and it may be these immediate, positive effects that help to produce the long-term impact on caring for others, intellective functioning, motivation, and persistance.

This argument maintains that positive mood or the absence of a negative mood may be an important vehicle by which illusions achieve these other, more distal outcomes. This reasoning may especially apply to motivation and persistance. Manipulated positive mood does enhance the subjective probability of success and the tendency to attribute success to personal stable factors (Brown, 1984). People in a naturally occurring or an experimentally induced positive mood are more likely to believe they have succeeded and to reward themselves (Mischel, Coates, & Raskoff, 1968; Wright & Mischel, 1982). Manipulated negative mood is associated with lower expectations for future success, and attributions of success to unstable factors and with less self-reward (Brown, 1984; Mischel et al., 1968; Wright & Mischel, 1982).

The importance of mood in fostering beneficial social outcomes also has some basis. Positive mood is also known to evoke positive behavior toward others (see Taylor & Brown, 1988, for a review). Thus, mood may be the route whereby self-aggrandizing illusions facilitate social functioning as well as motivation and persistence.

Several issues concerning the centrality of mood to the impact of positive illusions remain unaddressed by this research program. For the most part, our research program has not examined mediational paths, and until such data are available, whether or not positive mood or the absence of negative mood is central to the other beneficial effects of positive illusions remains to be seen (cf. Aspinwall & Taylor, 1991). To date, we have discussed positive and negative mood only in general terms, without specifying the specific emotional experiences that might be involved. Clearly, different emotions have different consequences, both cognitive and behavioral (e.g., Frijda, Kuipers, & Ter Schure, 1989). Consequently, specifying more clearly the specific emotional states involved in these relations will be a useful direction for further investigation. A third remaining issue is the importance of positive versus negative emotional states. Several of the studies conducted thus far suggest that positive illusions may operate more to keep negative emotions at bay than to enhance the experience of positive emotions. Whether or not such an asymmetry exists in these self-regulation processes needs to be investigated more fully (cf. Taylor, 1991).

In closing, we reiterate our stance that the achievement of positive emotional states and the avoidance of negative ones appear to constitute important, though perhaps implicit, self-regulatory goals. Mild positive distortions of one's personal characteristics, one's degree of personal control, one's future, and one's circumstances more generally appear to assist in this task by enabling people to construe situations in a more favorable way than might be objectively warranted or justified. Our research also consistently shows that these processes are incomplete or lacking in individuals who are low in self-esteem, depressed, or under threat. Otherwise, these positive illusions, as we have called them, appear to be robust, and to operate not only intrapsychically, but also interpersonally, to help people manage information flow in ways that enhance their emotional functioning.

ACKNOWLEDGMENTS

Preparation of this manuscript was supported by MH 42152 from the National Institute of Mental Health to the first author. The second author was supported alternately by a National Science Foundation Graduate Fellowship and by an NIMH training grant (MN 13750).

REFERENCES

Abramson, L. Y., & Alloy, L. B. (1981). Depression, non-depression, and cognitive illusions: A reply to Schwartz. *Journal of Experimental Social Psychology, 110,* 436–447.

Affleck, G., Allen, D. A., Tennen, H., McGrade, B. J., & Ratzan, S. (1985). Causal and control cognitions in parents coping with chronically ill children. *Journal of Social and Clinical Psychology, 3,* 367–377.

Affleck, G., Tennen, H., & Gershman, K. (1985). Cognitive adaptations to high-risk infants: The search for mastery, meaning, and protection from future harm. *American Journal of Mental Deficiency, 89,* 653–656.

Alicke, M. D. (1985). Global self-evaluation as determined by the desirability and controllability of trait adjectives. *Journal of Personality and Social Psychology, 49,* 1621–1630.

Alloy, L. B., Abramson, L. Y., & Viscusi, D. (1981). Induced mood and the illusion of control. *Journal of Personality and Social Psychology, 41,* 1129–1140.

Alloy, L. B., & Ahrens, A. H. (1987). Depression and pessimism for the future: Biased use of statistically relevant information in predictions for self versus others. *Journal of Personality and Social Psychology, 52,* 366–378.

Allport, G. W. (1943). *Becoming: Basic considerations for a psychology of personality.* New Haven, CT: Yale University Press.

Amoroso, D. M., & Walters, R. H. (1969). Effects of anxiety and socially mediated anxiety reduction on paired-associate learning. *Journal of Personality and Social Psychology, 11,* 388–396.

Andreasen, N. J. C., & Norris, A. S. (1972). Long-term adjustment and adaptation mechanisms in severely burned adults. *Journal of Nervous and Mental Disease, 154,* 352–362.

Aspinwall, L. G. (1991).*The effect of upward and downward social comparisons on affect, self-evaluation, and expectations of future success.* Unpublished doctoral dissertation, University of California, Los Angeles.

Aspinwall, L. G., & Taylor, S. E. (1991). *Social comparison and mood repair: The affective consequences of upward and downward social comparison.* Manuscript submitted for publication.

Beck, A. T. (1967). *Depression: Clinical, experimental, and theoretical aspects.* New York: Harper & Row.

Brehm, J. W. (1956). Post-decisional changes in desirability of alternatives. *Journal of Abnormal and Social Psychology, 52,* 384–389.

Brehm, J. W., & Cohen, A. R. (1962). *Exploration in cognitive dissonance.* New York: Wiley.

Brock, D. W., & Wartman, S. A. (1990). Sounding board: When competent patients make irrational choices. *The New England Journal of Medicine, 322,* 1595–1599.

Brown, J. D. (1984). Effects of induced mood on causal attributions for success and failure. *Motivation and Emotion, 8,* 343–353.

Brown, J. D. (1986). Evaluations of self and others: Self-enhancement biases in social judgments. *Social Cognition, 4,* 353–376.

Buunk, B. P., Collins, R. L., Taylor, S. E., VanYperen, N. W., & Dakof, G. A. (1990). The affective consequences of social comparison: Either direction has its ups and downs. *Journal of Personality and Social Psychology, 59,* 1238–1249.

Campbell, J. D. (1986). Similarity and uniqueness: The effects of attribute type, relevance, and individual differences in self-esteem and depression. *Journal of Personality and Social Psychology, 50,* 281–294.

Cantril, H. (1938). The prediction of social events. *Journal of Abnormal and Social Psychology, 33,* 364–389.

Clements, C. D., & Sider, R. C. (1983). Medical ethics' assault upon medical values. *Journal of the American Medical Association, 250,* 2011–2015.

Collins, B. E., & Hoyt, M. F. (1972). Personal responsibility-for-consequences: An integration and extension of the "forced compliance" literature. *Journal of Experimental Social Psychology, 8,* 558–593.

Collins, R. L., Taylor, S. E., & Skokan, L. A. (1990). A better world or a shattered vision?: Changes in life perspectives following victimization. *Social Cognition, 8,* 263–285.

Coyne, J. C., & Gotlieb, I. H. (1983). The role of cognition in depression: A critical appraisal. *Psychological Bulletin, 94,* 472–505.

Crary, W. G. (1966). Reactions to incongruent self-experiences. *Journal of Consulting Psychology, 30,* 246–252.

Crile, G. (1972). *What women should know about the breast cancer controversy.* New York: Mac-Millan.

Crocker, J. (1982). Biased questions in judgment of covariation studies. *Personality and Social Psychology Bulletin, 8,* 214–220.

Crocker, J., & Gallo, L. (1985, August). *The self-enhancing effect of downward comparison.* Paper presented at the annual meeting of the American Psychological Association, Los Angeles, CA.

Danoff, B., Kramer, S., Irwin, P., & Gottlieb, A. (1983). Assessment of the quality of life in long-term survivors after definitive radiotherapy. *American Journal of Clinical Oncology, 6,* 339–345.

Diener, E. (1984). Subjective well-being. *Psychological Bulletin, 95,* 542–575.

Erikson, E. H. (1950). *Childhood and society* (2nd ed.). New York: Norton.

Festinger, L. (1957). *A theory of cognitive dissonance.* Stanford: Stanford University Press.

Festinger, L., & Carlsmith, J. M. (1959). Cognitive consequences of forced compliance. *Journal of Abnormal and Social Psychology, 58,* 203–210.

Fiske, S. T., & Taylor, S. E. (1984). *Social cognition.* New York: Random House.

Frijda, N. H. (1986). *The emotions.* Cambridge, England: Cambridge University Press.

Frijda, N. H. (1987). Emotion, cognitive structure and action tendency. *Cognition and Emotion, 1,* 115–144.

Frijda, N. H., Kuipers, P., & Ter Schure, E. (1989). Relations among emotion, appraisal, and emotional action readiness. *Journal of Personality and Social Psychology, 57,* 212–228.

Fromm, E. (1955). *The sane society.* New York: Rinehart.

Gibbons, F. X. (1986). Social comparison and depression: Company's effect on misery. *Journal of Personality and Social Psychology, 51,* 140–148.

Golin, S., Terrell, T., & Johnson, B. (1977). Depression and the illusion of control. *Journal of Abnormal Psychology, 86,* 440–442.

Golin, S., Terrell, T., Weitz, J., & Drost, P. L. (1979). The illusion of control among depressed patients. *Journal of Abnormal Psychology, 88,* 454–457.

Hakmiller, K. L. (1966). Threat as a determinant of downward comparison. *Journal of Experimental Social Psychology,* (Suppl. 1), 32–39.

Helgeson, V. S., & Taylor, S. E. (1991).*Social comparison and affiliation processes among recovering cardiac patients.* Manuscript submitted for publication.

Jahoda, M. (1958). *Current concepts of positive mental health.* New York: Basic Books.

Janoff-Bulman, R., & Frieze, I. H. (1983). A theoretical perspective for understanding reactions to victimization. *Journal of Social Issues, 39,* 1–17.

Janoff-Bulman, R., & Wortman, C. B. (1977). Attributions of blame and coping in the "real world": Severe accident victims react to their lot. *Journal of Personality and Social Psychology, 35,* 351–362.

Jourard, S. M., & Landsman, T. (1980). *Health personality: An approach from the viewpoint of humanistic psychology* (4th ed.). New York: Macmillan.

Kanouse, D. E., & Hanson, L. R., Jr. (1972). Negativity in evaluations. In E. E. Jones, D. E. Kanouse, H. H. Kelley, R. E. Nisbett, S. Valins, & B. Weiner (Eds.), Attribution: *Perceiving the causes of behavior* (pp. 47–62). Morristown, NJ: General Learning Press.

Kiesler, S. B. (1966). Stress, affiliation, and performance. *Journal of Experimental Research in Personality, 1,* 227–235.

Kuiper, N. A. (1978). Depression and causal attribution for success and failure. *Journal of Personality and Social Psychology, 36,* 236–246.

Kuiper, N. A., & Derry, P. A. (1982). Depressed and nondepressed content self-reference in mild depression. *Journal of Personality, 50,* 67–79.

Kuiper, N. A., & MacDonald, M. R. (1982). Self and other perception in mild depressives. *Social Cognition, 1,* 233–239.

Kuiper, N. A., MacDonald, M. R., & Derry, P. A. (1983). Parameters of a depressive self-schemata. In J. Suls & A. G. Greenwald (Eds.), *Psychological perspectives on the self* (Vol. 2, pp. 191–217). Hillsdale, NJ: Lawrence Erlbaum Associates.

Kuiper, N. A., Olinger, L. J., MacDonald, M. R., & Shaw, B. F. (1985). Self-schema processing of depressed and nondepressed content: The effects of vulnerability on depression. *Social Cognition, 3,* 77–93.

Langer, E. J. (1975). The illusion of control. *Journal of Personality and Social Psychology, 32,* 311–328.

Langer, E. J., & Roth, J. (1975). Heads I win, tails it's chance: The illusion of control as a function of the sequence of outcomes in a purely chance task. *Journal of Personality and Social Psychology, 32,* 951–955.

Larwood, L., & Whittaker, W. (1977). Managerial myopia: Self-serving biases in organizational planning. *Journal of Applied Psychology, 62,* 194–198.

Lemyre, L., & Smith, P. M. (1985). Intergroup discrimination and self-esteem in the minimal intergroup paradigm. *Journal of Personality and Social Psychology, 49,* 660–670.

Lewinsohn, P. M., Mischel, W., Chaplin, W., & Barton, R. (1980). Social competence and depression: The role of illusory self-perceptions. *Journal of Abnormal Psychology, 89,* 203–212.

Lund, F. H. (1975). The psychology of belief: A study of its emotional and volitional determinants. *Journal of Abnormal and Social Psychology, 20,* 63–81.

MacFarland, C., & Ross, M. (1982). The impact of causal attributions on affective reactions to success and failure. *Journal of Personality and Social Psychology, 43,* 937–946.

Malinak, D. P., Hoyt, M. F., & Patterson, V. (1979). Adults' reactions to the death of a parent. *American Journal of Psychiatry, 136,* 1152–1156.

Marks, G. (1984). Thinking one's abilities are unique and one's opinions are common. *Personality and Social Psychology Bulletin, 10,* 203–208.

Marsh, H. W., & Parker, J. W. (1984). Determinants of student self-concept: Is it better to be a relatively large fish in a small pond even if you don't learn to swim as well? *Journal of Personality and Social Psychology, 47,* 213–231.

Maslow, A. H. (1950). Self-actualizing people: A study of psychological health. *Personality, Symposium No. 1, 11*–34.

McGuire, W. (1960). A syllogistic analysis of cognitive relationships. In M. Rosenberg, C. Hovland, W. McGuire, R. Abelson, & J. Brehm (Eds.), *Attitude organization and change* (pp. 65–111). New Haven, CT: Yale University Press.

Menninger, K. A. (1930). What is a healthy mind? In N. A. Crawford & K. A. Menninger (Eds.), *The healthy-minded child.* New York: Coward-McCann.

Miles, M. S., & Crandall, E. K. B. (1983). The search for meaning and its potential for affecting growth in bereaved parents. *Health Values, 7,* 19–23.

Miller, D. T., & Ross, M. (1975). Self-serving biases in attribution of causality: Fact or fiction? *Psychological Bulletin, 82,* 213–225.

Mischel, W., Coates, B., & Raskoff, A. (1968). Effects of success and failure on self-gratification. *Journal of Personality and Social Psychology, 10,* 381–390.

Morse, S., & Gergen, K. J. (1970). Social comparison, self-consistency, and the concept of self. *Journal of Personality and Social Psychology, 16,* 148–156.

Nosanchuk, T. A., & Erickson, B. H. (1985). How high is up? Calibrating social comparison in the real world. *Journal of Personality and Social Psychology, 48,* 624–634.

Perloff, L. S., & Fetzer, B. K. (1986). Self-other judgments and perceived vulnerability of victimization. *Journal of Personality and Social Psychology, 50,* 502–510.

President's Commission for the Study of Ethical Problems in Medicine and Biomedical and Behavioral research. (1983). *Deciding to forego life-sustaining treatment: A report on the ethical, medical, and legal issues in treatment decisions.* Washington, DC: U.S. Government Printing Office.

Pruitt, D. G., & Hoge, R. D. (1965). Strength of the relationship between the value of an event and its subjective probability as a function of method of measurement. *Journal of Experimental Social Psychology, 5,* 483–489.

Rhuehlman, L. S., West, S. G., & Pasahow, R. J. (1985). Depression and evaluative schemata. *Journal of Personality, 53,* 46–92.

Rizley, R. (1978). Depression and distortion in the attribution of causality. *Journal of Abnormal Psychology, 87,* 32–48.

Robertson, L. S. (1977). Car crashes: Perceived vulnerability and willingness to pay for crash protection. *Journal of Community Health, 3,* 136–141.

Ross, M., & Fletcher, G. J. O. (1985). Attribution and social perception. In G. Lindzey & E. Aronson (Eds.), *The handbook of social psychology* (3rd ed., pp. 73–122). Reading, MA: Addison-Wesley.

Salovey, P., & Rodin, J. (1984). Some antecedents and consequences of social-comparison jealousy. *Journal of Personality and Social Psychology, 47,* 780–792.

Schulz, D. (1977). *Growth psychology: Models of the healthy personality.* New York: Van Nostrand Reinhold.

Sherman, S. J. (1980). On the self-erasing nature of errors of prediction. *Journal of Personality and Social Psychology, 39,* 211–221.

Shrauger, J. S., & Terbovic, M. L. (1976). Self-evaluation and assessments of performance by self and others. *Journal of Consulting and Clinical Psychology, 44,* 564–572.

Silver, R. L., Boon, C., & Stones, M. H. (1983). Searching for meaning in misfortune: Making sense of incest. *Journal of Social Issues, 39,* 81–102.

Silverman, I. (1964). Self-esteem and differential responsiveness to success and failure. *Journal of Abnormal and Social Psychology, 69,* 115–119.

Stockwell, S. (1983). Debate heats up over breast informed consent legislation. *Oncology Times, 5,* 1, 29.

Taylor, S. E. (1983). Adjustment to threatening events: A theory of cognitive adaptation. *American Psychologist, 38,* 1161–1173.

Taylor, S. E. (1989). *Positive illusions: Creative self-deception and the healthy mind.* New York: Basic Books.

Taylor, S. E. (1991). The asymmetrial impact of positive and negative events: The mobilization-minimization hypothesis. *Psychological Bulletin, 110,* 67–85.

Taylor, S. E., & Aspinwall, L. G. (1990). Psychological aspects of chronic illness. In G. R. VandenBos & P. T. Costa, Jr. (Eds.), *Psychological aspects of serious illness* (pp. 3–60). Washington, DC: American Psychological Association.

Taylor, S. E., Aspinwall, L. G., Giuliano, T., Dakof, G. A., & Reardon, K. (1991). *Storytelling, social comparison and coping.* Manuscript submitted for publication.

Taylor, S. E., & Brown, J. D. (1988). Illusion and well-being: A social psychological perspective on mental health. *Psychological Bulletin, 103,* 193–210.

Taylor, S. E., Helgeson, V. S., Reed, G. M., & Skokan, L. A. (1991). Self-generated feelings of control and adjustment to physical illness. *Journal of Social Issues, 47,* 91–109.

Taylor, S. E., Kemeny, M. E., Aspinwall, L. G., Schneider, S. C., Rodriguez, R., & Herbert, M. (1991). *Optimism, coping, psychological distress, and high-risk sexual behavior among men at risk for AIDS.* Manuscript submitted for publication.

Taylor, S. E., Kemeny, M. E., Reed, G. M., & Aspinwall, L. G. (in press). Assault on the self: Positive illusions and adjustment to threatening events. In G. A. Goethals & J. A. Strauss (Eds.), *The self: An interdisciplinary perspective.* New York: Springer-Verlag.

Taylor, S. E., Lichtman, R. R., & Wood, J. V. (1984). Attributions, beliefs in control, and adjustment to breast cancer. *Journal of Personality and Social Psychology, 46,* 489–502.

Taylor, S. E., Wood, J. V., & Lichtman, R. R. (1983). It could be worse: Selective evaluation as a response to victimization. *Journal of Social Issues, 39,* 19–40.

Tempelaar, R., de Haes, J. C. J. M., de Ruiter, J. H., Bakker, D., van den Heuvel, W. J. A., & van Nieuwenhuijzen, M. G. (1989). The social experiences of cancer patients under treatment: A comparative study. *Social Science and Medicine, 29,* 635–642.

Tesser, S., Millar, M., & Moore, J. (1988). Some affective consequences of social comparison and reflection processes: The pain and pleasure of being close. *Journal of Personality and Social Psychology, 54,* 49–61.

Testa, M., & Major, B. (1988, April). *Affective and behavioral consequences of social comparison.* Paper presented at the annual meetings of the Eastern Psychological Association, Buffalo, NY.

Thompson, S. C. (1981). Will it hurt less if I can control it? A complex answer to a simple question. *Psychological Bulletin, 90,* 89–101.

Veronen, L. J., & Kilpatrick, D. C. (1983). Rape: A precursor of change. In E. J. Callahan & K. A. McCluskey (Eds.), *Life span development psychology: Non-normative events.* New York: Academic Press.

Wagener, J. J., & Taylor, S. E. (1986). What else could I have done? Patients' responses to failed treatment decisions. *Health Psychology, 5,* 481–496.

Watson, D., & Clark, L. A. (1984). Negative affectivity: The disposition to experience aversive emotional states. *Psychological Bulletin, 96,* 465–490.

Weinstein, N. D. (1980). Unrealistic optimism about future life events. *Journal of Personality and Social Psychology, 39,* 806–820.

Wheeler, L., Shaver, K. G., Jones, R. A., Goethals, G. R., Cooper, J., Robinson, J. E., Gruder, C. L., & Butzine, K. W. (1969). Factors determining the choice of a comparison other. *Journal of Experimental Social Psychology, 5,* 219–232.

Wicklund, R. A., & Brehm, J. W. (1976). *Perspectives on cognitive dissonance.* Hillsdale, NJ: Lawrence Erlbaum Associates.

Wills, T. A. (1981). Downward comparison principles in social psychology. *Psychological Bulletin, 90,* 245–271.

Wright, J., & Mischel, W. (1982). Influence of affect on cognitive social learning person variables. *Journal of Personality and Social Psychology, 43,* 901–914.

9 Emotions and the Psychology of Freedom

George Mandler
University of California, San Diego and University College London

During the past several years, we have all witnessed events of great emotion in the context of the political upheavals in Eastern Germany and Europe, as the constraints of foreign and domestic repression were lifted. The emotional reactions to the achievement of freedom were particularly pronounced in those countries that had previously experienced liberal democratic freedoms, such as Czechoslovakia (until 1938) and Eastern Germany (until 1933). Apart from the results of wars, such as the relatively brief, though brutal, German subjugation of most of Western Europe, these emotions were somewhat alien to our experience in modern liberal democratic states. Though not true for all their citizens, constraints on political and personal liberty in liberal democracies have been relatively tempered and infrequent. The absence of constraints tends to be taken for granted.

The imposition of unfreedom and repression, as well as their removal, in modern nation states presents a psychology of emotion with a challenge to our understanding that we have, understandably, not been forced to face before. There should be no doubt that what we witnessed, and what the subject populations experienced, were truly intense emotional experiences. This chapter is an attempt to respond to that challenge. In particular, I wish to address a psychology of emotion both in the context of our understanding of the liberal values of freedom, and in terms of the effect of constraints on such liberties on emotional experience.

In the course of the study of human emotional experience, I have been increasingly led into a study of human value—the evaluation of experiences and events as good or bad, attractive or noxious. I present here the latest stage in that exploration, the relation of the experience of freedom to more general principles

241

of emotional experience. I start with an exposition of discrepancy/evaluation theory as the main explanatory vehicle. I then show the role that values play in a number of different emotional situations, primarily in order to lead into a discussion of the experience of freedom.

The experiences of freedom and unfreedom address a variety of values and ensuing emotions that have escaped the attention of emotion theorists in the past. The social and political arenas engender emotions that are highly relevant to daily existence and concerns. In the process of asking for more attention to these states, I try to illustrate how varied and complex affective and emotional reactions can be, going beyond the limited domains that the psychology of emotion has previously considered.

DISCREPANCY/EVALUATION THEORY:
AROUSAL AND VALUES

The focus of this discussion of emotion is on subjective emotional experiences. It is an approach in the analytic, constructivist tradition, forerunners of which can be found in Aristotle and Descartes, and in the specific, though varied, proposals that have been advanced by the French philosopher Frederic Paulhan and the philosopher/psychologists William James and John Dewey (cf. Mandler, 1979). I present first a brief sketch of the theory, followed by some theoretical elaborations on facial displays, discrepancies, the nature and source of values, and applications of the theoretical approach.

The theoretical outline presented here does not claim omniscience about emotion, and there are aspects of human emotion that the theory cannot (or does not intend to) handle. The theory proposes two basic underlying processes, autonomic (sympathetic) nervous system arousal and evaluative cognitions. In addition it suggests that the majority of occasions for sympathetic nervous system (SNS) arousal come about by the occurrence of discrepancies in perception, action, and thought. Specifically, SNS arousal accounts for the physical dimension (body), whereas evaluation incorporates the socially situated aspects of emotion (mind). Unitary conscious emotional experiences are constructed out of activated underlying cognitive representations and the registration of SNS arousal (cf. Mandler, 1985, Ch. 3; 1990a).

The notion that autonomic (sympathetic) arousal is important for the intensity of emotional experience was enshrined in psychological theory by James (1884, 1894) and Lange, and it was James who noted that if all feelings of bodily symptoms (by which he meant primarily, but not exclusively, autonomic symptoms) were abstracted from the felt emotion, all that would remain would be a "cold and neutral state of intellectual perception" (1884, p. 193). My own view of the importance of visceral arousal goes back to my initial explorations of interruption (Mandler, 1964) and has been elaborated since then (Mandler, 1975, 1984). Most recently, experimental evidence has provided strong support for that position. MacDowell (1991) showed that experimentally produced subjective states show a linear, monotonic relationship between reported intensity of feelings and the preceding autonomic events (heart rate increases and skin resistance rates).

Discrepancies (and interruptions) do not constitute emotions, they only produce the "passionate" contribution of the sympathetic nervous system. Discrepancies exist in positive as well as negative situations and provide the fuel for both types of emotions. In addition, positive emotions arise out of the opportunity to complete interrupted or discrepant actions and thought (Berscheid, 1983). On the other hand, discrepancy is not the only source of "emotional" arousal; emotions can be energized by arousal arising from a variety of sources, such as effort, exercise, drugs, conditioning, and so on.

I discuss evaluative states and cognitions in greater detail later. I should stress here a point I have made in the past, namely that the variety of different intra- and extra-psychic situations that produce subjective emotional states is in principle infinite. Different situations, evaluations, and kinds of knowledge produce different cognitive states that inform the subjective experiences we call "emotions."

Subjective emotional states have direct motivational effects. Organisms will seek out occasions that are evaluated as beneficial, that make them feel "good," and avoid those that are evaluated as noxious and make them feel "bad"; they will act to generate "positive" states and to eliminate "negative" ones.

Approaches such as the one advocated here have been sometimes described as (unnecessarily?) reductionist. I am not sure whether a theoretical analysis of a complex psychological event should be called reductive, but be that as it may, consider the alternatives. Philosophers and psychologists have been trying to define emotions for at least 2,500 years, and we still have little if any agreement about the "nature" of human emotions, the full panoply of situations and feelings that they entail, or the range of phenomena implied by the natural language uses of "emotion." It may well be that common sense is not always a good guide to reality in psychology, anymore than it is in physics (*pace* Einstein). I have previously argued that a necessary first step is to develop a theoretical system that can account successfully for a reasonably large number of "emotional" phenomena (see also McNaughton, 1989).

The theory does not claim explanatory power for all phenomena that may be considered emotional. Emotions are too pervasive, and different interpretations of the natural language uses of *emotion* are too diverse to be derived from a single source. They are also too important in the daily life of *homo sapiens* to have a single evolutionary origin. Emotions emphasize our values, color our actions, motivate much of our behavior, and are likely to have several sources. Among other sources of emotions are so-called conditioned emotional reactions, some aesthetic values, behaviors of the self or others that are interpreted as emotional, unusual (including pathological or drug induced) brain states, and some motivational states such as lust.

THEORETICAL ELABORATIONS

I have previously discussed some of the myths that surround the psychology of emotion (Mandler, 1992b). The main ones are the expectation that an unequivocal answer to the question, "What is an emotion?" is possible, that there exists a specific set of fundamental or basic emotions, and that facial displays are structurally and developmentally tied to the emotions that they "express." I do not wish to discuss here further the first two myths (but see Mandler, 1990a; Mandler, 1992b; Ortony & Turner, 1990), but I do want to make some further comments about the issue of facial expression because it is particularly relevant to a discussion of value.

Facial Displays

In 1975 I made the suggestion that facial displays are ancient, preverbal communicative devices and as such are displays of values (indicating what is good or bad, useful or useless, etc.) that are frequently part of the emotional concatenation. Rather than expressing some preceding or contemporaneous emotional state, facial displays derive from social and communicative needs and, inter alia, play a role in emotion. Recently there has been extensive systematic work on the function and structure of facial displays. For example, Fridlund (1991, 1992) analyzed such displays from a social psychological point of view and noted that facial displays are consonant with current evolutionary views of signaling, and that even displays previously considered involuntary are in fact social and communicative devices. Fridlund has shown how a social interpretation of these displays, depending in part on the presence or absence of an audience, best fits with existing knowledge about the function of displays in emotion and their apparent universality. He has elaborated a scenario of the evolutionary origin and utility of facial displays in which these displays function to communicate intentions and situational evaluations in the absence of verbal devices. Extensive experimental work on facial displays has further substantiated the view of facial displays as communicative (i.e., nonverbal language-like) devices. Facial displays are mediated by communicative situations (Chovil, 1991) and they convey syntactic and semantic information in close connection with speech (Chovil, in press). Bavelas, Black, Lemery, and Mullett (1987) summarized extensive work on body displays and motor mimicry with the relevant comment that "nonverbal expressions [such as facial displays] can occur during, before, or after an emotional state; they are independent of such feeling, to the same degree that words are" (1987, p. 336). Facial displays exemplify evaluative reactions just like words (and verbal language in general) provide evaluative information. Verbal and nonverbal languages contribute to emotional constructions; verbal and other bodily displays reveal evaluative reactions. Emotions are constructed, in part, of these verbal and nonverbal displays, but the displays have independent functions and histories.

Discrepancies

An aspect of the theory that deserves further exploration is the widespread nature of discrepancies. First, discrepancies, as usually defined, are practically always present. All events are somewhat discrepant from what is expected; the world changes continuously. As a result, some degree of arousal is present in many, possibly most, day to day situations. And so is some degree of feeling or mood. It is the very pervasiveness of discrepancies that keeps the SNS at a fairly continuous, but low, level of arousal, and that accounts for the continuous background of feeling states. On the other hand, the passionate, strongly felt emotions require significant levels of SNS arousal, much above the usual background level.

Second, expectations tend to be fairly specific, and even apparently expected events can be followed by emotional episodes. Consider the loss of a loved one who has been ill and whose death has been anticipated. Thus, one expectation is confirmed, but the actual emotions that are experienced are due to a number of other expectations—all different from the expected death. The actual loss is always different from the anticipated one. It is unlikely that the grieving person has rehearsed (anticipated) all the possible situations that are changed as a result of the loss of the loved one. And one expectation that is usually violated is the hope that the person may not die after all. Friends remind one of past interactions that cannot be recreated and thus generate discrepancies; actions and plans must be envisaged that are often discrepant with previous experiences and expectations; in short, one's life changes and the changes produce emotions (cf. Berscheid, 1982).

In brief, emotions, just as other human thought and action, are multidetermined. We do not live in our world with simple, single expectations, and similarly their violations (the discrepancies) are not unidimensional. Unconscious expectations of the state of the world not only encompass a large number of different aspects of our environment at the same time, but also involve conflicting expectations about the same event.

Demonstrations of these conflicts can be found in the positive emotional states. The intensity of these states is often related to the fact that at the same time that we expect (hope for) the positive outcome, we also expect (fear) the negative one. Combinations of competing expectations are found everyday in the job situation, in close relationships, and even in rather mundane scenarios such as the dentist's office, a restaurant, or a food market. What is discrepant? The anticipation of most events is rarely devoid of doubts and fears, of hopes and dreams, though not necessarily in very intense degrees. The world of romantic love for example, is full of such ambivalences, and wherever there are ambivalences the actual event will be discrepant with some of them. In contrast, consider a positive event that is fully anticipated, in all its details and nuances. For example, a lottery has been won and some time later the check arrives in your mail. The value is still there, but the intensity will be relatively low. Ambivalences operate, of course, in negative as well as positive events. For every expected "good" there are thoughts of disappointments and slip-ups, and for every expected "bad" there are hopes of redemption and relief.

Discrepancies most frequently occur in our interactions with the real world, which may counter our expectations. However, wishes and ideals also frequently produce discrepancies, both intrapsychically and in our interactions with the external world. I may wish for my favorite team to win an important game, and its failure to do so creates a discrepancy (and an emotional state). I may have a desire to speak a foreign language fluently, but my realization that I do not and cannot produces discrepancies. Ideal conditions (and people) can be envisaged, but fail to be encountered in reality, and sometimes even fail in fantasy. In a repressive society my expectations may not be violated because I expect repression and it actually occurs, but my hopes and wishes are dashed.

More generally, the detection of discrepancies is one of the most useful adaptive devices that humans (and at least all other mammals) have developed. The utility of such an ability can best be described as the possession of a difference detector (Mandler, 1992b), which informs the organism that the situation it is in is different than expected, that the world has changed, that new ways of dealing with it need to be developed, and that preparation for further action is needed. That preparation by the autonomic nervous system (cf. Cannon, 1930) speaks directly to the origins and utility of emotional experience.

Sources and Origins of Values

Values are cognitive representations that shape our likes, dislikes, preferences, prejudices, and social attitudes. They are expressed in judgments of what is good or bad, acceptable or unacceptable, in our choices and preferences. We usually exercise simple values unconsciously; we usually know what we like without reflection—without deliberation.[1] For example, sweet substances are "good," pain is "bad," rock may be preferred to classical music, and one may rather have a bar of chocolate than a dish of spinach. All of these demonstrate the operation of values. By themselves, values are just preferences, and so forth, but in

---

[1]Complex values, such as moral values, usually do require deliberation and justification (cf. Mandler, 1993a).

conjunction with sympathetic arousal, they provide the cognitive representations in the construction of subjective emotional states. Similar uses can be found in other theoretical approaches: for example in Lazarus' (e.g., 1991) use of the notion of *appraisal,* the outcome of which is usually some value, or in the many different cognitive structures explored by Ortony, Clore, and Collins (1988). Frijda's concept of *concerns* is also related to values; concerns refer to "dispositions that motivate the subject, that prompt him to go in search of given satisfactions or to avoid given confrontations" (Frijda, 1986, p. 334).

Values, as expressed, for example, in judgments of good and bad and in preferences and dislikes, have a number of different sources. However, any single such value is likely to be multidetermined. The three major sources of values—innate, social, and structural—are briefly sketched here.[2]

Some values arise out of *innate* approach and withdrawal tendencies, as seen in the preference for sweet substances and the avoidance of pain-producing events. The most likely mechanism for the transformation of these behaviors into cognitive values lies in our self-observations of these tendencies and actions, that is, the experience and perception of our approaches and withdrawals (cf. Bem, 1967). In humans, these values inform only a small part of our lives and are overshadowed by social (as well as structural) sources.

Social values arise out of a variety of interactions with our cultural, social, and personal environment. the mental representation of objects and events—and in particular their evaluative characteristics—is largely determined by the social context. The predication of values, such as preferences and dislikes, arises out of a number of different learning mechanisms operating in social situations. We acquire such predications often without any contact with the actual events. Prejudices and tastes (in food, clothing, pulchritude) are adopted from the cultural context—usually without question or deliberation.

Structural sources of values arise out of the patterning, consistency, and discrepancy of mental representations of objects and events. Both the consistency and the potential discrepancy of representations contribute to the change of values. These factors are best seen within the context of schema theory (cf. Mandler, 1985). The properties of schemas are dispositional; that is, schemas are "created" or assembled at point of use. It is useful not to conceptualize schemas as neurophysiologically localized entities. Rather they are constructed out of distributed features (Rumelhart & McClelland, 1985), which are available for a variety of different schematic structures. Currently available information and evidence constructs a particular representation that responds both to the immediate situation and to the regularities (schemas) generated by past events. Schemas are dispositional organizations of mental content that represent past experiences and in turn organize perception and experience; they represent regularities of past experiences, often in an abstract form, but they may also be very concrete

---

[2]For a detailed discussion see Mandler (1993a).

representations. Schemas determine what will be expected and, consequently, what is different or discrepant. A particular schema, a concatenation of features, defines an object or event, such as an automobile or a social encounter. Different patterns or organizations of these features determine whether it is a beautiful or ugly automobile, a proper or improper greeting.

Well established schemas that represent frequently encountered objects or events, that is, that are consistent with the current scene, generate a feeling of familiarity, of acceptance and, in general, positive evaluations. Such increasing familiarity may even change initially negative evaluations to positive ones (cf. Gaver & Mandler, 1987; Mandler & Shebo, 1983). In general, novel events are often seen as discrepant and unpleasant, but may over time change to a more positive evaluation. This gives rise, in part, to an essentially conservative human being, who prefers the known to the unknown, the familiar to the unfamiliar. Well-known habits and fashions are usually preferred to new ways of acting and thinking—in a sense as a means of avoiding mental and physical effort. Preferences usually go to the typical and known event.

At the same time that we tend to prefer the familiar, we are faced with discrepancies that are a frequent characteristic of our experience, and they become important in establishing new values, new ways of seeing the world. Following Piaget, I have noted that assimilation is one mode of adapting to the world, leaving basic values and approaches unchanged. The other mode is accommodation—the change of existing mental structures in order to deal with new events and changing conditions. In contrast as well as in complement to the conservative influence of familiarity, humans may also seek novel, discrepant, challenging events. The positive evaluation of the novel derives in part from the satisfaction of dealing with the unknown, the sense of completing and the feeling of achievement when new situations are mastered and brought under our control (cf. also Berscheid, 1982, 1983); in part it finds it origins in social values that reward creativity and novel adaptations. However, novel situations are always discrepant and are always occasions for autonomic arousal: the emotions that follow will depend on other expectations, such as the social acceptance of creativity and achievement. In the absence of value systems that favor dealing with new situations, they usually will be seen as somewhat disturbing and anxiety arousing. A very similar point has been made by existentialist thinkers, as when Kierkegaard (1844/1957) spoke of the inevitability of anxiety as the maturing individual is faced with possibility and choice.

Discrepancies are not only indicative of novelty, they also, by the very act of accommodation, create new ways of seeing the world, new ways of perceiving and thinking. The accommodation to new ways of creating music, art, or literature is marked by initial unease (and often dislike), which is then followed, with increasing exposure and analysis, by increasing appreciation and eventual acceptance. More generally, contradictions in our personal and social environment require changes in mental structures, accommodations that inevitably create new likes and dislikes, new values. The result is human vacillation between the acceptance and comfort of the familiar and the challenge and restructuring of the novel.

Applications:
Interactions of Discrepancies and Values

A wide variety of situations produces different values, and, in concert with interruptions and discrepancies, generates a wide variety of different emotions. I summarize a number of demonstrations of the application of discrepancy/evaluation theory as a prelude to moving to new ground in a discussion of freedom.

The complex designated as *stress* refers at various times—and sometimes in the same context—to environmental conditions and/or organismic response. Stress represents an example of the operations posited by discrepancy/evaluation theory (cf. Mandler, 1993b). The environmental conditions usually ascribed to stress involve almost without exceptions some form of discrepancy or interruption. Whether it is the stress of excessive demands at work or of the uncertainty of personal relationships or of the lurking dangers of driving at high speeds or of the change of residence or occupation (cf. Mandler, 1990b), they all involve expectations and the uncertainty of their outcome. Dealing with stress involves dealing with autonomic arousal, and the values that are assigned to stress situations are predominantly negative. The negative values are often signaled by attempts to remove such stimuli or to remove oneself from the situation.

The effects of emotion on *memory and thought* processes involve arousal as well as evaluation (Mandler, 1992c). Arousal operates on memory by restricting the limited capacity of consciousness (Mandler, 1992a). The perception of arousal preempts part of that capacity and therefore restricts the conscious aspects of memory retrieval, which in part accounts for poorer recall under conditions of emotional arousal. The operations of values and the evaluative aspects of emotion are demonstrated in the effects of mood on memory. The reinstatement of mood states (persisting values) at the time of recall favors recall of information acquired under the influence of that particular mood.

I noted earlier the importance of discrepancies in the perception and evaluation of *musical and artistic productions*. William Gaver and I (Gaver & Mandler, 1987) discussed the conditions that produce the appreciation of musical works, and particularly the reaction to new arrangements and the development of positive and negative evaluations. The emotional reactions to artistic productions (whether visual or auditory) all involve some discrepancies, violations of expectations, and values that are engendered both by the structure of the work and by social contexts (cf. Mandler, 1993a).

Relatively little attention has been paid to the interaction between emotion and the *acquisition of knowledge*. There are a number of different such interactions, but I have concentrated on the effect of errors and successes (Mandler, 1989). Social learning produces the context that defines errors as bad and successes as good and these values interact with discrepancies. Any discrepancy in the course of learning and problem solving produces a potential emotional episode. Errors and unexpected successes are obvious discrepancies, and they contribute both to the impairment and to the success of learning. Errors produce interruptions, arousal, and constriction of available conscious capacity. As such they are deleterious. However, the occurrence of errors during the learning process makes it possible for the individual to anticipate such interruptions and to make them less disruptive, that is, less surprising and therefore less interfering. Errors are inevitable, and it is advantageous for the individual to anticipate them, specifically so as not to be overwhelmed when unexpected errors occur. Errors will at first be associated with negative valuations, but with experience such errors will be seen as a natural part of the learning process and will have a less negative, possibly neutral, value associated with them. Conversely, successes, and especially unexpected ones, will be occasions for positive evaluations, but they may also have deleterious consequences on the learning process, that is, they produce arousal and conscious constriction.

With the theoretical background established, and with its applicability demonstrated, I now move to a new endeavor—the exploration of a psychology of freedom.

FREEDOM, CONSTRAINTS, AND POWER: WHAT DOES IT MEAN TO FEEL FREE?

To venture into an analysis of the psychological meaning of human freedom is daunting indeed, and I do so with a sense of tentativeness.[3] However, the attempt is motivated by any commitment to the central task of psychology, which is to understand the mechanisms and processes that eventuate in everyday human thought and action. A search for these underlying variables is based on a rejection of facile explanations of complex human behavior, frequently couched in appeals to innateness, and to apparently inevitable evolutionary adaptations. Such approaches reveal a certain scientific laziness; one should not accept apparently inescapable (but often untestable) biological explanations until one has explored in depth other alternative explanations. I have tried to do that in my approach to emotion and its evolutionary background (Mandler, 1990a, 1992b),

---

[3]None of my discussion is intended to intrude on the use of such concepts as liberty, freedom, and power within political, sociological, or philosophical contexts. Arguments about the relative advantages of liberty or the use of power in democratic and other societies are at a different level from those advanced here (e.g., Hall, 1985; Mann, 1986). I am addressing the issue of personal, psychological meanings of freedom and power.

in analyses of aggressive behaviors (Mandler, 1992b), and now in an approach to human freedom. I cannot let go unchallenged an appeal to an innate "instinct for freedom" (Chomsky, 1991), any more than I can accept unidimensional evolutionary stories about "human aggression," or accounts about the apparently unheralded, sudden and full grown emergence of human language. Aggressive actions are often situation specific, have different social and evolutionary histories, and cannot be squeezed into a single evolutionary account. Nor is verbal language a singular evolutionary event, but rather the complex outcome of phonological, cognitive, and social precursors.[4] In general, complex human actions and thoughts are the least likely candidates for unique, singular evolutionary events. And the concept of freedom is surely characterized by complexity and multiple determination.

Natural (Negative) and Constructed (Positive) Liberties

I start with a distinction between two different concepts of human liberty, a negative one and a positive one (Berlin, 1969), though for reasons elaborated later I shall call them natural and constructed liberties.

The central concept of freedom in the modern Western liberal tradition was defined by John Stuart Mill in stating that "liberty consists in doing what one desires." However, to do "what one desires" requires that no impediments be placed in the path of one's desires. As a consequence, it has been noted that this "liberal" definition is negative, in the sense that such freedom (or liberty) requires "the absence of coercion or constraints imposed by another person" (Partridge, 1967, p. 222). Such absence may be enlarged to "the absence of obstacles to possible choices and activities" (Berlin, 1969, p. xxxix), but the classical reference is always to the ability to do as one wants without constraints; the crucial event is the constraint that *does not happen*. It is understood, of course, that society generally and normally will accept some obvious constraints, such as the overworked constraint against yelling "fire" in a crowded theater. I will primarily address this "negative" (natural) sense of freedom.

Before dealing in some detail with the negative freedoms, I need to address the positive ones. Positive/constructed liberty involves the sense in which I consider myself free to act in the service of more abstract reasons, purposes, and goals, or in the interests of a higher good or higher self.[5] The notion of these constructed freedoms can be traced to classical Greek ideas that freedom involves knowing the "good" (through learning and social experience) and deliberately choosing it. Some examples from major contributors to the Western tradi-

---

[4]See the reference above to facial displays as nonverbal communicative precursors and alternatives to verbal language.

[5]The arguments for "positive," constructed freedoms frequently involve appeals to rationality, which, in turn, requires extensive psychological investigation.

tion (cf. Oppenheim, 1968) assist in defining this concept. Epictetus stated that "freedom is not acquired by satisfying yourself with what you desire, but by destroying your desire"; Spinoza said that "I will call him free who is led solely by reason"; and Rousseau observed that "obedience to a law which we prescribe to ourselves is liberty." As Isaiah Berlin eloquently argued, positive/constructed freedoms may require commitments to higher ideals or goals that themselves may be corrupted and that may be subject to abuse, both frivolous and evil (cf. Berlin, 1969). Hartley Coleridge summed up the problem by defining freedom as a "universal license to be good," which leaves open to mischief or chance the public or personal definition of what constitutes the "good." More generally, "if 'freedom' becomes available for anybody's moral or political ends, then . . . all will agree that liberty is a supreme good, but they will agree on nothing else" (Oppenheim, 1968, p. 558).

I prefer to call the negative freedoms "natural," because they arise out of the absence of constraints, and positive freedoms "constructed," because they arise out of social constructions. Natural freedom means the absence of constraints and it is "natural" because universally it invokes emotional reactions to constraints and their removal. The constructed freedoms, on the other hand, are socially constructed; they vary from time to time and from society to society; they often reflect contemporary social conventions and mores, in terms of current views of human nature, rationality, or social structure. The prohibitions involved in natural freedoms are, to be sure, also frequently social products, but the reaction to these constraints and their absence is not.

Constructed liberties are not usually the occasion for true emotional experiences; they are essentially cognitive in structure and intent. However, some constructed liberties may be constrained just as natural ones are, that is, they have both natural and constructed components, and as a result may engender emotional reactions. For example, it has been argued that positive/constructed freedoms endow the individual with the power or ability to be part of the political process, particularly in decision making. In that sense, individuals are free to the extent that they are in a position to participate in government, in the distribution of public goods, and importantly in necessary restrictions of natural liberty. And at least some of these liberties may, of course, be constrained. However, these constructed liberties may refer more to the empowerment of individuals in the political process, rather than in their "wish" to participate in it (cf. Dworkin, 1991, for a relevant argument and a practical application of Berlin's distinction).

I cannot deal here with the problems of determinism and free will that are implied in most definitions of freedom, that is, in freedom to choose or act. Suffice it to say that I am primarily concerned with the availability of alternatives and choices, and the presence or absence of constraints on them. William Kessen and I (Mandler & Kessen, 1974) have noted that a belief in free will may, by itself, provide many of the subjective experiences usually assigned to the concept of free will. Such a belief is likely to produce delays in decision making, considerations of alternatives and other consequences, which will have the effect of producing more deliberate choices.

I am concerned primarily with a psychological understanding of the "negative"/natural liberal sense of freedom or liberty. I should note, though, that this does not imply that I accept this definition as the only or the preferred sense. However, the concern with this particular use in the Western tradition motivates my attempt to understand its psychological underpinnings. I return later to possible alternative social goals.

The Psychology of Constraint and Freedom

To be constrained from initiating some action or from continuing to act are prime examples of discrepancies and interruptions. One usually expects to initiate an intended action and to continue and complete an action once it has been initiated. It is irrelevant to the present discussion whether one wants to or wishes to act or whether the action is automatic or deliberate—questions of voluntarism or free will do not affect the fact that an action is initiated and prevented from completion. We wish to be able to do "what we want." With respect to freedom or liberty, constraints are actions or conditions that prevent the execution of a particular act or a class of behaviors. Prohibiting people from associating with one another, keeping them from traveling abroad, confining them because of their unpopular or prohibited beliefs, restricting the occupations in which they may engage, are just a few examples of constraints that denote the absence of freedom. All of these constraints are discrepancies or interruptions—of hopes and expectations, actions, and incipient actions.

It is obvious what the emotional consequences of an absence of liberty (i.e., the presence of constraints) are. Actions are contemplated or even tentatively initiated, and are then interrupted or diverted. As a result, arousal occurs and the ensuing emotional reaction is negative. The negative affect is, of course, a result of the negative evaluation of being prevented from doing what one "wants" to do. The most frequent emotional reactions are resentment, frustration, a sense of oppression, and—very frequently and partly related to all of them—anger. The emotion of anger is usually associated with being blocked from reaching a desired goal (cf. Mandler, 1992b; Ortony, Clore, & Collins, 1988), and the central value is presumably the desirability of the goal: the freedom to do what one desires to do. To the extent that we fail to have any alternative action available, the very consideration of a prohibited act generates anxiety; we imagine the desired state of affairs, but also become aware of the obstacles that prevent its achievement and of our impotence in the face of these obstacles. Such a view restates part of Kierkegaard's (1844/1957) discussion of freedom.

Kierkegaard related freedom to our ability to become aware of possibility (i.e., possible choices). We create possibility, and the very consideration of such possibility generates conditions of anxiety and dread.

It is a truism that living in a human society means living with constraints. Common cultural norms and social roles constrain a vast array of behaviors, beliefs, attitudes, and so forth. All societies constrain. They prescribe pervasive and commonplace concerns; to name just a few: how we act as a function of our gender, what we wear and when and where, what are acceptable foods, how and when we vote (if we do), whether we live in apartments, tents, houses, and so on, how we form families, whom we can or cannot marry, and how we engage in social and sexual intercourse. Many of these prescriptions produce no conscious constraints, and are not discrepant; they are accepted as "right and proper." In the areas of social and political thought and behavior we encounter the same dialectic of the familiar and the discrepant that I discussed earlier with respect to individual behavior. There are aspects of society and culture that are accepted unconsciously without deliberation or further consideration. These aspects (including some areas of food, dress, and social intercourse) provide the acceptable "familiar" and even reassuring features of our daily existence. The question of whether these cultural constraints are desirable or not does not, in the majority of cases, even arise. They are.

It is possible to divide the various constraints that exist in society rather roughly into three categories. First, are the cultural norms just discussed; they do not give rise to discrepancies; there are typically no wishes or desires that are discrepant with them. Second, there is a set of constraints on choice that we encounter that are either not of great importance—we care, but not too deeply, about being constrained in these desires or wishes—or that are constraints of only temporary, although possibly great, importance. We may be conscious of these constraints, which include some social rules ("do not cross when the light is red"), as well as idiosyncratic obstacles. Among these are the many daily annoyances in which we are prevented from doing what we "wish to do." These too vary over a wide range and include such wishes/wants/desires as wanting to exceed the speed limit, wanting, as a child, to stay out after midnight or to eat only chocolates for dinner, desiring to let one's hair grow long, wanting to smoke in a restaurant, and so on. Finally, there are the natural liberties, essentially the political freedoms. These are lasting, important, and considered to be part of our "rights" as citizens in a democratic society. The constraints imposed on the first category are rarely considered as such; those in the intermediate category refer primarily to restrictions on group or individual preferences and wishes, whereas those in the third category are generally considered violations of "rights."

The "habits" of the first category outlined above are rarely subject to the kind of emotional reactions that I have sketched here, but the wishes and rights of the second and third categories usually evoke emotional experiences. When these wishes and rights are constrained we are faced with discrepancies, autonomic arousal, and subsequent emotional reactions. The emotions may vary from embarrassment when we exercise our social norms in a different social or cultural setting and discover that they are not acceptable, to negative feelings of usually temporary nature when our desires are thwarted, and to lasting social disaffections when rights are blocked or frustrated.

It is also the case that the habits, desires, and rights are subject to change that may be slow or may take place rather suddenly. Cultural norms change over time and personal desires change; for example. as we shift our position in the social group. But political rights also change as societies and their structure changes. Political rights were different in Roman society from medieval times and from modern rights, and we should keep in mind that in terms of recorded history the liberal concept of freedom is relatively recent. Furthermore, some of the apparently nonpolitical desires (and their constraints) may become politicized, as, for example, length of hair became both a political statement and subject to social constraints in some places in the 1960s.

To return to a more specific question about the psychology of freedom, what are the emotional conditions when natural liberty does in fact exist? Negative liberty implies the ability to complete actions that may or may not have been frustrated at some earlier time, or to engage in actions that are now and always have been available. I want briefly to consider the latter—liberties that are in fact available and have rarely if ever been constrained in the past. These are not usually considered as liberties; they are taken for granted; they actually become part of the cultural background and are accepted unconsciously. In addition to this usual cultural background, in most established democracies the choice of (available) foods, the selection of reading materials, and similar everyday "liberties" produce little if any recognition as freedoms, and no affective reaction. Societies that have little history of previous constraints or authoritarianism should show little emotional/affective reactions to the liberties available in everyday life, just as there is little reaction to the other "habits" and norms of the culture.[6]

Now consider the cases in which liberties are available that have been previously constrained. Such events may occur in nearly all societies. The lifting of rationing restrictions after a war permits people to do things they were previously constrained from doing. The emotional scenario may be quite complicated. On the one hand, prior experience expects one to encounter that which are now removed. This is just another case of violation of an expectation, with arousal to follow, but the evaluation, and the ensuing emotional state, would be positive.

---

[6]In contrast, as I have indicated earlier, nations that have previously enjoyed democratic liberties generate particularly strong emotional reactions to repression and its removal; they "know" what is constrained. Conversely, it would be of interest to investigate formally the proposition that in the absence of repression societies that have always enjoyed unrestricted liberties value these freedoms less.

On the other hand, the very ability to carry out an act that had previously not been available produces the evaluative cognition of completion (Berscheid, 1983), which, together with the arousal derived from its relative unexpectedness, generates a "joy of completion" (Mandler, 1985). In the case of societies that switch—slowly or suddenly—from repression to freedom, these effects are much greater, the emotional reaction is much stronger (if for no other reason than that the arousal will be much greater). The best recent example is, of course, found in the European revolutions of 1989. This sense of freedom, expressed in Martin Luther King's "free at last," of being able to act as one "wishes," produces the positive sense of freedom that natural liberties can engender.[7] It should be clear now that the "freedom emotion" is more likely to occur under conditions where previous constraints and prohibitions have existed. The values that inform this emotional reaction include the desired end goals (e.g., unconstrained speech and association), as well as the more general removal of constraints in principle.

There is another side to the psychological reaction to a lack of freedoms. I have noted above that extensive experience with situations and events will generate very stable schemas. And stable schemas generate the stable aspects of society—a condition necessary for the very fact of social organization. Successive encounters with such events will produce an easy "fit" with the underlying schemas and will generate the subjective experience of familiarity—and eventual acceptance. Briefly entering the arena of sociological and political analysis, I offer the following only as illustrative and by no means complete. Authoritarian societies that generate basic satisfactions for their members will, despite many constraints and prohibitions, produce acceptance of the *status quo*. This may be particularly true if the government in power can produce satisfaction of other— real or imagined—desires or wishes. The widespread acceptance of a fascist regime in Germany during the late 1930s existed in the absence of many natural freedoms. Their absence was counterbalanced by the availability of employment, the appeals to German hegemony, the defeat of "foreign" influences and domination, and promises of increasing power to the German nation.[8] The lure of familiarity, coupled with obvious (but often superficial) benefits, may lead to the acceptance of a state of affairs that objectively, constrains many actions and restricts freedom. In addition, the restriction to certain permitted actions, the satisfaction of perceived needs and desires, and the power derived from the protection of a powerful government will be perceived as producing other benefits. If one is at ease—to some extent—with current life, one need not entertain novel, unfamiliar actions with uncertain outcomes that may themselves lead to arousal and failure. Stories of long-term prisoners reluctant to leave the famil-

---

[7] I find this another difficult case for the proponents of a limited number of basic emotions. It is, like love and lust, never mentioned in lists of such emotions.

[8] I shall return to the issue of the meaning of power later; in the present context, it refers to the fact that the individual shares some real or imaginary ability to constrain others and to be free from constraints themselves.

iarity and "safety" of prison illustrate how constraints may be preferred to the uncertainties and dangers of the "free" life.

There is a sense in which the citizen of a fascist state and the prisoner in jail are psychologically "free." They do not, for different reasons, request freedom of speech or of movement, and as a result do not experience the deleterious effects of the constraints that are in force. The constraints have become cultural norms. Such an analysis does not, of course, address the political or philosophical issues involved in the absence of these freedoms.

The Psychological Meaning of Power

The exercise of liberty—the absence of constraints—requires controls over the means of attaining desired ends and goals. In its most general sense, "power is the ability to pursue and attain goals through mastery of one's environment" (Mann, 1986). In addition, power may be defined as the possession of desired goods and the control of scarce means and of the conditions for action and communication.[9] But "when there is conflict between individuals and groups for possession or control of scarce means and conditions of action, control over means is a condition of the availability of alternatives, and hence of choice and freedom" (Partridge, 1967, p. 224).

Groups that have "power", that is, privileged access to the goods of society, protect that access by the domination/restriction of less powerful groups. Under those conditions, it is the groups that hold power who enjoy maximum freedom in a society. Conversely, the powerless will be deprived of goods and constrained from exercising actions to the extent that such access and exercise restricts the "freedoms" of the powerful, as in Isaiah Berlin's felicitous phrase: "Freedom for the wolves has often meant death to the sheep" (Berlin, 1969, p. xlv). But, as I have noted above, in a stable society the powerless may accept the constraints and are, in that sense, psychologically free. It is only if one posits some basic human needs for expression, sustenance, shelter, association, or movement that the associated freedoms can be said to be generally relevant to people under all conditions.

The psychological satisfaction for those in power is the exercise of freedoms, particularly when such "freedom" becomes evident by the fact that others in the society are constrained from its exercise. And it is irrelevant whether these freedoms are trivial or crucial. It is the mark of subjective satisfaction by the powerful in a restrictive society to enjoy the use of a private car as much as the availability of adequate food, the privilege of criticizing "their" government as much as the availability of sumptuous houses. In the extreme cases, feudal rulers were often able to command any satisfactions available in their societies. This is not to say that the problems and contradictions of power do not generate their

---

[9]For present purposes I shall not employ the otherwise very useful distinction among economic, ideological, and political power (cf. Hall, 1985; Mann, 1986).

own conflicts and dissatisfactions, but the distinction between powerful and powerless groups is obvious.

Since the last century, the primary analysis of power and control has been in terms of economic classes. Marx saw the basic locus of power in the control over the "economic surplus" through the control of the means of production. Subsequent thinkers in that tradition have tended to subsume other power relations under the economic ones. However, it has become increasingly clear that, whereas economic dominance is important, dimensions other than control over the economy have to be considered seriously. Control and power have been exercised by Whites against Blacks, men against women, hetero- against homosexuals. In all of these cases, privileges and controls (including, of course, economic ones) are preserved by the powerful over the less powerful groups. The powerless experience less freedom, because they are constrained from exercising certain roles and actions, and therefore tend to experience negative states.

If power is identified as the ability to restrict others and to entertain actions without restraint, then membership in groups of power is something that is likely to be desired by those who are in fact constrained. More generally, though, it appears that actual membership is not necessary to derive some, at least temporary, satisfaction from identifying with powerful groups.[10] If I feel constrained and deprived of goods and the possibility of actions, then I may well seek some other role or social identity that will restore at lest a sense of possible power. Such identifications are more likely, the more confused the state of society, the more uncertain one's future status. We see such identification with actual or potentially powerful groups in the conflicts that have swept the world in recent decades. Catholics versus protestants in Northern Ireland, Serbs versus Croats in Yugoslavia, Azeris versus Armenians in the former Soviet Union, Hindus versus Muslims in India are examples of identification with groups that are seen to generate power, which implies empowerment to their followers. Class, nationality, religion, and other groupings represent social forces with varying salience and attraction at different points in history (Hall, 1985). Members of such groups, in general, are likely to find a sense of empowerment in group membership, and such group membership may in fact give them "liberties" (lack of constraints) they would otherwise not possess. Conversely, the ruling, powerful groups may confer partial "rights" to the powerless, in the expectation that even a minimum sense of being freed of constraints will divert attention from restraints actually still in force.[11]

---

[10]Freud's notion of "identification with the aggressor" exemplifies this phenomenon in part.

[11]In an analysis of nationalism in Eastern Europe, Gellner noted that with modernity and industrialism a new context-free "High Culture" became the style of the entire society, and citizenship required its mastery. If one could not "assimilate into the dominant High Culture" then one needed "to ensure that one's own [national] culture becomes the defining one." (1991, p. 130). It is the identification with such a national culture in the context of the "High Culture" (e.g., Eastern European/former Soviet culture) that is powerless or unattainable or economically impotent that provides some of the psychological background for extreme nationalism.

Alternatives and Additions
to the Concept of Liberty

The two major "democratic" revolutions of the 18th century nailed the cry for natural liberty to their banner.[12] As part of both "liberty, equality and fraternity" and "life, liberty, and the pursuit of happiness" they insured the, at least partial, triumph of the liberal concept of freedom.[13] But, as we have seen, that concept speaks to rights that are defined by the absence of complementary constraints. And it appears to have overshadowed in the popular imagination the other goals of those powerful movements, such as fraternity and the right to "happiness." Are these human goals and rights that can supplement natural liberties?

I have indicated earlier the problems with constructed liberties—the sometimes pernicious ends that some higher goals may trap us into. On the other hand, constructed liberties do speak to informed principles of human association and possibly to rights of participation in decision making and to access to public goods. The political question—not to be addressed here—is to define such higher goals and to assure such rights and access without falling into the trap of subverting the public good in the name of some higher good. Political and philosophical anarchism, and also its contemporary offspring of the often unfraternal and antisocial "libertarianism," see their goals in the free association of people and the absence of concentrations of power in groups or state machinery. A similar goal—the classless society with the state having "withered away"—is represented in Marx and his followers. But we have experienced how such a goal can be subverted into authoritarianism in the service of final or higher goals.

When constructed liberty is defined as "knowing the good," such knowledge implies deep understanding, educated choices, and social consensus. With these conditions, the subversion of constructed liberties might be avoided. The analysis of such "knowledge" is a complex cognitive problem, requiring an analysis of how we understand the sociopolitical-economic world and how we develop our sociopolitical consciousness. In part, the recognition of group rights—the empowerment of significant social groups—might lead to an understanding of group freedoms. Such conditions and extensions might well be applied to constructed liberties such as fraternity, equality, and the pursuit of happiness. They embody ideals that exclude constraints and that envisage access to goods and participation in decision making. Their psychological consequences have rarely been pursued, but they are likely to include a variety of social satisfactions. Fraternity responds to the social nature of human beings, who are biologically

---

[12]Though it should be noted that some of the leaders of the French revolution, following Rousseau, were advocating constructed liberties as well, thus producing another case of compounded natural and constructed liberties.

[13]The fact that "pursuit of happiness" was substituted for John Locke's "property" in an early draft of the American Declaration of Independence illustrates how changes in the social definition of rights and liberties may overcome the attempt by empowered groups to enshrine their privileges as "rights."

and psychologically bound to the social matrix. Its exercise may generate such emotional satisfactions as helping others, being one's neighbors' support, avoiding doing physical or psychological harm, and the positive values of contributing to and benefiting from cooperative social action.[14]

CONCLUSIONS

One aim of this essay was to show how the analytic, constructivist approach of discrepancy/evaluation theory can be useful for an understanding of complex individual and social phenomena. In the process, this excursion into the psychology of freedom and unfreedom has come a long way from the explication of simple interruptions and straightforward judgments of good and bad. We have seen how social constraints and proscriptions can act as powerful discrepancies and interruptions. The exploration has also led to a discussion of values such as the negatively valued presence of constraints on the one hand, and their positively valued absence on the other. Values—preferences and choices—pervade human social interactions. Not least among them are the democratic values embodied in our views of freedom. And I have tried to show how these values operate in individual and social thought, action, and emotion.

One product of this exposition may be the demonstration that psychological analyses can usefully supplement and contribute to our understanding of complex social and political questions. It should provide further impetus to an interdisciplinary approach to such questions, using the insights of political science, sociology, history, and psychology. Psychologists are relatively new to the analysis of such concepts as liberty and power, but I trust that I have demonstrated the possibility of relevant psychological analyses. There is no doubt that questions of freedom and choice engender strong emotions. The psychology of emotion cannot avoiding addressing these issues, and whether one chooses the present framework or some other one, the challenge must be faced.

ACKNOWLEDGMENTS

I am grateful to Tim Shallice and to Jean, Michael, and Peter Mandler for important psychological, philosophical and political critiques of earlier versions of this chapter. Correspondence to: George Mandler, Center for Human Information Processing 0109, University of California, San Diego; La Jolla, CA, 92093–0109.

---

[14]See also my discussion of consensual moral values that represent common social goals and rights in Mandler (1993a).

REFERENCES

Bavelas, J. B., Black, A., Lemery, C. R., & Mullett, J. (1987). Motor mimicry as primitive empathy. In N. Eisenberg & J. Strayer (Eds.), *Empathy and its development* (pp. 317–338). Cambridge: Cambridge University Press.

Bem, D. J. (1967). Self-perception: An alternative interpretation of cognitive dissonance phenomena. *Psychological Review, 74,* 183–200.

Berlin, I. (1969). *Four essays on liberty.* London: Oxford University Press.

Berscheid, E. (1982). Attraction and emotion in interpersonal relationships. In M. S. Clark & S. T. Fiske (Eds.), *Affect and cognition: The Seventeenth Annual Carnegie Symposium on Cognition* (pp. 37–54). Hillsdale, NJ: Lawrence Erlbaum Associates.

Berscheid, E. (1983). Emotion. In H. H. Kelley, E. Berscheid, A. Christensen, J. H. Harvey, T. L. Huston, G. Levinger, E. McClintock, L. A. Peplau, & D. R. Peterson (Eds.), *Close relationships* (pp. 110–168). San Francisco: Freeman.

Cannon, W. B. (1930). The Linacre lecture on the autonomic nervous system: An interpretation. *Lancet, 218,* 1109–1115.

Chomsky, N. (1991). *Deterring democracy.* London: Verso.

Chovil, N. (1991). Social determinants of facial displays. *Journal of Nonverbal Behavior, 15,* 141–154.

Chovil, N. (in press). Discourse-oriented facial displays in conversation. *Research on Language and Social Interaction.*

Dworkin, R. (1991). Liberty and pornography. *The New York Review of Books, 38 (No. 14),* 12–15.

Fridlund, A. J. (1991). Evolution and facial action in reflex, social motive, and paralanguage. *Biological Psychology, 32,* 3–100.

Fridlund, A. J. (1992). The behavioral ecology and sociality of human faces. In M. Clark (Ed.), *Review of Personality and Social Psychology* (Vol. 1, pp. 90–121). Beverly Hills, CA: Sage Publications.

Frijda, N. H. (1986). *The emotions.* Cambridge: Cambridge University Press.

Gaver, W., & Mandler, G. (1987). Play it again, Sam: On liking music. *Cognition and Emotion, 1,* 259–282.

Gellner, E. (1991). Nationalism and politics in Eastern Europe. *New Left Review,* (September–October, No. 189) 127–134.

Hall, J. A. (1985). *Powers and liberties.* Oxford: Basil Blackwell.

James, W. (1884). What is an emotion? *Mind, 9,* 188–205.

James, W. (1894). The physical basis of emotion. *Psychological Review, 1,* 516–529.

Kierkegaard, S. A. (1957). *The concept of dread* (2nd ed.). Princeton, NJ: Princeton University Press. (Original work published 1844)

Lazarus, R. S. (1991). *Emotion and adaptation.* New York: Oxford University Press.

MacDowell, K. A. (1991, June). *Autonomic (sympathetic) responses predict subjective intensity of experience.* Poster presented at American Psychological Society Convention, Washington, D.C.

Mandler, G. (1964). The interruption of behavior. In E. Levine (Ed.), *Nebraska Symposium on Motivation: 1964* (pp. 163–219). Lincoln, NE: University of Nebraska Press.

Mandler, G. (1975). *Mind and emotion.* New York: Wiley.

Mandler, G. (1979). Emotion. In E. Hearst (Ed.), *The first century of experimental psychology* (pp. 275–321). Hillsdale, NJ: Lawrence Erlbaum Associates.

Mandler, G. (1984). *Mind and body: Psychology of emotion and stress.* New York: Norton.

Mandler, G. (1985). *Cognitive psychology: An essay in cognitive science.* Hillsdale, NJ: Lawrence Erlbaum Associates.

Mandler, G. (1989). Affect and learning: Causes and consequences of emotional interactions. In D. B. McLeod & V. M. Adams (Eds.), *Affect and mathematical problem solving: A new perspective* (pp. 3–19). New York: Springer Verlag.

Mandler, G. (1990a). A constructivist theory of emotion. In N. S. Stein, B. L. Leventhal, & T. Trabasso (Eds.), *Psychological and biological approaches to emotion* (pp. 21–43). Hillsdale, NJ: Lawrence Erlbaum Associates.

Mandler, G. (1990b). Interruption (discrepancy) theory: Review and extensions. In S. Fisher & C. L. Cooper (Eds.), *On the move: The psychology of change and transition* (pp. 13–32). Chichester, England: Wiley.

Mandler, G. (1992a). Toward a theory of consciousness. In H. G. Geissler, S. Link, & J. G. Townsend (Ed.), *Cognition, information processing and psychophysics: Basic issues* (pp. 43–65). Hillsdale, NJ: Lawrence Erlbaum Associates.

Mandler, G. (1992b). Emotions, evolution, and aggression: Myths and conjectures. In K. T. Strongman (Ed.), *International Review of Studies on Emotion* (Vol. II, pp. 97–116). Chichester: Wiley.

Mandler, G. (1992c). Memory, arousal, and mood: A theoretical integration. In S.-A. Christianson (Ed.), *Handbook of emotion and memory* (pp. 93–110). Hillsdale, NJ: Lawrence Erlbaum Associates.

Mandler, G. (1993a). Approaches to a psychology of value. In M. Hechter, L. Nadel, & R. E. Michod (Eds.), *The origins of values* (pp. 229–258). Hawthorne, NY: Aldine de Gruyter.

Mandler, G. (1993b). Thought, memory, and learning: Effects of emotional stress. In L. Goldberger & S. Breznitz (Eds.), *Handbook of stress* (2nd ed., pp. 40–55). New York: Free Press.

Mandler, G., & Kessen, W. (1974). The appearance of free will. In S. C. Brown (Ed.), *Philosophy of psychology* (pp. 305–324). London: Macmillan

Mandler, G., & Shebo, B. J. (1983). Knowing and liking. *Motivation and Emotion, 7,* 125–144.

Mann, M. (1986). *The sources of social power.* Cambridge, England: Cambridge University Press.

McNaughton, M. (1989). *Biology and emotion.* Cambridge, England: Cambridge University Press.

Oppenheim, F. E. (1968). Freedom. In D. L. Sills (Ed.), *International encyclopedia of the social science* (pp. 554–559). New York: Macmillan and Free Press.

Ortony, A., Clore, G. L., & Collins, A. (1988). *The cognitive structure of emotions.* New York: Cambridge University Press.

Ortony, A., & Turner, T. J. (1990). What's basic about basic emotions? *Psychological Review, 97,* 315–331.

Partridge, P. H. (1967). Freedom. In P. Edwards (Ed.), *The encyclopedia of philosophy* (pp. 221–225). New York: Macmillan and Free Press.

Rumelhart, D. E., & McClelland, J. L. (1985). *Parallel distributed processing: Explorations on the microstructure of cognition* (Vol. 1–Foundations). Cambridge, MA: MIT Press.

10 The Lex Talionis: On Vengeance

Nico H. Frijda
University of Amsterdam

THE DESIRE FOR VENGEANCE

Desire for vengeance certainly is one of the most potent of human passions. It has been one of the major preoccupations in the world literature. Witness Euripides' Medea, the Oresteia, Hamlet, or Tess, Cain's killing of Abel, God's expulsion of Adam and Eve from paradise, and his near destruction of the human race with the Flood. It is a major theme in history as well. Jews were massacred on the grounds of what they were supposed to have done to Jesus. And it is a dominant theme in recent and current affairs. Lidice and Putten were destroyed, and their male populations killed because of the attacks by resistance fighters on Heydrich and some other German officer. Serbian violence in Croatia obtained added stength and motivation from fury about the collaboration and atrocities committed by Ante Pavelitch and his bent 50 years ago. The Imam Abou Kheireidinne, in December 1991, cried out for the establishment of people's tribunals to "try the traitors" for offenses against the sharia in Algeria. The Israeli air force, February 1992, killed the Hezbollah leader Abbas Musawi to revenge a Palestinian attack on an Israelian village, and Hezbollah forces retaliated by prolonged rocket shelling of northern Israel.

Nor is the force of vengeance restricted to religious or political action. A woman called Jean Harris killed Dr. Tarnower, a famous doctor, for his unfaithfulness to her with another, younger lover. A man called Richard Herrin killed his former girlfriend, Bonnie Garland, for having ended their affair (both examples from Jacoby, 1983). In 1989, a Dutch man killed four women in a subway station: Women had betrayed him, because his girlfriend had rejected him.

The power of the desire for vengeance can be inferred from the very existence of the Law of Talion. An eye for an eye, a tooth for a tooth. The law of Talion is stated in the book of Exodus (21:24), among a number of other prescriptions that God gave to Moses, and which were to serve to regulate interactions within the tribe. The law of Talion represented a major advance in lawfulness. It served to hem in blind vengeance. For an eye, no more than an eye; for a tooth no more than a tooth; that is the significance of the law of Talion (Hirzel, 1907–10; Jacoby, 1983). Evidently a need existed for such regulation, then as now. Were it not so, no law of the kind would have been needed. Desire for revenge itself is immoderate.

The Old Testamentic law of Talion attests to the immense power of the urge for private vindication. In fact, curtailing personal vengeance is considered to be one of the major general sources of criminal law, next to the protection of society and re-education of the criminal. Society needs protection from the destructive effects of this power, both because of its unbounded strength when not curtailed, and its endless repetitive cycle, of vengeance begetting vengeance. Where centralized law is absent, as is the case with independent tribes, personal vengeance is indeed the traditional mode of response to intratribal offence (Black-Michaud, 1975).

Desire for vengeance is not restricted to a few individuals, nor only to desires that lead to murder. In a questionnaire study on emotions that we recently ran, 46% of the respondents, 41 students between 18 and 25 years old, admitted to remembering at least one instance of a vengeful impulse. In another, small study, all of 22 participants recalled an instance of desire for revenge. Ten of those rated the intensities of their emotion as strong or very strong (6 or 7 on the 7-point scale, even if short lasting). Vivid thoughts of revenge were felt, and some enacted, for erotic unfaithfulness, indiscretions, having been slighted, being cheated, having one's bicycle stolen, and the like. Thoughts consisted of vengeful fantasies of the offenders' possible misfortunes, inflicted by the participant, by others, or by fate. Vengeful fantasies, of course, vastly outnumber actual vengeful acts; the latter are by no means absent, though, among civilized people in daily circumstances. Vengeful acts in everyday life (as mentioned in the studies, or coming from people I know) include destroying some of the offender's cherished possessions, going to bed with her or his best friend, publicly making a fool of him or her, blackening him or her by gossip, degrading his or her performances.

Vengeance might thus be expected to form one of the major topics in the psychology of emotion. Not so. No major psychological study has appeared on the topic during the last 70 or 80 years. A literature search from 1967 to 1991 yielded not a single study having "vengeance" or "revenge" as its main subject. Many studies dealt with "retaliation," but few addressed the core issues of its reasons, power, and extent. Anthropology does somewhat better, as it extensively studies revenge in specific societies. Outside anthropology the situation appears to be little different from that in psychology. I found only one work that dealt explicitly with vengeance: Susan Jacoby's (1983) excellent study "Wild Justice"; and of course, Bob Solomon's (1989; chapter 10, this volume) recent publications.

One might explain the absence of discussion on vengeance in the psychology of emotion by arguing that it is not an emotion. One may even assert that it is not a psychological phenomenon at all, but a social one with a political or judicial motivation; or merely a mode of behavior that follows from cultural example or norm.

Of course, vengeance is not an emotion. But the desire for revenge, the urge to retaliate, most certainly is. It is, I think, a mere coincidence that no word for this emotion exists in current English. As a matter of fact, the English language has exactly the right word for it, but it has gone out of usage: Wrath. Its Latin equivalent, *ira,* indiscriminately referred to anger and the impulse for revenge (see Seneca's *De Ira).* The desire is an emotion, in that it has all the usual features of one: It is a state of impulse, of involuntary action readiness, generated by an appraisal, often accompanied by bodily excitement, and with every aspect of control precedence: preoccupation, single-minded goal pursuit, neglect of extraneous information, and interference with other activities. Anyway, it should be a task of the psychology of emotion to devote attention to the properties of wrath, that is, of such anger as leads to vengeful fantasies and actions.

The fact that discussion is possible on whether desire for revenge is or is not an emotion is worth a moment's reflection. It shows the primitive state of our science that grapples with "substance concepts" in true Aristotelian fashion, rather than fully going over to the side of function concepts, as in Galilean science (the oppositions come from Cassirer, 1908, and Kurt Lewin, 1935). It is not of interest whether or not vengeance (or any other phenomenon) falls within a given class. What is important is to understand particular functional features, and see how they relate to other functional features. It is such features that should hold center stage.

THE PROBLEMS POSED BY VENGEANCE

Vengeance and the desire for vengeance present several remarkable features that form the reason for interest in the subject. Because of these features (or inasmuch as it has these features), vengeance poses problems of general relevance to the study of emotion. The features are its apparent uselessness and even occasional self-destructiveness, its often extreme intensity, and its often extended duration. The purpose of this chapter is to explore these features and to try to form some hypotheses for understanding them.

The first feature is shown with clarity in the very definition of vengeance. I define *vengeance* as an act designed to harm someone else, or some social group, in response to feeling that oneself has been harmed by that person or group, whereby the act of harming that person or group is *not* designed to repair the harm, to stop it from occurring or continuing in the immediate confrontation, or to produce material gain. Let us not quibble about this definition; let us not quarrel about whether some acts that are called vengeance yet serve material profit or defense. The definition points to a delay between offense and response, or to some lack of continuity between them, and thus delimits an interesting class of events, setting them apart within anger and aggression in general. Events answering to the definition do exist; they are manifold, and they have considerable social consequences.

The definition refers to the first feature of interest and the first major problem that desire for vengeance poses. What use has vengeance? What is it good for? Why commit it or want it, when no obvious gain is to be had? Current psychology of emotion takes a functional perspective. Emotions are supposed to serve a purpose, or to be appropriate in dealing with the emotion-arousing situation. They may not always be appropriate, but they are so in principle. Fear motivates self-protection. Anger motivates defense, or the overcoming of frustrating obstacles. But what gain has vengeance? By definition, it is concerned with actions that do not intend to right the suffered wrong and are quite often incited by wrongs that cannot be put right or undone, and this the individual knows. Violence springing from jealousy, which means more than anything else taking revenge (like Othello's murder of Desdemona), neither undoes the unfaithfulness nor brings back the unfaithful spouse. So what is the use?

Vengeance may even be harmful to the individual, to the point of being self-destructive, and this too he or she knows. The clearest example again is a literary one: Euripides' Medea. Not only does she kill her rival, but also her own children, in order to strike Jason a most devastating blow. She puts her life in jeopardy, and would indeed have been killed, were it not for Athena's *deus ex machina* spiriting her off to the abodes of the gods. Real-life examples are not too hard to come by: Schopenhauer, when discussing this issue, mentions "that Spanish bishop who, during the last war (1808–1814), poisoned himself and the French generals at his table" (Schopenhauer, 1819, p. 446). Ramon Mercader, who killed Trotsky, could have foreseen that he would spend his life in prison; and so it goes.

The immediate purpose of revenge, as the definition states, is to make the object of vengeance suffer. This points to the second striking feature of vengeance, and to its second major problem: Whereto the violence of violence? Why such immoderation, why the power of its impulse, the degree of violence it tends to incite, and the risk, time, and effort people invest in its execution? No systematic study exists, so we have to rely on literary illustration and historical example. Medea illustrates the degree of violence in mind. The extent of her violence is extreme: Jason's bride cringing in a poisoned cloak; the murder of his children "to break your heart" (Euripides, *Medea,* line 1398). Medea is a character of drama, but her cruelty appears true to life. Real-life examples are indeed readily available. Take the lynchings of suspects of rape of a White woman in the American South. Take the notorious example of the killing of the commander of the Bastille who, when presenting himself to the masses, was wildly accused of what he was supposed to have done to the prisoners, was stabbed by a baker stepping forward from among the public, and had his head cut off, which was carried through the town on top of a lance by the cheering crowd (Schama, 1989). Or take the cruel revenges in war. In war, revenge is difficult to separate from pure hostility; but all hatred in active fighting readily takes on a vengeful coloring. A few examples come to mind. Isaac Babel writes about "the reckless journal *Red Cavalerist* that every soldier in the foremost lines wants to read, to thereupon with true heroic courage slaughter those bastardly Polish gentry" (Babel, 1924/1957, p. 57). A certain Private West, of Charlie Company, recalled that they went out to My Lai "in a mood to get even" (Tiede, 1971), for the casualties suffered earlier by their platoon. Civil wars and guerilla wars abound with instances of extreme cruelty, and it seems plausible to assume that this is because of the numerous accounts to be settled. The Violencia, in Colombia, was a civil war that erupted at the level of villages and neighborhoods. Between 1948 and 1953, it took 150,000 lives. Its reports abound with the most horrifying examples of cruelty, from peasant to neighboring peasant: stabbing out eyes, cutting off genitals, cutting open pregnant women (Pearce, 1990). Similar reports come from the recent Serbian-Croatian conflict (Glenny, 1992), from incidents perpetrated by the Vietnamese against the Americans, the Americans against the Vietnamese, the Dutch against the Indonesians, the Indonesians against the Dutch, and so on, in all of which vengeance for previous wrongs and for suffered casualties among comrades figure prominently among the accounts of why they did what they did. The cruelty in sexual murders is as staggering, or even more so, and is mainly motivated by diffuse revenge, or so it seems (Leyton, 1989). Or take another class of physical assaults, or killings, those of wife by husband, husband by wife. A large proportion of murders occurs within the family, within the confines of the house, in the kitchen or bedroom. One may assume that vengeance plays a role, for unfaithfulness or years of frustration. These murders are more violent than other ones: The number of knife stabbings or bullets fired is significantly higher than in the average murder (Wolfgang, 1958).

The cruelty of revenge can be brutal, as in the examples given. It is often mixed with defamations. Take the Lebanese muslim's revenge upon the people of Damour for the horrid killings by the Phalangists of the muslim population in Karantina:

> The Christian militiamen were executed. The civilians were lined up against the walls of their homes and sprayed with machine-gun fire. Their houses were then dynamited. . . . Many of the young women had been raped. Babies had been shot at close range in the back of the head. . . . And at some point they vented their

wrath on the old Christian cemetery, digging up the coffins and tearing open the gates of vaults, hurling Damour's past generations across the graveyard. They lay there for days, the long dead, skeletons and withered cadavers still dressed in the nineteenth-century Sunday-best in which they had been buried before mandate Palestine even existed. (Fisk, 1991, p. 100)

Similarly, Saddam Hussein's Revolutionary Guards destroyed the graveyards in the Shia's holy cities of Kerbala and Nahaf, after the Iraqui Shia's revolt. The cruelty can also be more subtle and refined. A woman who felt denied appreciation by her husband, after leaving him for someone else, while still in possession of his credit-card deluged him with huge debts. Marie Antoinette was accused of incest with her son, to which she could only respond with: "*Messieurs,* I am a mother" (Schama, 1989).

As to the violence of revenge's violence: The commander of the Phalangist forces that wrought the horrors in the Chatila camp in Lebanon in 1982—Elie Hobeika—was betrothed to a woman killed in Damour (Fisk, 1991, p. 387).

Vengeful desire only very partially appears in violent acts. Most of it remains at the level of desire and is expressed in fantasies. However, vengeful fantasies, it seems, are remarkably violent even in the everyday instances of the small questionnaire study mentioned. They quite often have a virulent quality, including impulses at physical destruction of objects, images of stabbing the offender, wishes that he or she may be killed or tumble into great, great misery.

The persistence of vengeful desire over time is the third remarkable feature with which the psychology of emotion has to deal. Desire for vengeance may stretch out over years. The thirst remains unquenched, or is evoked with ease, even decades after the events. When thoughts of the offending events come up, resentment, vengeful fantasies, and malign joys lie ready. A couple of years ago, there was an outcry in the newspapers and in the gallery of the Dutch parliament when a discussion arose in parliament about releasing the three remaining war criminals languishing in a Dutch prison since 1945. Occasional murders of Turkish representatives continue until the present day, in retaliation for the outrages to the Armenian people in 1915 and following years. Current Serbian violence towards Croatians is partly motivated by Pavelitch's fascist collaboration in the Forties; at any rate, that betrayal was constantly invoked (Glenny, 1992). At an individual level, the story of Ferdi E. serves as an illustration of how long vengefulness can last. Ferdi E. is a Dutch engineer, who in 1983 with two colleagues founded an industrial development company. Some time after starting the company, his colleagues decided to drastically cut E.'s salary and to remove him from his responsible position in the company. He withdrew and continued to live quietly with his wife and children in an Amsterdam suburb. Meanwhile he pondered revenge. Precisely what revenge he planned has remained unclear, but it included the need for a considerable sum of money. To obtain this, he decided to abduct a rich man for ransom. He selected Gerrit-Jan

Heyn, the acting director of Holland's major supermarket chain. Carefully, over a period of weeks, he studied the man's habits. One day in September, in 1987— 4 years after the insult—he accosted his victim when the man left his house for work one morning, dragged him into his own car, and took him to a wood that he, E., knew well. There they chatted for awhile and had lunch with sandwiches prepared by E. beforehand. Then E. murdered Heyn, cut off the man's thumb to later serve as proof of having him in his power, put it in a small tin that he had brought for the purpose, buried the corpse, and set out to put in his claims for ransom: one million guilders, in uncut diamonds and banknotes. He managed to collect half the ransom; then silence reigned. Some 5 months later he was traced and caught, after having carelessly spent one of the (marked) ransom bills in a supermarket near his home. The story is intriguing for many reasons. For the psychology of revenge the main remarkable features are the sequences of humiliation, vengeful planning, the amount of thought and preparation put into its execution, and the time span that made the desire into a "passion," in the old sense of that word: 4 years of emotion-fed work towards an emotion-fed goal.

The duration of vengeful impulse appears at different levels: In the time span over which vengeful feelings can be evoked, in the time span from event to execution of the revenge, in the time that the impulse outlives acute emotional upset. At the small time scale of a psychological experiment, intensity of revenge does not appear to decay during a delay between offense and retaliation during which manifest bodily excitement disappeared (Sapolsky, Stocking, & Zillmann, 1977).

Many of the above illustrations may look like examples of violence instigated by other impulses than those of revenge: jealousy, hatred, mere political motive, war, or instrumental purposes. Yet I think they are appropriately given as illustrating revenge. Revenge is involved when thoughts of having suffered at the hands of the object contribute to the force of violence. Such thoughts are documents in most of the examples—witness the words of private West, the accusations of the Parisian crowd, the reproaches in the Serbian press—and are almost inevitably aroused in fighting at close quarters. Vengeful feelings, it seems, are aroused with surprising ease in any situation of animosity.

These, then, are the three main features: the absence of evident gain or usefulness; the degree of violence; and the duration, the persistence over time. These three features are not unique to desire for vengeance. Instances of shame, guilt, and jealousy too may show these features: cases of shame and guilt that may destroy a life and bring one to suicide, jealousy that may destroy the life of both the individual and his object. Proust (1925/1954) gives us illustrations of the latter. These instances indeed pose the same problems, and their analysis may profit from the analysis of vengeance. They all confront us with the problem of what makes an emotion a self-destructive passion, what can account for its extreme intensity, and for its long persistence.

In trying to find some tentative answers, we may employ the clues that current psychology of emotion provides. First, quite generally, we assume that the nature of the emotional feeling and impulse are determined by the individual's mode of appraisal of the situation. This appraisal, in turn, is determined in part by the fine grain or context of the situation and its significance, and in part by the individual's available modes of coping with the situation (e.g., Frijda, 1986; Lazarus, 1991; Ortony, Clore, & Collins, 1988; Scherer, 1984). Explanation of the features of revenge mentioned has to be found, in part, in such appraisal and context. Second, we assume that the intensity of an emotion is determined by the number and strength of the concerns that are engaged by the emotional event, and by the seriousness of that event with respect to those concerns (Frijda, Ortony, Sonnemans, & Clore, 1992; Sonnemans, 1991). One may expect that the power of vengeance, and the violence of its violence, derive from what and how many concerns are at stake, and how deeply the offenses threaten or damage them. Third, we assume that duration and other aspects of emotional intensity are relatively independent and have each their different determinants (Frijda, Mesquita, Sonnemans, & van Goozen, 1991; Frijda et al., 1992; Sonnemans, 1991). We assume that extended durations result when an emotion has changed into a sentiment and, possibly, into a passion. A sentiment is defined as a persistent disposition to appraise an object in a particular concern-relevant way or, equivalently, as a disposition for emotions to arise upon confrontation with the object or with signs associated with it. A passion is defined as a persistent endeavour to obtain an emotional goal. The sentiment connected with revenge is hatred, defined here as the disposition to appraise an object as of evil nature, and thereby to desire its diminished existence: its destruction or the loss of its enjoyment of life. Emotions change into sentiments, we assume, when events stretch out over time, or when the issue, evoked by dealing with an event, has not been resolved after the event is over (Frijda et al., 1991). They change into a passion when the issue is felt as intolerable, and one feels the strength to do something about it. The conditions for change of an emotion into a sentiment, presumably, are the conditions for anger to lead to desire for revenge.

THE SOCIAL FUNCTIONS OF REVENGE

Let us take the first feature as our lead. What is the purpose of revenge? What gain does it yield?

At the level of society, an answer is easy to find. Vengeance serves power equalization. When individuals or groups endeavour to impose their will upon others, vengeance serves to correct them. Revenge is the social power regulator in a society without central justice. Vengeance is "a system of defining and controlling conflict by avoiding any recourse to a third party, i.e., the state. We can see that this is an attempt to maintain social order without resorting to the obedience model" (Marongiu & Newman, 1987, quoted from Solomon & Murphy, 1990, p. 247/8).

In addition, revenge serves as a deterrent to infliction of harm. Fear of revenge instills reticence in the exercise of violence and greed. Even if the power of an individual is sufficient to get away with it at one moment, he or she may be called to answer at a later time. Revenge is punishment for harm inflicted upon others by those others and, as in any punishment, aims to inhibit the recurrence of the punished behavior. Of course, there is another side to this: Fear of retaliation often inhibits standing up for one's rights, as in those who fear reporting an offense to the authorities (e.g., Bandura, 1983; Ohbuchi & Megumi, 1986). Yet, in circumstances of relatively equal power, the deterrent function may well dominate.

Vengeance thus can have value in stabilizing society. It may well have been invented as a rational strategy. In fact, it is a rational strategy. "Tit for tat" has been shown to be the superior strategy in bringing a rival in line for cooperation. Occasional revenge for noncooperation shows cooperation to be the ultimately most profitable procedure in situations like the prisoner's dilemma game (Axelrod, 1984). Of course, we know that vengeance often blatantly destabilizes society, and may be disruptive and destructive to it. That, again, is what the Law of Talion sought to attenuate. Vengeance tends to elicit vengeance in response, with endless feuding as a consequence. Feuds may even bring about the extinction of the feuding tribes; that, after all, is one of the messages of Greek tragedy. However, there are conditions under which vengeance does stabilize: when the victim recognizes that abstaining from returning revenge is to his or her benefit, as in the situations described by Axelrod, or when the harm expected from subsequent retaliation outweighs the gains expected from one's own. Such was the case when Syria and Lebanon ordered the South Lebanese Hezbollah to discontinue their rocket offensive, in view of the Israeli retaliations. Also, evolution has developed conciliatory procedures along with offensive ones (De Waal, 1991); humans have developed strategies such as the paying of blood money. Destabilization through revenge may be restricted to conditions of revenge ideology that pervert the purpose and erode the conciliatory modes. We do not know how widespread the functional occurrence of revenge is, as compared to its destructive one, because only the destructive ones are depicted in tragedy. In fact, we may propose that the principal stabilizing power of vengeance springs from the fear of its occurrence, rather than in its actual execution. The function of vengeance is best served when the urge for it is forestalled. It is, as I said, a threat, a deterrent that should be enacted only as often as needed to remind one of its force, as a proper partial reinforcement, which is precisely how it functions in the strategies leading to cooperation between rivals, analyzed by Axelrod.

Societies, then, may discover vengeance as a means for deterrence and equalization of power. Even if, as the definition given earlier states, vengeance serves no purpose in the immediate confrontation, it may do so with regard to possible future confrontations, and flow from foresight with regard to them. Also, it can be argued that evolution has on that basis created an emotion of desire for vengeance, an innate propensity to punish an offense towards the self or one's kin. Other emotions exist with the function of motivating efforts to prevent their occurrence. Pain and grief are among these (see Averill's, 1968, analysis of the latter), but shame and guilt even more clearly have such a function. Anticipation of shame motivates behavior of norm-conformity, so that shame will not arise; anticipation of guilt-feeling motivates being careful in social interaction, and the assistance of suffering others, so that guilt feeling will not arise.

Thus vengeance serves a function in social regulation. It does so in situations of continuous or continued social interaction. Vengeance is often explicitly instigated for such regulation, as in the Israeli action just cited. However, the problems in understanding vengeance are thereby not resolved. It does not explain the emotion, the desire and its urge, the content of the desire, "to get even." Recall that at the level of emotion and urge, vengeance represents a puzzle: What is it that one strives after, what is it that is gained? The deed is done, the harm inflicted; it cannot be prevented or undone. Or is there no gain for the individual, and is the desire for revenge nothing but an inherited impulse, blind and senseless with regard to the individual?

THE GAINS OF VENGEANCE:
RESTORING THE BALANCE OF SUFFERING

I think that the gains of revenge are real enough. Desire for vengeance is as "rational" as any other emotion, and functional in the same way as are these other emotions. This implies that there are many instances of nonrational desires for vengeance, in the same way as there are many nonrational angers and fears. But, in principle, there are proper gains in vengeance. That this is so, as I just said, appears from the content of the desire: to get even, to retaliate, where retaliation means ensuring a return payment. An offender should pay for what he did. He should not escape with impunity, he should get tit for tat. Expressions like these are the usual motivations or justifications for vengeance. These sound as though they express a basic sense of justice, but the question is what that basic sense of justice means. What is it that should become even? Is it indeed that something should be equally distributed? It is doubtful, because the Law of Talion had to impose proportionality or equivalence upon a desire that by itself does not include it. Without the Law of Talion, or some still stronger attenuation of vengeance like turning the other cheek, desire for revenge tends to be immoderate, an unquenchable thirst. That we must take as a basic datum on vengeance. As several investigators argued (e.g., Donnerstein & Hatfield, 1983; Solomon, 1989), vengeance seeks retribution rather than equal distribution; but what profit does the offender's return payment yield?

The social function of revenge, of course, can be expected to have its reflection in the individual. The offender has to be punished for what he did, because that might serve as a deterrent in future interactions. Sometimes, there is clear anticipatory planning and calculation of effects, as in many military examples; at other times, one may be driven by emotions about unfair advantage and the restoration of unfair inequity (Donnerstein & Hatfield, 1983; Rabbie & Lodwijkx, 1991), or fear of recurrence and, in general, by a dim sense that taking revenge turns the world into a safer place than if the offender were left alone.

Much as deterrence may play a role in vengeance, it cannot be the only thing. It cannot be a meaningful cause for taking revenge for offenses that do not allow of recurrence: a death, for instance. It does not account for urge for revenge when there is no prospect of continued interaction with the offender. It does not explain the major features of revenge that I enumerated: that vengeance tends to outweigh the harm incurred, that it has the features of extravagance, the often extreme violence and persistence over time. It does not explain the meaning of "getting even." Most of all, it does not explain the focus of revenge, which is to make the offender suffer, rather than to prevent him or her from repeating the mischief. That is what guides vengeful action: the aim to hurt the offender. Pain or discomfort is what vengeance seeks to produce. Indeed, that is why judicial punishment rarely seems to satisfy desires for vengeance; it only does when the offender is known to suffer by it. It is true that in some civilizations, revenge can be bought off by payment of blood money (Black-Michaud, 1975), but that, quite clearly, is a compromise. It is not what desire for vengeance strove after and, as one of the anecdotes to come illustrates, acceptance of a payment may be recanted, or later declared void as settlement of the feud.

The problem thus shifts to explaining in what way the offender's suffering can alleviate the subject's suffering. In what sense does the suffering subject get even when the offender suffers in return? An older psychology of vengeance sought the answer in an additive theory of affect. Steinmetz (1894/1928) proposed that vengeance diminishes suffering because the pleasure of seeing the offender suffer annuls one's own suffering, or subtracts from it. Or, in a slightly different conception: Because the mind has place for only one affect at a time, one's suffering is pushed aside by the pleasure of seeing the offender suffer. The idea is attractive in its neatness, but the affect mechanics are too simple to satisfy our current cognitive view of emotions. The mechanics may even be wrong. The evidence goes counter to an additive view. Bad moods are not necessarily improved by pleasurable events; they may even be exacerbated by them (Biglan & Craker, 1982; Hammen & Glass, 1975).

Current views of emotion allow some more satisfactory insight into the profit gained from seeing one's offender suffer. In those views, feelings do not add up or subtract but respond to patterns of appraisal. These patterns of appraisal are structured patterns. They result from the multiple concerns touched upon by an emotional event and its implications; they include the multiple ways in which an event can be emotionally relevant. It is not that different affects add up or substract, but that different relevances summate, conflict, or keep each other in balance.

Being subjected to offense indeed has several implications with an emotional significance. One is one's harm or loss. A second is that the harm or loss is caused by someone, the offender; a third is that the offender remains unscathed, or even stands to profit by the event. A fourth is that the offender knows what he or she has caused, and enjoys it. The victim's appraisal of the event includes all that; it includes awareness of the offender's experience, as well as his or her own. It all adds up in that appraisal: what I feel, and what the offender feels or is supposed to feel.

And it all contributes in shaping the resulting affect. Quite generally, one's pleasures and pains are measured not in absolute but in relative terms. They are determined by what I have called the Law of Comparative Feeling (Frijda, 1988). They depend on how one's fortunes or misfortunes compare with one's fortunes or misfortunes at earlier times, or with those that were possible, or those of others. Here, the comparison is particularly poignant. My awareness includes his glory in having inflicted suffering upon me and, in the event, his glory in having gotten away with it; all that contrasts with my own situation. He walks in pleasure and I in suffering.

This is one of the implications of offense. He walks in pleasure and I in suffering. It is one of the most unbearable aspects of having suffered at the hands of someone else. In fact, it is an aspect of unavenged misery that haunts victims of torture or persecution, or the kin of murder victims. I mentioned the upset caused by the discussion of whether to free three war criminals, the leaders of the political police in the Netherlands during the Occupation. Much of the upset and disturbance precisely concerned the hallucinatory vision of these released criminals leading a quiet and happy life, while one's pain of the old suffering and one's irremediable loss remain. That serious pains and losses indeed never pass is evident from the literature. Wortman and Silver (1989) studied responses to loss of a child, and found such loss often to engender distress even scores of years after. Silver, Boon, and Stones (1983) found that victims of sexual child abuse never find peace with what happened to them, and often continue to try to make sense of what befell them as children. Parallel to that is a persistent rise of pain upon recurrence of the thought that the perpetrator has remained unpunished and may even enjoy his memories (Sprang, McNeil, & Wright, 1989).

The victim's appraisal of offense thus includes the offender's gains. Vengeance does take this away. It takes away his or her gains. Medea says it quite precisely: "You were mistaken if you thought you could dishonour my bed and live a pleasant life and laugh at me" (Euripides, *Medea*, lines 1354–56), and "My pain's a fair price, to take away your smile" (line 1362). Vengeance actually works in equalizing the suffering. It makes part of the suffering disappear. Not all of it—the loss and the recollection of harm remain—but some of it, the poignancy of it, the loneliness of it, goes, the being-less-than-he or she, the thought of his or her gain. You get even in suffering.

All this is personal and emotional. It has nothing to do with a sense of justice.

But the dolorous inequalities can be transformed onto an abstract and general plane and become formulated in a moral way, and so can the restoration of the balance of suffering. Then it indeed becomes a sense of justice. Those who cause pain should suffer in return, and, if possible, at least to an equal degree. The sense of justice derives, I think, from reflection upon comparative suffering. Comparative suffering, though, would seem to come first, or be among the primary sources.

Obviously, these things also work the other way. There is glory after successful revenge, there is joy about the spoils that revenge may have yielded, and there is added joy because of Comparative Feeling.

Equalization of Power

The added pain of seeing the offender go unscathed and enjoying his or her glory does not depend only on the processes of Comparative Feeling. The inequality between victim and offender has further and more tangible aspects. Revenge yields further and more tangible gains.

When someone willfully harms another, he or she manifestly has the power to do so, and the other lacks the power to prevent it or do likewise. There is power inequality. The offender has or had power over you, and you are or were powerless. The offender was able to do with you as he or she willed, handle you, walk over you, use you for his or her purposes. He or she is the actor, you are the object; he or she was the master, you were the slave. The power inequality applies not only to conditions of physical offense or social subjugation, but also to emotional offense. Being confronted with unfaithfulness in love, or being abandoned—whether by quitting or by dying—are results of unilateral actions about which one's opinion was not asked, and against which reciprocal action is not appropriate or possible, or in any case can only come later. Even in a simple domestic quarrel, a jibe that one cannot counter scores a point in the power contest. The emotional load of powerlessness or helplessness when facing painful events needs no elaboration. It is a cornerstone of stress theory, and it is the factor responsible for the escalation of quarrels.

Power inequality is effectively diminished or annulled by revenge. One is no longer the inferior one, the one to whom things can be done. Revenge precisely achieves in the individual's emotion what a social or societal analysis of vengeance indicates might be its purpose: power equalization. Through revenge, one gets even in power.

Restoring power inequality, or reestablishing superiority, are more important to one individual than to another, and to one social group than to another. Cultures where social power is a central value are also those where power rivalries and revenge are prominent: in the "subcultures of violence," for instance, where each arrogance is immediately countered (Wolfgang & Ferracuti, 1967); in societies such as Albania, Sicily, or Sardinia where revenge is institutionalized (Black-Michaud, 1975, Marongiu & Newman, 1987); and in Renaissance Italy, where the power-and-prestige symbolizing towers of San Geminiano were built over the recurrent revenges for slightings to honor of every kind (Burckhart, 1860/1935; Cellini, in his *Autobiography*). Power equalization and revenge tend to go hand in hand even without such explicit cultural values; and they also do so at subtler and more individual levels. Every offense upsets power equality to some degree, and diminishing inequality or gaining the upper hand is an aspect of every revenge and maybe always contributes to its satisfactions. For instance, I know of someone who experienced great triumph in being called as a witness in the interrogation of a former officer in the German security police, when this took place in the same room of the same prison where that officer previously had interrogated and beaten him, but now sitting at the other side of the green cloth. But in situations like that, power equalization is not the only thing. Even with relatively minor insults, retaliation may reduce some of the inequality, without thereby reducing the instilled bad feelings (Atkinson & Polivy, 1976).

Restoration of Self-Esteem

Closely linked to power equalization is the restoration of threatened or damaged social prestige and self-esteem. Damage to one's prestige and self-esteem, or to that of one's social group, is one of the major sources of vengeful impulse and can be expected to give it much of its emotional force (Tajfel & Turner, 1979). Revenge does restore some of the damage, and even attempted revenge may yield some of this gain.

That offense to self-esteem influences propensity for revenge is fairly obvious. When, in an experiment, threat to self-esteem is used to instigate aggression, retaliation is more severe than without such threat (Caprara, Bonanno, Carrabbia, & Mazzotti, 1988). Self-esteem can be hurt in many ways and at many levels. There is, for instance, damage that is predominantly socially defined, or felt to be so (e.g., Felson, 1978). Rushdie, in *Shame* (1983), tells the story of a man who, in his club, publicly courts a lady. His brother-in-law enters, cuts in, and departs with her. The man, with ten brutes, then rides to the brother-in-law's country house, has them wreck the place, in the meanwhile shouting from his saddle to his sister, who sits knitting on the porch, that he couldn't have done otherwise since that fool had humiliated him in front of everyone. From a different order is the case described by Mergaree (1966) of a man who buys a trifle at his front door from a 6-year-old girl. Not knowing what to do when he finds that he had only a dollar in his pocket, he feels humiliated when she helpfully suggests that he go look for change. According to the report, his pain because of his clumsiness and the small girl's self-assuredness was such that he invited her in, raped her, and strangled her.

Damage to self-worth may go still deeper. Having been the object of maltreatment or insult may extend beyond mere power inequality or loss of social prestige and self-esteem. It may attack the individual's very sense of personal value and identity. It does so precisely because one has been treated as an object. Self-determination, at the very basic level of deciding about one's movements and about sensations to be experienced or avoided, is probably the rock bottom upon which one's sense of worth and identity rests. One's self-schema, the awareness of one's particular properties, would appear to be a mere embellishment or elaboration of that basic sense of being able to determine one's actions. This is the sense that is offended in many acts of violence and in other forms of maltreatment. One could not control, one could not resist, one could not do what one wished, one had to submit. Even when offense is not explicitly directed against one's self-determination, another person's power to inflict harm is a potential source of damage to one's sense of self. In many offenses, however, that sense is actually and purposefully severely violated.

It is difficult to exaggerate the disruptive effects of having been subjected to willfully inflicted harm. It defines basic humiliation such as is involved in rape, torture, and subjugation under threat. The effects are probably irreversible, being due to a destruction of a basic sense of identity and trust in oneself. "Anyone who has been tortured, remains tortured. . . . Anyone who has suffered torture never again will be able to be at ease in the world, the abomination of the annihilation is never extinguished" is what Primo Levi (1989, p. 25) quotes from Jean Améry, the Austrian philosopher. It cannot be a coincidence that so many of the persecution survivors who tried to take stock of their experience committed suicide, even if 40 years after the events: Améry, Kozynski, Primo Levi himself.

Revenge may be truly instrumental in restoring self-worth and identity. One has the initiative, one is once again the cause of one's acts, and one is so in the relationship with the individual who once took it away. Vengeance—destructive activity generally—probably is the most distinct proof of effectance, of being a cause of events and, what is more, of events with relevance for one's well-being. It staunches some of the repercussions that being a helpless victim and the object of someone else's arbitrary action may have had upon self-esteem. The gain of revenge, in this respect, is again tangible and real. Revenge may be seen as an attempt to restore self-identity, and the attempt probably is effective. The gain is so deep, so vital, that it is worth losses in other respects. "My pain's a fair price." Loss of life is among these losses. Preserving self-esteem and the sense of self form the motives of self-sacrificial acts in altruistic risks, and they do likewise in vengeance, as in the cases of Medea, the Spanish bishop, and the executors of Kamikaze acts in political contexts.

Involvement in damage to self-esteem and self-identity explains a number of aspects of vengeance. For one thing, it explains the very considerable importance of offenses to one's group, and to the identity of one's group, in the emergence of revenge, because self-esteem and self-identity are so closely dependent on those of the group. For another thing, it explains the duration of vengeful desire.

Damage to self-esteem is like the gown that Nessos threw over Hercules. It clings, it envelops and does not go away. It does not diminish in time, because it colors one's dealings with both the self and the environment, as well as being resuscitatable upon signs that recall the humiliating events. I mentioned the study by Silver, Boon, and Stones (1983) that found that having been the subject of sexual child abuse remains a topic for rumination and efforts to find some sense in it even into advanced age. We indicated earlier what it might be that transforms an emotion into a sentiment or passion: the presence of an unresolved issue (Frijda et al., 1991). Severe damage to self-esteem is not easily resolved, if ever. Shame is notorious for its incessant, burning duration. Indeed, successful revenge is perhaps the only way to achieve such resolution, when damage is caused by a particular actor or can be charged to his or her account.

It is obvious that power inequality and damage to self-esteem are not objective facts. Beyond a bottom layer of subjugation and humiliation they depend on cognitive appraisals and, through them, on the individual's prior expectations and the norms of his or her social environment. Individual expectations and social norms influence both the appraisal of what constitutes powerlessness and damages to self-esteem, and the appropriateness to seek redress by vengeance. As I was told, being brutally ordered to make and remake one's mattress neat and straight in the concentration camps was a burden to the men, who took it as both a failure and a humiliation, and led only to a shrugging of one's shoulders by the women, who were more used to humiliation anyway, or did not feel the same urgency to be in control; obviously, seeking redress was out of the question.

Strong cultural differences exist in the importance of "honor" and in what defines an infringement upon honor and self-esteem; and, for that matter, in the socially prescribed honorableness of revenge, or one's obligations in this regard. Honor, obligation, desire for revenge, and other emotions do not necessarily match. A Turkish man in the Netherlands told how he suffered because he had to avenge a dishonor to his sister. He felt no inclination to do so, but was under the obligation (Mesquita, personal communication). I remember the story (I found it at the time in the newspaper *Le Monde,* in March 1990) of two Mahgrebian boys who committed suicide after having killed the sister of one of them, who had dishonored their family. Individual sense of honor also differs. Black-Michaud (1975) repeated a story by Durham (1990) of a feud in an Albanian mountain tribe in the 19th century. By accident a man killed his friend when he lost control of his axe while working. The victim's family, on the urging of the tribal elders, let itself be compensated by a payment of blood money. However, the victim's son, 6 years old at the time of the accident, revived the feud 20 years later, claiming that he was not bound by an agreement made without his involvement.

Honor and self-esteem contribute to the gains from revenge over and beyond restoration of inflicted harm. Taking revenge may add to glory in cultures valuing machism. In our culture, it has been demonstrated that retaliatory aggression is stronger toward a pair with an offending male and watching female, than towards offending pairs of other composition (Thompson & Richardson, 1983).

Escape From Pain

The direct motor of vengeful desire is pain: the pain of insult or harm or loss, of having been slighted, of having been subjected to another person's power or whim, or of humiliation. I use the word "pain" on purpose. Physical as well as mental pains, or "anguish," possess a particular phenomenal quality: Their urge, their physical quality, their inescapability. Pain, mental as well as physical, pervades the body and makes it cringe. There is evidence that both kinds of pain are related physiologically, in that they activate the opiate system (Panksepp, 1989).

Perhaps all vengeful acts are attempts to escape pain; it may be regarded as the basic pushing power. Pain explains the persistence of the desire for revenge: The desire continues as long as the pain lasts. It also explains why revenge, if let loose, is immoderate; its direct focus is to get rid of pain, and not to get even. Pain is not neutralized by an equal amount of pain but only by taking away its causes. Often this is not possible. The efforts are often in vain. One cannot undo the harm or wipe out the insult, the irreversible loss or one's destabilized self-esteem and sense of identity. Such attempts are doomed, like those of writhing and cringing in physical pain. What one can do, as discussed earlier, is to take away the added sting of the other's gains. What one can do is remove every trace of his or her gains, every recollection of it, and everything that might remind one of the offense. The nearest one can come to terminating the pain, perhaps, is to secure the object's total destruction, removing him or her from the face of the earth, erasing him or her from the records of history. Each one of these attempts, in fact, is what one can see happening. "Domitian, Vespasian's son, whose monstrous behaviour left such a mark upon the Romans that even when they had carved up his whole body they did not feel that they had exhausted their indignation against him: the Senate passed a decree that not even the name of this emperor should remain in inscriptions, nor any statue of portrait of him be preserved" (Procopius, [1981, p. 78]).

One may attempt to escape from pain by means of destructive actions even when the cause of pain is not appropriate to such attempts, that is, when there is an offense but no offender. One may construct a responsible, blameworthy agent. One may smash the kitchen shelf against which one had hit one's head, or in fury smash the portrait of the one who deserted by dying. Stanley Hall (1899) reports as an anger instance that someone fetched a hammer from his barn to smash a stone against which he had hurt himself. In another such instance, a man who had stumbled over his own coil of barbed wire took up the coil, carried it to a brook one mile further downstream, and threw it into the water.

There are more serious vengeful impulses, in which revenge is cooled upon an innocent object, or in the event upon society as a whole. Scapegoating provides one group of examples. In the Middle Ages, Jews were massacred in revenge for supposedly having caused the black death (Girard, 1982). Some serial murders have been explained, both by their perpetrators and by commentators, as revenges for feeling slighted by "those others" or not being accepted by the valued section of society (Leyton, 1989). Frequent are the acts of vengeance enacted upon merely felt offense. Many or all acts of rape are to be understood as acts of vengeance, "vengeance toward all women enacted upon the body of one" (Jacoby, 1983, p. 193), instigated by blaming on Woman that she exerts disturbing power, that her very existence is a suggestion of a promise that she then withholds, that her existence epitomizes independent power and assurance of which the man falls short and is humiliated by (Brownmiller, 1976). It may go as far as murder; the accounts of serial murderers contain examples in which the murderer explicitly refers to revenge and feelings of humiliation of the kind indicated (Leyton, 1989).

Pain perhaps explains that further feature of so much vengeance, the tendency towards extreme violence and cruelty. Extreme cruelty is not restricted to vengeance, but there seems to be an affinity. Examples were given before, and I also recall here the high scores on the 7-point scale ("very strong") for the impulse at revenge for a stolen bicycle, or upon hearing that your friend had slept around.

Why such cruelty? I have not been able to find much literature on the subject. As a special topic it only occurs, as far as I know, in the 19th century literature (Bain, 1876; Steinmetz, 1894/1928).

Several possible explanations come to mind that have indeed been advanced in this context (Steinmetz). One is that infliction of pain enhances one's happiness or reduces one's unhappiness by the sense of contrast. So Hume stated, "The comparison of ourselves with others seems to be the source of envy and malice. The more unhappy another is, the more happy do we ourselves appear in contrast" (Hume, 1759, quoted from Steinmetz, 1894, p. 35). This combines the affect-equalization notion rejected earlier in this paper with the Law of Comparative Feeling and, specifically, the appeasing effects of downward comparison (Taylor & Lobel, 1989). The explanation is a weak one. A more pertinent hypothesis holds that cruelty provides the most unambiguous proof of power over someone else. One fully controls the victim's most inner feelings. One can see each twitch of his or her feelings, and see them as contingent upon one's actions. The explanation is proposed by Schopenhauer (1819) and by Bain (1876). The sense of power relevant here is of a different sort from the social power involved in power equalization as discussed earlier. Rather, it is the counterpoint to the power loss involved in being the victim of offense and, in particular, of torture. It is the elementary power to act upon the environment, to control it; it is self-efficacy at its most basic, in its most extreme form. There is support for the thought that something like this is involved in cruelty in statements by sexual murderers. Cheney (1976) cited the killer Edmund Emil Kemper: "Alive, they [the women he killed] were distant, not sharing with me. I was trying to establish a relationship and there was no relationship. . . . When they were being killed, there wasn't anything going on in my mind except that they were going to be mine. . . . That was the only way they could be mine" (p. 108, quoted by Leyton, p. 59). The explanation would seem to apply also to cruelty in revenge. Each stab, each whimper of the victim is a tangible tit for a particular tat, and that one is capable of delivering.

Yet this explanation of cruelty, whether in revenge or outside, does not appear to explain enough. As regards cruelty in general: Why did Nero indulge in it, why did Caligula, why did Tiberias, all of whom had all the power and efficacy they could wish? Their cruelty has puzzled writers and philosophers for centuries, from Suetonius onward. I do not pretend to understand it, but some associations come to mind. Need for proof of power or self-efficacy at this level has a ring of need for proof of a sense of self—again as the counterpoint of being a victim. Most certainly Kemper's statement about relationships and possession had that ring. Thinking about a weakness of sense of self or identity, it is relevant to remember that cruelty supposes some degree of empathy with the victim: It is his or her suffering that is aimed at, and that somehow must be appreciated. There is a suggestion of ego–object fusion, of effort to find awareness of the self through the feelings of someone else.

This empathy may have another aspect to it, particularly in revenge. Vengeance, I said, basically is an attempt to get rid of the pain. The victim's pain may act as an anaesthetic. The hypothesis comes from a similar hypothesis with regard to self-injurious behavior, and advanced to explain the self-injurious behavior of animals in prolonged stressful conditions (battery breeding). Increased endorphin release through self-injury might serve to attenuate severe discomfort. The same explanation can be advanced (and has been advanced) to explain self-injurious behavior that is frequent in conditions that would (and do) also elicit vengeful impulses, namely, child sexual abuse (Ensink, 1992). In a similar way, pain might be dampened by empathic participation in the extreme injury one inflicts upon someone else.

LEVELS OF OFFENSE, LEVELS OF GAIN,
AND THE MEANING OF REVENGE

I began this paper by stating a puzzle: People seek revenge, whereas revenge does not yield the tangible gains of warding off harm or of undoing offense. If my analysis is correct, the gains are nonetheless real. Revenge represents gain at five different levels that correspond to five levels in the appraisal of offense. At the uppermost level stands protection against the general sense of threat that infliction of harm by others presents through the possible correction of future harmful behavior; it corresponds to the harm as such. Second is the re-equilibration of gains and losses, the restoration of the equality of pleasure and pain, the correction of the offender's profit and glory. Third, there is the re-equilibration of power inequality that was implied by not having been able to prevent the offense or to return it in kind. Then follows recapturing self-esteem, the restoration of one's sense of self and self-efficacy, when this was hurt by having been a victim who had had things done to one, or when one's group had been rendered powerless or deprecated. Restoration of self-worth, if only to a small degree, is possible even when revenge is of little actual effect. Finally, there is relief from pain, through exertion of elementary power over the offender, and perhaps by other ways.

Five levels of gain. All these can be obtained by revenge, and together they seem to represent the root of what is meant by the feeling that revenge flows from one's desire to get even, or satisfies one's sense of justice. Not all offense and revenge reach all five levels. Cool political revenge includes only the first, although for most politicians, soldiers, and policemen, power inequality readily comes in: Who do these unruly elements think they are? Inequality of gain probably is a feature felt in response to any willful offense. Reparation of power inequality or power loss, and of self-esteem or social prestige—the third and fourth levels—may enter every offense. They will do so more readily as the social environment puts emphasis on power and prestige in its norm system. The deeper layers of self-esteem—identity, self efficacy—presumably are engaged mainly or only, when offense is pervasive and cuts deeply, as in torture, enslavement, or rape; or, drawing from criminal examples, when self-esteem is critically vulnerable.

All aspects mentioned, those of offense and those of the gains of revenge, though part of the individual's emotions, are also interpersonal. I should emphasize an obvious aspect to the losses as well as the gains: Vengeance is as interpersonal as the offense that gave rise to it. Vengeance is not only *my* affair, it is also *his* or *her* affair. Vengeance may not restore my loss or undo the harm I have suffered, but it takes away his or her gain or glory; it hides *my* shame behind *his* or *her* shame, and my pain behind his or hers.

The desire for vengeance thus is "rational," in the sense of the rationality of emotions generally (DeSousa, 1988): their being appropriate to their conditions. Vengeance is rational and functional, in the broad sense defined. As I said before, not every individual instance of desire for vengeance is rational, as little as each individual instance of anger or fear is. The appraisal may be irrational, given the actual events. The impulse or its intensity may be irrational, given other options that were available under the prevailing conditions. The destructive power of the actual revenge may be irrational, given the power of the retaliation that might have been foreseen. But as such, as emotional phenomena, revenge and the desire for it are rational.

Desire for vengeance is rational in restoring security, equality of gains, power equality, self-esteem, and identity, and trust in social dealings as a whole. Note that this rationality does *not* include equality between harm received and harm returned, or proportionality between them. That is not among vengeance's primary considerations and, moreover, whereas the received harm *per se* can be graded, its major implications cannot. Being a helpless subject of maltreatment, being unable to control one's conditions, losing one's sense of self-determination, all have something absolute in them.

All of this means that the desire for revenge is not a senseless emotion, a mere instance of emotional irrationality. As with any other emotion, it knows senseless expressions and disruptive manifestations. As elsewhere, in desire, lust, or fear, its adaptive functioning requires moderation. It requires a measure of control with regard to being proportional to circumstance, adaptation to context, anticipation of repercussion, and the appropriate degree of regard for others. But by itself it is tailored to be for the individual's benefit. Revenge is a natural thing to desire, and sometimes it is a natural thing to take. It leads to the few things that a not-so-powerful individual can do, when offended, to repair a disturbed position in the social environment or in the power relationship with a particular other individual. It is the only thing he or she can do with respect to the damages that are secondary to the material harm. Material harm can be repaired by compensation or by blood money. Power inequality can sometimes be repaired by formal means; but for damage to self-esteem and sense of identity, little or no other reparation exists. We have seen, after World War II, how little emotional benefit restoration money can bring.

Non-revenge or impossibility of revenge perpetuates the harm or damage. It is one more indication of the other's power to control or the continuation of his or her glory, the cumulative effect of encountering the traces of the subjugation that was in the original offense, and that the passage of time may not have undone.

Of course, other means than revenge exist to handle damage to one's position and sense of self-efficacy. There exists a number of alternatives in the various techniques of intrapsychic coping, and the complex social-emotional play of forgiveness. Rare are the situations though that an individual will have good reason to make efforts to forgive, unless the offender makes real efforts to show remorse.

Mild revenges are possible, and frequent, in the relatively mild offenses within the interchanges of love; they are, however, impossible and inadmissible when it comes to vigorous desire, and revenge adequate to extreme offense. Simultaneously, judicial punishment rarely administers to such desire; it offers little in the way of the gain that is sought, and the offended person often is entitled to. As Solomon (1989; chapter 11, this volume) argued: Civilized society would do well to try to find more of a solution than it currently does. At least, it should recognize vengeful desire for what it is: a natural emotion seeking natural relief for unnatural suffering inflicted by unnatural offense. That is not what society does. Jacoby (1983), as an instance, describes how all witnesses in the trial of a supervisor from the Maidanek death camp, survivors from that camp, were asked by the accused's attorney whether they were "out for revenge" (p. 2).

WHERE DOES THE DESIRE FOR REVENGE COME FROM?

Desire for revenge is, I think, a universal or near-universal emotion. It is a "basic" emotion, in the sense that it is universally elicited by a particular condition: receiving intentional harm that is not considered justified, that one has not been able to avert or counter, and that has continued to have material or psychological repercussions.

That it is a universal emotional response does not imply that it also is a necessary answer to such eliciting events. It is not. There are alternative ways of responding. Alternative solutions exist for having been the subject of offense. One may suffer in silence, abandon oneself to despair, fully submit to or identify with the aggressor, become angry and leave it at that. Revenge is one solution among several. Said otherwise, there are additional conditions for ensuring wrath and revenge to ensue, rather than one of the other solutions. These additional conditions are, one may expect, reflected in the structure of the individual's appraisal. They include, first of all, the relative weakness of signs of threat of the offender's re-retaliation (e.g., Bandura, 1983; Baron, 1977) or of other inhibitory influences, such as friendship (e.g., Kanekar, Bulsara, Duarte, & Kolsawalla, 1981). They further include those appraisal aspects that contribute generally to the occurrence of anger rather than some other emotion, and to the intensity of that anger. I enumerate: the attribution of malevolent intent to the offender (Dyck & Rule, 1978; Ohbuchi & Kambara, 1985; Zumkley, 1984), the felt unfairness, injustice, or norm-violating character of the offense (e.g., Ohbuchi & Megumi, 1986), or the absence of mitigating circumstances (e.g., Johnson & Rule, 1986); the sense that events could have been otherwise, that the world offers alternative possibilities, which is what I called the appraised modifiability (Frijda, 1986); the inclination not to let offenses pass, the expectation that one could or should control events; the expected approbation for taking a stand, and for aggressive action in particular. There also are factors that are not specific to revenge, or anger generally, such as prevailing state of excitation (Russell, DiLullo, & DiLullo, 1988; Zillmann, 1983). Then there are those factors that account for the transformation of an emotion into a sentiment or passion: the depth or magnitude of the offense (Ohbuchi & Izusu, 1984), the durability of its effects, the involvement of honor, self-esteem or sense of identity.

All these factors, as can be readily seen, can be more or less prominent by receiving support from actual properties of the events—actual evil intent, actual harming of self-esteem and so forth—and from the powers and propensities of the individual—powers to retaliate, propensities to attribute evil intent to others, and the like. They can also, and in particular, be more or less prominent due to social factors: social example and acclaim, and the prevailing value system (e.g., Harvey, 1981).

Many of the facts and stories in the preceding sections illustrate the considerable role of social factors in revenge. I mentioned the influence of the values of power and honor, of norms and obligations regarding taking revenge and, more pervasively, of cultural standards with respect to manliness, social prestige, or assertiveness. Operative in the other direction are values with respect to forgiveness, nonviolence, and "civilization." Societal models of revenge can be expected to facilitate the choice of revenge as the solution to the problem of how to cope with the offense. I also mentioned the influence of group belongingness, when it is the group or its identity that has been offended. In addition, social example and acclaim from the direct social environment are powerful, and in many circumstances decisive in the occurrence and violence of revenge. Revenge by groups has been shown to be considerably fiercer than when one reacts as an individual (Rabbie & Lodewijkx, 1991), and the same probably applies when one acts individually as the representative of a group (Tajfel & Turner, 1979).

Yet vengefulness would not seem to reduce to these social factors of social learning, example, acclaim, and values. They do not show that revenge is of sociocultural origin. It would seem that neither desire for revenge nor actual revenge is so. Sociocultural norms may render revenge normative, prescribed, laudable, or more readily thought of; at the same time these norms can be held to find ready acceptance in norm-independent emotional propensities. Some revenge, moreover, obviously does not conform to cultural rules or expectations. The case of Ferdi E. provides an illustration, and so do the vengeful yearnings and actions of individuals who feel rejected by society as a whole, as did some of the serial killers whose cases are reported in Leyton (1989). Also, absence of revenge in a particular culture does not indicate that it is culturally formed elsewhere. Sociocultural norms can suppress overt revenge, up to and including gossip and blackening someone, and they can even suppress one's urges. One may well assume desire for revenge to be still present whenever it is suppressed; blood will tell. There is sufficient indication that vengeful dreams and fantasies abound in our cultural circles where revenge, except in contexts of love, is almost wholly condemned. At least, I know of someone who blocked the professional promotion of a man because the latter's friend had once, in his view, slighted him, and later actually admitted to have done so out of spite. And, as earlier mentioned, occasional vengeful impulses were acknowledged by almost half of the student respondents in our small inquiry. The social influences selectively encourage or discourage the propensities of the individual (Rabbie & Lodewijkx, 1991). They do not, however, create the urge for vengefulness. They do not ensure that pain arises that seeks relief, and to which revenge is one gate, and on occasion the only one.

Is desire for revenge thereby an innate emotion? I think not. There is no need for such an assumption. Revenge and desire for revenge are fitted to offense in such a manner that each individual may easily discover them for him- or herself. They are "solutions" to a problem at hand, indicated by features of the problem situation, when the individual has an eye for them. They can be supposed to be universal and unlearned, even without being innate.

CONCLUSIONS

What can we conclude? I started out by saying that the analysis of vengeance may provide some clues to help us understand certain highly prominent, disturbing, and puzzling kinds of emotions and emotionally motivated behaviors: those with the features of irrationality, in the sense of providing no obvious gain, of sometimes extreme intensity, and of extended duration. The analysis has shown, I think, that such emotions and behaviors can be meaningfully approached from the perspectives of current emotion theory. The specific structure and conditions of vengeful impulse can be at least hypothetically described; there are features that differentiate wrath from anger. The irrational emotional impulse can be understood as fitting the general functional framework in the analysis of emotions, through the multiple gains of vengeance that can be plausibly inferred. The features of intensity and duration can be shown to fit reasonably into the assumptions from emotion theory. The violence of revenge can be understood from the extent and depth of the offense; its persistence both from the duration of the offense and the nature of the concerns that are injured or trampled by it.

The analysis has also shown, although only in passing, how deeply the interpersonal penetrates into emotion and emotional impulse. The profit of the offender's suffering through revenge has to do with one's sense of the social relationship; the pain of offense has to do with awareness of the offender's pleasure. The interpersonal aspect of emotion and feeling is still to be fully explored.

One conclusion is specific to vengeance: When the offense is real and unacceptable, desire for revenge is acceptable. Society would do well to recognize this, and should find ways to deal with desire for revenge beyond denying or condemning its existence.

ACKNOWLEDGMENTS

I am grateful to Beulah MacNab for her careful correction and improvement of my English text, to Jaap Rabbie for his useful criticism, and to the editor, Stephanie van Goozen, for her comments and patience.

REFERENCES

Atkinson, C., & Polivy, J. (1976). Effects of delay, attack, and retaliation on state depression and hostility. *Journal of Abnormal Psychology, 85,* 570–576.

Averill, J. R. (1968). Grief: Its nature and significance. *Psychological Bulletin 70,* 721–748.

Axelrod, R. (1984). *The evolution of cooperation.* New York: Basic Books.

Babel, I. (1924). The letter. In *Red cavalry* [In The collected stories.] W. Morisson, trans. London, 1957].

Bain, A. (1876). The gratification derived from the infliction of pain. *Mind, 1,* 429–431.

Bandura, A. (1983). Psychological mechanisms of aggression. In R. G. Geen & E. I. Donnerstein (Eds.), *Aggression: Theoretical and empirical reviews (Vol. I,* p. 1–40). New York: Academic Press.

Baron, R. A. (1977). *Human aggression.* New York: Plenum Press.

Biglan, A., & Craker, D. (1982). Effects of pleasant activities manipulation on depression. *Journal of Consulting and Clinical Psychology, 50,* 436–438.

Black-Michaud, J. (1975). *Feuding societies.* Oxford: Basil Blackwell.

Brownmiller, S. (1976). *Against our will: Men, women and rape.* New York: Bantam Books.

Burckhart, J. (1935). *Die Kulturgeschichte der Renaissance in Italien* [The history of renaissance culture in Italy]. Wien: Phaidon. (Original work published 1860).

Caprara, G. V., Bonanno, S., Carrabbia, D., & Mazzotti, E. (1988). Experiments on delayed aggression: A methodological contribution. *Archivo di Psicologia, Neurologia e Psichiatria, 49,* 28–37.

Cassirer, E. (1908). *Substanzbegriff und Funktionsbegriff* [Substance concepts and function concepts]. Leipzig: B. Cassirer.

Cellini, B. (1986). *Autobiography.* Harmondsworth, Middlesex: Penguin Books.

Cheyney, M. (1976). *The co-ed killer.* New York: Walker.

DeSousa, R. (1988). *The rationality of emotions.* Cambridge, MA: MIT Press.

DeWaal, F. (1991). *Peacemaking among primates.* Harmondsworth, Middlesex: Penguin Books.

Donnerstein, E., & Hatfield, E. (1983). Aggression and inequity. In J. Greenberg & R. C. Cohen (Eds.), *Equity and justice in social behavior* (pp. 309–336). New York: Academic Press.

Durham, M. E. (1909). *High Albania.* London: Edward Arnold.

Dyck, R. J., & Rule, B. G. (1978). Effect on retaliation of causal attributions concerning attack. *Journal of Personality and Social Psychology, 36,* 521–529.

Ensink, B. J. (1992). *Confusing realities: A study on child sexual abuse and psychiatric symptoms.* Amsterdam: VU University Press.

Euripides. (1966). *Medea* (P. Vellacott, Trans.). Harmondsworth, Middlesex: Penguin Books.

Felson, R. B. (1978). Aggression as impression management. *Social Psychology, 41,* 205–213.

Fisk, R. (1991). *Pity the nation: Lebanon at war.* Oxford: Oxford University Press.

Frijda, N. H. (1986). *The emotions.* Cambridge, England: Cambridge University Press.

Frijda, N. H. (1988). The laws of emotion. *American Psychologist, 43,* 349–358.

Frijda, N. H., Mesquita, B., Sonnemans, J., & van Goozen, S. (1991). The duration of affective phenomena, or emotions, sentiments and passions. In K. Strongman (Ed.), *International review of emotion and motivation* (pp. 187–225). New York: Wiley.

Frijda, N. H., Ortony, A., Sonnemans, J., & Clore, G. (1992). The complexity of intensity. In M. Clark (Ed.), *Review of personality and social psychology* (Vol. 13, pp. 60–89). Beverly Hills, CA: Sage Publications.

Girard, R. (1982). *Le bouc émissaire* [The scapegoat]. Paris: Grasset.

Glenny, M. (1992). The fall of Yugoslavia: The Third Balkan War. Harmondsworth, Middlesex: Penguin Books.

Hall, G. S. (1899). A study of anger. *American Journal of Psychology, 10,* 516–591.

Hammen, C. L., & Glass, D. R. J. (1975). Depression, activity, and evaluation of reinforcement. *Journal of Abnormal Psychology, 84,* 718–721.

Harvey, M. D. (1981). Outcome severity and knowledge of "Ought": Effects on moral evaluations. *Personality and Social psychology Bulletin, 7,* 459–466.

Hirzel, R. (1907–1910). Die Talion. *Philologos, Zeitschrift für das classische Altertum, 9* (Suppl. 155), 407–482.

Hume, D. (1759). *A dissertation on the passions.* [quoted from Steinmetz, 1894].

Jacoby, S. (1983). *Wild justice.* New York: Harper & Row.

Johnson, T. E., & Rule, B. G. (1986). Mitigating circumstance information, censure, and aggression. *Journal of Personality and Social Psychology, 50,* 537–542.

Kanekar, S., Bulsara, R. M., Duarte, N. T., & Kolsawalla, M. B. (1981). Perception of an aggressor and his victim as a function of friendship and retaliation. *Journal of Social Psychology, 113,* 241–246.

Lazarus, R. S. (1991). *Emotions and adaptation.* New York: Oxford University Press.

Levi, P. (1989). *The drowned and the saved* (R. Rosenthal, Trans.). New York: Vintage Books.

Lewin, K. (1935). On Aristotelian and Galilean science. In K. Lewin *Towards a dynamic theory of personality* (pp. 16–23). New York: McGraw-Hill.

Leyton, E. (1989). *Hunting humans.* Harmondsworth, Middlesex: Penguin Books.

Marongiu, P., & Newman, G. (1987). *Vengeance.* Toronga, NJ: Rowman & Littlefield.

Mergaree, E. I. (1966). Undercontrolled and overcontrolled personality types in extreme antisocial aggression. *Psychological Monographs, 80*(Whole No. 613).

Ohbuchi, K., & Izusu, T. (1984). Retaliation by male victims: Effects of physical attractiveness and intensity of attack of female attacker. *Personality and Social Psychology Bulletin, 10,* 216–224.

Ohbuchi, K., & Kambara, T. (1985). Attacker's intent and awareness of outcome, impression management, and retaliation. *Journal of Experimental Social Psychology, 21,* 321–330.

Ohbuchi, K., & Megumi, S. (1986). Power imbalance, its legitimacy, and aggression. *Aggressive Behavior, 12,* 33–40.

Ortony, A., Clore, G., & Collins, A. (1988). *The cognitive structure of emotions.* Cambridge: Cambridge University Press.

Panksepp, J. (1989). The psychobiology of emotions: The animal side of human feelings. *Experimental Brain Research, 18,* 31–55.

Pearce, J. (1990). *Columbia: Inside the labyrinth.* London: Latin American Bureau.

Procopius. (1981). *The secret history* (G. A. Williamson, Trans.). Harmondsworth, Middlesex: Penguin Books.

Proust, M. (1954). *A la recherche du temps perdu: La prisonnière* [In search of times past: the prisoner]. Paris: Gallimard. (Original work published 1925)

Rabbie, J. M., & Lodwijkx, H. F. M. (1991). Aggressive reactions to social injustice by individuals and groups: Toward a behavioral interaction model. In R. Vermunt & H. Steensma (Eds.), *Social justice in human relations* (Vol. 1, pp. 279–309). New York: Plenum Press.

Rushdie, S. (1983). *Shame.* London: Jonathan Cape.

Russell, G. W., DiLullo, S. L., & DiLullo, D. (1988). Effects of observing competitive and violent versions of a sport. *Current Psychology Research and Reviews, 7,* 312–321.

Sapolsky, B. S., Stocking, S., & Zillmann, D. (1977). Immediate and delayed retaliation in male and female adults. *Psychological Reports, 40,* 197–198.

Schama, S. (1989). *Citizens: A chronicle of the French revolution.* New York: Albert Knopf.

Scherer, K. R. (1984). Emotion as a multicomponent process: A model and some cross-cultural data. In P. Shaver (Ed.), *Review of personality and social psychology* (Vol. 5, pp. 37–63). Beverly Hills, CA: Sage Publications.

Schopenhauer, M. (1819). *Die Welt als Wille und Vorstellung* [The world as will and mental representation]. Leipzig: Reclam, no year.

Seneca, L. A. (1985). On anger. In J. W. Basore (Ed. and Trans.), *Moray essays* (Vol. I). Cambridge: Harvard University Press, The Loeb Classical Library.

Silver, R. L., Boon, C., & Stones, M. H. (1983). Searching for meaning in misfortune: Making sense in incest. *Journal of the Social Issues, 39,* 81–102.

Solomon, R. C. (1989). *A passion for justice.* Reading, MA: Addison-Wesley.

Solomon, R. C., & Murphy, M. C. (Eds.). (1990). *What is justice?* Oxford: Oxford University Press.

Sonnemans, J. (1991). *Structure and determinants of emotional intensity.* Unpublished doctoral dissertation, University of Amsterdam.

Sprang, M. V., McNeil, J. S., & Wright, R. (1989). Psychological changes after the murder of a significant other. *Social Casework, 70,* 159–164.

Steinmetz, S. R. (1928). *Ethnologische Studien zur ersten Entwicklung der Strafe, nebst einer psychologischen Abhandlung über Grausamkeit und Rachsücht* [Ethnological studies on the first development of punishment, next to a psychological treatise on cruelty and desire for vengeance]. *Vol. I,* (2nd ed.). Groningen: Noordhoff. (Original work published in 1894)

Suetonius. (1980) *Life of the twelve Cesars.* Harmondsworth, Middlesex: Penguin Books.

Tajfel, H., & Turner, J. C. (1979). An integrative theory of intergroup conflict. In W. G. Austin & S. Worchel (Eds.), *Psychology of intergroup relations* (pp. 33–47). Monterey, CA: Brooks/Cole.

Taylor, S. E., & Lobel, M. (1989). Social comparison activity under threat: Downward evaluation and upward contacts. *Psychological Review, 96,* 569–575.

Thompson, H. L., & Richardson, D. R. (1983). Same-sex rivalry and inequity as factors in retaliative aggression. *Personality and Social Psychology Bulletin, 9,* 415–425.

Tiede, T. (1971). *Calley: Soldier or killer?* New York: Pinnacle Books.

Wolfgang, M. E. (1958). *Patterns of criminal homicide.* Philadelphia: University of Pennsylvania Press.

Wolfgang, M. E., & Ferracuti, F. (1967). *The subculture of violence.* New York: Barnes & Noble.

Wortman, C. B., & Silver, R. C. (1989). The myths of coping with loss. *Journal of Consulting and Clinical Psychology, 57,* 349–357.

Zillmann, D. (1983). Transfer of excitation in emotional behavior. In J. T. Cacioppo & R. E. Petty (Eds.), *Social psychophysiology: A sourcebook* (pp. 215–240).

Zumkley, H. (1984). Einflusse von individuellen Differenzen der Agressivität bei kausaler Ambiguität. Zeitschrift für Differentielle und Diagnostische Psychologie [The influence of individual differences in aggressiveness under causal ambiguity]. 5, 131–140.

11

Sympathy and Vengeance: The Role of the Emotions in Justice*

Robert C. Solomon
The University of Texas at Austin

"WHAT IS JUSTICE?"
(THEORIES VERSUS FEELINGS)

> *"Any doctrine that eliminates or even obscures the function of choice of values and enlistment of desire and emotions in behalf of those chosen weakens personal responsibility for judgment and for action."*
> —John Dewey, in *Commentary* (July, 1946)

"What is justice?" Socrates asked that question 25 centuries ago, and it has been, ever since, one of the leading questions of Western thinking. But from Plato to contemporary theories, philosophical discussions of justice have emphasized the supremacy of reason and rationality, and there has been little talk about feelings. Plato (1985) did insist on "harmony" between passions and reason, but he also warned us—often—against the unbridled emotions. Rawls (1971) did devote a late section or two to "the moral sentiments," but by these he seemed to mean no more than certain dispositions to act on rational principles. Many lesser authors,

*This essay is based on several lectures and papers I have been giving over the past several years, including a Memorial Lecture at the University of Massachusetts, Boston for I.S.R.E. member Shula Sommers in April of 1989, as an informal presentation at the I.S.R.E. meeting in Paris in March of 1988, at the conference of N.A.S.S.P. at Oxford University in 1988, and in an essay for Mel Lerner in *Social Justice Research* in 1991. Pieces of this essay are adapted from portions of my book *A Passion for Justice*, (New York: Addison-Wesley, 1990). My special thanks to Nico Frijda for his encouragement and support as well as his vigorous criticism of many of the ideas expressed in this essay.

291

of course, have simply dismissed all sentiments as mere "sentimentality" and insisted that the emotions only confuse and distort the rational deliberations of justice. My thesis in this chapter and in my book, *A Passion for Justice,* (Solomon, 1990) is that there can be no adequate understanding of our sense of justice without an appreciation and understanding of the emotions. This includes not only those benign "moral sentiments" such as sympathy, care and compassion, and other "fellow-feelings" that are presupposed by justice but also the nastier emotions of envy, jealousy, resentment, and, especially, vengeance.

Justice, we are reminded again and again and again, is a matter of rational principles, and if those principles or their consequences should turn out to be "callous"—as Nozick (1974) declared in his preface to *Anarchy, State and Utopia*—so much the worse for our feelings. It is this utter dismissal of the passions that I want to reject. I do not suggest that we in turn dismiss reason from the proceedings, but rather I argue that the distinction between reason and the passions is itself overblown and the source of much mischief. Indeed, much of what is called "reason" in philosophy is rather callousness, insensitivity, distrust of our own (or others') sensibilities and pigheadedness in the pursuit of a proof of the obvious, and the impersonality and detachment with which we philosophers so often identify and on which we so pride ourselves may, in the instance of social philosophy, in particular, be exaggerated if not misplaced. What is essential to justice, I want to argue, is our supposedly unphilosophical sense of compassion and various other passions, too long swept under the carpet laid down by Kant and so many other sarcastic critics of "melting compassion" and the "inclinations." And perhaps even more controversial, I want to argue that "negative" emotions such as indignation and vengeance are part and parcel of our human nature and equally essential to justice, not just character flaws or human weaknesses.

It is often said that a life ruled by the passions is dangerous. I would like to suggest, in response, that it is the ideal of rational justice that is dangerous. It encourages passivity, mere judgment and not motivation and action. It leaves us uninvolved in the world, as if justice is merely to be hoped for and not a personal virtue to be cultivated and exercised. Perhaps it is the very word, "justice," that tends to awe us, transfix us, mislead us. It seems to refer to something heroic and awesome, perhaps even divine. It is always at a distance, something "other," a state to be hoped for, prayed for, or perhaps desperately worked for but not as such something already "in us," something very much our own. Justice is an abstract belief, what Lerner (1980) called "the belief in a just world," but it is out of our hands, a matter of personal concern perhaps but not a matter of individual responsibility. The aim of my efforts to inject emotion back into discussions of justice is first of all an attempt to get people to care and not just think abstractly about justice. Better indignation and even vengefulness than indifference, when such emotions can make a difference.

The problem with all of our lofty philosophical conceptions is that they seem to descend upon us from nowhere (literally, "u-topia"); "out of thin air" is a phrase commonly associated with philosophical discussions of rights and rationality, and our obsessive need to "ground" our claims may have something to do with this. Meanwhile, we ignore the very down to earth and human emotional foundations of justice and neglect those passions that make justice necessary and also make it possible. Justice is not, first of all, a set of principles or policies; it is, first of all, a set of personal feelings, a way of participating in the world. Without the cultivation of those feelings—and some of them are by no means attractive—the principles of justice are nothing but abstract "ideals," and the policies that would make us just, however justified, seem overambitious and even irrelevant, but in any case unsuited for application in the so-called real world. The question of justice, then, may be very much in the spirit of Nico Frijda's own scholarly ecumenticalism. It is not just a matter of philosophy but also a topic for psychologists, sociologists, anthropologists, not to mention novelists, filmmakers, and poets as well. My main aim in this essay, accordingly, is to encourage cooperation between philosophy and the social sciences, and urge both of them to pay more attention to the often neglected intelligence of the emotions.

"WHAT IS AN EMOTION?"
(EMOTIONS AND RATIONALITY)

"What is an Emotion?" asked William James (1884) as the title of an essay he wrote for *Mind* over 100 years ago. But philosophers have been concerned and often worried about the nature of emotion since Socrates and the "preSocratics" who preceded him, and although the discipline has grown up (largely because of Socrates and his student Plato) as the pursuit of reason, the emotions have always lurked in the background, as a threat to reason, as a danger to philosophy and philosophers, as just plain unreasonable. Perhaps that is why one of the most enduring metaphors of reason and emotion has been the metaphor of master and slave, with the wisdom of reason firmly in control and the dangerous impulses of emotion safely suppressed, channelled or, ideally, in harmony with reason. But nowhere have the unruly and threatening power of the emotions been more at odds with what has often been called "reason" than in the realm of justice, where both compassion and its vicious "negative" counterpart, vengefulness, have been condemned as disruptive, irrelevant and, at worst, downright dangerous.

The arguments tend to focus on the alleged "capriciousness" and "prejudice" of emotions, although, alternatively, they are attacked for their "intractibility" and their stupidity. On the one hand, conservatives love nothing more than to lambast the "do-gooders" and "bleeding hearts," namely those who express their feelings rather than stick by some abstract and often ruthless, but in any case "hard-headed" theory. On the other hand, there is the age-old insistence on "the rule of law," shared by both liberals and conservatives, which insists on "not returning evil for evil," and, accordingly, the foreswearing and condemnation of revenge. (That said, of course, liberals and conservatives then go on to have very different ideas about the aims and arguments for punishment.) But compassion and revenge are but two sides of the same coin, and against the wisdom that goes back to Plato, I would call that coinage "justice." Reason is not the master here, nor should it be. (Nor, of course, should it be slave.) What must be shown is that the emotions do not and should not play an inferior role in deliberations about justice, and that it is false that emotions are more primitive, less intelligent, more bestial, less dependable, and more dangerous than reason. Reason and emotion are not two conflicting and antagonistic aspects of the soul. Rational emotions constitute justice, which is neither dispassionate nor merely emotional.

The conjunction of emotions, reason, and justice would make little sense if emotions were only that which they have often been said to be, mere short-term, disruptive physiological disturbances. Plato (1984) seemed to so treat them, at least in his more ethereal discourses on reason (e.g., in his early dialogue, *Crito*, in which Socrates reprimanded Crito for appealing to emotions and the opinions of *hoi poloi*). James (1884) treated them as such, in his famous "What is an Emotion?" essay and so did C. G. Lange (1922). But recent work on emotion has shown that what was once called a "passion" is neither so unintelligent nor so opposed to reason as is often supposed. Frijda (1986) in particular highlighted and analyzed the "cognitive" ingredients and preconditions of emotion and the purposes they serve. Emotions themselves are ways of coping, products of assessment and evaluation, modes of rational action. In his presidential address to I.S.R.E. in 1990, Frijda emphasized the very important and often neglected point that many emotions have and require *duration* and should not be considered (as they typically are) in terms of merely episodic, short-term responses (Frijda et al., 1991). This is nowhere more important than in the emotions of justice, where the sense of justice (and injustice) as well as more particular feelings such as caring and vengefulness are by their very nature not merely immediate but emotional commitments for the long haul. The sense of justice (and injustice) is not an "episode." It is often, for better or for worse, a way of life.

My own argument, briefly stated here, is that emotions already "contain" reason, and practical reason is circumscribed and defined by emotion (Solomon, 1976, 1991). (Nietzsche: "as if every passion didn't contain its quantum of reason!") Our emotions situate us in the world, and so provide not so much the motive for rationality much less its opposition but rather its very framework. Every emotion involves what Gordon (1987) designated a conceptual "structure" of judgments that can be well wrought or foolish, warranted or unwarranted, correct or incorrect. Anger involves judgments of blame, jealousy includes judgments about a potential threat or loss. Love involves evaluative judgments, typically overblown, but so does hatred. Grief involves recognition of a loss, and vengeance—often maligned in philosophy—already involves a small scale theory of justice, an "eye for an eye," or what Kant (1889) less violently but more ambiguously called "equality." In all of these examples, one can readily recognize what can go wrong in the emotion—and consequently what is required for it to go right. In anger one can be confused about the facts. He or she is still angry, but wrongfully so. And if one lept to conclusions or did not examine the readily available evidence, he or she is foolishly so. One can be right about the facts but wrong about the harm done or the blameworthiness of the person with whom one is angry. (The "intensity" of anger, I want to suggest, has much more to do with the harshness of such evaluations than with the physiological accompaniments of the emotion.) One can be right about the facts and justified about the warrant for anger but yet go wrong in its expression, misdirecting it (a common problem with vengeance) or overdoing it. (The irrationality of emotions is often a fault in performance or timing rather than a mistaken emotion as such.) The fault may be the aim or purpose of the emotion, what Jean-Paul Sartre (1948) called an emotion's *finalité*. But Sartre then goes on to accuse all emotions of escapism, strategies for avoiding difficult circumstances. Similar analyses are available for love and grief and every other emotion, even the seemingly simplest of them. Fear, for example, is not just a rush of adrenalin but the recognition of a danger, and one can be wrong about the danger, its imminence, or its seriousness. Fear can be irrational, which means that it is composed of and subject to the judgments of rationality. It can therefore be rational as well. So, too, the sense of compassion, the desire for revenge, the sting of injustice, and the generalized sense of justice. To say that these can go wrong and be irrational is just to say that, properly exercised, they can be rational as well.

What is more striking and more provocative in this analysis is that the concepts and judgments that are constitutive of our emotions are in turn constitutive of the criteria for rationality as well. If an offense is worthy of anger it thus becomes rational (that is, warranted) to be angry about it, and if one argues that it is even more rational (for example, more effective in terms of self-esteem or common prudence) not to get angry, that only shows, I want to suggest, how firmly entangled are the life of the emotions and the various meanings of rationality. Indeed, rationality begins to look more and more like emotional prudence, presupposing, of course, the right emotions. My point, then, is not just to defend the rationality of the emotions, a now well-established and much-mulled over thesis, but to establish what one might call the emotional grounding of rationality. What I want to reject here is the now-prevalent idea that rational criteria are simply the presuppositions of emotion or the external standards by which emotions and their appropriateness may be judged. That would leave standing the idea of a rational framework within which the emotions may be appropriate or inappropriate, warranted or unwarranted, wise or foolish. I want to suggest rather that emotions constitute the framework (or frameworks) of rationality itself. Of course, a single emotion does not do this, any more than a single correct calculation makes a student intelligent. A single emotion (or even an entire sequence of emotions) may be dictated by character, the circumstances, and the overall cultural context, but altogether our emotions (appropriate to the general circumstances) dictate that context (as well as character). Our sense of justice, as well as the grand theories that are constructed in expression of that sense of justice, is thus not a single emotion but rather a systematic totality of emotions, appropriate to our culture and our character. What I have in mind here is a holistic conception of the personality in which the whole field of one's (or one's culture's) experience is defined and framed by his or her engagements and attachments, in which truly "dispassionate" judgment is more often pathological than rational and detachment more likely signals alienation than objectivity. Martin Heidegger's (1962) punsical conception of mood (*Stimmung*) as our mode of "being tuned" (*Bestimmen*) to the world is instructive here, both because of its welcome shift in emphasis from detached knowing to holistic personal caring (*Sorge*) but also because of the not insubstantial fact that he emphasizes moods— which are general, diffuse, and devoid of any determinate object—rather than, for example, love, an emotion whose character is marked first of all by its particularity and attachment. But what is important about both moods and emotions is the fact that they thoroughly permeate our experience and they are not, as several honorable ancient views would have it, interruptions, intrusions, or brief bouts of madness that get in the way of the otherwise calm and cool transparency of rational objectivity.

The idea that emotions as such are not rational thus begins with a basic misunderstanding of both the nature of emotions and the nature of rationality, and the idea that emotions as such are irrational is a confusion of certain sorts of specialized procedures—appropriate perhaps to the seminar room and the negotiating table—with rationality as such. But even in the seminar and at the negotiating table, it is caring that counts first of all, and as a matter of strategy, it is obvious that even as a negotiating tool emotion is often appropriate and, well used, effective. Love is sometimes said to be irrational because it over-evaluates the beloved. But here as always we should be very suspicious: Is the enthusiastic idealization of someone about whom one cares a great deal a falsification and thereby irrational, or is it part and parcel of any intimate connection, recognizing another as more important than others ("to me") and being engaged in life rather than a merely disinterested, dispassionate spectator? So, too, with almost all of the emotions, including many of those that have typically been dubbed "negative," even "sins," one must be very careful about dismissing their admittedly biased vision of the world as merely "subjective" or "irrational," for what is the alternative—not caring at all? ("apatheia"). No affections or offenses whatever? No commitments or attachments—the dubiously "rational" approach to a life without loss suggested by various ascetics and religious thinkers (e.g., the Arab philosopher al-Kindi in the 9th century[1]) (see Goodman, 1989). These are the

---

[1]See L. E. Goodman (1989) on Medieval Jewish and Islamic Philosophers, In Biderman and Scharfstein (Eds.), *Rationality in question: On eastern and western views of rationality* (pp. 95–99).

targets of Nietzsche's (1967) reknowned attack on the hypocrisy of asceticism in Part III of his *Genealogy of Morals,* where he claimed that ascetics (like everyone) seek power and self-assertion but obtain it, as it were, backwards, by stealth and self-denial. Caring about the right things—one's friends and family, one's compatriots and neighbors, one's culture and environment, and, ultimately, the world—is what defines rationality. It is not reason (as opposed to emotion) that allows us to extend our reach to the universal, but rather the expansive scope of the emotions themselves. What one cares about is defined by one's conception of the world, but one's conception of the world is itself defined by the scope and objects of one's emotional cares and concern (Frijda, 1986).

Not only is every emotion structured by concepts and judgments, most of them learned (at least in their details and applications), but every emotion is also engaged in a strategy of psychological as well as physical self-preservation. Thus it is readily understandable that emotions should first of all emerge as self-interested, even selfish, then concerned with kin and kinship rather than a larger sense of community, chauvinistic rather than cosmic. But part of cultivation, or "civilization," is internalizing the larger concepts of history, humanity, and religion, conceptions of morality and ethics that go beyond provincial self-interests. But this is not to say that the emotional nature of these concerns is replaced by something more abstract and impersonal; the emotions and the persons themselves become more expansive. Emotions are not just "reactions," and although they undoubtedly have an evolutionary history that precedes the arrival of the human species by hundreds of millions of years, they have evolved not only along with but hand in hand with the evolution of reason and rationality, which means in part an awareness of the larger human and global context in which all of our fates are engaged and our interests involved. There is, however, nothing particularly human about emotion as such (a dog or a horse can be as rightfully angry or sad as a person) although there are particularly human emotions, for instance romantic love and moral indignation. Indeed, some of those particularly human emotions—for instance, religious passion and scientific curiosity—are precisely the passions that are typically designated as proof of our rationality.

One might, of course, object to all and any philosophical theories of emotion as mere "armchair" speculation, devoid of the empirical support supplied by psychologists and other social scientists, but this objection ignores the fact that most philosophers, contrary to their own self-styled reputations as men and women of pure reason, have emotions themselves. As Descartes (1989) insisted, in his introduction to the subject of *The Passions of the Soul,* "everyone has experience of the passions within himself, and there is no necessity to borrow one's observations from elsewhere in order to discover their nature" (p. 14). No one who has been in a philosophy department tenure meeting could possibly doubt the propensity of these practitioners of pure reason to compassion and vindictiveness (though rarely both in the same professor at the same time). Extensive experience does not always require an experiment, and ultimately, there is no need for the century-old feud between philosophy and psychology.

Both one's own experience and the experience of others, as the subject of reflection, can serve the purpose of understanding the role of emotion in our affairs. And when the topic is as large as justice, we need all the varied experience and reflection we can get.

THE CARING FACE OF JUSTICE: THE MORAL SENTIMENTS

No man is devoid of a heart sensitive to the suffering of others. . . . Suppose a man were, all of a sudden, to see a young child on the verge of falling in a well. He would certainly be moved to compassion, not because he wanted to get in the good graces of the parents, nor because he wished to win the praise of his fellow villagers or friends, nor yet because he disliked the cry of the child. From this it can be seen that whoever is devoid of the heart of compassion is not human, whoever is devoid of the heart of shame is not human, whoever is devoid of the heart of courtesy and modesty is not human, and whoever is devoid of the heart of right and wrong is not human. (Mencius, 1970)

How selfish soever man may be supposed, there are evidently some principles in his nature, which interest him in the fortune of others, and render their happiness necessary to him, though he derives nothing from it except the pleasure of seeing it. Of this kind is pity or compassion, the emotion which we feel for the misery of others. . . . The greatest ruffian, the most hardened violator of the laws of society, is not altogether without it. (Adam Smith, 1880)

The awareness of the importance of emotions that is emerging in psychology is a welcome antidote to the dangerous obsession with abstract reason in philosophy. But philosophy has not always been so abstract and emotionally alienated. The ancient Greeks, for all of their emphasis on reason, never excluded the emotions and in fact discussed their importance at considerable length. But much more recently, in the 18th century, philosophers in Scotland and France, in particular, developed an elaborate theory of the emotions' important place in ethics and social philosophy. The Scottish moralists included David Hume (1978) and Adam Smith, who made his reputation with his *Theory of the Moral Sentiments* (1880), the proceeds of which allowed him the time to write his bible for capitalism, *The Wealth of Nations* (1948). Hume and Smith argued that the basis of all morality had to be emotion, not reason, and that we were all endowed by nature (if not our creator) with the all-important natural sentiment of sympathy. Hume famously argued that reason itself cannot move us to action, only passion can do that, and so "reason is and ought to be the slave of the passions." It was an extreme statement, problematic in part because it reinforces (rather than challenges) the strict separation of the two, but it had the virtue of shifting the emphasis onto the "natural" aspects of human nature rather than the "artificial" constructions of reason and society. Hume and Smith put an enormous emphasis on the notion of personal "character" and devoted a good portion of their works to developing theories of the virtues and accounts of those emotions that should be cultivated to bring up a virtuous person in a just society.

If we wanted to capture a single culprit who, in reputation at least, is responsible for the philosophical obsession with "reason" and rational principles and abusive to the passions, it would be Immanuel Kant, although Kant himself was not nearly so one-sided as many of his latter-day followers. It was Kant (1980) who argued so fervently against reliance on the "inclinations" in moral matters, insisting instead that all evaluations of "moral worth" should rely on obedience to principles and practical reason rather than having the right feelings or displaying a proper "character." Emotions, according to Kant, were too capricious, too easily shifted, too readily influenced by other people. Emotions, unlike reason, differed from culture to culture, even from person to person. Emotions, for the most part, were concerned with particular situations, particular attachments to particular people, and often "blind" to larger considerations. Morality and justice, by contrast, were rational ideals that had to remain constant, even eternal. Morality consisted of universal principles, applicable everywhere and equally to everyone. Kant was reacting, in part, to the tradition that preceded him, the work of the 18th century Scottish moralists, and he was concerned to provide a view of morals and justice that did not depend on the vicissitudes of emotion and the peculiarities of individual character, though he did not, again, deny the importance of either emotions or character. It is worth noting that Kant was answered by that cranky but always perceptive post-Kantian, Arthur Schopenhauer (1965). And it was the moral sentiment theorist Hume (1978), who, on other matters had "awakened [Kant] from his dogmatic slumbers." But Kant's emphasis on "practical reason" won out over both the generation that preceded and the century that succeeded him in philosophy, and today's largely uncritical acceptance of the Kantian paradigm—especially in the realm of social philosophy—should be juxtaposed against the healthy tradition that Kant was rejecting. There is no justice without feeling and sympathy in particular, and I think that Schopenhauer hit the Kantian nail right on the head when he pointed out that Kant's theory of morality had in fact left out the very basis of morals—namely, the sentiment of compassion.

The emphasis on emotions in ethics, the "theory of the moral sentiments," in a broad sense, goes back to Aristotle (1985), although he did not so sharply separate the emotions that prompted action from the action itself and from rational considerations that preceded it. But he did recognize that the right emotions were as essential to right action and insisted that a just man was moved by just feelings as well as just thoughts. Augustine (1956) and many other Christian thinkers placed a special premium on the emotions, not just faith and love but on all of those sentiments that defined the various virtues (and, of course, those deadly passions that constituted the worst vices). But moral sentiment theory really comes of age in the 18th century, in Scotland, with the idea of an "innate moral sense" in the work of Francis Hutcheson (1755). Hutcheson did more than just recognize the importance of feeling in the appreciation of values; he developed a detailed taxonomy and account of these feelings and their relation to different kinds of value. But Hutcheson's, it should be noted, is not so much a sentiment theory as it is a moral sense theory. Pleasure and pain, which are the primary ingredients in his taxonomy, are treated more like perceptions than like emotions. Although he has much to say about feeling, he does not mean by this that genuine feelings or emotion play a part in our value appreciation (Calhoun, 1981). It is Hume (1978) who picked up Hutcheson's theory and converted it into a theory of moral sentiments. For this, he needed a theory of genuine feelings, emotions, and a way of distinguishing those peculiarly moral feelings. Hume retained Hutcheson's account of value-feelings as painful or pleasant sensations, and this remains the primary defect in his theory. Pleasure and pain (and with them, the derivative notion of "positive" and "negative" emotions) are just too simplistic—like most such dualisms—to capture the enormous richness of our our emotional life and the extent of our engagement in the world. Ironically, it was Kant who started correcting this aspect of Hume's philosophy (though he does not use the results to undermine his own overly rationalistic view of morality). The primary breakthrough (in fact harking back to Aristotle and some later Greek philosophers) is the recognition of a distinctively conceptual component in emotion, anticipated by Hume but retarded by his "pleasure and pain" view of the passions. Later European philosophers would develop this "cognitive" theory of emotion even further, and one might mention in particular the work of Brentano (1889), who ably combined conceptual and empirical research in his "psychognosy" and his thesis of the "intentionality" of emotion as the source of a fundamental axiology of social values, and Scheler (1954), who brought to bear the new research in "phenomenology" on an updated theory of sympathy as the core of our social experience. But my concern here is not the history and development of moral sentiment theory but rather its results. And those results, if taken as theory, tend to undermine the favorite prejudice of contemporary Anglo-American moral and social theory, namely that morality and justice are first of all *a priori* functions of reason rather than matters of emotion. Justice is not to be found or looked for in the world, whether as reality or as potential; justice is and must be, first of all, "in us," in our attitudes towards each other rather than any particular set-up with which the world presents us.

Several of the moral sense theorists (particularly Hume) identified sympathy with benevolence, noting the motivational power of the latter, whereas sympathy too readily remains nothing but a "feeling with" or "feeling for." But benevolence too need not lead to action (it is a "wishing well" rather than the "making well" of "beneficence") and it need have nothing to do with "feeling with" or even "for." (One can want to help others on principle, for example, or because one cannot abide their noisy suffering.) In such cases, one may well "care" but not care primarily for the well-being of the other. But this is just the problem with sympathy. It always seems to suggest more than it actually provides. It is one thing to say that one is upset and has kindly feelings towards a fellow creature in pain, that one in some sense "shares" the suffering. But feeling sorry for someone is not the same as wanting to help them, and whereas benevolence typically leads to beneficence and helping behavior, "feeling sorry for" too often stops at pity.

"Sympathy" (like "compassion") literally means and is often meant to mean "shared feeling," but, what is it to "share" a feeling—individuation problems aside (i.e., can one and the same feeling be shared by two people, or can each person have his and only his own feeling?) Insofar as sympathy involves actually sharing feelings, it is clear that the suffering one shares with the sufferer is, for the most part, pretty limp stuff and not nearly adequate to motivate ethical behavior. I may in fact feel slightly ill because you have just broken your leg in three places, but it would be absurd to compare my feelings to yours much less to say that I am "sharing" your suffering. Indeed, it seems absurd to talk at all about "sharing" feelings in most such cases. I may feel upset to hear that you have just lost your grandfather, been called for a general audit by the Internal Revenue Service or have been fired from your job. But the fact that I too have negative feelings (sadness, fear, indignation) because of you and even for you hardly adds up to a sufficiently equal measure of mutual emotion to call this "shared feelings." Of course, if indeed we share the situation, if it is our grandfather who died, our partnership that is to be audited or we both who are to be fired, it is perfectly plausible to say that we share the appropriate feelings. But this would not be a matter of "sympathy," for the whole idea behind moral sentiment theory is that I can and do feel for you on the basis of your suffering and not my own.

I may have a fairly mild sense of pathos caused by and in my concern about your rather awful suffering, and it makes little sense to compare the two much less to talk about them as "shared." It is for this reason that Smith, in particular, suggested that a sense of justice is needed to supplement sympathy, which by itself is not nearly powerful enough to counter the inevitably self-serving motives of most people. Justice, for Smith, is an internalized sense of fair play, and it is justice, not sympathy, that provides the main "pillar" that supports the whole society. Justice, unlike sympathy, is a passion with a determined content, albeit a negative one; justice is the sense that one should not cause harm to one's neighbor. Sympathy and justice, together with a sense of benevolence, provide Smith with a portrait of human nature in his *Theory of the Moral Sentiments* (1880) that is very different from the usual Hobbesian interpretations of his later work, *The Wealth of Nations* (1948), in which the wheels of capitalism are (wrongly) said to be moved by individual greed alone. Sympathy is "fellow-feeling," feeling not so much for as with one's fellow citizens, whatever their particular passions happen to be. Our sense of justice moves us to avoid harming one another, and between the two, the Hobbesian picture of human life as "a war of all against all" and as "nasty, brutish and short" gets replaced by the much more flattering portrait of a society of citizens who care, feel for, and naturally avoid harming one another.

Sympathy is often confused with "empathy," which is also defined as "identification with another," "putting oneself in the other's shoes" and vicariously sharing his or her emotions. Certainly Smith, in particular, used the one term to mean the other, and Cropsey's explicit identification of the two (in *The Theory of the Moral Sentiments: 1880*) is not at all inappropriate as an interpretation of some of Smith's text. "[Smith argues that] every human being has the power to feel the passions of those other beings who come under his observation. The man who observes joy of another will himself experience joy."[2] But empathy, too, has been characterized not so much as an emotion but as a technique or a strategy for sharing and understanding emotions, an ability to "put oneself in the other's place," as well as the actual sharing of feelings that results from such identification, and Smith elsewhere denies that we can ever actually share the feelings of another. Moving from the 18th century to our own, however, we find that much the same debate and confusion continues, especially in the social sciences, where the validity of the "method" of empathy is much in dispute, for example, in anthropology.[3] Recent studies of sympathy and empathy in psychology by Wispé (1986) and Natsoulas (1988) strongly suggest that the distinction has become largely a stipulative matter. But we can take a strong hint from etymology and the observation that sympathy means "feeling with," (a) "agreement in feelings" and (b) "sharing feelings, especially sorrow or trouble," whereas empathy means "feeling into" and "identification with or vicarious experiencing of the feelings or thoughts of another person."[4] Empathy, in other words, might better be thought of as shared feeling, whereas sympathy is a more specific feeling, feeling sorry for, a kind of caring, but caring at a distance, as an observer rather than a "caretaker."

THE VINDICTIVE FACE OF JUSTICE: VENGEANCE AND THE "NEGATIVE" EMOTIONS

There is no denying the aesthetic satisfaction, the sense of poetic justice, that pleasures us when evil-doers get the comeuppance they deserve. The impulse to punish is primarily an impulse to even the score. . . . That satisfaction is height-

---

[2]Joseph Crospey (1954). *Polity and Economy* (p. 12) Westport, CT: Greenwood Press.

[3]For instance, in the now classic dispute between Margaret Mead and Marvin Harris and in the more recent debate over Jean Briggs' book on eskimo emotions, *Never in Anger*, (Harvard University Press). See, for an extensive and varied account of this dispute, Levine and Schweder, eds., *Culture Theory* (Cambridge University Press, 1984).

[4]The Random House Dictionary, 1980.

ened when it becomes possible to measure out punishment in exact proportion to
the size and shape of the wrong that has been done. . . . *mida k'neged mida*—
measure for measure, *lex talionis.*—Arthur Lelyveld (1971)

My argument is that justice is a passion to be cultivated, not an abstract set of
principles to be formulated, mastered, and imposed upon society (whether or not
this is "for our own good" or in accordance with our presocietal inherent "na-
tures"). Justice begins not with Socratic insights but with the promptings of some
basic emotions, foremost among them such "negative" emotions as envy, jealousy, and resentment, a keen sense of having been personally cheated or neglected and the desire to "get even."[5] This is not the usual list of "moral sentiments," to be sure. In Smith (1880), in Hume (1978), across the channel and a
border or two in Rousseau (1983), what we hear a great deal about are those
supposedly basic feelings of fellow-feeling, compassion, and sympathy. Of
course these are essential, but the problem is that they are only a small piece—
albeit an absolutely essential piece—of the picture. (It may be worth noting,
with some sense of irony, that sympathy and the other undeniably positive
passions—"pity" may be a problem here—are often not just neglected but actually denied, for example, by those cynics who don't even think of denying the
existence of the antipathetic passions—envy and resentment in particular.) But
could one have sympathy much less empathy with one's fellows if one did not
know what it was to be envious, humiliated, or embittered? Could one be
resentful without at least the capacity to be sympathetic as well? What both
conceptual analysis and empirical research will show, I anticipate, is that the
emotions of justice essentially come in a "package." Just as one cannot feel love
without the potential for grief and one cannot feel pride without the capacity for
shame, one cannot have or develop a passion for suprapersonal justice without a
primary sense of personal injustice (Thomas, 1983). The emotions of justice
must be particular as well as general, and when we speak of a "sense of justice" it
cannot be just a universal sensibility, a Platonic love of the good, that we have in
mind.[6] The sense of justice includes not just the noble or sympathetic emotions
but the often nasty even hateful antipathetic emotions as well.

---

[5]The term "negative emotions" has been effectively employed by Lawrence Thomas, for example, in an essay on "Grief and Guilt" in Myers, Irani, eds., *Emotion* (New York: Haven, 1983). He
lists as his basic list of "negative" emotions, not only grief and guilt (which I do not here discuss) but
also envy, hatred, and so on. The idea is that these are distinctively unpleasant and undesirable in
themselves (unlike joy and love, for instance) but are to be valued rather for the "support" they give
to such "positive" emotions. My argument here is somewhat different, but the overall point is much
the same.

[6]Martha Nussbaum recently argued similarly with regard to "love and the moral point of view."
She noted that Adam Smith, who defended the importance of all sorts of emotions, nevertheless
denied love the status of a moral sentiment on the grounds that it was too exclusive and particular. See
her *Love's Knowledge* (Oxford, 1990) especially p. 338f. Nussbaum also made the astounding claim
that theorists of emotion have virtually ignored "the connection between emotions and beliefs about
what is valuable and important" (p. 293 and n. 15).

The usual set of altruistic or what Rescher (1974) calls "vicarious" passions is too limited to account for justice. The antipathetic emotions are as essential as the sympathetic passions to our sense of justice. Envy and jealousy have as much to do with the origins and development of justice as pity and compassion. At the very beginning of our historical sense of justice (antidating our own rather ethnocentric notion of "distributive justice" by several millenia) is the sense of justice as revenge and outrage. (Whatever the cynic's doubts about such emotions as pity or compassion, he or she will probably have few doubts about the reality of the all-too-human passion for revenge. Nietzsche is obviously a case in point.) It is too easily assumed that a fully developed sense of justice, because it is such a noble sense, must be derived only from equally noble (though perhaps more primitive) emotions. I think that this is wrong. Our sense of justice emerges as a generalization and a rationalization (not in the bad Freudian sense but rather in the good Hegelian sense) of a personal sense of *in*justice.

Our sense of injustice isn't a general sense of outrage—that comes later and already involves a number of grand generalizations. That sense of injustice begins with a personal slight, a perceived inequity, probably at a very young age, perhaps even in infancy. But the "negative" emotions are not all that negative after all. It has been argued, for instance, that envy is itself an important emotion, an engine of capitalism and the consumer society that encourages us to want more and to be more competitive (Schoeck, 1970). Nietzsche (1967) argued at length that resentment is the main ingredient in much of what we call morality, and Dostoevsky (1960) (or one of his most famous characters) maintained that spite is the very essence of the free and autonomous self. The argument that I want to suggest, if not pursue, here is that our sense of justice cannot ignore and to some extent even develops out of these rather vile emotions. This is not to deny that justice requires and presupposes compassion, respect, and a sense of duty as well, but justice also involves the often despised and dismissed emotion of vengeance, which may, in fact, be (both historically and psychologically) the seed from which the entire plant of justice has grown.

Vengeance is the original passion for justice. The word "justice" in the Old Testament virtually always refers to revenge. In Kant (1889) and Hegel (1967), the word "Gerechtigkeit" refers to retribution, and throughout most of history the concept of justice has been far more concerned with the punishment of crimes and the balancing of wrongs than it has been with the fair distribution of goods and services. "Getting even" is and has always been one of the most basic metaphors of our moral vocabulary, and the frightening emotion of righteous, wrathful anger has been the emotional basis for justice just as much as benign compassion. "Don't get mad, get even"—whether or not it is prudent advice—is conceptually confused. Getting even is just an effective way of being mad, and getting mad already includes a generous portion of revenge. The pleasure, the aesthetic satisfaction referred to by Lelyveld—an extremely important concept to which the "measure" of vengeance is often appealled—indicates the depth of the passion, and the need for "proportion" already indicates the intelligence involved in this supposedly most irrational and uncontrollable emotion. Our response to the many revenge novels and films is an indication of not only our deep-seated sense of vengeance but also the concept of fairness that is built therein. (Consider the uncomfortable response one has to Woody Allen's recent *Crimes and Misdemeanors,* where such justice is so obviously denied us.)

This is not to say of course, that the motive of revenge is therefore legitimate or the action of revenge always justified. Sometimes vengeance is wholly called for, even obligatory, and revenge is both legitimate and justified. Sometimes it is not, notably when one is mistaken about the offender or the offense. But to seek vengeance for a grievous wrong, to revenge oneself against evil—that seems to lie at the very foundation of our sense of justice, indeed, of our very sense of ourselves, our dignity, and our sense of right and wrong. Even sentimentalist Smith wrote, in *The Theory of the Moral Sentiments* (1880), "The violation of justice is injury . . . it is, therefore, the proper object of resentment, and of punishment, which is the natural consequence of resentment" (p. 115). We are not mere observers of the moral life, and the desire for vengeance seems to be an integral aspect of our recognition of evil. But it also contains—or can be cultivated to contain—the elements of its own control, a sense of its limits, a sense of balance. Thus the Old Testament instructs us that revenge should be limited to "an eye for an eye, a tooth for a tooth, hand for hand, foot for foot, burning for burning, wound for wound, stripe for stripe" ("*Lex Talionis*"), *Exodus* 21:24–5). It was such "equality" that Kant took to be an absolute rational principle in his *Philosophy of Law* (1889), and, in more modern, jovial guise, there is Gilbert's musical *Mikado:* "an object all sublime/make the punishment fit the crime." The New Testament demands even more restraint, the abstention from revenge oneself and the patience to entrust it to God. Both the Old and New Testaments (more the latter than the former) also encourage "forgiveness," but there can be no foregiveness if there is not first the desire (and the warrant) for revenge.

Vengeance is not just punishment, no matter how harsh. It is a matter of emotion, often delayed, protracted or frustrated emotion, and like punishment, it is always for some offense, not just hurting for its own sake (even if, in some other sense, it is deserved). Vengeance, then, always has its reasons (though, to be sure, these can be mistaken, irrelevant, out of proportion, or otherwise bad reasons). Vengeance is no longer a matter of obligation and it certainly can't claim to be rational as such but neither is it opposed to a sense of obligation (e.g., in matters of family honor) or rationality (insofar as rationality is to be found in every emotion, even this one). Vengeance is the emotion of "getting even," putting the world back in balance, and this simple phrase already embodies a whole philosophy of justice, even if (as yet) unarticulated and unjustified. Philosophers have been much too quick to attribute this sense of "balance" or "retribution" to reason, but I would want to argue that it is rather a function of emotion—cultivated, passionate cognition, not calm and cool reason. (And yet we know, nevertheless, that vengeance is a dish that is best served cold.) Kant (1965), of course, immediately opted for the former, dismissing the latter suggestion virtually altogether. Vengeance, he suggested, is purely subjective, wholly irrational, undependable, and unjustifiable. It is wholly without measure or reason, devoid of any sense of balance or justice. So, too, Gerstein (1985), for example, wrote: "Vengefulness is an emotional response to injuries done to us by others: we feel a desire to injure those who have injured us. Retributivism is not the idea that it is good to have and satisfy this emotion. It is rather the view that there are good arguments for including the kernel of rationality to be found in the passion for vengeance as a part of any just system of laws" (pp. 75–79). But I want to suggest that vengeance just is that sense of measure or balance that Kant (and so many other philosophers) attributed to reason alone. But, of course, it is ultimately the same old dichotomy that is most at fault here, the supposed antagonism between reason on the one side and passions on the other. Where would our reasoning about punishment begin if not for our emotional sense of the need for retaliation and retribution? (We should stress here that retaliation and retribution should not be confused with reparation and mere compensation, which may in some cases "undo" the damage but in no case by themselves count as punishment.) And what would our emotion be if it was not already informed and cultivated by a keen sense of its object and its target, as the mores and morals of the community in which the offense in question is deserving of revenge? Indeed, one might surmise that all vengeance has a single object, namely, the undoing or payback for humiliation. And though humiliation may sometimes be without measure, more often than not its antidote comes in carefully measured, knowing dosages.

Perhaps nowhere is the denial of what is most human about us (that is, our passions) more evident than in the various debates and concerns that surround the problems of punishment in criminal justice. The ongoing dispute between the "utilitarians" (who believe in a "deterrence" theory of punishment) and the "retributivists" (who believe that punishment is necessary in order to satisfy the demands of justice as such) not only neglects but explicitly dismisses any mention of that passion that alone would seem to give some fuel to the notion of punishment, namely the emotion of vengeance. This is not to say that punishment should serve only to revenge, but it is to say that punishment is in part the satisfaction of the need for vengeance, and punishment makes no sense without this. Several years ago, Jacoby (1983) argued that our denial of the desire for vengeance is analogous to the Victorian denial of sexual desire, and we are paying a similar psychological price for it. But as with our hunger for sex, we do not succeed very well in suppressing our thirst for revenge.

How did our passion for retribution—our need for vengeance, come about? I think that evolutionary speculations can go a long way in answering this question. Earlier in this essay, I stressed the accounts of the moral sentiment theorists as an important insight into "human nature," but I hope that I was sufficiently careful not to give the impression that we are naturally "nice" in any ridiculous sense. Evolutionary theory has shown, conclusively I think, that there is demonstrable advantage for groups and species—if not always for individuals—in the evolution of cooperation. But cooperation has two sides, the willingness to cooperate, first of all, but then the resentment and punishment of those who do not cooperate as well. (This includes the expectation that one will be punished oneself if one does not cooperate.) One cannot imagine the evolution of the cooperation without the evolution of punishment, and Axelrod's (1984) now-classic "tit-for-tat" model of the former explains as well the latter. In a repetitive "prisoner's dilemma" type situation, or in any ongoing situation in which one person frequently has the ability to "cheat" the other(s), an optimum strategy for discouraging such cheating is to respond, dependably, with retribution. A creature endowed only with compassion, who would "understand" the motives of the criminal in every case, would be just as much of an evolutionary failure as a creature who did nothing but watch out for his or her own advantage and cheated every time. Swift and dependable retaliation is thus in the nature of social animals as well as the lesson of game theory. Vengeance is not the antagonist to rationality but its natural manifestation. To breed a social animal who has "the right to make promises," is to understand the evolution of a creature who has the natural urge to punish as well as natural sympathy and a sense of social solidarity.

Perhaps the point was overstated in the majority opinion in United States Supreme Court decision *Gregg v. Georgia* (1976): "The instinct for retribution is part of the nature of man, and channeling that instinct in the administration of criminal justice serves an important purpose in promoting the stability of a society governed by law. When people begin to believe that organized society is unwilling or unable to impose upon criminal offenders the punishment they 'deserve,' then there are sown the seeds of anarchy—of self-help, vigilante justice, and lynch law." But at least the emotion of vengeance was taken seriously and not merely sacrificed to the dispassionate authority of the law. Retributive justice, however rationalized, is not as such a purely rational matter—but neither is it thereby "irrational" either. Most of the arguments that have been advanced against vengeance, for example, the charge that "all punishment is the return of evil for evil," could with only slight modifications be applied to the standard notions of retributive justice as well—which is not surprising if vengeance and retributive justice are in the end identical. But in the end, it is perhaps not just a question of whether revenge is rational or not, but whether it is—at the bottom of our hearts as well as off the top of our heads—an undeniable aspect of the way we react to the world, not as an instinct but as such a basic part of our worldview and our moral sense of ourselves that it is, in that sense, unavoidable.

Vengeance is assumed to be wholly without measure or reason, devoid of any sense of balance or justice. Vengeance, unlike justice, is said to be "blind" (though it is worth reminding ourselves which of the two is depicted in established mythology as blind-folded). Vengeance, it is said, knows no end. It is not just that it gets out of hand; it cannot be held "in hand" in the first place. Vengeance is always violent, we assume, but reciprocating a snub, blocking an invitation to a party, or having a forbidden sexual encounter can be vengeance just as surely as a Clint Eastwood finale. Of course, we can agree: There is danger in vengeance. It can become increasingly violent, disrupting the present order of things in an often impossible attempt to get back to a prior order that has itself been violently disrupted. Such an impossibility breeds frustration, and violence—even justified as vengeance (if, indeed, this is possible)—typically leads to more violence. An act of revenge results in a new offense to be righted, and when the act is perpetrated not against the same person who did the offense but against another who is part of the same family, tribe, or social group (the logic of "vendetta"), the possibilities for escalation are endless. Accordingly, the limitation of revenge through institutionalization is necessary. But it does not follow that vengeance itself is illegitimate or without measure or of no importance in considerations of punishment. To the dangers of vengeance unlimited it must be added that if punishment no longer satisfies vengeance, if it ignores not only the rights but the emotional needs of the victims of crime, then punishment no longer serves its primary purpose, even if it were to succeed in rehabilitating the criminal and deterring other crime (which it evidently, in general, does not). The restriction of vengeance by law is entirely understandable, but the wholesale denial of vengeance as a legitimate motive may be as much of a psychological disaster as its unlimited exercise is dangerous.

Just to be clear, I have not tried to defend vengeance as such, but my claim is that vengeance deserves its central place in any theory of justice and, whatever else we are to say about punishment, the desire for revenge must enter into our deliberations along with such emotions as compassion, caring, and love. Any system of legal principles that does not take such emotions into account, which does not motivate itself on their behalf, is not—whatever else it may be—a system of justice. Vengeance as such, I do not deny, is in any case dangerous.

As the Chinese used to say (and no doubt still do) "if you seek vengeance, dig two graves." But I think that the dangers and destructiveness of vengeance is much overblown and its importance for a sense of one's own self-esteem and integrity underestimated.

Many people believe that vengeance is the primary cause of the world's troubles today, unending feuds and vendettas that block every rational effort at resolution and peace. But vengeance is not the same as vendetta and feuds and vengeance is not the same as protracted, cultivated group hatred for which "vengeance" is often a mere cover and an excuse. I would argue that the passionate hostilities of the world that are fueled by revenge are only secondary and in many cases caused or at any rate aggravated and rendered unresolvable not by passion at all so much as by supposedly rational ideology, abstracting and elevating personal prejudices to the status of absolute truths and giving vengeance a set of reasons far less negotiable than any feud or mere urge to "get even." Vengeance, at least, has its measure. Ideology, however "reasonable," may not.

CONCLUSION: THE BELIEF IN A JUST WORLD

We do not live in a just world; on this every thinker in history has agreed, even those who, like the great early 19th-century German philosopher Hegel (1967), used their work to try to get us reconciled to the world ("the actual is rational and the rational is actual"). But the importance of justice is not thereby diminished; on the contrary, it becomes all the more urgent, to (re)define, once again, the meaning of that honorific term. My suggestion here is that we shift our focus from large theories to personal and suprapersonal feelings, from the merely awesome awareness of global injustice to our own actions and attitudes. Such a shift brings edification as well as understanding, and it helps avoid what Melvin J. Lerner (1980) called the "fundamental delusion" of a "belief in a just world." Lerner showed, in distressing detail, how we tend to misperceive or interpret recipients of rewards and victims of injustice in order to maintain this belief and how far we will go to do so. But he also demonstrated the extent to which this belief in a just world is a deeply emotional matter, a question of deep personal investment, heavily tied up with self-esteem and other questions of self-worth, rather than an abstract philosophical belief. One is reminded of Albert Camus, who argued in his *Myth of Sisyphus* (1955) for what he called "the Absurd," that devastating sense of disappointment and outrage that any adult and aware human being experiences on discovering that the world is not and could not be fair. What Camus then defended as "keeping the Absurd alive," I suggest, is a dramatic and mock-heroic emphasis on seeing through Lerner's "delusion" as a prerequisite of becoming a just person.

The idea of justice as a personal virtue rather than an ideal state of society and therefore a matter of emotion rather than the basis of an all-embracing theory is a very old idea. Socrates argued this in *The Republic* (1985), and Aristotle (1985) later agreed that justice is first of all a state of character. Of course, Socrates (and presumably Plato) wanted it both ways, justice as a virtue and justice as the ideal state, but, nevertheless, the former was as important as the latter, an idea too easily lost sight of in the modern philosophical world of contracts and rights. There cannot be a "value-free" theory of justice (or of the emotions) and one cannot develop a theory of justice without a substantial grounding and engagement in the empirical knowledge of how people actually feel and behave. Philosophy needs psychology; indeed an adequate theory of justice cannot but be both. We need more philosopher-psychologist-activists like Nico Frijda who will move beyond the self-defeating belief that justice is a delusion and close the gap between the world they envision and the world they live in. Depressing realism and abstract idealism cannot be the only alternatives. Justice is neither in the heavens nor is it merely in the mud of self-deception. It is, as Socrates argued, to be found in ourselves, as a virtuous state of character based on the appropriate emotions. The danger is that, like country singers looking for love, we are looking for justice in all the wrong places.

ACKNOWLEDGMENTS

For Nico Frijda, for his good feelings, first of all.

REFERENCES

Aristotle. (1985). *Nichomachean ethics* (T. Irwin, Trans.). Indianapolis: Hackett.

Augustine. (1956). *The city of God* (Philip Levine, Trans.). Cambridge, MA: Harvard University Press.

Axelrod, R. M. (1984). *The evolution of cooperation.* New York: Basic Books.

Brentano, F. (1889). *The origin of our knowledge of right and wrong.* London: Routledge.

Calhoun, C. H. (1981). *Feeling and value.* Unpublished doctoral dissertation, University of Texas, Austin.

Camus, A. (1955). *The myth of Sisyphus* (J. O'Brien, Trans.). New York: Vintage.

Cropsey, J. (1954). *Polity and Economy,* Westport CT: Greenwood.

Descartes, R. (1989). *The passions of the soul* (S. Voss, Trans.). Indianapolis: Hackett.

Dewey, J. (1946). The crisis in human history. *Commentary, 1*(5), 9.

Dostoevsky, F. (1960). *Notes from underground* (R. Matlaw, Trans.). New York: Dutton.

Frijda, N. H. (1986). *The emotions.* Cambridge, England: Cambridge University Press.

Frijda, N. H., Mesquita, B., Sonnenemans, J., & van Goozen, S. (1991). The duration of affective phenomena or emotions, sentiments and passions. In K. Strongman (Ed.), *International review of studies on emotion* (Vol. 1, pp. 187–225). New York: Wiley.

Gerstein, R. S. (1985). Capital punishment: A retributivist response. *Ethics, 85,* 75–79.

Goodman, L. E. (1989). Medieval Jewish and Islamic philosophers. In S. Biderman & B. Scharfstein (Eds.). *Rationality in question.* Leiden: Brill.

Gordon, R. (1987). *The structure of emotions.* Cambridge, England: Cambridge University Press.

Hegel, G. W. F. (1967). *The philosophy of right* (T. Knox, Trans.). Oxford: Oxford University Press.

Heidegger, M. (1962). *Being and time* (J. Robinson, Trans.). New York: Harper & Row.

Hume, D. (1978). *A treatise of human nature.* Oxford: Oxford University Press.

Hutcheson, F. (1755). *A system of moral philosophy.* Hildesheim: Olms.

Jacoby, S. (1983). *Wild justice.* New York: Harper & Row.

James, W. (1884). What is an emotion? *Mind, 9,* 188–205.

Kant, I. (1889). *Philosophy of law* (T. Hastie, Trans.). Edinburgh: Clark.

Kant, I. (1965). *The metaphysical elements of justice* (J. Ladd, Trans.). Indianapolis: Bobbs-Merrill.

Kant, I. (1980). *The grounding of the metaphysics of morals* (Ellington, Trans.). Indianapolis: Hackett.

Lange, C. G. (1922). *The emotions.* Baltimore, MD: Williams & Wilkins.

Lelyveld, A. (1971). *Punishment: For and against.* New York: Hart.

Lerner, M. J. (1980). *Belief in a just world.* New York: Plenum.

Mencius. (1970). *The mind of Mencius* (D. Lau, Trans.). New York: Penguin.

Natsoulas, T. (1988). Sympathy, empathy and the stream of consciousness. *Journal of the Theory of Social Behavior, 18*(2) pp. 169–196.

Nietzsche, F. (1967). *Genealogy of morals* (W. Kaufmann, Trans.). New York: Random House.

Nozick, R. (1974). *Anarchy state and utopia*. New York: Basic Books.

Plato. (1984). *Crito*. In G. M. A. Grube (Ed. and Trans.), *The life and death of Socrates*. Indianapolis: Hackett.

Plato. (1985). *The republic* (Grube, Trans.). Indianapolis: Hackett.

Rawls, J. (1971). *A theory of justice*. Cambridge: Harvard University Press.

Rescher, N. (1974). *Unselfishness*. Pittsburgh: University of Pittsburgh Press.

Rousseau, J.-J. (1983). *Discourse on the origin of inequality* (D. Cress, Trans.). Indianapolis: Hackett.

Sartre, J.-P. (1948). *The emotions: Sketch of a theory*. New York: Philosophical Library.

Scheler, M. (1954). *The nature of sympathy* (P. Heath, Trans.). London, Routledge.

Schoeck, H. (1970). *Envy: A theory of social behaviour* (M. Glenny & B. Ross, Trans.). New York: Harcourt, Brace & World.

Schopenhauer, A. (1965). *The basis of morality* (E. Payne, Trans.). Indianapolis: Bobbs-Merrill.

Smith, A. (1880). *The theory of moral sentiments*. London: George Bell and Sons.

Smith, A. (1948). *An inquiry into the nature and causes of the wealth of nations*. New York: Hafner.

Solomon, R. (1976). *The passions*. New York: Doubleday.

Solomon, R. (1990). *A passion for justice*. Reading, MA: Addison-Wesley.

Solomon, R. (1991). Existentialism, emotions and the cultural limits of rationality. *Philosophy East and West,* Fall. Vol. XLII. no. 4 pp. 597–622.

Thomas, L. (1983). Morals, the self, and our natural sentiments. In Myers & Iran (Eds.), *Emotion* (pp. 144–163). New York: Haven.

Wispé, L. (1986). The distinction between sympathy and empathy: To call forth a concept, a word is needed. *Journal of Personality and Social Psychology, 50,* 314–321.

Author Index

Numbers in *italics* denote pages with complete bibliographical information.

Subject Index